TOWARDS MORE EFFECTIVE MONETARY POLICY

Proceedings of International Conferences organized by the Institute for Monetary and Economic Studies, Bank of Japan

MONETARY POLICY IN OUR TIMES, Ando, Eguchi, Farmer, and Suzuki, eds, MIT Press, 1985

FINANCIAL INNOVATION AND MONETARY POLICY, Suzuki and Yomo, eds, University of Tokyo Press, 1986

TOWARD A WORLD OF ECONOMIC STABILITY, Suzuki and Okabe, eds, University of Tokyo Press, 1988

THE EVOLUTION OF THE INTERNATIONAL MONETARY SYSTEM, Suzuki, Okabe, and Miyake, eds, University of Tokyo Press, 1990

PRICE STABILIZATION IN THE 1990s, Shigehara, ed., Macmillan, 1993

FINANCIAL STABILITY IN A CHANGING ENVIRONMENT, Sawamoto, Nakajima, and Taguchi, eds, Macmillan, 1995

Towards More Effective Monetary Policy

Edited by

Iwao Kuroda
Director, Institute for Monetary and Economic Studies
Bank of Japan

in association with
BANK OF JAPAN

First published in Great Britain 1997 by
MACMILLAN PRESS LTD
Houndmills, Basingstoke, Hampshire RG21 6XS and London
Companies and representatives throughout the world

A catalogue record for this book is available from the British Library.

ISBN 0–333–66668–2

First published in the United States of America 1997 by
ST. MARTIN'S PRESS, INC.,
Scholarly and Reference Division,
175 Fifth Avenue, New York, N.Y. 10010

ISBN 0–312–16526–9

Library of Congress Cataloging-in-Publication Data
Towards more effective monetary policy / edited by Iwao Kuroda.
p. cm.
Proceedings of the seventh international conference organized and sponsored by the Institute for Monetary and Economic Studies, Bank of Japan.
Includes bibliographical references and index.
ISBN 0–312–16526–9 (cloth)
1. Monetary policy—Congresses. 2. Monetary policy—United States—Congresses. I. Kuroda, Iwao, 1943– .
HG230.3.T68 1997
332.4973—dc20 96–34663
CIP

This book is printed on paper suitable for recycling and made from fully managed and sustained forest sources.

10 9 8 7 6 5 4 3 2 1
06 05 04 03 02 01 00 99 98 97

Printed and bound in Great Britain by
Antony Rowe Ltd, Chippenham, Wiltshire

Contents

Preface

In a rapidly changing world, no more so than in the financial industry, central bankers are no exception in that they have to keep abreast of an ever expanding array of subjects. Hence, communication, including the exchange of views among central bankers and academia, is of the utmost importance, and it is with this thought in mind that the Bank of Japan's Institute for Monetary and Economic Studies has organized and sponsored a biennial International Conference since 1983.

This book contains the proceedings of the Seventh International Conference that focused on the theme of "Towards More Effective Monetary Policy," and which was held on 26–27 October 1995. The conference explored the operational and institutional framework for effective monetary policy implementation against the background of recent developments in economics and central banking practice.

In planning and organizing the conference, we received invaluable advice from many individuals including Allan H. Meltzer and John B. Taylor, both Honorary Advisers of the Institute. In addition to the authors of the papers which were presented and discussants, many in the Institute also contributed; in this context, I would especially like to thank Kunio Okina, Yoshiaki Shikano, Wataru Takahashi, and Michio Kitahara for organizing the conference, and Miho Yamaguchi for her secretarial support.

IWAO KURODA
Director
Institute for Monetary and Economic Studies

List of Participants

Teresita D. Adamos is Deputy Director, Department of Economic Research, Central Bank of the Philippines.

Koos Alders is Assistant Manager, Monetary and Economic Policy Department, De Nederlandsche Bank N.V.

Ismail Alowi is Deputy Manager, Economics Department, Bank Negara Malaysia.

Krister Andersson is Chief Economist and Director, Economics Department, Sveriges Riksbank.

Jack H. Beebe is Senior Vice President and Director of Research, Federal Reserve Bank of San Francisco.

Boediono is Managing Director, Bank Indonesia.

Clive B. Briault is Head, Monetary Assessment and Strategy Division, Bank of England.

Franco Bruni is Professor of International Monetary Economics and Director of Department of Economics, Bocconi University.

Bo-Yung Chung is Director, Institute for Monetary and Economic Research, Bank of Korea.

Benjamin M. Friedman is William Joseph Maier Professor of Political Economy, Harvard University.

Toshihiko Fukui is Senior Deputy Governor, Bank of Japan.

Marvin Goodfriend is Senior Vice President and Director of Research, Research Department, Federal Reserve Bank of Richmond.

Thomas M. Hoenig is President, Federal Reserve Bank of Kansas City.

Jerry L. Jordan is President and Chief Executive Officer, Federal Reserve Bank of Cleveland.

Keimei Kaizuka is Professor of Economics, Chuo University.

Mervyn A. King is Executive Director and Chief Economist, Bank of England.

Linda Koh is Deputy Director, Domestic Money and Capital Markets Division, International Department, Monetary Authority of Singapore.

Donald L. Kohn is Director, Division of Monetary Affairs, Board of Governors of the Federal Reserve System.

Reiner König is Head of Economics Department, Deutsche Bundesbank.

Iwao Kuroda is Director, Institute for Monetary and Economic Studies, Bank of Japan.

David Laidler is Professor of Economics, University of Western Ontario and C.D. Howe Institute.

David Longworth is Chief, Department of Monetary and Financial Analysis, Bank of Canada.

Ian J. Macfarlane is Deputy Governor, Reserve Bank of Australia.

Yasuo Matsushita is Governor, Bank of Japan.

David Mayes is Chief Manager, Economics Department, Reserve Bank of New Zealand.

Bennett T. McCallum is H.J. Heinz Professor of Economics, Carnegie Mellon University and National Bureau of Economic Research.

Allan H. Meltzer is University Professor of Political Economy and Public Policy, Carnegie Mellon University, Visiting Scholar, American Enterprise Institute, and Honorary Adviser, Institute for Monetary and Economic Studies, Bank of Japan.

Cathy E. Minehan is President and Chief Executive Officer, Federal Reserve Bank of Boston.

Frederic S. Mishkin is Executive Vice President and Director of Research, Research and Market Analysis Group, Federal Reserve Bank of New York, Graduate School of Business at Columbia University, and National Bureau of Economic Research.

Michael H. Moskow is President, Federal Reserve Bank of Chicago.

David W. Mullins, Jr is President, Long-Term Capital Mangement, L.P.

Michael Mussa is Economic Counsellor and Director, Research Department, International Monetary Fund.

Manfred J.M. Neumann is Professor of Economics, University of Bonn.

Bandid Nijathaworn is Deputy Director, Economic Research Department, Bank of Thailand.

Kunio Okina is Chief Manager, Institute for Monetary and Economic Studies, Bank of Japan.

Tommaso Padoa-Schioppa is Deputy Director General, Bank of Italy.

Robert Raymond is Director General, European Monetary Institute.

Robert Reynders is Director, National Bank of Belgium.

Georg Rich is Director, Deputy Head of Department I, Swiss National Bank.

Kumiharu Shigehara is Head, Economics Department, Organisation for Economic Cooperation and Development.

Gary H. Stern is President and Chief Executive Officer, Federal Reserve Bank of Minneapolis.

Guido Tabellini is Professor, Bocconi University and IGIER.

Wataru Takahashi is Manager and Senior Economist, Institute for Monetary and Economic Studies, Bank of Japan.

John B. Taylor is Professor of Economics, Stanford University, and Honorary Adviser, Institute for Monetary and Economic Studies, Bank of Japan.

Kazuo Ueda is Professor of Economics, University of Tokyo.

Alain Vienney is Head of Research Department, Bank of France.

Xiaoyi Wang is Deputy Director, Research and Statistics Department, The People's Bank of China.

William R. White is Economic Adviser, Head of Monetary and Economic Department, Bank for International Settlements.

Opening Remarks

Yasuo Matsushita

It is a great pleasure to be with you today for the Seventh International Conference organized by our Institute for Monetary and Economic Studies. I welcome this opportunity for the Institute, and also for the Bank of Japan as a whole, to be engaged in a dialog with such distinguished participants from all over the world, and to be able to discuss various issues with respect to monetary policy, the implementation of which constitutes one of the principal functions of a central bank.

This year's conference is entitled "Towards More Effective Monetary Policy," and its primary purpose is to discuss and develop a new operational and institutional framework for effective monetary policy. I am sure that, in the course of this conference, I will find new evidence of the strength and the adaptability of central banks, and the wisdom of professional economists, all within the framework of our discussions about sound monetary policies.

Issues of monetary policy have always been complex and challenging, and never more so than today. Central bankers must confront a variety of economic circumstances over time. A consensus has developed among monetary authorities about the need to maintain a credible long-run commitment to price stability in order to achieve a stable and sustainable path of growth. The need to achieve such price stability in an effective manner calls for the elaboration of an optimal monetary policy framework.

In order to come up with such a framework, what are the factors we should take into account? I believe there are three major ones.

First, the nature of our changing financial environment. As a result of changes in communications and information technology, and the new instruments and risk management techniques that they have made possible, financial markets have become far more efficient today than a decade ago. Such new technologies and new instruments have presented new opportunities and challenges to central bankers, but they have brought new stresses as well. The emergence of financial derivatives has improved the risk management of market participants, yet it has also increased the activities that central bankers are having difficulty in monitoring.

Second, the expectations of the general public. The recent academic literature on the assessment of monetary policy effectiveness has emphasized the importance of public expectations *vis-à-vis* such policy. I would say that central banks must determine the appropriate monetary policy for the current economic circumstances, and then they must pursue that policy in a way that builds their credibility with the public, both in terms of their policy statements and in terms of the consistency of their actions over time. Now, of course circumstances do change, and the central banks must respond accordingly; but if a change or an adjustment in monetary policy is required, then it must be articulated in a consistent manner and it must be explained to the public in a way that demonstrates an ongoing coherence and consistency, even in the face of changing circumstances. And the subsequent actions must also demonstrate this ongoing coherence. We see in the literature that there are still questions about whether central banks should adopt a discretionary policy framework or a rule-oriented policy framework, nevertheless I believe in the importance of establishing the central banks' credibility.

Third, the environment of high uncertainty in which central banks have to conduct monetary policy. In order to make policy decisions, we base our judgments on forecasts, theory, and empirical evidence, all of which are subject to uncertainties. Forecasts are normally based on various assumptions, not all of which prove to be as reliable as we would like. Theories of monetary policy have various influential streams. Empirical evidence is difficult to establish; many of the statistical relationships which are useful for policymakers have become fragile because of evolving changes in the financial system.

With these factors in mind, what should we do? One sure thing is that we have to act. Central bankers need to continue to make a convincing case that price stability enhances economic welfare and helps economic growth, and that inflation is an impediment to growth.

When we closely watch the trends of the actual world, we find evidence of innovations. Innovation is not the byword for the private sector alone, however. Central banks should be also innovative in designing relevant monetary policy, and in elaborating the institutional framework that is most suitable for pursuing it.

In this regard, central banks need wisdom not only from within their own ranks but also from distinguished economists world-wide. It is my hope today that this conference will help us to integrate the wisdom of academics and central bankers so that we can better meet the challenges from the evolving financial market, and that it will also help us to bridge some of the existing gaps between theory and practice.

In closing, I would like to thank you for your attention, and to assure you that I will be paying very close attention to the outcome of the Seventh International Conference.

Part I
Keynote Speeches

1 On Making Monetary Policy More Effective Domestically and Internationally*

Allan H. Meltzer

The organizers of the Seventh International Conference have chosen a theme and a set of issues that, I believe, should be revisited frequently by all central banks. How can monetary policy be made most effective? What task or tasks should the central bank undertake in its role as protector of the value of money and all nominal obligations nationally and internationally? What institutional arrangements are most useful for fulfilling these responsibilities? How have recent developments in academic research and central banking practice changed our answers to these questions?

As is well-known, there is no single response to these questions that is applicable to all central banks and all time periods. Small and large countries have different opportunities. The opportunities are interdependent. At least since Keynes's *A Tract on Monetary Reform* (1923), economists have known that a country's potential gain from the choice of monetary arrangements depends on the choices that other countries make. Countries can only minimize the excess burden that arises from fluctuations in prices and exchange rates if this joint problem is solved.

One solution, that I have proposed at several earlier conferences, is for the leading monetary economies – the United States, Germany, and Japan – to adopt rules for price stability. By maintaining price stability, these countries would provide an opportunity for smaller countries to voluntarily fix their exchange rates and import zero inflation. The small economies would gain what they could not otherwise gain: both a fixed external value of money and zero or low inflation. Prices would fluctuate, but expected inflation would be zero. The large countries would gain also. They would each have expected inflation equal to zero. Their bilateral exchange rates would adjust to real disturbances, but monetary disturbances would be damped or absent. Further, large countries would benefit from trading at the fixed exchange rates maintained by smaller countries.

* I am indebted to Bennett McCallum and Charles Plosser for helpful suggestions.

This proposal is rule-based and distinguishes between countries with different problems and opportunities. Large countries would have activist, rule-based policies to maintain zero expected inflation. Smaller countries could choose to follow a fixed exchange rate rule or could pursue an independent course if they chose to do so. I believe that a proposal of this kind would realize most of the potential welfare gains that monetary policy can provide, so monetary policy would be effective in raising welfare. I will return to this proposal in the concluding section, after discussing recent academic research on monetary policy and credibility, some relevant bits of monetary history, recent changes in practices at several central banks, and the possibility of achieving zero expected inflation.

Much recent academic research on monetary policy has sought to develop positive theories of monetary policy. Many of these theories are based on game-theoretic models that treat the policymaker as a constrained welfare maximizer concerned about credibility and aware of the relation between central bank credibility, independence, and the opportunities for reaching low or zero inflation. Within this framework, rules dominate discretion and adaptive rules typically dominate fixed rules. The dominance of rules over discretion follows from the assumption about information: The central banker and the public have access to information on the same terms and at the same cost. If this is not so, it is a fault of the central banker who always has the option of revealing information instead of exploiting it to surprise the public. The models recognize shocks, surprises or new information that was not available when the rule was formulated. An adaptive rule takes this information into account by adjusting the stimulus from policy action. Hence, it may be superior to a fixed rule. Whether it is superior in practice depends on the nature of the new information, particularly the persistence of changes, and on the rate at which the public adjusts or adapts. If all changes are transitory, there is no reason to adapt. An adaptive rule would have no advantage over a fixed rule.

Accompanying these developments in the theory of economic policy are some major changes in central banking practice. Three are of particular interest here. First, several central banks have announced that price stability is their primary or exclusive objective. Second, many central bankers recognize far more clearly than in the recent past that pursuit of a single objective – whether price stability or exchange rate stability – is more likely to be achieved if the central bank is independent of the political authority. Hence there is renewed interest in central bank independence, and several countries have adopted laws declaring the central bank "independent." Rule-based policies are another, possibly more effective, way to achieve central bank independence. Third, independence is seen as a step

– perhaps a major step – toward establishing credibility. Central bankers and market participants now recognize that lack of credibility reduces the value of central bank announcements and raises the cost of achieving central bank objectives. Indeed, in the absence of credibility, the cost of achieving policy objectives may make the objectives unattainable in practice.

The common concern of theorists and practitioners with price stability, independence and credibility may suggest more convergence of practice to theory than has, in fact, occurred. The activist central banker of the post-war years, who regarded the maintenance of the value of money as one of many objectives, and not the most important or overriding objective, is a historical aberration. Traditional central banks were private institutions to prevent governments from controlling money. They did not always succeed but those that followed gold standard rules were concerned first and foremost about the value of money. Central banks were wary of politicians interested in the use of monetary policy to give the appearance of prosperity, and on guard to prevent inflation or devaluation. Archetype central bankers of this century, like Britain's Montagu Norman or his American friend Benjamin Strong, were very aware of the risks of political pressure, though they did not always escape these pressures. They would not be surprised to learn that many of today's central bankers are struggling to establish or regain their independence so as to pursue as their main objective the maintenance of the internal or external value of money.

Perhaps convergence has gone the other way – from central bankers' concerns to the positive theory of central banking. Here, too, there is reason for skepticism. The central banker – or policymaker – captured in current models is an unusual creature. Although central bankers traditionally have supported price or exchange rate stability in their public statements and private diaries, they have rarely achieved either. The current generation of positive theories has some difficulty explaining past or recent history. Although there are differences about why and where the failure occurred, there is now near unanimity that monetary failure caused the Great Depression. And, though positive theories of central banking can explain inflation, many have difficulty explaining rising inflation in the 1970s and disinflation in the 1980s. The solution in most of these models is a positive steady rate of inflation, not rising inflation followed by disinflation.[1]

1 INFLATION THEORY AND MONETARY HISTORY

The twentieth century has a rich monetary history, much of it at variance with positive models of central banking or monetary policy. The history includes the common experience of the Great Depression of the 1930s, the great inflation of the 1970s, and the disinflation of the 1980s, but it also includes some notable individual country experiences. In the interwar period, there was hyperinflation in Germany and Hungary and Britain's return to a gold parity at an overvalued exchange rate that required deflation in Britain and the countries that pegged their currencies to the pound sterling. In the post-Bretton Woods era, central banks in Argentina, Bolivia, Brazil, Chile, Israel and, most recently, Russia produced high inflation or hyper-inflation for many years.

These experiences and many others raise a question: Why did central bankers or governments adopt the policies that produced these outcomes? My reading of history suggests not one but two answers. First, central bankers, policymakers and most others hold some core set of beliefs that they use to interpret events and decide on actions to be taken or avoided. Second, recognition of mistakes and revision in basic beliefs is often slow and costly.

With some exceptions, central bankers and government policymakers have been practical men who paid little attention to abstract ideas. Their beliefs are not cast as formal theories. Nevertheless theories function as guides to action and help to distinguish acceptable outcomes from those that require new initiatives.

At the beginning of the twentieth century, two beliefs were firmly accepted by the practical men who managed central banks. The first was that the gold standard maintained long-run stability of both price levels and exchange rates. Neither the deflationary experience in the last quarter of the nineteenth century, nor the gradual inflation following the expansion of gold production late in that century, changed this belief.

The second belief was in the real bills or commercial loan theory of central banking. The proponents of this theory claimed that central bank discounts should be restricted to credits that arise in the financing of commerce and agriculture. If this were done, credit expansion would be limited and non-inflationary (see Mints, 1945).

Experience in Britain held that the discount rate at the Bank of England should remain between 2 percent and 10 percent. During the deflation phase of the gold standard, when many countries joined the system, at the end of the nineteenth century, the Bank held to the 2 percent minimum rate for long periods, thereby requiring deflation as a solution for Britain and, given Britain's monetary role at the time, contributing to deflation in other gold standard countries. At the 2 percent discount rate, real costs of borrowing were high relative to profitability, so money growth remained deflationary. The deflationary phase was brought to an end not by a decision of central bankers to lower interest rates but by the expansion of gold production near the turn of the century (see Friedman and Schwartz, 1963a).

The Federal Reserve, founded just as World War I began in Europe, was too small and powerless to stop the inflow of gold in its early years. Moreover, under gold standard rules, it was not much inclined to act. Its initial policy was passive; it permitted inflation based on gold inflows. This was followed by a financing of wartime budget deficits, as in all of the belligerent countries.

Neither the prewar nor the wartime experience conforms to current positive theories of inflation. Nor is there evidence in the movements of interest rates that the inflation was expected to last. Nominal yields on long-term treasury bonds remained below the rate of inflation.

The early postwar experience of all the belligerents was continued inflation followed by deflation, stabilization, and a return to a fixed exchange rate regime based on gold. Delays in reestablishing a fixed exchange rate tied to gold are attributable much more to factors such as the pressure to finance government borrowing, the size of prospective reparations, and demands for repayment of war debts than to any modern theory of the efficient rate of inflation (Chandler, 1958). Beliefs about gold were a more powerful force than any theory of optimal inflation. Only a few critics questioned the return to a type of gold standard in which gold was supplemented by foreign exchange reserves. This arrangement is called the gold exchange standard.

In the USA, the period from 1922 to 1929 is one of the few episodes in which the Federal Reserve delivered price stability and economic growth over a sustained period of five or more years. There were two mild recessions, followed in 1929–30 by another recession. That recession, as we know, became the Great Depression. Instead of delivering an optimal or efficient rate of inflation, most central bankers presided over a severe deflation. Reading the speeches, writings, and Federal Reserve minutes for the period suggests that mistaken beliefs were a main reason for the failure to act.[2] What were those beliefs?

French officials did not like the gold exchange standard for many of the same reasons that they did not like the Bretton Woods system a generation later. Pride or caution encouraged them to hold only gold as a reserve, as in the USA and the UK, and prudence taught them that the gold exchange standard was vulnerable if several countries behaved as they did. Acting on these beliefs, they converted their foreign exchange balances into gold. The effect was to impose a deflationary impulse on falling world price levels (Eichengreen, 1992).

In the writings and discussions of Federal Reserve policy at the time, the word "inevitable" appears repeatedly. Deflation and depression were considered an inevitable consequence of the inflationary policies that had gone before. To a current observer, there are few signs of inflation in the late 1920s. To contemporary observers, however, the Federal Reserve had financed a stock market boom. Credit had been used for speculative purposes, not to finance real bills. Hence, the dominant belief of central bankers, bankers, and practical men was that the financial system had to undergo a correction. The correction could only end, they believed, when the demand for commercial loans encouraged banks to borrow by rediscounting real bills.

One notable exception is Sweden. Sweden, following Britain, left the gold standard in the fall of 1931. Thereafter monetary policy, guided by three leading economists, aimed at price level stability. Their policy avoided much of the subsequent decline in output experienced elsewhere (Jonung, 1981).

There was no place for the current positive theory of optimizing social policy as long as belief in the gold standard or the real bills theory dominated central banks and many governments. Experience after World War II under the Bretton Woods system comes closest to the implications of the positive model. Although some policymakers in the Kennedy administration favored higher inflation as a means of increasing employment and achieving other social goals, I have found no evidence that the Federal Reserve under Chairman Martin accepted these arguments or acted on them. The inflation that occurred seems much more the result of two factors working together. The first is flawed operating procedures, particularly the use of free reserves as the principal indicator of the policy stance. Once operating errors produced inflation, the Federal Reserve was unwilling to pay the political cost of disinflating to maintain the exchange rate system. This is a point of contact with the positive theory of central banking. However, the positive theory does not explain why inflation increased from 1 percent to more than 10 percent a year between 1960 and 1980. The second reason is that the Federal Reserve had an incomplete and partially formed theory of inflation. There were different ideas about what caused inflation; speculators, cost push, and government spending are examples commonly cited. The connection to monetary policy was not entirely clear to many Federal Reserve officials until much later.

Outside the United States, application of the positive theory is limited to countries that devalued repeatedly. France and the UK are in this group, but many countries were not. Some like Italy or Japan accepted the inflation coming from the United States. Germany and Holland revalued their currencies to avoid some of the imported inflation. No country maintained price stability. The main reason that countries other than the United States inflated, however, is their acceptance of the Bretton Woods rules.

The 1970s was a period of rising inflation and rising average unemployment in many countries. Monetary policymakers, freed of the constraints of Bretton Woods, responded in different ways to the oil shocks and other one-time commodity price increases. By the end of that decade, policymakers in many countries had given up any vestigial belief in their ability to manage a tradeoff between inflation and unemployment. Reducing inflation at acceptable social cost became a main policy goal in most developed countries.

Many of the European central banks in the 1980s repeated the mistake made by the British in the 1920s. They attempted to lower inflation by fixing the exchange rate, as Britain's Governor Norman had tried to do in 1925 (Chandler, 1958). The fixed exchange rate policy had a similar result in several countries – a persistently high unemployment rate. Until currency markets overwhelmed Italy, Britain, France, Spain, Portugal, and Sweden, governments and central banks in these countries continued to insist that a fixed exchange rate with Germany was the key to price stability or low inflation. I do not find much evidence for the socially optimizing central banker in these experiences.

Latin American countries are prominent among non-industrial countries that have recently declared their central banks to be independent. Here, too, there is not much support for the optimizing model of central bank behavior. Chile's inflation in the 1970s had such features as wage increases with prices controlled and rapid money growth to finance rising wages and transfer payments. Such policies seem better described as confiscation and transfer of wealth, based on beliefs or ideology, than as optimization of social welfare. Peru in the 1980s is similar to Chile in the 1970s. In Brazil, there was repeated denial that inflation was caused by money growth and several efforts to stop inflation based on these beliefs. Argentina and Bolivia are other examples of countries with high inflation or hyperinflation that is better explained as the result of policies based on mistaken beliefs than as the outcome of optimizing behavior. Mexico's monetary problems in 1976, 1982, and 1994 occurred in election years. Socially optimal policies would not produce this pattern or its aftermath.

2 CREDIBILITY

The modern case for rules highlights the role of credibility. Analysis of credibility became an active research topic once Kydland and Prescott (1977) put a new foundation under earlier work on policy rules. Since that time, and particularly following Barro and Gordon's (1983) influential paper, there has been an explosion of literature on this topic. Much less has been done empirically. The brief survey of twentieth-century monetary policy in the previous section finds little evidence that central banks generally behave as implied by positive models of the Barro–Gordon type. The stable inflation rate implied by these models is rare in practice. These models do not explain variable inflation, deflation or hyperinflation. Something is missing from these models that is present in practice.

Informally, credibility is easily defined. It is a measure of the confidence that the public has that the central bank (or other policymaker) will follow the policy path to which it is committed. A more precise generic definition brings in the problem of time consistency (Kydland and Prescott, 1977). A policy is credible if, given his objectives, the policymaker maximizes by choosing the expected policy action when the time comes to act.

Some of the empirical problems are immediately apparent. Suppose the policy rule is inferred, not announced. How does the analyst or the public learn the policy rule other than by observation? With many possible contingent states, there will be uncertainty about how well a state contingent rule is known. The credible policy depends on the objectives of the policymaker, on the expectations of the public, on the public's knowledge of the rule. All of these are non-observables. Later work, for example influential work on the reputation of the policymaker, does not narrow the number of non-observables. Further, these models assume away a major part of a central bank's problem – the control of the money supply. As some central bankers have noted, economists seeking to test the credibility of a rule-based policy cannot assume a close short-run relation between money and the price level (Issing, 1995; Rich, 1995).

The literature has two or three attempts to give quasi-operational definitions. For the case in which the policymaker announces targets, Cukierman and I (1986) defined *average* credibility as the extent to which the public expects the policymaker to deviate from the action consistent with the prior announcement. *Marginal* credibility is the response of the public's expectations to the announcement of a target. Notice that the expected rate of inflation can change continuously. Notice also that assuming a policy announcement gets rid of one problem but does not eliminate all non-observables – for example, expectations of the public and intentions of the policymaker.

Some additional, significant problems arise in testing credibility models. Most credibility modeling focuses on the policy rule for issuing money, the money supply, but does not model the supply. Moreover, money is used as a medium of exchange because it saves on information costs and transaction costs. These costs are not constant. Changes in intermediation and the growth of intermediaries are important for the rate of growth of the demand for money. Bordo and Jonung's (1987) empirical studies suggest that these changes in costs have brought large, permanent changes to the demand for money. Such changes are relevant for the choice of a policy rule. The policymakers' response to these changes must be part of any model that tests for credibility.

Further problems arise in empirical testing of credibility because there is uncertainty about the true model of the economy, and most policymakers do not announce rules. A policymaker finds it is in his interest to be ambiguous about the rule he follows (Cukierman and Meltzer, 1986). Simply put, the combination of neglect of inflation costs and intermediation, non-observables, ambiguity, and economists' inability to develop an empirically supported, dynamic model of the economy with low forecast errors makes empirical testing of credibility models an exceptionally challenging venture (see Weber, 1991).

Central bankers are adept at making ambiguous statements about their decisions and future actions. Ambiguity obscures the procedures they follow, the timing of policy actions, and the size of prospective changes. Ambiguity increases opportunities for discretionary action. Policymakers do not maximize credibility – whatever that would mean. Many build credibility to use when they choose to surprise the public. Ambiguity contributes to surprises by keeping the public uncertain about the precise rule that is followed.

Evidence suggests that, in the absence of an announced, explicit rule, credibility is achieved only by performance. Three of the five countries with the lowest inflation since the Bretton Woods system formally ended in 1973 – Germany, Switzerland, and Japan – relied on a quasi-monetary rule during much of the period, and a fourth, the Netherlands, followed a fixed exchange rate rule by pegging its currency to Germany's. The fifth country, Singapore, followed what appears to an outsider to be an eclectic policy.

Each of the five countries had an average inflation rate of 4 percent or less for the period. The degree of formal independence differs. The Bank of Japan is nominally responsible to the Ministry of Finance, although practice varies. Cukierman (1992, p. 451) assigns it the same independence as the Federal Reserve. Yet Japan has had a lower inflation rate than the United States consistently. During much of the period, the Bank of Japan used a broad monetary aggregate to guide its policy. Difficulties began when this policy was replaced in 1985 by a policy of managing the exchange rate.

Germany and Switzerland are two of the most independent central banks.

Each uses preannounced monetary targets to guide policy. Both banks have missed their targets several times.

When explaining performance, theories of credibility do not add much to what one learns from the mean and variance of quarterly or annual inflation rates. People are right to believe that Japan, Switzerland and Germany have relatively credible monetary policies because they deliver lower rates of inflation than most other countries. Would we find their policies less credible if they delivered the same inflation rates but did a poorer job of hitting their announced or projected targets? Conversely, would we find them more credible if they hit their targets precisely but had a higher average rate of inflation. Our theories of inflation are not good enough to predict short-term changes in the rate of inflation accurately or to use our models to assign credibility rankings.

What seems important is that Germany and Switzerland promptly correct large errors. George Rich (1995) showed that there were three big misses in Swiss money growth after 1970. Money growth of 60 percent in 1971 is followed by minus 20 percent in 1972; 35 percent in 1978 is followed by minus 25 percent in 1979; 20 percent in 1987 is followed by minus 10 percent in 1988. I submit that these instances of decisive correction have more influence on the Swiss National Bank's credibility than either small annual departures or exact hits on a target. This should not suggest that targets are useless or that monetary targets are unnecessary. Switzerland would have experienced less variability and lower excess burden if monetary growth had been less variable. The three episodes show that Switzerland ignored its monetary target at times. They do not show that Switzerland gained from doing so.

Targeting money growth means the price *level* will be a random walk (or nearly so) whatever the expected rate of inflation. Suppose money growth is set to keep expected inflation at zero. A one-time price level change, distributed over time, can give rise to serially correlated, transitory, non-zero rates of price change. At times data will show prices rising or falling while the maintained rate of inflation is zero.

Suppose the central bank follows, but does not announce, a rule that keeps money growth equal to real output growth so that the unknown but true value of expected inflation is zero. There is no permanent inflation. There are transitory and permanent changes in the price *level* that make the rate of price change deviate from zero. For example, real shocks, changes in commodity taxes, or changes in intermediation may raise or lower the price *level* without changing the maintained or expected rate of inflation.

This is, of course, artificial. The public would eventually learn the rule.

Nevertheless, it brings out a problem in measuring credibility that should not be ignored, particularly where the rule is opaque and changing. Discussion of inflation for the past twenty-five years has been plagued by the failure to distinguish temporary and permanent changes in the price *level* from permanent changes in the rate of inflation.

The Netherlands is an informative case. Here simple observation is clearly consistent with the definitions of credibility but not with most positive models of inflation. The Netherlands follows an easily observed rule. It pegs the guilder to the D-Mark and takes whatever inflation rate results. Since 1960, the Netherlands has revalued the guilder with every revaluation of the mark except one. One can treat the exchange rate as an announcement and observe what it is. We know the objective and we can use observation of the exchange rate to judge the credibility of the Netherlands central bank in carrying out its policy.

Or can we? Suppose the Netherlands does not follow Germany in the next revaluation of the mark. That experiment has been run. A one-time failure to revalue increased the interest rate differential between German and Dutch bonds. It took many years to remove the differential by restoring the policy of always revaluing with Germany. This suggests that market measures, such as the interest rate spread on comparable debt, may be useful as measures of credibility.

However it is measured, credibility is a stock that rises or falls with policy outcomes. Is the optimal degree of credibility the same as maximum credibility? Should a country build a stock and never use it so as to satisfy time-consistency properties? Is it not more useful to analyze a political economy world where the policymaker is interested not only in the public interest but in his own interest and the two are not always the same. Even relatively independent central banks have been known to expand money growth in election years, as much research shows.

After Sweden, the UK, and Mexico each spent about $30 billion or more to defend a fixed exchange rate, should they have borrowed more to maintain their credibility (assuming someone would lend)? Each of these countries was forced to devalue by from 20 percent to 60 percent. Defending the parity cost about $700 per capita in Sweden and more than $150 in Mexico. Was Ricardo right when he told the Bank of England to deflate by 50 percent to reestablish the pound at the former gold parity? (He later changed his mind.) Economists generally agree with Keynes's *ex post* judgment that it was a mistake to restore the pound at its prewar parity in 1925.

After World War I, Montagu Norman and Benjamin Strong agreed that both the USA and the UK should deflate to restore prewar gold parities and price levels. Would it not have been socially better to use up some credibility and avoid the social costs of deflations in at least one country?

Consider recent experience in Latin America. After experience with inflation, devaluation and exchange rate problems in two previous election years, Mexico was able to establish sufficient credibility to return to world capital markets after 1989 by adopting institutional reform, and promoting privatization, budget balance, and other reforms. After decades of high inflation, default, devaluation, and workouts, Argentina reformed in 1990. In 1994 Brazil promised to reform for the sixth or seventh time in the past twenty years. Each of these countries received large loans and equity investments from presumptively rational investors abroad. Credibility appears to have increased despite long histories of trouble. This suggests a model in which large discrete changes in credibility can occur following reforms that are perceived as permanent.

Argentina is a particularly interesting example of the use of institutionalization to increase credibility. In the past, I have been skeptical about the practical relevance of the literature on trigger strategies used to punish a policymaker who inflates (Barro and Gordon, 1983). These models eliminate a most difficult problem by assuming a representative individual who metes out the punishment. This abstracts from a highly relevant, possibly central, problem of coordinating individual actions to get a social response.

Argentina adopted a currency board but it added an important feature. The public can hold its deposits in dollars or pesos. Any risk of inflationary action can be followed by a shift into dollar deposits. This is an uncoordinated, but so far effective, punishment technique.

Until the EMS ran into difficulties in 1992–93, many papers discussed the role of the EMS in extending credibility from Germany to its neighbors. It is true that inflation rates fell in Europe, but the accompanying cost of unemployment was often higher in the EMS than in countries with flexible exchange rates. And unemployment rates fell more slowly in the EMS than outside – about 50 percent slower in my comparison. Germany had one of the slowest rates of decline, although its maximum unemployment rate was lower than in most of the EMS and non-EMS countries.

Of course, factors other than credibility affect these observed differences. But Germany's credibility did not reduce costs for the EMS countries below those in the United States, the UK, Japan or Sweden. Each of the later (non-EMS) countries experienced more rapid decline in unemployment rates than Belgium, Denmark, Germany, France, Ireland or Italy – members of the EMS.

My conclusion is *not* that credibility is unimportant in practice. We do not know that one way or the other. Our models give either implications that lead to their easy rejection or implications that are not easily tested.

At the subjective level, commitment by Britain to the EMS as a means of lowering the cost of inflation did not work as expected by its proponents. Nor has the EMS worked to lower social costs of disinflation in Spain, France, and Italy. Reported rates of inflation have fallen, but unemployment rates ranged from 12 percent to 24 percent several years after disinflation began. This is hardly a testament to the social benefits of commitment to the European Monetary System or the gain in credibility that such commitment achieves.

My conclusion is that game-theoretic literature teaches us some wrong lessons. Yes, ambiguity is important and so are credibility and the design of institutions. But recent game-theoretic literature fails as a positive theory of inflation. The Great Depression and the great inflation were not preplanned. There were mistakes. It was not a central banker or an obscure economist working in the bowels of the central bank that convinced much of the profession and many policymakers that the Phillips curve tradeoff could be used to get permanent or long-lasting increases in employment. It was Samuelson and Solow, leaders of our profession.

Much evidence suggests that the error has been recognized. Central banks are now trying to avoid their past mistakes. Inflation has fallen in the industrial countries. Positive theories of inflation based on optimizing behavior did not predict this.

3 INFLATION TARGETS

Five countries – New Zealand, Canada, Britain, Sweden and Finland – have now adopted some type of inflation target as the sole or principal objective of monetary policy. The targets vary as do the time frames within which the target is to be achieved and the institutional arrangements under which the central bank operates. New Zealand has a formal contract that requires the central bank Governor to offer his resignation if the target is not achieved. In Finland and Sweden the inflation target is chosen by the central bank with, at most, a tacit understanding between the government and the central bank.

The common characteristics of these countries include the choice of an explicit target for inflation and a commitment to achieve the target within a few years (Leiderman and Svensson, 1995). Central banks in Germany, Japan, and Switzerland have followed low-inflation policies for a longer time, but they have expressed their targets in terms of some monetary aggregate. These countries choose the growth rate of the monetary aggregate to lower the inflation rate toward zero, but there is no commitment to a specific range for inflation or a time when inflation will be in that range. The United States is further removed from an inflation target. The current Chairman of the Federal Reserve often expresses his wish, or perhaps his personal intention, to reduce the inflation rate to a negligible value, but neither Congress nor the administration nor the Federal Reserve has endorsed the commitment, and there is no way of knowing whether the next Chairman would continue the commitment or wish to maintain it. Despite these differences, inflation has been reduced in each of these countries.

The choice of an explicit inflation target and a formal contract are, I believe, useful steps. In August 1988, I proposed a scheme to the Reserve Bank of New Zealand that differs modestly from the plan they later adopted.[3] I suggested the use of a monetary aggregate as an intermediate target. The goal was to reduce inflation. The central bank would choose the target and conduct policy independently. However, the Governor would be required to offer his resignation if the target was not achieved. The Governor would be allowed to offer an explanation of any failure, and the government would have the option to accept the explanation instead of the Governor's resignation. The aim was to increase accountability by the political authorities, maintain the independence of the central bank over operations and choice of policy target, and increase the central bankers' incentives to achieve the targets they set.

The New Zealand contract improved on my proposal by binding the government and the central bank to the same goal. Elimination of the intermediate target may not be an improvement. It remains to be seen whether inflation targeting can maintain low inflation as well as monetary targeting has done in countries such as Germany, Japan (before 1986) and Switzerland.[4]

Central banks with inflation targets can, of course, choose a monetary aggregate as an indicator of inflation. None has announced its intention to do so. Some have developed feedback rules from interest rates or exchange rates to monetary instruments. I believe each has retained discretionary authority to change implementation and procedures when and as they choose.

Restricting the goal or objective either by contract or announcement limits discretion. Central bankers are less free to shift objectives or to trade more inflation for temporary reductions in unemployment. They can, of course, announce their intention to let inflation rise temporarily, but such an announcement would eliminate the effect of surprise and, therefore, reduce or eliminate any desired response in employment or output.

Announcement of an inflation target moves in the direction of rule-like behavior. The extent of the move depends on how reliably central banks can achieve the targets and how serious they are about developing and explaining procedures to reduce the size and frequency of deviations from announced rates of inflation.

If economists could provide a validated, dynamic model of the inflation process that delivered accurate forecasts, achieving an inflation target with acceptable accuracy would be easier. Absent such models, several problems arise in the implementation of inflation targeting. Although there is some overlap, I will mention four problems: (1) the variability of lags between a monetary impulse and its effect on inflation; (2) the problem of forecasting; (3) the problem of measurement; and (4) political interference.

Every policy rule or procedure depends for its successful implementation on a theory that relates the instruments that can be controlled to the objectives to be achieved. The instruments are open market operations, changes in the discount rate or some money market rate and the like. The objective of an inflation target is, of course, to keep inflation within a band that is sufficiently narrow to be both credible and acceptable to the public. Band widths of 2 percent are commonly used. Let me therefore take as a goal keeping inflation within a 2 percent band.

How much in advance must the central bank act to achieve that goal? Economists differ about the length of lags. Friedman and Schwartz (1963b) concluded that lags in the USA were long and variable. Real business cycle theorists claim the lags everywhere are constant at (or near) zero or would be if policy were fully credible.

Uncertainty about the average length of lags and the variability of lags poses a greater problem for a policy of judgmental adaptation or discretion than for a rule-based policy. The reason is that the length of the lag depends on structural parameters of the system. These parameters are not invariant to changes in operating procedures. Discretionary changes in procedure may accelerate or decelerate responses. Variability of lags adds to the uncertainty about whether the target will be achieved and puts pressure on the central bank to respond to dominant market interpretations or misinterpretations.

Successful discretionary policy requires relatively accurate forecasts of inflation and other variables. The record of central bank and private forecasting of inflation shows errors much larger than the bands used by central banks. Mean square errors of 60 percent to 100 percent of the average rate of inflation one quarter or one year ahead are common during the 1970s and 1980s (Meltzer, 1987). McNees (1995) reports root mean square errors for US inflation one year ahead of 1.2 percent for the years 1980 to 1994 and 0.9 percent for 1983 to 1994. This suggests that the width of a 95 percent confidence interval for the USA would be 4 to 5 percent; a target of zero expected inflation would produce inflation rates between minus and plus $2^1/_2$ percent.

Many forecasters use some type of Phillips curve relating inflation to the unemployment rate and other variables, including past inflation. A recent study by King, Stock and Watson (1995) found that this method produced root mean square forecast errors of approximately 1.6 percent for one-year ahead forecasts and 3.9 percent for two-year ahead forecasts during the period 1954–94.[5] Moreover, the authors found considerable variance around the estimated value of the equilibrium level of unemployment, or NAIRU, at which inflation begins to rise. Their work suggests that a central bank that relies on the Phillips curve relation would be unlikely to remain consistently within a 2 percent band for inflation one or two years ahead.

Rasche (1995) reports similar results for several different sample periods. His lowest root mean square error is 1.1 percent for quarterly data from 1980 through 1993. Rasche shows that most of the forecasting power from his Phillips relation comes from the lagged values of inflation. The unemployment rate contributes to the forecast, but its contribution is small.

A necessary condition for inflation is a sustained growth rate of money in excess of the growth rate of output. A considerable body of evidence for many different countries and time periods supports this proposition. A recent study by McCandless and Weber summarizes evidence from other recent studies and adds additional evidence for 110 countries. In the authors' words (1995, p. 4):

> In the long-run, there is a high (almost unity) correlation between the rate of growth of the money supply and the rate of inflation. This holds across three definitions of money and across the full sample of countries and two subsamples.[6]

Cecchetti (1995) computed correlations of seventeen different possible indicators of inflation with the US inflation rate at leads of three months to three or four years. Using monthly data for 1967 to 1994 the highest correlation at a three-month or one-year lead was the growth rate of M1 (0.72). The next highest correlations were for M2 at three months and the monetary base at one to two years, but these correlations were lower, 0.43 and 0.66 respectively. In a shorter monthly sample, 1982 to 1994, the three highest correlations at a three-month lead are the rate of change of the nominal exchange rate, average hourly earnings and the monetary base. The last of these has a correlation of 0.8 for a three-month lead.

Contrary to the often repeated view that narrow monetary aggregates have little predictive power, Cecchetti's evidence suggests that growth of the monetary base has much more information about future US inflation than most of the other sixteen variables he considered. At the two-year frequency, relevant for inflation targeting, growth of the monetary base is correlated to 0.66 in the full sample and 0.98 in the shorter sample. The federal funds rate is uncorrelated with inflation at all frequencies in the full sample and at all but the one- to two-year frequency in the shorter sample.[7] Further, Cecchetti reports that the root mean square error for one year ahead rolling forecasts of inflation using only the growth of the monetary base is 1.6 percent in the longer sample and 1.1 percent in the shorter sample, 1982–94. This compares favorably to Phillips curve estimates. Other commonly used measures such as the term structure spread or the spread between commercial paper and the federal funds rate have zero or low correlations.

The monetary rule I have proposed requires the central bank to target the rate of growth of the monetary base, a variable over which it can exercise close control (Meltzer, 1987).[8] The rule is adaptive; the current growth rate of the monetary base adjusts to past rates of growth of velocity and real output.

I have arbitrarily chosen a four-quarter moving average of the growth rate of the base as the variable to be controlled (or monitored) by the central bank and a twelve-quarter moving average of the growth rates of base velocity and real output to guide changes in the growth rate of the base. As in equation (1.1), expected inflation $E(p)$ is zero when the four-quarter growth rate of the base, b_4, is equal to the twelve-quarter growth rate of the difference between growth of output and base velocity, $y_{12} - V_{12}$.

$$E(p) = 0 \quad \text{for} \quad b_4 = y_{12} - V_{12} \tag{1.1}$$

By definition, $V = y + p - b$; substituting, we get that for $E(p) = 0$

$$b_4 = b_{12} - p_{12} \tag{1.2}$$

The expected rate of inflation for the next four quarters is

$$E(p_4) = b_4 - (b_{12} - p_{12}) \tag{1.3}$$

Equation (1.1) is an identity if b, y and V have the same time dimension, and the same is true of equation (1.3). The right side of (1.3) describes the permanent or expected trend rate of inflation based on information currently available. It does not assure that all of the inflation will be realized in the next quarter. There are reasons for the differences. First, given the uncertainty about the length of lags and the arbitrary choice of the period over which to average b and $b - p$, some of the expected inflation may have occurred; actual inflation can exceed or fall short of the trend rate shown on the right side of (1.3). As is well-known, inflation rates show considerable persistence. I use quarterly measured rates of inflation to adjust expected inflation for recent inflation. Second, as suggested by McCallum's version of a similar monetary rule (1988 and elsewhere), it may be useful to recognize that the inflation is affected systematically by fluctuations in output or employment such as occur during a business cycle.[9] Third, changes in the terms of trade, excise taxes, oil shocks and other one-time price level changes introduce temporary changes in the rate of inflation. These changes will be left for the random term in a regression equation.

To introduce these changes in (1.3), let the four-quarter expected rate of inflation equal next quarter's inflation rate plus actual inflation for the past three quarters plus an error term to allow for one-time changes in the price level.

$$E(p_4) = Ep_{t+1} - (p_t + p_{t-1} + p_{t-2}) \tag{1.4}$$

where

$$E(p_{t+1}) - p_{t+1} = \varepsilon_{t+1} \tag{1.5}$$

Further, let U_t allow for business cycle fluctuations in the measured rate of inflation.

With these changes, the rule becomes part of a regression equation to forecast inflation as shown in (1.6). The equation has the monetary rule, an autoregressive equation and a type of Phillips curve. The rule implies that the coefficients on b_4 and $(b_{12} - p_{12})$ are equal. The statistical findings below do not reject this implication.

$$p_t = a_0 + a_1 b_{4,t-1} + a_2(b_{12} - p_{12})_{t-1} + a_3 p_{t-1} + a_4 p_{t-2} + a_5 p_{t-3} + a_6 U_{t-1} + \varepsilon_t \tag{1.6}$$

Table 1.1 compares forecasting equations for the percentage rate of change of the GDP deflator using (separately) an autoregressive equation, a Phillips-type equation, and equation (1.6) with and without the lagged unemployment rate. All equations use quarterly data for the USA at annual rates for the period 1962: I to 1995: I.

Table 1.1 Forecasts of measured inflation
(one-quarter inflation rate at annual rates)

Period	*1962:I–1995:I*				*1980:I–1995:I*
	(1)	*(2)*	*(3)*	*(4)*	*(5)*
p_{-1}	0.40	0.38	0.39	0.29	0.38
	(4.85)	(4.41)	(4.50)	(3.36)	(2.89)
p_{-2}	0.27	0.29	0.27	0.24	0.24
	(3.05)	(3.29)	(2.92)	(2.72)	(1.71)
p_{-3}	0.23	0.25	0.20	0.25	0.28
	(2.74)	(2.89)	(2.28)	(2.96)	(1.99)
B_{-1}			0.10	0.34	0.17
			(1.11)	(3.22)	(1.52)
			−0.10	−0.21	−0.07
$(\overline{B} - \overline{p})_{-1}$			(0.33)	(2.18)	(0.47)
U_{-1}		−0.18		−0.39	−0.26
		2.18		(3.73)	(1.42)
see	1.47	1.43	1.46	1.39	1.15

Notes: *t*-statistics (absolute value) in parentheses.
p = quarterly measured inflation rate at annual rates (deflator).
B = four-quarter growth rate of monetary base.
$(\overline{B} - \overline{p})$ = twelve-quarter moving average of real base growth.
U = unemployment rate.
Subscripts denote lag length.

Column 1 shows the autoregressive forecast. As is well-known, inflation persists, so the autoregressive equation captures much of the systematic variance in the measured inflation rate. Adding the lagged unemployment rate has a modest effect on the standard error of estimate (see). As Rasche (1995) suggests, the unemployment rate is statistically significant in the equation but contributes little explanatory power for the range of unemployment rates observed in postwar recessions. Column 3 uses the monetary rule with the lagged measured rates of inflation. Again, there is not much improvement over the autoregressive forecasts. Column 4, using equation (1.6), shows some improvement over the autoregressive equation. This version of the rule implies that, on average, a 1 percent change in the growth rate of the monetary base maintained for four quarters increases the quarterly rate of inflation by more than 0.3 percent at annual rates, other things equal. A 3-percentage-point reduction in the growth rate of the base reduces inflation, directly, by one percentage point within a year and, indirectly, reduces inflation by nearly one percentage point more by changing

Table 1.2 Forecast errors, US inflation, 1994:II to 1995:I

	Full sample (1962–95)	*Shorter sample (1980–95)*	
	Rule	*Rule*	*Autoregressive only*
1994:II	1.33	1.65	1.87
:III	0.23	0.24	0.34
:IV	–0.66	–0.70	–0.74
1995:I	0.29	0.18	0.27

the lagged inflation terms. Part of the reduction is, temporarily, offset by any increase in unemployment or change in real base growth that results.

The last column of Table 1.1 reestimates the McCallum-type rule for the period 1980 to 1995. Both the monetary and unemployment variables are much weaker than in the full sample, but the standard error of estimate is lower. Forecast errors for four recent quarters, however, are not uniformly lower using the equation for the shorter sample. The monetary and unemployment terms contribute to forecast accuracy. Forecast errors are generally larger in this period using the autoregressive equation. Table 1.2 shows these errors.

A by-product of Table 1.1 is the evidence showing that, on average, the standard error of measured inflation is large relative to the bands within which central banks seek to hold the inflation rate. One reason is that inflation, as measured, includes one-time price level changes from oil shocks, changes in commodity taxes, the terms of trade, weather and other non-monetary events. A monetary target abstracts from all or most of these changes; a price level or measured inflation target makes the central bank appear responsible for all such changes. In practice, central banks often exclude the most common types of one-time shocks by redefining the price level or rate of price change that they target. By excluding one-time price level changes, the central bank allows the price level to vary around the rate of inflation produced by monetary growth.

Although the rule contributes to forecast accuracy, the benefit of the rule lies less in its contribution to forecasts than its contribution to policymaking. The base can be controlled directly, so a central banker can use the base rule as a guide to policy action. If nominal and real base growth have remained on paths consistent with zero expected inflation, the policymaker should not react to changes in lagged rates of price change that temporarily raise or lower the current measured rate of price change. The difference between recent nominal and lagged real base growth gives information about the expected rate of inflation. For example, if increased intermediation reduces desired real money balances and raises monetary velocity, the gap between nominal and real base growth will widen. This implies that expected inflation will be higher, so the growth of the monetary base should be reduced to keep expected inflation at zero.

In the past I have suggested that the central bank should not choose either the price level or the measured rate of inflation as its target. The target I have proposed is the *expected* rate of inflation. Using this target, the objective of the central bank is to prevent the public from making decisions based on anticipations of inflation. A monetary rule helps to make this important distinction clear to the public. Prices and measured inflation would not be constant, but changes in the rate of price change would be one-time events. Some of the public would interpret the changes as inflation or deflation. Since many of these changes are distributed over time, the ideal of no response would not be fully realized. Nevertheless, the proposal has an advantage that should not be neglected. The central bank would not be expected to roll back increases or decreases in the price level, so the public would avoid the real costs of these adjustments.

This description brings out a choice that governments and central banks must make in a world of zero (or low) inflation. Economic theory does not tell us whether it is better to keep the anticipated price level or the anticipated rate of inflation constant. One choice imposes costs of reversing price level changes; the other increases the variance of the long-run price level. One choice imposes costs of adjustment if there are lags, contracts or other impediments to price level adjustments; the other imposes long-term costs of uncertainty about the future price level. Research comparing or measuring these costs would be highly desirable.

4 CONCLUSION: RULES AND DISCRETION AGAIN

Much has happened both to practice and theory since Henry Simon proposed a rule for monetary policy or since Milton Friedman's *Program for Monetary Stability* (1959). Recently, several central banks seeking increased independence from their governments and more freedom to control inflation have tried to develop procedures that are understood by market participants and more predictable than in the past. Yet, in their public statements, they oppose rules. It may be useful to end by reconsidering the meaning of rules and discretion.

Friedman's lectures contain one of a very few efforts to define and measure discretion (1959, pp. 85–6 and 95–8). Most discussion of rules and discretion leaves entirely open what is meant by discretion.

Central banks do not behave haphazardly. Many try hard to behave in a consistent way so as to avoid misinterpretations. Governors and staff members speak and write frequently to inform market participants and the public about their procedures and their intentions. Market participants watch the same variables that central bankers watch, and they anticipate policy actions. In short, central bankers typically follow rules of behavior, but they do not like to make precise statements about the rules. They want to adjust rules flexibly and preserve the right to depart from the rule temporarily or change the rule permanently. There are many examples. The Federal Reserve has changed its target from free reserves to the federal funds rate, to some measure of reserve growth, and back to the federal funds rate. The Bank of Japan shifted in the mid-1980s from principal reliance on a broad measure of money growth to a policy of targeting the exchange rate. The Bundesbank has deviated from its announced monetary targets at times and has changed the monetary aggregate that it targets. The Swiss National Bank has intervened to manage the exchange rate by allowing the monetary base to exceed its announced growth rate. Most of these changes by the central banks were accompanied by announcements, speeches and papers that informed interested parties about some of the new procedures. I use the term discretion to refer to these changes in processes or procedures whether open or hidden in ambiguity. I know of no evidence that these changes have generally increased welfare. Some have clearly been costly.

Many central banks now express concern about the credibility of their policies for reducing and controlling inflation. Although major central banks continue to respond to rising unemployment rates, central bankers talk much less than in the past about a broad range of objectives and much more about the social cost of inflation and the social gain from price stability. It is difficult to conceive of credibility independently of a rule or rule-like behavior at least as to the objective of policy. It is difficult also to conceive of a credible policy of inflation control achieved by frequent changes in process or procedure. Frequent discretionary changes increase costs of information and raise doubts about the commitment to the central bank's announced objective.

I believe that central banks in the industrial countries no longer choose between rules and discretion as these terms were used in the past. The choices that many central banks now make are (1) the degree of ambiguity they maintain in announcing their rule, (2) the consistency with which they maintain procedures, and (3) the extent to which the rule covers both procedures and objectives, not just objectives. Evidence suggests that central banks that give most weight to the growth of monetary aggregates in the implementation of policy have had the lowest average rates of inflation and less variable inflation. Most models of central banking do not reach this conclusion. The models typically assume that the central bank can achieve its objective and they do not distinguish between maintained inflation and one-time price level changes.

The normative implications of available evidence are much less than fully general. As noted in the introduction, central banks cannot control both the internal and external values of money unless they act cooperatively. Economic theory does not give clear guidance about the relative merits of internal and external price stability, but it does suggest how countries can gain from cooperation.

I suggest three types of institutional arrangements to internalize the gain from cooperation. The United States, Germany and Japan should follow an adaptive monetary rule to achieve zero expected inflation. This would maintain the internal value of money in these countries, allow bilateral exchange rates to adjust to real shocks, and provide a public good for all other countries. Very small countries should eliminate the monetary operations of their central banks by establishing a currency board or a permanently fixed exchange rate and, to enforce their commitment, these countries should permit their citizens to use a non-inflating foreign currency as a medium of exchange or parallel currency. The central bank in a small economy can do much harm but has little prospect of improving on a fixed exchange rate, low-inflation solution. The remaining countries can choose between the advantages of a fixed exchange rate in a world of zero expected inflation or an independent monetary policy to prevent domestic inflation. Any other choice would fail to provide the benefits that countries can expect to gain from a stable world monetary order and more effective monetary policies. It is up to each country to decide whether it is small or medium-sized and whether it wishes to join the club of stability or undertake its own policy actions. Only the three largest countries should be restricted by a common commitment to a rule that maintains zero expected inflation and provides public benefits for them and for any country that accepts the requisite monetary discipline.

The proposal I have made is close to the practice of the Bundesbank (Issing, 1995) and fits well with the recent statement of Governor Matsushita of the Bank of Japan. Last spring Governor Matsushita wrote (1995, p. 6):

> Firstly, each country should take appropriate policy responses to achieve the common objective of non-inflationary sustainable growth in accordance with domestic circumstances . . . and, secondly, each country should make every effort to acquire the market's understanding of its firm policy

stance, and thereby to eliminate uncertainties to as great a degree as possible.

A rules-based policy, with common rules in the largest countries, seems the most effective way to realize these objectives and, in the process, increase the contribution that central banks make to policy effectiveness and economic welfare domestically and internationally.

Notes

1. Some exceptions are Cukierman and Meltzer (1986) and Cukierman (1992).
2. Meltzer (1994) develops this argument in greater detail.
3. The proposal was based on a 1981 recommendation by the Shadow Open Market Committee but its antecedents lie in the nineteenth-century practice of finance ministers who resigned if they devalued the currency.
4. Japan abandoned monetary targeting to control its exchange rate in 1986 and has had difficulty regaining economic stability since that time.
5. For the more stable years 1954–73, the error is 1.1 percent.
6. See also Capie (1995) who summarizes the history of inflation and concludes that the only periods when inflation occurred were times when money expanded persistently.
7. The correlation is 0.89, however, in the 1982–1994 sample at the one- to two-year frequency.
8. The complete statement of the rule also requires the central bank to post a penalty discount rate and provide the services of a lender of last resort.
9. McCallum uses the difference between current output and its trend growth. I use lagged unemployment to compare to a Phillips curve.

References

Barro, R.J. and Gordon, D.B. (1983) "A Positive Theory of Monetary Policy in a Natural Rate Model," *Journal of Political Economy*, 91, pp. 589–610.

Bordo, M. and Jonung, L. (1987) *The Long-Run Behavior of the Velocity of Circulation: The International Evidence* (New York: Cambridge University Press).

Capie, F. (1995) "Money and Prices in the Long Run," *Economic Affairs*, 15 (Autumn), pp. 15–20.

Cecchetti, S.G. (1995) "Inflation Indicators and Inflation Policy," National Bureau of Economic Research Working Paper No. 5161, June.

Chandler, L.V. (1958) *Benjamin Strong, Central Banker* (Washington, DC: Brookings Institution).

Cukierman, A. (1992) *Central Bank Strategy, Credibility and Independence* (Cambridge, Mass.: MIT Press).

Cukierman, A. and Meltzer, A.H. (1986) "A Theory of Ambiguity, Credibility and Inflation under Discretion and Asymmetric Information," *Econometrica*, 54, pp. 1099–1128. Reprinted in A.H. Meltzer, A. Cukierman and S. Richard (eds), *Political Economy* (New York: Oxford University Press, 1991).

Eichengreen, B. (1992) *Golden Fetters: The Gold Standard and the Great Depression* (New York: Oxford, University Press).

Friedman, M. (1959) *A Program for Monetary Stability* (New York: Fordham University Press).

Friedman, M. and Schwartz, A.J. (1963a) *A Monetary History of the United States, 1867–1960* (Princeton, NJ: Princeton University Press for the National Bureau of Economic Research).

Friedman, M. and Schwartz, A.J. (1963b) "Money and Business Cycles," in *The State of Monetary Economics, Review of Economics and Statistics*, 45, supplement (February), pp. 32–64.

Issing, O. (1995) "Stability of Monetary Policy, Stability of the Monetary System: Experience with Monetary Targeting in Germany," prepared for the Symposium of the Swiss National Bank, Gerzensee, March. *Journal of Monetary Economics* (forthcoming).

Jonung, L. (1981) "The Depression in Sweden and the United States: A Comparison of Causes and Policies," in K. Brunner (ed.), *The Great Depression Revisited* (Boston, Mass.: Martinus Nijihoff).

Keynes, J.M. (1923) *A Tract on Monetary Reform* (London: Macmillan and St Martin's Press for the Royal Economic Society, 1971).

King, R.G., Stock, J.H. and Watson, M.W. (1995) "Temporal Instability in the Unemployment–Inflation Relationship," *Economic Perspectives*, Federal Reserve Bank of Chicago (May/June), pp. 2–12.

Kydland, F. and Prescott, E.C. (1977) "Rules Rather than Discretion: The Inconsistency of Optimal Plans," *Journal of Political Economy*, 85 (June), pp. 473–92.

Leiderman, L. and Svensson, L. (1995) "Inflation Targets: Introduction," in L. Leiderman and L.E.O. Svensson (eds), *Inflation Targets* (London: CEPR, forthcoming).

McCallum, B. (1988) "Robustness Properties of a Rule for Monetary Policy," Carnegie–Rochester Conference Series on Public Policy, 29 (Autumn), pp. 173–204.

McCandless, G.T., Jr and Weber, W.E. (1995) "Some Monetary Facts," *Quarterly Review*, Federal Reserve Bank of Minneapolis (Summer), pp. 2–11.

McNees, S. (1995) "An Assessment of the 'Official' Economic Forecasts," *New England Economic Review*, Federal Reserve Bank of Boston (July/August), pp. 13–23.

Matsushita, Y. (1995) "Global Economic Integration and the Central Bank," *Quarterly Bulletin*, Bank of Japan.

Meltzer, A.H. (1987) "Limits to Short-Run Stabilization Policy," *Economic Inquiry*, 25 (January), pp. 1–13.

Meltzer, A.H. (1994) "Why Did Monetary Policy Fail in the Thirties?," unpublished manuscript, Carnegie Mellon University.

Mints, L.W. (1945) *A History of Banking Theory* (Chicago, Ill.: University of Chicago Press).

Rasche, R.H. (1995) "How Useful and Reliable is the Unemployment Rate in Forecasting Inflation?," unpublished, Michigan State University (September).

Rich, G. (1995) "Monetary Targets as a Policy Rule: Lessons from Swiss Experience," prepared for the Symposium of the Swiss National Bank, Gerzensee, March. *Journal of Monetary Economics* (forthcoming).

Weber, A. (1991) "Credibility, Reputation, and the European Monetary System," *Economic Policy*, 12, pp. 57–102.

2 Policy Rules as a Means to a More Effective Monetary Policy*

John B. Taylor

The purpose of the Seventh Bank of Japan International Conference is to discuss ways in which monetary policy can be made more effective. There are many routes to a more effective monetary policy – through more accurate measurement of inflation, greater knowledge of the monetary transmission mechanism, better ways to supervise banks and other financial institutions, and so on. But the most basic route of all, in my view, is through the development of a set of monetary policy rules or guidelines to help guide monetary policy decisions.

The use of monetary policy rules is a theme which has repeatedly come up at previous Bank of Japan conferences – Milton Friedman (1985) and James Tobin (1985) discussed policy rules in their keynote addresses at the First Bank of Japan International Conference in 1983 and such rules are discussed in most of the chapters in this volume. Continuing in that tradition, my aims are (1) to briefly review historical developments in the empirical design of policy rules – with an emphasis on what has happened since the rational expectations revolution began to transform econometric policy evaluation methods in the early 1970s, (2) to give the reasons why setting explicit targets and using policy rules to achieve those targets can make monetary policy more effective, and (3) to discuss some of the differences and similarities between some recent policy rules which have been proposed for practical application in the United States and other economies.

1 MODELS, TRADEOFFS, AND TARGETS

A basic principle of economic policy analysis is that recommendations for policy actions – including proposals for policy rules – be based on a

* This research was supported by the Center for Economic Policy Research at Stanford University and by a grant from the National Science Foundation at the National Bureau of Economic Research.

coherent explanation, or theory, of how policy actions affect the economy, backed up by empirical facts in support of the theory. The most formal way to provide an empirically supported theory is through a well-specified and tested econometric model, but less formal descriptions of theories and facts have their use as well. The introduction of rational expectations to macroeconomics by Robert Lucas in the 1970s (see Lucas, 1972, for example) had major impacts on our models – both theoretical and empirical – of how monetary policy actions affect the economy.

1.1 No Long-Run Tradeoff

The rational expectations revolution laid to rest the notion of a long-run tradeoff between the rate of inflation and the rate of unemployment, as first put forth by Milton Friedman and Edmund Phelps. That is, when averaged over long periods of time, such as decades, higher rates of inflation are not associated with lower levels of unemployment, and lower levels of inflation are not associated with higher levels of unemployment. Whether average inflation is high or low in a given decade, unemployment hovers around a natural rate of unemployment during that decade. Experience with inflation and unemployment during the decades of the 1970s and 1980s in the United States and other countries has confirmed this view.

The natural rate of unemployment is not a constant, however. For example, the rise in unemployment in Europe compared to the United States since the 1980s is due to a rise in the natural unemployment rate in Europe relative to the United States.

Moreover, the non-existence of a long-run tradeoff between inflation and unemployment does not mean that inflation does not have long-run effects on economic growth and productivity. Cross-country evidence suggests that countries with higher rates of inflation tend to have lower long-term economic growth rates.

1.2 A Short-Run Tradeoff?

The introduction of rational expectations into macroeconomics was less definitive, however, about the short-run tradeoff between inflation and unemployment. Today, many remain tentative about the existence of such a tradeoff, or at least about how to describe it and take account of it in policymaking. Some early econometric models with rational expectations (Sargent, 1976, for example) implied there was no short-term tradeoff in the sense that short-run anticipated *changes* in inflation or money growth would not affect the level of the unemployment rate. Models without a short-run tradeoff – which today includes most real business cycle models – usually assume perfectly flexible prices.

But other econometric models, for example, the one which I built about the same time as Sargent's (Taylor, 1979), do imply a kind of short-run tradeoff, and this tradeoff has implications for monetary policy decisions. Such models are usually based on some degree of temporary price or wage rigidities. I have found the short-run tradeoff best described and estimated in terms of a tradeoff between the *variability* of inflation and the *variability* of unemployment: that is, in terms of the short- run fluctuations in these variables rather than their levels over time. In particular, I find that there is a tradeoff between the size of the fluctuations in inflation and the size of the fluctuations in real GDP (or the fluctuations in unemployment because deviations of real GDP from potential GDP are highly correlated with deviations of the unemployment rate from the natural rate).

The best way to understand this short-run variability tradeoff is to consider some scenarios which bring it about. Consider a situation where the unemployment rate equals the natural rate of unemployment (or real GDP equals potential GDP) and where inflation is equal to the target rate of inflation, perhaps zero inflation. Now suppose that there is a upward shock to velocity. Assuming that monetary policy cannot react to offset the velocity shock immediately, the shock will cause real GDP to rise above potential GDP, probably with a lag of several quarters. Most likely this boom in the economy will cause the inflation rate to rise above its target, again with a lag. In such a situation the central bankers have a policy decision (if they were following a policy rule their decision would be stipulated by the rule): How much should we "tighten" policy? If the central bank tightens policy sharply letting short-term interest rates rise by a large amount in response to the rise in inflation, the inflation rate will return to target quickly, but the economy will slow down and perhaps go into recession. Alternatively, if the central bank is more cautious in tightening policy, the inflation rate will return to target more gradually, but there will be a smaller slowdown in real GDP. One monetary reaction results in more inflation stability and less real GDP stability, while the other monetary reaction results in less inflation stability and more real GDP stability. Hence, the tradeoff.

Many other shocks would give rise to the same set of choices. For example, the monetary response to an unanticipated change in potential GDP growth, a run-up in oil prices, or simply a past error in setting or measuring the money supply, would affect the size of the fluctuations of inflation versus real GDP.

1.3 The Rationale for Inflation Targets

Whether or not there is an inflation–output variability tradeoff, the finding that there is no long-run tradeoff has unambiguous normative policy implications in my view. It implies that central banks should choose a target for inflation and then consistently stay with the target. Because higher inflation has higher costs and no benefits in terms of lower unemployment, a low target for the inflation rate is better than a high target for the inflation rate. Due to biases in the measure of inflation, a target of slightly greater than zero would be reasonable, and may be near an actual inflation rate of zero.

Even with such an inflation target for monetary policy, the actual inflation rate would tend to fluctuate around the target. Or if the target is stipulated as a range then the inflation rate would fluctuate within that range. If all the major central banks adopted inflation targets and stuck with them then a major source of uncertainty about exchange rates would be removed and we would likely see a much greater stability of exchange rates.

It should be noted that an inflation target is not a maximum for inflation; if inflation falls below the target (deflation if the target is zero) then that is as poor an outcome as inflation being above the target. For example, an explicit target of 1 percent inflation would imply easing of monetary policy if inflation were below 1 percent.

In my view this same theory also implies that the central bank should *not* set a long-run target for the unemployment rate or for the gap between potential GDP and real GDP. According to the theory neither the unemployment rate nor the GDP gap can be affected by monetary policy in the long run. Of course, a higher inflation rate can affect the growth rate of potential GDP and since the inflation rate is affected by money growth the central bank can implicitly affect the growth rate of potential GDP; but setting a low target of inflation is apparently the best monetary policy for potential GDP growth.

1.4 Targets versus Rules

This conclusion that the central bank should set a long-run target, or a target range, for inflation, but not for real variables like real GDP or unemployment, does not imply any particular policy rule to achieve that target. In fact, as I will show, there is a whole range of policy rules which will give the same average target rate of inflation. The long-run average rate of inflation is determined by the long-run average rate of money growth, but there are many different monetary policy rules which generate the same long-run money growth. An important question, in my view, is which of those policy rules works best in keeping the fluctuations of inflation around the stated target small. That depends on the nature of the short-run tradeoff.

2 RULES FOR SETTING THE INSTRUMENTS OF MONETARY POLICY

I have already begun to use the term "policy rule" without defining what I mean by policy rule. In my work I have focused on policy rules that describe explicitly what the central bank should do with its instruments of policy. Currently we can think of two broad classes of monetary instruments – monetary aggregates, such as the monetary base, and short-term interest rates, such as the federal funds rate. I recognize that this is a somewhat more narrow focus than in recent research. In my view, if a policy rule is to be useful in making monetary policy more effective to policymakers it should stipulate exactly how the instruments of policy should be set in response to events in the economy.

A broader focus on policy rules might include nominal GDP targeting, which simply states that the central bank should keep the growth rate of nominal GDP at a certain target or target range. However, a nominal GDP target does not specify the actions that must be taken regarding interest rates or the monetary aggregate to achieve that target. Similarly, simply setting a target for the inflation rate or the price level does not tell the central bank what to do. Setting targets without policy rules is like telling a sailing ship's crew to "head zero degrees north" without stipulating how to turn the rudder, tack, or trim the sails when the wind or current changes. One could simply say that sailing is a "technical problem" the crew can figure out on its own, but it would be constructive for those giving policy advice to endeavor to at least comment on this important (and as interesting as sailing) technical problem.

2.1 Money Rules

By far the most widely cited monetary policy rule is the constant growth rate rule for the money supply put forth by Milton Friedman. Friedman's justification for this rule – summarized nicely in Friedman's (1985) address to the First Bank of Japan Conference – was based on monetary theory and extensive empirical research which documented the dynamic effects of changes in the money stock on inflation and output. Friedman explicitly rejected price level or inflation targeting as a substitute for a monetary policy rule – "I think this is the wrong kind of rule" (Friedman, 1962) – because of a lack of a close short-term connection between the money stock and the price level. Friedman also rejected proposals that money growth be adjusted to events in the economy though he had earlier advocated using money to finance the budget deficit and thereby have money growth vary counter-cyclically.

However, armed with a new class of rational expectations econometric models, extensions of Friedman's constant growth rate rule to allow for contingencies began to be examined in the late 1970s. For example, I designed and proposed an alternative money rule using a rational expectations econometric model; this rule called for money growth to respond to real GDP, but not to accommodate inflation. In particular, money growth would average the Friedman *k*-percent rate, but would be increased when real GDP dropped below potential GDP and decreased when real GDP rose above potential GDP. The optimal rule (derived from the model) had the feature that (as an approximation) the money supply should not respond to inflation at all. In other words, if inflation picked up the money growth would stay constant, reducing real money balances, slowing down the economy, and thereby bringing inflation back under control. As a matter of econometric estimation I found that it was not optimal to decrease the money supply when inflation rose or increase it when inflation rose (even if there were a supply shock).

Simulation of the model showed that such a policy rule would outperform a constant growth rate rule for the money supply, though the constant growth rate rule was better than the actual policy at the time. This calculation was based on the inflation–output variability tradeoff previously discussed.

2.2 Velocity Shocks and the Rise of Interest Rate Rules

In the mid-1980s research on monetary policy rules aimed at guiding the instruments of policy experienced two significant developments. I believe both developments were related to a decrease in the observed stability of several velocity measures.

First, there was an increased emphasis of interest rate rules rather than money supply rules. For example, during this period I was working on a multi-country econometric model with rational expectations with the aim of experimenting with alternative money supply rules. My first working paper reporting the results – which argued in favor of flexible exchange rates – was based entirely on simulating money supply rules in which the money supply in each of the developed economies responded to various indicators. However, because of the large estimated money demand shocks in my estimated money demand equations, it quickly became apparent that interest rate rules would result in less instability than money rules; at least that was what was implied by the model simulations, as could be expected from the analysis of different instruments by Poole (1970). For this reason I began to focus on interest rate rules, examining which variables should be in the policy rule and what the size of the response coefficients should be. Also during this period, the Fed and other central banks began moving toward interest rate setting in their policy deliberations – a move which is now complete and transparent at the Federal Reserve. In any case virtually all the policy rule analysis in my final multi-country model (Taylor, 1993) was conducted in terms of interest rate rules.

The other development in research on policy rules consisted of the proposals by McCallum (1988) and Meltzer (1987) for money rules which automatically adjust to shifts in velocity. Bennett McCallum has since done extensive experimentation with such money rules by simulating their performance in different models and for different countries, including Japan (McCallum, 1993).

This research on policy rules – both money and interest rate rules together – has now become quite substantial. The book edited by Bryant, Hooper and Mann (1993) has assembled much of this research in one place. Rational expectations model simulations by Jeffrey Fuhrer and George Moore (1995) have been in a similar vein though focused on a single economy framework. Work by Judd and Trehan (1995) and others at the San Francisco Fed and by John Lipsky and others (1995) at Salomon Brothers has investigated the use of policy rules for both historical analysis and forecasting. In fact, virtually all academic policy evaluation research on monetary policy in recent years has focused on policy rules.

In my view this research is providing information which can be quite useful in making monetary policy more effective. But the results of the different researchers do not always agree and are hard to reconcile. For example, while it is possible to glean a slight consensus about policy rules from the Bryant, Hooper and Mann study, in many cases the experiments were not conducted in the same way by different researchers.

2.3 Advantages of Policy Rules

There are several reasons to recommend policy instrument changes through policy rules rather than as one-time changes in the instruments of policy. The most commonly cited reason is the time-inconsistency problem which states that, without commitment to a rule, policymakers will end up choosing a suboptimal monetary policy – with a higher average inflation rate and the same unemployment that could be achieved with a lower average inflation rate (see Kydland and Prescott, 1977). But the time-inconsistency problem is only one of many reasons for using policy rules, and, as I first argued in comments on the Kydland and Prescott (1977) and Barro and Gordon, 1983) papers (see Taylor, 1983), it is difficult to see why the time-inconsistency problem should be that tough for a political system to solve in the case of the unemployment–inflation tradeoff.

There are several other good reasons to make use of policy rules. First, if people are forward-looking one needs to stipulate future as well as current policy actions in order to evaluate the effects of policy. Second, policy rules can reduce uncertainty about policy actions and thereby can reduce risk premia in financial markets. Without a policy rule to describe monetary policy actions, market participants find it difficult to forecast future actions or even interpret current actions of policymakers. Third, policy rules can be useful as a way to instruct policymakers about actions to take to achieve their goals. If there were a school for central bankers the early lessons might indeed be conducted in terms of policy rules describing what they ought to do in certain circumstances. Fourth, policy rules can make it easier to teach students and educate the public about the actions of one of the most powerful agencies of government. Fifth, policy rules provide a way to increase the accountability of policymakers: if the policy rule is reliable then policymakers would find themselves having to account for differences between their actions and the recommendations of a policy rule. Of course, I recognize that, at least with our current knowledge, events like the 1987 stock market crash may require that the central bank depart from the rule, and that some discretion is still necessary in working with a rule. But with a policy rule the analysis of policy – including justifying whether a deviation from the rule is warranted – will tend to focus less on discretion and more on the rule.

3 THE SIMILARITY BETWEEN MONEY RULES AND INTEREST RATE RULES

Although interest rate rules and money supply rules are frequently viewed as quite different there is an important similarity between them. First, consider a money supply rule which calls for constant growth rate of the money supply. Recall that the demand for money is a demand for real money balances – the money supply divided by the price level (P) – which is a function of some scale variable such as real income or real GDP (*Y*), an opportunity cost variable such as the short-term interest rate (*R*), and some other taste variables which may change from time to time. If money growth is fixed then the money demand function can be viewed as a relationship between three variables: (1) the price level (*P*) or its percentage change – the inflation rate, (2) real GDP (*Y*) and (3) the short-term interest rate (*R*). If we isolate the interest rate as one variable then this relationship says that the interest rate depends on the inflation rate and on real GDP. This relationship many be quite complex, but over long periods of time the signs are remarkably stable: along this relationship a higher level of real GDP raises the interest rate and a higher level of inflation also raises the interest rate (assuming a constant rate of money growth).

The similarity between money supply rules and interest rate rules is that many interest rate rules that have been proposed – including the ones that I have proposed (Taylor, 1993) – have exactly the same properties: a rise of real GDP calls for the central bank to increase the interest rate and an increase in the inflation rate calls on the central bank to increase the interest rate. In fact, when I simulate the effects of interest rate rules in econometric models I replace the money demand function with the policy rule as a determinant of the short-term interest rate. (The money demand function then becomes a way to project money growth, though not with much accuracy because of the volatility of the shocks to money demand.)

I think this close connection between money rules and interest rate rules is important. First, it helps us in the design of rules: the good properties of one type of rule can be copied in the other. In the case of the interest rate rules I have proposed the effect of real GDP and inflation on interest rates are carried over from money supply rules but the volatility of velocity is left behind. Second, the connection reminds us that if interest rate rules become unreliable – perhaps because inflation gets very high or very low (deflation) and short-term nominal interest rate movements become dominated by expectations of inflation or deflation – then money rules can be emphasized. For example, in Japan in recent years the deflation has, in my view, made an interest rate rule unreliable, calling for greater emphasis on money supply rules and the need to keep money growth from falling. Another example was the Great Depression in the United States in the 1930s. I would argue that interest rate rules need to be supplemented by money supply rules in cases of either extended deflation or hyperinflation.

The similarity between money supply rules and interest rate rules suggests that both have a role as a consistency check on monetary decisions. For example, in recent work Wall Street economists interested in projecting Fed behavior have consulted both types of rules (see Lipsky *et al.*, 1995).

3.1 The Role of Real GDP in Interest Rate Rules

The connection between money rules and interest rate rules helps resolve a puzzle that many have raised about interest rate rules. As I stated earlier, modern macroeconomic theory implies that it is not wise for a central bank to have a long-run target for real output or unemployment as it should for an inflation rate. But then why is real output a variable in the interest rate policy rule I have suggested? The answer is that non-target variables have an important role in policy rules; effectively real GDP plays a role in moving interest rates when the central bank keeps money growth fixed: this is one of the attractive features of money supply rules, because the interest rate increase helps moderate the boom in real GDP and thereby helps stabilize both inflation and real GDP. Real GDP appears in interest rate policy rules for exactly the same reason: the increase in the interest rate helps moderate the boom and stabilize inflation.

3.2 Future Developments Relating to Monetary Policy Rules

I am getting old enough to see the development of monetary policy rules from a long-term perspective. My first experience with research on monetary policy rules was when I was in college nearly thirty years ago. In my senior thesis (Taylor, 1968) I built a dynamic simulation model to evaluate different types of policy rules for monetary policy. In fact the rule which I found worked best was a money rule in which the money supply growth rate increased when real GDP fell below potential GDP and decreased when real GDP rose above potential GDP – an adaptation of the Friedman *k*-percent rule. Needless to say that model was before rational expectations entered macroeconomics, and involved no formal policy optimization. It is nice to see the progress we have made since then. In my view, future progress will occur not only in improving policy rules, but in finding ways for them to be more useful to practitioners of monetary policy.

Are policy rules of the type I have described here applied in practice? Some have characterized the Federal Reserve policy of the late 1970s and early 1980s as monetarist, but Milton Friedman (1985) argued in no uncertain terms that that was far from what the Fed was doing during that period. Similarly many have commented on the similarity of the interest rate policy rule I developed and the actual action of the Federal Reserve since 1987, but Federal Reserve officials say that at most they look at such a rule as a reality or consistency check, and I think this is true.

A challenge for future research is to find ways for policy rules to be used more directly by policymakers. The 1990 *Economic Report of the*

President devoted a chapter to describing policy rules, showing how they can be useful, and describing in words an interest rate policy rule for the Fed. One of the advantages of explicit policy rules is that they can be used in real time at least in parallel with other means of formulating policy decisions. The experience can then prove useful in modifying the policy rule for the future.

In assessing future work on policy rules I think it is useful to close with a quote from Milton Friedman written after proposing the *k*-percent rule:

> I should like to emphasize that I do not regard my particular proposal as a be-all and end-all of monetary management, as a rule which is somehow to be written in tablets of stone and enshrined for all future time. It seems to me to be the rule that offers the greatest promise of achieving a reasonable degree of monetary stability in light of our present knowledge. I would hope that as we operated with it, as we learned more about monetary matters, we might be able to devise still better rules, which would achieve still better results (Milton Friedman, 1962, pp. 54–5).

References

Barro, R. and Gordon, D. (1983) "Rules, Discretion, and Reputation in a Model of Monetary Policy," *Journal of Monetary Economics*, 12, pp. 101–22.

Bryant, R., Hooper, P. and Mann, C. (1993) *Evaluating Policy Regimes: New Empirical Research in Empirical Macroeconomics* (Washington, DC: Brookings Institution).

Friedman, M. (1962) *Capitalism and Freedom* (Chicago, Ill.: University of Chicago Press).

Friedman, M. (1985) "Monetarism in Rhetoric and Practice," in A. Ando, H. Eguchi, R. Farmer and Y. Suzuki (eds) *Monetary Policy in Our Times* (Cambridge, Mass.: MIT Press), pp. 15–28.

Fuhrer, J.C. and Moore, G. (1995) "Monetary Policy Tradeoffs at the Correlation between Nominal Interest Rates and Real Output," *American Economic Review*, 85, pp. 219–59.

Judd, J.P. and Trehan, B. (1995) "Has the Fed Gotten Tougher on Inflation," *Federal Reserve Bank of San Francisco Weekly Letter*, No. 95–13.

Kydland, F. and Prescott, E. (1977) "Rules Rather than Discretion: The Inconsistency of Optimal Plans," *Journal of Political Economy*, 85, pp. 473–92.

Lipsky, J., Di Clemente, R., Herring, S. and Jones, B. "Comments on Credit," Salomon Brothers, 29 September 1995.

Lucas, R.E., Jr (1972) "Expectations and the Neutrality of Money," *Journal of Economic Theory*, 4 (April), pp. 103–24.

McCallum, B. (1988) "Robustness Properties of a Rule for Monetary Policy," Carnegie–Rochester Conference Series on Public Policy, 29, pp. 173–204.

McCallum, B. (1993) "Specification and Analysis of a Monetary Policy Rule for Japan," *Monetary and Economic Studies*, Bank of Japan, 11, pp. 1–45.
Meltzer, A.H. (1987) "Limits of Short-Run Stabilization Policy," *Economic Inquiry*, 25, pp. 1–13.
Poole, W. (1970) "Optimal Choice of Monetary Policy Instruments in a Simple Stochastic Macro Model," *Quarterly Journal of Economics*, 84 (2), pp. 197–256.
Sargent, T. (1976) "A Classical Macroeconometric Model of the United States," *Journal of Political Economy*, 84 (2), pp. 207–37.
Taylor, J.B. (1968) "Fiscal and Monetary Stabilization Policies in a Model of Cyclical Growth," Working Paper, Econometric Research Program, Princeton University.
Taylor, J.B. (1979) "Estimation and Control of a Macroeconomic Model with Rational Expectations," *Econometrica*, 47 (5), pp. 1267–86.
Taylor, J.B. (1983) "Comments," *Journal of Monetary Economics*, 12, pp. 123–5.
Taylor, J.B. (1993) *Macroeconomic Policy in the World Economy: From Econometric Design to Practical Operation* (New York: W.W. Norton).
Tobin, J. (1985) "Monetary Policy in an Uncertain World," in A. Ando, H. Eguchi, R. Farmer, Y. Suzuki (eds), *Monetary Policy in Our Times* (Cambridge, Mass.: MIT Press), pp. 15–28.

3 Styles of Monetary Management*

Tommaso Padoa-Schioppa

1 INTRODUCTION

Although the task of providing "sound money" to the economy was attributed to central banks as early as the late eighteenth century, the importance of price stability has grown significantly for both central banks and the general public since the high inflation of the 1970s. Through that experience a new generation became aware of the association of fiat money regimes with inflationary bias in public and private economic behavior and recognized how much the public good of monetary stability contributes to the material and moral welfare of society. Of the three measures of the value of money – expressed respectively in terms of the goods and services available in the country of the currency (the index of prices), of other currencies (the exchange rate), and of the currency itself in the future (the interest rate) – the first is now generally deemed to be the most important. Price stability today is viewed as a precondition for lasting economic growth: this was not the case twenty-five years ago, when I joined the central bank of my country.

Over the years, the focus of theoretical discussions concerning monetary policy has shifted from the inflation–unemployment tradeoff and the choice of monetary control instruments to the institutional features affecting central banks' activity and the information they disclose about their actions, aims and strategies. Notions such as precommitment, credibility, reputation, independence and accountability, once absent from the vocabulary of central banking, have assumed a key role in discussing central banks and the effectiveness of their action.

In addition to recent experience and theoretical developments, two other factors have tended to foster greater transparency and more active communication. In the first place, technological and financial innovation has led to

* The author expresses his gratitude to Paolo Del Giovane and Valeria Sannucci for assistance and advice in the preparation of this paper. I. Angeloni, L. Guiso, M. Magnani, D. Terlizzese also provided useful comments and suggestions. Responsibility for opinions and errors belongs to the author.

a world in which market participants are equipped with the same analytical and statistical instruments as central banks and are thus able to monitor the latter's actions in real time; in such conditions central bankers' best course is to complement this "passive" transparency with a more active communication strategy. In the second place, central bankers have had to balance their growing independence *vis-à-vis* the political sphere with increased accountability for their actions to the government, parliament and the public.

As the debate about monetary policy has gradually shifted away from the *priorities* and *techniques* the central bank should adopt, reflecting a growing consensus on the priority to be attributed to price stability and a common understanding of how the monetary mechanism works, the way in which a stability-oriented monetary policy operating through the money market should formulate and communicate its action in order to maximize its effectiveness has become the central issue. This is what can be called the *style* of monetary policy, that is to say, the way in which central bankers make their strategy known to the other agents in the economy. I define a "style" as being a course of behavior which is held with sufficient continuity through a variety of circumstances: a later paragraph will explain in what way a style differs from a "rule."

This chapter is concerned with styles of monetary management. I shall deal with the subject by first reviewing some basic reference points that central bankers take into account when designing their strategies, that is, developments in economic theory, the information on which they can draw and the working of financial markets. I shall then outline and discuss the four styles of monetary management that, in my view, represent the options open to central banks today. Three of them involve a formal, quantified and time-specific precommitment in terms of a single target variable: the exchange rate, the money supply or the rate of inflation itself. The fourth, which I shall call the "classic" style, relies instead on action and openly gives consideration to a multiplicity of variables, thus foregoing both the advantages and the risk of formal precommitments with respect to a single variable. More specific attention will be devoted to inflation targeting, which is perceived today as "the" novelty in monetary management. I will then survey the experience of the G-7 countries with regard to their choice of style and show how at times in the past twenty-five years central bankers have adhered to a different style from the one they professed to have adopted. I will conclude with some general remarks.

2 THE THEORY KIT

Saying that economic theory is a fundamental reference point for central bankers in the conduct of monetary policy is not such an obvious statement as it might seem. It could not have been made with the same strength thirty or forty years ago. Nor can it be made today for other policy functions such as banking supervision or the payment system. I can only try to flag the concepts that, on the basis of my own education and professional experience, I regard as the key theoretical reference points for monetary policy.

In a few words, I would say that among the theoretical contributions of the past sixty years there are five which constitute the theory kit that central bankers possess regardless of the depth of their academic background. First, they owe to Keynes the notion of instability, in both real and financial markets, and the recognition of the role of uncertainty and speculation. Second, from Milton Friedman they have reinherited the conviction that, in the long run, money is neutral, and that monetary policy cannot contribute to solving the structural problems of the economy. Third, game theorists have clarified that private agents and policymakers interact strategically, anticipating each other's responses, and have thus shifted the picture of the economy from one of mechanistic determinism to one of multiple equilibria in which history matters. Fourth, Robert Lucas has made all policymakers aware that economic agents cannot be assumed to maintain expectations which are systematically falsified. Finally, from the neo-Keynesians, they have gained a clearer understanding of the many obstacles to the ideal functioning of markets, stemming from the asymmetric distribution of information, the inertial role of institutions and contracts, and the existence of market power.

In parallel with the debate on the propositions put forward by these various schools of thought, there was a debate on the choice between "rules" and "discretion" in the conduct of monetary policy. And if we push our retrospective observation of economic thinking to embrace the nineteenth century, this would still hold true, with Keynes and Friedman finding their precursors in Thornton and Ricardo respectively. In the earlier phases of the theoretical debate, "rules" and "discretion" were not necessarily mentioned explicitly. Yet, in most cases the disagreement basically reflected different views on the desirability and effectiveness of discretionary action by policymakers.

Though the issue never seems to be settled, the arguments set forth in support of the two positions have changed considerably over the years. Supporters of the superiority of discretion have abandoned the idea that there exists a tradeoff in the long run between inflation and unemployment, while finding it desirable to maintain a capacity to react flexibly to unforeseen shocks. The idea that fine-tuning of the economy is possible has given way to the view that some smoothing action may be helpful in the face of excessive fluctuations. On the other hand, those who argue in favor of rules no longer necessarily base their case exclusively on the fact that monetary policy can exert no more than a temporary influence on real variables and then only after long and variable lags, or on the the claim that market forces alone are able to ensure an efficient allocation of resources. Only a few radical adherents to the rational expectations school would actually claim that unbiased expectations prevent monetary management from being effective even in the short term. The literature based on game theory has shifted the focus of the debate, in that it has shown that rules are often not enforceable, so that a substitute has to be found in "strong" institutions, so that the issue becomes that of defining a strong institution.

Since the proposed rule was the highly simplified one of constant money growth, the alternative "rules versus discretion" tended at first to coincide with the choice between non-activism and activism. It later became clear that rules could be complicated and allow for activism by designing a "state contingent" policy response to shocks. However, I believe that the conflict between activism and non-activism is still present, at a deeper level, once one fully acknowledges the implications of uncertainty. Adding uncertainty to a model does not simply involve adding a stochastic term to its equations. What uncertainty really implies is that there are unforeseeable events that cannot be incorporated in a stochastic rule, no matter how sophisticated it may be. Not only do we not know which, or which combination, of all the possible – known – events will be drawn from the urn; we do not know what the urn actually contains. Recognizing that we do not have perfect knowledge of what is in the urn is, in my opinion, the only way to avoid the dangers inherent in a deterministic view of the branch of social sciences called economics.

In the academic world the various schools have often been drawn up in opposition to each other, almost as if the aim was mutual exclusion. Nevertheless, there have always been leading economists seeking to achieve a synthesis of the different contributions rather than monistically presenting a new discovery as an interpretative passkey and unique prescription for action – John Hicks, Franco Modigliani, Robert Solow, James Tobin are names that spring to mind. Thanks to their efforts, and partly in the light of the events of recent decades, there is now a broad consensus on the long-run neutrality of money, on the influence monetary policy can have on real variables in the short run, on the priority to be assigned to price stability among central banks' objectives, on the limits to the effectiveness of monetary policy in promoting price stability when other economic policies act in the opposite direction, and on the desirability of it not remaining inactive in the face of major economic perturbations.

Apart from the efforts aimed at producing a synthesis within academia, it appears to me that central bankers, precisely because they are faced with *practical* problems, approach these issues in a non-doctrinaire fashion. The opposition between rules and discretion, activism and non-activism loses some of its force in the face of institutional and practical considerations: once the two extreme hypotheses of deterministic rules and arbitrary action are rejected, experience shows that rules, even when provisos are added, must allow for discretionary action by central banks to cope with the complexity of real life, changes of a structural nature and extraordinary events. A strong central bank is an institution which is in a position to act in a discretionary way.

A final point concerns the limits of the theory kit. The fundamental strands of the theoretical debate just recalled refer to a highly stylized economic system. Central banks, however, are faced with the structural characteristics of their particular economy and have to interpret economic doctrine accordingly.

I will not go into this vast subject here, except to stress the importance of the specific features of a country's economic and financial structure for the choice of the style of monetary management. For example, while large and relatively closed economies have considerable freedom of choice and are unlikely to opt for a fixed exchange rate regime, small and open economies are virtually excluded from pursuing an independent monetary policy and may prefer a fixed exchange rate. Similarly, the financial structure – the range of instruments available to firms and households for financing their expenditure, the menu of financial assets available for investing their savings, and the degree of competition prevailing in the financial markets – may be crucial in determining the financial aggregate to be chosen if a strategy based on intermediate targeting is adopted, because the predictability of the relationship between GDP and the various definitions of money or credit depends on the relative stability of the saving, investment and money demand functions. The structural features of both the goods and the financial markets also play a role in the choice between a direct and an indirect targeting system, because the more difficult it is to control inflation (owing, for example, to major budgetary problems or to features of the labor market), the less likely the shift from indirect to direct inflation targeting will be.

3 THE INFORMATION KIT

The other fundamental reference point for central banks is provided by the data on the economy. While the content of the theory kit is rather stable – even more so once the necessary qualifications dictated by the structural features of the economic system are taken into account – the data kit is in continuous turmoil.

Not only does the data kit include a vast assortment of information on all the main economic variables, but it actually provides the picture of a virtual reality – just as the configuration of the stars we see at night at a distance of light-years does not actually exist, and in fact never existed, because of the different times it takes light from the various sources to reach the earth. Delays, noise, and other problems in statistical data can affect the choice of targets and indicators central banks use to guide their actions and the temptation to give greater weight to the most easily observed variables – which are not necessarily the most meaningful ones – is very strong. Thus, if markets may sometimes find it hard to read the day-to-day behavior of the central bank, the latter may find it just as difficult to interpret the information they produce.

Consider the case of prices, the crucial variable for a stability-oriented monetary policy. To assess their behavior accurately, central banks refer to a variety of indices, ranging from consumer prices to more selective ones.[1] They keep track of the variables – such as the prices of raw materials, labor costs, profits and, in small, open economies, exchange rate movements – that influence consumer prices, albeit to a varying degree and with different lags. Furthermore, they use both aggregate and sectoral information in order to identify potential bottlenecks.[2]

Given the importance of preemptive action, central bankers face the problem of measuring inflation expectations. Opinion surveys, which are a natural and widely used method, suffer from a number of drawbacks: they cannot be updated continuously and the reference time horizon is normally shorter than that required for the conduct of monetary policy. As to market interest rates, it is far from easy to separate out the component associated with inflation expectations. Thanks to the development of indices of implicit volatility based on the prices of options on securities and exchange rates, we now have information on the uncertainty present in the underlying markets and the related risk premia. Nonetheless, the different components of interest rates remain difficult to interpret.

4 THE MARKET: FROM MECHANISM TO ACTOR

Equipped with theory and data, central banks used to exercise their judgment and experience to define (sometimes also through discussions and negotiations with the government) their course of action. In doing so, they had in front of them "the economy." The banking system and the money market of course existed and were the first link in the transmission mechanism. But to a large extent they were just a "mechanism," that is, a system of wheels, belts and shafts that passively – that is, without producing any unpredictable reactions of its own – passed on the impulses to the rest of the economy.

This is no longer the case. In recent years the financial markets have increasingly become an active interlocutor of the central bank. They have acquired an autonomous and almost irresistible force, which at times works for monetary stability and at others against it. Dialoguing and interacting with the markets, sometimes strategically, is an essential part of central banking today.

The availability on computer screens of a continuous stream of economic, financial and political information concerning a large number of countries, coupled with the rapidity with which operators translate these news flashes into buy-or-sell decisions regarding a vast range of financial products, results, for better and for worse, in highly reactive markets, which end up exercising active control over national economic policies. Since traders have a very short time horizon, privilege marginal news over more important but "slow" events, and look at price changes rather than levels, the prices expressed by markets may temporarily deviate from the levels corresponding to the underlying economic conditions. Over- or undershooting, noise, protracted misalignments are inherent to a world in which financial transactions are a high multiple of real transactions. And such deviations are not without effect on the economy, even if markets themselves eventually make the necessary correction. It is impossible, with the instruments available, to separate the two aspects (volatility and basic trends) of the behavior of financial markets.

We may wonder whether the implications for policymaking of the rise of an active financial market have been fully understood yet. In choosing between alternative targets, central bankers cannot ignore, for example, that their ability to control the exchange rate has been severely curtailed by markets' ability to generate massive capital movements. The growth of financial markets may well enhance the effectiveness of monetary policy, if announcements of policy objectives pursued over a definite time horizon do indeed guide expectations: in such a case the market adds power to the process. The same market, however, can exert enormous pressure on exchange rates and the prices of government paper, if policies are perceived as inadequate by reference to the announced objectives: the resulting perturbations not only serve as an indicator of a country's economic health, but also tend to destabilize the economy and create difficulties for monetary and economic policy. Markets have become an amplifier, or a damper, of policy impulses, depending on their judgment of both the economic situation and the adequacy of policy actions. Policymakers therefore have to weigh the potential benefits of official and formal precommitments with the costs markets may impose if they take a different view, or if the announced goals are missed.

Central banks also have to reckon with another, more puzzling, aspect of the development of financial markets. The thousands of traders who move enormous sums across the world no longer trust only their intuition, profit motives and market feeling. More and more their trading activity translates theoretical convictions concerning the conduct of macroeconomic policies into price movements, which may end up by validating the original theoretical premises, regardless of whether or not they are sound. The ammunition they can put at the service of a particular policy paradigm forces policymakers to come to terms with economic doctrine in a new and tangible way that has nothing to do with an intellectual contest. Until recently, a theory could affect the economy if policymakers believed it to be correct; today it may suffice that market operators believe it to be correct.

5 STYLES OF MONETARY MANAGEMENT

The guidance offered by theory, the continuous movement of markets and the uninterrupted flow of data and news are the elements that central banks consider in conducting monetary policy. Like sailors, who have to take account of charts, the weather and the boat itself, central bankers have to synthesize all these factors in order to set and hold their course. As in navigating, different styles of monetary management are possible. I shall briefly describe the four which cover, in my view, nearly all the methods used by central banks today. The first consists in pegging the exchange rate to another currency. The second and third can be named after the variable adopted as the target: respectively the money supply and the inflation rate. The last style, which I call the "classic" style, differs from the others in that it does not involve monetary policy on its own adopting a formal, quantified and time-specific commitment in terms of a single target variable, but relies more on action and on multiple variables.

Before describing the four styles, I would like to stress that a style is neither a rule nor a fashion. A style is a distinctive manner of behaving which may well not include a mechanistic rule or, if a rule is present, provide an interpretation of it that is not necessarily unique. For a line of behavior to become a "style" it must be implemented with sufficient continuity through a variety of circumstances. How long the period should be for this condition to be satisfied is an open question, of course. I would suggest, however, that a time span falling short of, say, a whole business cycle would prove ineffective in persuading economic agents of the central bank's determination to stick to the declared style. I would also say that the choice of a style should be recognized on the basis of stated intentions and actual behavior, rather than success in achieving the announced results. Failure to attain a target may be caused by a set of events, of which at least some could be beyond the reach of central bankers. Although deviations from the desired path for the targeted variable are, of course, important in assessing whether the choice was effectively implemented, they are not sufficient to prove that the authorities' commitment was weak. Finally, to be meaningful, the formulation should be such as to bind the behavior of the central bank: for instance, announcing a target range for the growth of a monetary aggregate equal to or more than twice the lower limit of the band would appear too loose to indicate that targeting had been adopted.

6 EXCHANGE RATE PEGGING

With the first style of monetary management the exchange rate link can be adopted unilaterally or through a multilateral agreement. The Bretton Woods system and the European Monetary System are the most important examples of multilateral fixed rate arrangements in the second half of the twentieth century. Austria and the Netherlands are examples of unilateral fixed rate regimes. The exchange rate style is the one used by the largest number of countries although, when account is taken of the size of each economy, floating rates are far more important than fixed exchange rates.

I shall not refer here to the vast literature on the choice of the optimal exchange rate regime because it is not really relevant for the issues discussed here. Indeed, a large part of this literature is concerned with the question of how relationships between currencies should be organized, and does not deal with the problem of the policy style the nth country or a particular country seen in isolation should follow. For the purpose of deciding whether a country should adopt the exchange rate style, it is sufficient to say that the success of exchange rate pegging in terms of price stability depends crucially on the policy line followed by the country (or group of countries) to which the currency is linked. As we all know, however, fixed rate regimes leave this policy line undetermined not only from a functional but, in most cases, also from an institutional point of view, because they do not indicate who will decide the stance of policy. Under Bretton Woods and the EMS, this indeterminateness caused policy conflicts and the eventual breakdown or the virtual suspension of the arrangements. Unilaterally chosen links have functioned well in some cases. In sum, exchange rate pegging ensures price stability only if the policy line is, in the first place, "good" and, in the second, accepted.

7 MONEY SUPPLY

Under the second style of policy, the central bank announces a target for the quantity of money in the coming year and pursues that quantity whatever happens. There are two conditions for this style to be effective: first, the central bank must be able to control the money supply and, second, there must be a sufficiently stable (and statistically observable) link between monetary growth and inflation.

In the second part of the 1970s many countries abandoned interest or exchange rate objectives and began to target variously defined quantities: domestic credit expansion, central bank money, M2, and so on. The two main reasons given for the switch were the changing nature of the shocks affecting the economy, then originating mainly in the goods market, and the increasing difficulty of setting a target level for interest rates in conditions of high and variable inflation. Behind these reasons there were the inroads made by the monetarist intellectual offensive in the media and the academic and central banking camps. The role of quantity targets diminished in the 1980s, as rapid financial innovation and deregulation undermined the stability of the relationship between intermediate targets and final variables. In some European countries participation in the ERM led to a reassessment of the importance of monetary targets. The United States, which had adopted new operating procedures under Volcker in 1979 aimed at strengthening the control over monetary aggregates, reverted to a more flexible approach once the stabilization had borne its fruits (and the "debt crisis" of 1982 exploded).

Only one country has elevated the monetary targeting approach into a style: this is Germany, which adopted it in 1975. Over the years the Bundesbank has formulated and presented the rule with varying degrees of stringency and exclusiveness, but it has never abandoned it, or at least never given the outside world the impression of allowing it to slip. Notably, in the period following German unification the Bundesbank continued to refer to a target for monetary growth despite the significant overshooting that occurred: the Bundesbank did not change its style and markets did not see the Bundesbank as having become permissive toward inflation.

Monetary targeting is not the only, nor probably the most important, reason for Germany's remarkable record of monetary stability. Other factors have been decisive: the strength of the country's economic structure; the slow pace of financial innovation; and, above all, the fact that, for historical and sociological reasons, the good associated with monetary security has permeated the psychology, behavior and value systems of all the components of society more deeply in Germany than in any other modern country. In its monetary rule the Bundesbank has found an effective catalyst for these deeply embedded sentiments. In the 1980s and 1990s the German style of monetary management has been exported to a number of countries via exchange rate pegging.

8 INFLATION

Inflation targeting, which is the "new" style currently receiving considerable attention, is usually described as a regime in which the central bank (a) makes a precommitment to an explicit quantitative inflation target; (b) is free to choose the means to pursue that target; and (c) is accountable for reaching its goal.[3] While the first characteristic is the essential one, the second and third, though they play a crucial role in this approach, are not specific to it and may also apply to other styles of monetary management.

Inflation targeting is not as novel as it might appear. Central banks have always had a desired, albeit implicit, price performance in mind, even when they resorted to intermediate objectives. Besides, central banks that resort to direct inflation targeting obviously still have to maneuver the variables under their control and to proceed judgmentally, just as they would if they were pursuing an intermediate target. The main difference is that with inflation targeting the announcement takes the form of a public commitment to a quantified objective over a defined time horizon, much as with M2 or M3 in monetary targeting.

The first countries to announce an objective in terms of inflation were New Zealand and Canada, between 1989 and 1991. In late 1992 and early 1993 they were followed by the United Kingdom, Sweden and Finland, which had abandoned their exchange rate anchors in the European currency storm. More recently, central banks of other countries – such as France and Spain – have announced an explicit objective for inflation, while retaining a target in terms of a monetary aggregate or the exchange rate. Inflation targeting differs across countries with respect to the reference price index, the length of the time horizon, the adoption of a target range or a single value, the existence of other macroeconomic objectives, and the institutional basis. More specifically, the responsibility attributed to the central bank in each country is quite different. In England the central bank acts as a technical body, which, since it does not even enjoy full instrument independence, is entrusted with the task of signaling the need for a tightening or easing of monetary conditions to the government; in New Zealand and Canada it sets the target jointly with the government but is directly responsible for its attainment; and in Sweden and Finland it is responsible for setting the target but the implications of failing to achieve are not clearly defined.

Direct inflation targeting has been used for too short a period and by too few countries to judge its effectiveness on the basis of experience. We can, for the moment, only discuss it *a priori*.

On theoretical grounds, the adoption of this style is primarily motivated by the desire to provide an anchor for monetary policy and serve as an effective coordination device for price and wage setters and for financial market operators; on a more practical plane, inflation targets are meant to fill the gap left by the abandonment of monetary targets, motivated in turn by empirical problems of instability. While the practical motivation stems from controllability considerations, the theoretical motivation relies on the signaling–catalyst role of inflation targets in influencing expectations and thus reducing the real costs of stabilization. Let me consider these two motivations in turn.

From the narrow viewpoint of *controllability*, it is very doubtful whether inflation targeting can perform better than monetary targeting. Since central banks do not exert fuller or more direct control over inflation than over M2 or M3, the former style of monetary management, by definition, does not overcome the difficulties that led to the abandonment of the latter. Indeed, by shifting from monetary to inflation targeting, the problems of controllability posed by the unreliability of the link between central bank instruments and monetary aggregates are not really avoided, if one still believes that such aggregates are crucial to the control of inflation. And a similar argument applies to other intermediate variables, such as interest rates, the exchange rate, and total credit. Moreover, such old problems are aggravated by new ones, arising from the segment of the transmission mechanism that goes from intermediate variables to prices. This is so because factors such as labor costs, the exchange rate and raw material prices undoubtedly influence prices and yet are partly outside the reach of monetary policy. And other factors, such as the state of the public finances, may also affect interest rates and the exchange rate and end up by being reflected in prices.

This leaves the *signaling–catalyst* role of inflation targeting. If inflation targeting proved more effective than – say – monetary targeting in influencing expectations and hence the pricing behavior of economic agents, it could be hoped that effectiveness would be regained through a shortcut. But the problem here is: what will bring inflation on track if the signaling–catalyst process does not work as planned, that is to say if it does not prove powerful enough to overcome the influence on price performance exercised by some of the other factors I mentioned above? This brings us back to the controllability problem. The introduction of escape clauses when announcing the target could alleviate the problem; but there are so many possible shocks that the addition of a string of provisos would result in the announcement of the target losing most of its signaling effect.

There is some circularity in the process. The solution to the controllability issue depends crucially on the hypothesis that inflation targeting, thanks to its signaling–catalyst power, does indeed enhance the role of expectations in the transmission of monetary policy impulses in comparison with alternative approaches. At the same time, this signaling–catalyst power is bound to depend on the credibility of the announcement, that is to say on the confidence that the central bank really is able to control inflation.

In view of these considerations, it has been suggested that to gain credibility in a relatively short time span, a more controllable target may be preferable, provided enough people pay attention to it, while a less controllable and more visible target may be adopted where the central bank has a solid reputation and can hence exploit the role of expectations more powerfully, without suffering a significant loss of credibility if the target is not achieved.[4] It is worth noting, however, that the Bundesbank, which is usually reckoned to have the highest reputation, remains faithful to indirect targeting. This is partly because financial innovation has not yet caused insurmountable measurement and control problems in Germany, but it also owes much to the considerable effort systematically deployed by the Bundesbank to explain its actions, thus increasing the number of people who pay attention to the results obtained even though the intermediate objective is not particularly visible.

It is often said that the greater the distance separating monetary policy from its objective under inflation targeting, the more transparency is required on the part of the central bank for its action to be effective. Both markets and the public must be given a detailed explanation of the factors and reasoning that guide its decisions in the short term. The inflation reports published by the Bank of England and the Swedish central bank are a response to this need. In practice, however, it is just as important for the central bank to explain policy with the other styles of monetary management, so that this distinction between direct and indirect targeting is not really valid.

Time will tell whether inflation targeting will become firmly established or wither away like other styles, such as that based on a target for nominal income, which I have not mentioned here. In several respects, inflation targeting does not appear to be dramatically innovative in comparison with intermediate targeting: it is unlikely to outperform the latter in terms of controllability and effectiveness in building a reputation; nor does it necessarily ensure more transparency and accountability. It undoubtedly has the merit of focusing attention on what central banks prize most, monetary stability. However, it is precisely this merit that also constitutes its most serious drawback, because it obliges the monetary authorities to make a formal commitment with respect to an economic variable that is beyond its full and direct control, especially in the short time horizon that is used for judging monetary policy actions. Inflation targeting may lead a central bank to gamble its credibility, and hence the effectiveness of its action, for want of caution or because of an excess of ambition. It is as if the police were to announce in figures the reduction in the rate of crime it plans to achieve in the coming year, instead of striving to reduce it "as much as possible."

9 THE "CLASSIC STYLE"

With the fourth style monetary policy relies on actions more than on precommitments, although all central banks now "speak up" their aims. Central banks using this style refer to the whole body of theoretical and empirical knowledge about the functioning of the economic system. In view of the complexity of functional relationships between economic variables, central banks know that the significance of any single indicator may vary with the circumstances. In a world of uncertainty, any commitment taking the form of a "simple" announcement may prove too costly in terms of credibility. These central banks do not make *formal, quantified* and *time-specific* commitments with regard to a *single* variable, either intermediate or final.

This style can be called "classic" for two reasons. First, because it is the one that has been in use longest in the majority of leading countries, including Japan and the United States. Second, because it is the one that makes the most complete use of the information available to central banks and takes the greatest account of the aspects of economic theory that bear on central banking. As in the case of supervision constructive ambiguity allows responsible behavior on the part of individual banks to be combined with the possibility for the authorities to prevent contagions that may have disruptive effects, in monetary management some degree of imprecision in stating central banks' intentions leads to an improved tradeoff between credibility and smoothing action.

The fundamental difference between the classic style and the three others is the lack of a formal and quantified precommitment by the central bank, so it is with reference to this that we have to discuss its validity.

On theoretical grounds, a policy based on an announced objective has the key advantage of offering a reference point for expectations. However, when such announcements are made in a formalized and quantified manner, there may be a down side if uncertainty or unforeseeable factors make it impossible to stick to the strategy that has been announced. In a continuously changing world, such a precommitment can prove very costly, especially if the process of establishing credibility is hampered by inflation-prone behavior on the part of other key economic agents (such as the government, employers and organized labor) and if markets are quick to punish and slow to forget. On the other hand, the potential advantages of a policy based on formal precommitments may be negligible if the central bank already enjoys a strong position.

A policy style that foregoes the technique of sound-bite announcements may appear unattractive in a modern information society, in which central banks and their actions receive daily media coverage and markets are constantly seeking new information and interpretations, with the corollary of an exasperated need to simplify and schematize. The classic style is not simple to explain, summarize or interpret; it calls for patience and is ill-suited to the "skimming" typical of newspaper readers and foreign exchange traders. On the other hand, it has the advantage of greater interpretative power and openness to new contributions, a broader statistical basis, and a long and illustrious tradition. The other styles are perhaps more useful for judging monetary policy than for implementing it.

The advocates of inflation targeting and of other approaches based on precommitments tend to use a very simplistic version of their approach when they intervene in the media to comment on central bank actions, but they are much more careful in their academic work, where they surround the proposed method with so many qualifications that much of the merit of simplicity and easy signaling they praised in the media is actually lost.

It would be unfair to extol the virtues of the classic style without recognizing the influence that the various schools of economic thought have had on its evolution. Twenty-five years ago adherence to the classic style implied central banks hardly ever talking on public occasions; communication with the outside world was restricted to the publication of official reports coming out perhaps once a year; "silence" ("le silence de la monnaie" in J. Rueff's words) was the key to the optimal behavior of those entrusted with the management of money. Attention was devoted to a fairly limited amount of financial data basically consisting in a long-term interest rate and the exchange rate. The desire to exploit a Phillips curve tradeoff played a large role in the decision-making process.

Since then, the classic style has evolved considerably, learning from and adapting to theoretical developments, the growth of the financial markets and the experience gained using the other styles. Compared with the time I moved from graduate school to the central bank, the classic style now assigns clearer priority to the objective of countering inflation, pays more attention to monetary aggregates, attributes greater importance to the exchange of signals with the market, gives more weight to the medium term than the short term, seeks to ensure consistency in its policies, and discloses more detailed information on its decisions, interpretations and intentions.

All these are positive features that the classic style partly owes to schools that have opposed it, although it should be noted that in the transition from theory to practice such schools have lost some of their inflexibility and rigidity. I still see a dividing line, however, between monetary policy on its own adopting and not adopting a style based on what I have called a formal, quantified and time-specific commitment in terms of a single target variable.

10 THE CHOICE OF A STYLE: THE PAST TWENTY-FIVE YEARS

With the qualifications outlined above, we can try to review where countries stand – or have stood – on the style of monetary management. If I were to take the 175 observations of the monetary policy style used by individual Group of Seven countries in each of the twenty-five years that I have worked in the Bank of Italy and weight them by the size of their economies, the resulting indicator would show the classic style to be way out in front. Let me explain this conclusion by briefly reviewing the record of each of the four styles. I will begin by illustrating a sketchy picture of targets for the exchange rate or for domestic variables in the G-7 countries since 1970 (Table 3.1).[5] I will then argue that the style actually practiced in many instances deviated from formally stated intentions and conclude that the classic style has been the predominant one (Table 3.2).

Inflation targeting cannot be judged yet because its appearance in the list of styles is too recent. I will simply observe that, leaving aside the somewhat

Table 3.1 Targets for the exchange rate and for domestic variables: the G-7 countries in 1970–94

	Exchange rate arrangements		*Announced targets for: money supply*	*inflation*
USA	BW	1970–71	1975–94	–
Japan	BW	1970–71	–	–
Germany	ERM	1979–94	1975–94	–
France	BW S ERM	1970–71 1972–73 1979–94	1977–94	–
United Kingdom	BW ERM	1970–71 1990–92	1976–92	1993–94
Italy	BW S ERM	1970–71 1972 1979–92	1985–94	–*
Canada	–		1976–82	1991–94

* Total Domestic Credit was targeted from 1974 onward; by the middle of the 1980s the role played by this aggregate had been openly de-emphasized.
BW: Bretton Woods system.
S: "Snake."
ERM: Exchange Rate Mechanism of the EMS.

extreme case of New Zealand, most of the countries adopting it view their inflation "target" much in the same way as many other countries – including my own – view a desired performance for prices over the medium term as a reference point guiding individual and collective behavior. It may be established on the basis of a scenario drawn up by the government as part of its general economic policy functions, or by the government and the central bank. With this benchmark in mind the central bank explains its conduct of monetary policy in its regular publications and in hearings before Parliament.[6] This reference to inflation does not have the structured procedure, or the binding character, or – for the moment – the protracted period of implementation that would make it a style. Even in those countries (such as Finland and Sweden) in which the target is set by the central bank alone, the announcement does not (or perhaps does not yet) have the strong features that make a style.

More extensive comments are required for the exchange rate and monetary targeting experiences, which are longer and more diversified. As concerns the exchange rate, I shall consider the cases during the past twenty-five

Table 3.2 Styles of monetary management actually followed: the G-7 countries in 1970–94

	Exchange rate pegging	*Money supply*	*Inflation*	*Classic style*
USA	–	1979–84	–	1970–78 1985–94
number of years		6		19
Japan	1970–71	–	–	1972–94
number of years	2			23
Germany	–	1975–94	–	1970–74
number of years		20		5
France	1970–71 1979–94	–	–	1972–78
number of years	18			7
United Kingdom	1970–71 1990–92	1980–83	1993–94	1972–79 1984–89
number of years	5	4	2	14
Italy	1970–71 1979–92	–	–	1972–78 1993–94
number of years	16			9
Canada	–	–	1991–94	1970–90
number of years			4	21
Total				
number of years	41	30	6	98

years in which the external value of a currency played the role of a nominal anchor. Among the G-7 countries, this occurred in the years preceding the collapse of the Bretton Woods system and, more importantly, under the European currency arrangements. The participation of France, the United Kingdom and Italy in the "Snake" was discontinuous and not very significant compared with their participation in the Exchange Rate Mechanism of the EMS: on the part of France during the whole period from 1979 to 1995, of Italy from 1979 to 1992, and of the United Kingdom for the two years in which it took part. Notwithstanding various realignments for France and, even more, for Italy, and in spite of the fact that Italy and the United Kingdom had a 6 percent fluctuation band, it is fair to say that adherence to the ERM in fact set the style of monetary management for the participating countries and played a key role in their achieving disinflation.

Of course the choices of the G-7 central banks were also guided by exchange rate considerations in a number of other cases. For instance, they were crucial in explaining the policy adopted by the Federal Reserve in 1985–86, when a depreciation of the US dollar was actively pursued. And the Bank of England appears to have had similar concerns in 1987–88, when the appreciation of the pound was deemed to be excessive. But these instances in no way fit a meaningful definition of the exchange rate style. Even the Canadian experience of *de facto* pegging of the exchange rate to the US dollar over the 1978–83 period is a dubious application of this style since the decision to abandon the exchange rate pegging policy was linked to the desire to alleviate the effects of the cyclical downturn.

As to monetary targeting, it seems, *prima facie*, to have been widely used in the past twenty years, replacing the "adjustable peg" regime that issued from the Bretton Woods Conference. If we leave aside Japan – which formulated forecasts, rather than targets, for money supply – all the other G-7 countries announced growth targets for one or more aggregates at some stage between the mid-1970s and the early 1990s.[7] Yet, if we take a closer look at each country's experience, we find that Germany is the only clear-cut example of a monetary targeting style having been adopted. Let me explain this point.

Considering the United States and the United Kingdom first, they introduced formal targets in 1975 and 1976 respectively, but pursued them in a relatively loose way until the end of the 1970s. In the USA the weakness of the commitment is shown by the recourse made to base drift and by the way interest rates were maneuvered. In the case of the UK, recourse was made to administrative controls (the "corset"). Money supply targeting was made more binding in 1979, after the second oil shock, when the Federal Reserve introduced new operating procedures and the Thatcher government adopted a Medium Term Financial Strategy in the UK. Monetary targeting was, however, *de facto* attenuated three or four years later in both countries. In the USA, the first indications of a style change can be seen in the new operating procedures that were introduced in the fall of 1982; the analysis presented by Benjamin Friedman in Chapter 6 of this volume suggests that the Fed's commitment to money supply targeting was significantly reduced after 1984. Partly as a result of the difficulties caused by financial innovation, targets were regularly exceeded in both the USA and the UK over the 1979–82 period. Since 1982 (in the USA) and 1984 (in the UK) a target range, which in most cases was greater than or equal to 100 percent of the lower limit, was announced. In the USA, over the whole period announcements referred to more than one aggregate; indeed, at times four measures of money supply were targeted, as well as a credit aggregate. In February 1993, the Chairman of the Fed announced that less weight was being given to money supply targeting. To sum up, if I had to single out the periods in which money supply targeting was viewed as "the" style of monetary management in the United States and the United Kingdom, I would choose, respectively, 1979–82 (or at most 1984) and 1980–3.

In Canada, money supply growth targets were announced at irregular intervals between 1976 and 1982; for most of the period, the Canadian dollar was *de facto* pegged to the US dollar; in 1981–82 the target range cannot be viewed as having been binding. As to France and Italy, targeting of a credit aggregate or of a money supply measure coexisted for quite a long time first with the application of credit ceilings, then with the adoption of the exchange rate as a nominal anchor, and has been played down even more over the past couple of years.

Germany is thus left as the only country that has consistently followed monetary targeting for a long period, well beyond the minimum required for it to be considered a style. The mechanism was revised a number of times, with central bank money being replaced by M3 and single value targets by ranges of 2 or 3 percentage points. But throughout the period an announcement was made, toward the end of the year, of the monetary growth set as the (only) objective for the coming year.

Targets were overshot nine times and undershot twice in the twenty-year period. Persistent overshooting occurred in 1975–8 and in 1986–8, but the fact that this did not undermine the Bundesbank's credibility was due to its reputation being underpinned by the excellent results achieved in terms of the stability of the D-Mark, both in the past twenty years and in the earlier postwar period.

This brief overview suggests that even when a country claimed to have adopted (monetary or exchange rate) targeting, there is scant evidence of the central bank behaving in accordance with the chosen approach over a long enough period or strictly enough to justify using the word "style." The classic style prevails.

Beyond the stated objectives that characterize the style, however, we have to look at the performance in terms of price stability, even though very few countries targeted inflation as such. Between 1955 and 1994 the annual increase in German consumer prices averaged 3.2 percent; it was below 3 percent in no less than twenty-one of these forty years and above 6 percent in only four years; it never exceeded 7 percent. In Japan, where the classic style has been consistently followed, the results were comparable to those achieved by Germany: Japanese inflation has averaged 3.6 percent since fixed exchange rates were abandoned in 1974 and was 4.6

percent over the forty-year period; it was below 3 percent in fifteen of the forty years and above 7 percent in eight years. Over the same forty-year period the average annual rate of inflation was 4.4 percent in the United States, 6 percent in France, 6.8 percent in the United Kingdom, and 7.7 percent in Italy. It was less than 3 percent in fourteen years in the United States, eleven in France, eight in the United Kingdom, and nine in Italy; it exceeded 7 percent six times in the United States, thirteen times in France and the United Kingdom, and fourteen times in Italy.

If we focus our attention on the two most successful and relatively unambiguous cases – that is, Germany's experience with monetary targeting and Japan's application of the classic style – we establish some points. First, both experiences show that credibility and flexibility are not necessarily incompatible; as the former is consolidated, the conflict with the latter diminishes and gives way to complementarity. German flexibility is shown not only by over- and undershootings but also by indications that counter-cyclical considerations were a factor in policy decisions. Second, the German case suggests that the causal link between monetary targeting and price stability probably acts in both directions; the former can be seen as an "expression" of the latter, not just one of its determinants. Third, a long time seems to be needed for attitudes oriented toward price stability to become firmly rooted in society and for them to be embodied in the expectations held by the markets, which are said to have a short sight but a long memory. Finally, the performances of Japan and Germany indicate that price stability can be successfully achieved through different styles and, more specifically, that precommitment may not be as important in practice as it might appear in theory. As a result, more than to the choice of the style in itself, attention should be paid to the process aimed at establishing a solid record in terms of strength, technical competence, time consistency, and good anti-inflationary performance. In turn, experience suggests that all these elements are more effectively gained and defended if adequate energies are devoted by the central bank to explaining the hypotheses underlying the formulation of its strategy, the uncertainties connected with them and the difficulties encountered in pursuing its goals. Once transparency is ensured, flexibility can enhance reputation.

11 CONCLUSIONS

Let me sum up. In the debate about monetary policy a consensus exists today on the priority to be attributed to price stability and on the need to operate through markets. The attention once paid to the definition of goals and the choice of techniques is now addressed to what I have called the "style" of monetary management.

A retrospective view of the past twenty-five years highlights the evolution undergone by the central banks' concept of the best way to implement their commitment to fighting inflation. If we leave aside the choice of an exchange rate regime, which only indirectly implies the choice of a style, we are left with the overwhelming impression that both the various styles based on precommitment and the one I have referred to as the classic style have been subject to a wide variety of interpretations. The former have profoundly influenced the latter, which however appears to have been the predominant choice.

The fact that precommitment does not appear to have been widely used does not imply that central banks are uncommitted and opaque. Rather, it suggests that commitment should not be identified with a formal, quantified and time-specific precommitment on the part of the central bank in terms of a single target variable and that transparency should not be reduced to announcements. Central banks adopting the classic style try to eschew both the gambles and the monistic bias of some recent strands of theory, while incorporating the useful elements that can be distilled from them and from experiences inspired by them. They surely "speak up before" and try to influence market expectations, but they do so knowing that they win their credibility with the results they achieve and the determination and consistency they show in their behavior. They are by no means inherently less transparent and accountable than central banks adopting inflation targeting.

In the pursuit of sound money the central bank can and does play a crucial role not only through its operations but also, and perhaps more, by determining the attitude of society toward price stability. For if the central bank fights its battle against inflation on the front line, the home front is no less important: in the end the whole country is responsible for its own rate of inflation. The ultimate secret of the monetary stability that Germany and Japan have enjoyed for more than forty years, and which they still enjoy today, is the extraordinary strength of the home front. This strength, in turn, owes much to the efforts of a central bank constantly seeking to inform, educate and clarify; such efforts are an integral part of the defense of the currency's value.

Notes

1. As calculated today in most countries, the consumer price index is open to several criticisms (see "Toward a more accurate measure of the cost of living,"

Interim Report to the Senate Finance Committee from the Advisory Commission set up to study the CPI, September 1995, New York). An example of the difficulty of obtaining an accurate measure of inflation when economic agents' behavior changes rapidly is provided by the Japanese CPI: the exclusion from the index of purchases at discount stores, which have increased continuously over the past few years, is generally deemed to cause it to underestimate the price deflation currently under way in Japan.

2. Additional difficulties in forecasting the intensity of potential inflationary or deflationary pressures can arise when factors affecting aggregate demand and supply change swiftly; the rapid asset price inflation and, later on, deflation, that have occurred in the Japanese real estate and equity markets over the past decade are a good example.
3. For this definition, see Leiderman and Svensson (1995), Debelle and Fischer (1994) and Goodhart and Vinals (1994). See also Svensson (1995).
4. See Cukierman (1995).
5. An interesting overview of the experience in 100 countries has been provided by Cottarelli and Giannini (1995).
6. The way inflation targeting is actually implemented in the countries adopting it is described in Del Giovane and Grande (1995) and in Leiderman and Svensson (1995).
7. Useful surveys of monetary targeting experience can be found in Bernanke and Mishkin (1992), Monticelli and Strauss-Kahn (1992), Passacantando (1995) and BIS (1991).

References

Bank for International Settlements (1991) *The Orientation of Monetary Policy and the Monetary Policy Decision-Making Process* (Basle), April.

Bernanke, B. and Mishkin, F. (1992) "Central Bank Behaviour and the Strategy of Monetary Policy: Observations from six Industrialized Countries," NBER Working Paper No. 4082, May.

Cottarelli, C. and Giannini, C. (1995) "Credibility without Rules? Monetary Frameworks in the Post-Bretton Woods Era," paper prepared for the Eleventh World Congress of the International Economic Association, Tunis, 18–22 December.

Cukierman, A. (1995) "Towards a Systematic Comparison Between Inflation Targets and Monetary Targets," in Leiderman and Svensson (1995).

Debelle, G. and Fischer, S. (1994) "How Independent Should a Central Bank Be?," in J.C. Fuhrer (ed.), *Goals, Guidelines and Constraints Facing Monetary Policymakers* (Federal Reserve Bank of Boston).

Del Giovane, P. and Grande, G. (1995) "Targeting dell'inflazione: principali aspetti teorici e di attuazione," mimeo, Banca d'Italia, December.

Goodhart, C.A.E. and Vinals, J. (1994) "Strategy and Tactics of Monetary Policy: Examples from Europe and the Antipodes," in J.C. Fuhrer (ed.), *Goals, Guidelines and Constraints Facing Monetary Policymakers* (Federal Reserve Bank of Boston).

Leiderman, L. and Svensson, L.E.O. (eds) (1995) *Inflation Targets* (London: CEPR).

Monticelli, C. and Strauss-Kahn, M.-O. (1992) "Broad Monetary Aggregates and

National Money Demand in Europe," in *Economie et Sociétés*, Série *Economie Monétaire*, M.O. 9, September–October.

Passacantando, F. (1996) "Building an Institutional Framework for Monetary Stability: the Case of Italy (1979–1994)," *Quarterly Review*, Banca Nazionale del Lavoro, March.

Svensson, L. (1995) "Optimal Inflation Targets, 'Conservative Central Banks' and Linear Inflation Contracts," paper prepared for the European Summer Symposium in Macroeconomics hosted by the Bank of Italy, Perugia, 28 June–2 July.

Part II

Exploration of a Framework for Effective Monetary Policy

4 Inflation Control and Monetary Policy Rules*

David Laidler

1 INTRODUCTION

If the 1990s turn out to be the decade in which a quarter-century of worldwide inflation comes to an end, that will be because policymakers have finally digested the message that inflation is a monetary phenomenon and a costly one at that. It will also be because institutional arrangements that permit price level behavior to become the main concern of central banks have been, or are in the process of being, put in place. Though details differ widely across countries, it is a fair generalization that in the past few years central banks have been granted (or have taken) increasing autonomy in the day-to-day conduct of monetary policy at the same time as they have become more single-minded about the control of inflation.

A particularly visible example of these tendencies is to be found in the European Union, where, as a preliminary step to the creation of a European System of Central Banks, the central bank laws of a number of countries have recently been amended to include an explicit price stability mandate as well as provisions to insulate their officers from political influence; and where the proposed European Central Bank will be organized on similar principles. In New Zealand, a new central bank law provides that the elected government and the Reserve Bank shall enter into a formal contract that sets explicit quantitative targets for price level behavior. The same forces are also at work in other countries in less dramatic ways. For example, in Canada there is now in place an explicit agreement between the government and the Bank of Canada which specifies quantitative targets for the inflation rate; though, in this case, the agreement is in no way required by the central bank law, and could be terminated without resort to legislation of any sort. In Britain too, the government has introduced

* I am grateful to John Crow, Peter Howitt, David Longworth, Alvin Marty, Allan Meltzer, Michael Mussa, Michael Parkin, and Bill Robson, and to participants in a Faculty Seminar at the Department of Economics, McGill University, as well as the Political Economy Workshop at the University of Western Ontario for many helpful comments. Loretta Nott provided able research and bibliographic help. I remain solely responsible for the views presented here.

inflation targets, and mechanisms have been put in place that provide for regular consultations between the Chancellor of the Exchequer and the Governor of the Bank of England, whose minutes are published with a "time lag." These mechanisms also call for the Bank to publish a quarterly inflation report whose content is not subject to Treasury control. However, though these measures have considerably enhanced the Bank of England's independent influence on policy, crucial tactical decisions, notably those involving setting interest rates, remain in ministerial hands.

It is tempting to characterize such developments as these as representing a triumph for "monetarism," so-called. To the extent that this doctrine always did emphasize the monetary nature of inflation, and the desirability of subjecting the conduct of monetary policy to clear-cut rules, this is accurate enough, but it is misleading to stop here. Over the past twenty years there have been important developments in both monetary theory and the theory of central banking, which have ensured that the ideas whose influence is so patently obvious in the current situation are significantly different from those described, for example, in Thomas Mayer's (1978) survey of monetarist doctrine.

This chapter explores the nature of those ideas, and their relationship to monetarism. It begins with a brief account of monetarism as it stood in the 1960s, just as inflation was beginning to get under way. It goes on to discuss what, with benefit of hindsight, seem to have been important weaknesses in that doctrine: namely, the inadequacy of its theory of money for dealing with normative questions about the costs of inflation, and the initial narrowness of its focus when it came to the treatment of inflation expectations and policy credibility. It analyzes the different senses in which the phrase "monetary policy rules" may be used, stressing in particular the relationships linking various policy rules to the political principle that the agents who undertake policy measures should be accountable to those whom their measures affect. Finally, the implications of the discussion for the appropriate configuration of the monetary policy regime are outlined.

In two important respects, this chapter is selective in its coverage. First, it is concerned with monetary policy and the control of inflation under central banking. It does not discuss the economics of hypothetical "free banking" regimes such as Selgin and White (1994) have recently surveyed. That is not because this missing material is uninteresting, but because I am here concerned with the economics that has underlain the actual evolution of policy over the past few years. Also, I pay no explicit attention to the role of exchange rate regimes, taking it for granted that there exists a regime under which national or, in the case of the proposed European system, supranational, central banks are, in fact, free to make meaningful choices about inflation. Thus, some sort of floating rate lies in the background of the discussion.

A fixed exchange rate is, of course, a monetary rule of sorts, and unless rigidly and perpetually fixed, it is a rule that can be abandoned in certain circumstances. From the perspective of this chapter, however, the rule in question is crucially incomplete, inasmuch as it leaves open the question of what form of monetary organization underpins the stability of the currency or basket of currencies against which the exchange rate is fixed.[1] The issues involved here, not to mention the principles to be observed in deciding how and when to adjust a pegged exchange rate, are nevertheless important and interesting. The only valid reason for not dealing with them here is that one can only cover so much in one chapter.[2]

2 THE MONETARIST VIEW OF INFLATION AND ITS CONTROL

The word "monetarism" was introduced into our vocabulary at the end of the 1960s to describe an already coherent body of macroeconomic doctrine. Monetarism thus existed prior to the onset of serious inflation in western economies, and though its subsequent evolution might have been a response to that inflation, its initial development was not. Empirical studies of inflation were important in early monetarist literature, but the episodes in question seemed remote from then recent American and European experience, and therefore cast only an indirect light on it, mainly by establishing the apparent ubiquity of an empirically stable aggregate demand function for money.[3] That monetary policy seemed to matter very much indeed for rapid inflation was interesting, but this result did not necessarily disturb then (i.e., "at that time") mainstream preconceptions about its lack of relevance for cyclical fluctuations which were taking place against a background of creeping (allegedly for cost-push reasons) inflation. It was monetarism's claim that creeping inflation was just as much a result of monetary expansion as was rapid inflation, and even more its claim that the cycle was also a monetary phenomenon, that were hard for that mainstream to accept.

Though this did not become clear until the mid-1970s, underlying early monetarism, or rather Friedman's version of it, was a macroeconomic model conventional in its overall structure – *IS–LM* plus Phillips curve – but special in its particular configuration – a stable, rather interest-insensitive demand for money function, a supply of money controllable by the authorities, and a Phillips curve that included endogenous inflation expectations among its arguments, with a unit coefficient. In any economy that was well-described by such a model, though cyclical fluctuations could still occur because of real shocks, their amplitude would in all likelihood remain modest unless money growth also fluctuated.[4] At the same time, the inflation rate would vary around an average value given by the money growth rate minus the real growth rate adjusted for the long-run real income elasticity of the demand for money. That is why the proposal, advanced by Friedman (1960), to reduce, by a legislated rule, monetary policy to the maintenance of a constant rate of growth for the money supply was also integral to monetarism. The case for a constant money growth rule was not that it was in any technical sense an optimal policy, but rather that its implementation would avoid major real fluctuations while simultaneously maintaining long-run price stability. That one could do better in principal was never denied, given enough knowledge about the actual economy's structure, and about the time lags to which policy effects were subject; but serious doubts about being able to do better in practice, given policymakers' ignorance of these matters, made a powerful case for not trying.

In the 1960s monetarism was controversial in its positive claims about the causes of cyclical fluctuations and creeping inflation; but, on the normative front, though the policy *means* – the money growth rule – it suggested was also controversial, the policy *ends* it advocated – price stability combined with minimal real fluctuations – were completely conventional. In the light of subsequent experience, the absence of debate about the desirability of price level stability in the early 1960s is worth highlighting. It was only late in the decade, once inflation had taken off, that the appropriateness of living with it began to be widely canvassed. And it was only with inflation's persisting for another two decades that the once universally accepted goal of price level stability became a minority taste. Prominent among the reasons for this was no doubt the reluctance of politicians to set a goal whose achievement would require temporary, but no less serious for that reason, contractions in real income and employment, and the closely associated reluctance of many economists to advocate unpopular policies with a slim chance of being implemented.[5] Paradoxically, however, a specific characteristic of monetarist doctrine also contributed to the attractiveness of a policy of living with inflation: namely, the absence of any careful analysis of money's functions in the theory of the demand for money which monetarism inherited from Friedman.

Friedman (1956) modeled the demand for real balances "as if" they were a consumer durable good, and his (1959) empirical formulation of the demand for money function was a special case of his permanent income hypothesis of consumption. It was a natural extension of this approach, pioneered by Martin Bailey (1956), to treat inflation "as if" an indirect tax levied on the services of this durable good, and to measure inflation's social costs as the area of a triangle, or trapezium, under its demand function. Friedman's (1969) paper on the "Optimum Quantity of Money" developed this approach further, and showed not merely that fully anticipated inflation reduced economic welfare, but also that, in the case of non-interest-bearing fiat money, welfare would actually be maximized where the price level fell at a rate equal to the economy's real rate of interest. The key insight underlying this result was that under a fiat money regime, as opposed to one in which money was a real commodity with alternative uses, the marginal social cost of real balances was zero; hence, it would be appropriate to drive the private opportunity cost of holding them to zero.

Friedman himself did not seriously argue that the Federal Reserve System, or any other central bank, should aim at a secularly falling price level, and his basic argument, considered in isolation, certainly did nothing to strengthen tolerance for ongoing inflation. One minor extension of that argument, however, to an economy in which the money stock was dominated by interest-bearing bank deposits did just that. In such an economy, if it really is appropriate to measure the economic impact of anticipated inflation "as if" it acts as a tax on the services of a durable good, then the only costs of inflation would arise from agents economizing on their holdings of that component of the money stock consisting of non-interest-bearing currency. On these assumptions, the welfare costs of anticipated inflation, to say nothing of the tax yield associated with it, though still positive, would verge on the negligible. Moreover, and crucially, the assumptions in question are not far-fetched. A competitive banking system would pay market-determined interest rates on its deposit liabilities, and these rates would vary with the inflation rate. Measures to eliminate monopoly power in banking, that is to say, would seem to do almost as much to reduce the welfare costs of ongoing inflation as the elimination of inflation itself.[6]

In the light of this conclusion, any dynamic cost–benefit calculation of the type pioneered by Phelps (1967), in which the short-run output and employment costs of bringing inflation down are compared to the long-term benefits accruing from having a lower, rather than a higher, stable and predictable inflation rate, seemed to lead inescapably to the conclusion that, once inflation had become embedded in the economy, the welfare-maximizing policy was probably to stabilize inflation and to live with it, while enforcing competition in banking. To the extent that this solution was complicated by the existence of contracts entered into before inflation began, as well as by other, not always very well-specified, nominal rigidities, resort to indexation seemed to be called for as a supplementary measure.

If monetarists were too uncomfortable with these conclusions ever to adopt them, and, with the exception of those concerning indexation, they were, their Keynesian opponents were more than willing to point out their apparent inconsistency in failing to do so. James Tobin's often quoted 1977 observation that "It takes a heap of Harberger triangles to fill an Okun gap," persuasively summarized the Keynesian position, and it was hard to disagree.[7] Something (or things) have clearly changed in the past twenty years to produce an intellectual underpinning for the configurations of monetary policies that we now observe. As I shall argue, the things in question were two in number: first, we have learned to pay much more careful attention than we once did to the complexity of the role played by the monetary system in a market economy, and to the implications of that complexity for the concept of anticipated inflation; and, second, we seem in large measure to have worked out the implications of our insights about these matters for the design of monetary policy rules and their place in the policy regime.

3 THE ROLE OF MONEY, THE ABSENCE OF INDEXATION AND THE COSTS OF INFLATION

To treat money "as if" a consumer durable good was a masterstroke as far as advancing our positive understanding of monetary phenomena was concerned. Once Friedman had suggested doing so, economists' attention shifted from armchair debates about why agents might hold money, and what that implied for the interest elasticity and overall stability of the demand for money function, to econometric work designed to provide empirical answers to these and related questions. If some of that early work seems in hindsight to have been naive, it nevertheless laid the groundwork for a permanent advance in our knowledge about these matters. This argument by analogy, however, neglected money's fundamental social importance as a means of exchange and unit of account, both for current transactions as well as those involving the passage of time. Interpreted literally, the standard macroeconomic models of the 1960s and 1970s had markets functioning without monetary exchange; and information about the structure of relative prices underlying the aggregates with which they dealt was apparently disseminated and processed without reference to the economies to be realized from the use of a reliable numeraire. This characterization is as true of the sticky price *IS–LM* model as of the flexible price New-classical framework that replaced it, including its "overlapping generations" variant.[8] Both types of model proved to be treacherous guides to normative questions about the social costs of inflation.

An older tradition in monetary theory, dating back to Carl Menger (1892) and beyond his work to such eighteenth-century writers as Adam Smith (1776), did, however, pay careful attention to money's role in market processes. From 1964 onwards, attempts to renew interest in, and indeed add to, the insights it yielded, while simultaneously linking those insights to monetarist empirical work on the demand for money, formed an important element in the monetarist research agenda of Karl Brunner and Allan Meltzer (e.g., 1964, 1971), an agenda which had been influenced not only by Friedman, but crucially in this respect, by their UCLA colleague Armen Alchian and later by Axel Leijonhufvud. Furthermore, in the mid-1970s, papers questioning the relevance of the "shoe-leather cost" model of inflation's costs in the light of money's unit of account and means of exchange role began to appear.[9] The work in question focused on money's central function as a unit of account and standard of deferred payment in disseminating information and incentives, and as a means of exchange in mediating trade in goods and services, and raised questions about the effects of inflation upon its capacity to perform these functions. It noted the tenuous correspondence of the theoretical concept of "fully anticipated" (i.e., expected and completely adjusted to) inflation to the complex phenomena associated with ongoing inflation in an actual economy, and therefore drew attention to the resulting scope for costly resource misallocations to arise from ongoing inflation's effect on the capacity of relative prices to convey accurate information and incentives to agents.

At roughly the same time, there also appeared Jo Anna Gray's important (1978) paper on the destabilizing effects of indexed wage contracts in the face of real shocks to the economy. This work attracted immediate attention and quickly undermined economists' optimism about the extent to which indexation could safely be deployed to turn an ongoing inflation into something more closely resembling a fully anticipated process. And in any event, as the 1970s and 1980s progressed, it gradually became apparent that the introduction of indexation on any widespread scale, even in areas such as taxation or capital market transactions, where it would not be destabilizing, was simply not going to happen. Whether the reasons for this were political or technical is irrelevant in the present context. It was the consequences which were important.

Accounting standards and taxation systems which largely took the stability of the economy's unit of account for granted remained in place throughout those decades, when, in many countries, inflation remained in the high-single to low-double digit range, with well-known results: standard debt contracts become "front-end loaded" as nominal interest rates rose to offset the real depreciation of capital values, giving borrowers strong incentives to shift towards projects promising high short-term gains; while inflation itself created private profit opportunities of dubious social value, and scarce resources, not least human resources, were diverted to their exploitation. As Howitt (1990) in particular has stressed, these effects fell not only on the level of real output but its rate of change too, to the extent to which resources were diverted from technical research and development activities that might otherwise have led to productive innovations. And in labor markets, inflation seemed to be associated with a higher level of industrial conflict.[10]

Ongoing inflation, in short, has turned out to do a great deal more than wear out a little shoe-leather. Even so, earlier assessments of the transitional costs involved in lowering inflation still seem to be valid; and so the foregoing arguments do not, in and of themselves, provide a sufficient reason for choosing price level stability as a goal for monetary policy. If even stable inflation is much more costly than we once thought, and if stability becomes harder to sustain the higher is the average rate of inflation, our assessment of what is a tolerable upper limit for the inflation rate might well be revised downward. But these factors, whether considered separately or in combination, do not also require that any ongoing inflation would best be reduced to zero. Indeed, many responsible commentators, in full awareness of their importance, have nevertheless expressed a preference for a more modest goal. Thus, at the 1991 Bank of Japan Conference, Stanley Fischer (1993, p. 43) advocated inflation targets in the 2–4 percent range, and John Taylor (1993, p. 6) noted, quite accurately, that there was no consensus at that conference as to whether this, or a lower range, was preferable.[11]

4 EXPECTATIONS AND POLICY CREDIBILITY

The choice between price stability and low inflation does not hinge upon comparing the gains to be realised in the long run by sustaining a stable inflation rate in the region of zero, rather than, say, 3 percent. The ultimate aim of price stability or low inflation targets is to render the operations of the price mechanism more efficient, and such targets are more likely to have that effect if agents believe in their durability. Advocates of eliminating inflation argue that a stable price level is a potentially durable policy goal, in a way that a low but stable positive inflation rate is not, and that its adoption will have a significant effect on expectations that would be hard to achieve by announcing a low inflation goal. Qualitatively speaking, their argument is compelling, but in the current state of knowledge, it is hard to see how the magnitude of the gains to be realized from the extra credibility of a price stability goal can be quantified.

Lucas's (1972) introduction of Muth's (1961) rational expectations idea into macroeconomics, and Sargent and Wallace's (1976) application of it to the modeling of monetary policy, laid the foundations for a notable advance in economic understanding.[12] This is so despite, indeed because of, the fact that the apparent policy implications of the rational expectations hypothesis which first attracted widespread attention in the late 1970s and early 1980s went badly wrong in a number of countries. The hypothesis had seemed to imply that monetary tightening, designed to lower the inflation rate, would succeed in doing so without significant transitional unemployment effects, only provided that it was clearly preannounced. Thus, for example, Robert E. Lucas Jr was quoted by *Time* (27 August 1979, p. 29) as follows: "Ideally we should announce a monetary expansion policy of 4% annually for the next seven years and then stick to it. People would respond, and inflation would be cured with a minimal risk of a deep recession." That is not how things subsequently worked out in practice. Neither in the United States, nor in the United Kingdom, for example, were the inflation reduction policies of the early 1980s implemented by stealth, but in each case their most apparent early consequence was recession. Announcement effects, it was soon realized, were unreliable.

To change behavior, statements of good intentions on the part of the authorities must be believed and acted upon. This requires not just that they be heard, but also that listeners find it plausible that the authorities will indeed keep their promises, and that the listeners in question are free to act upon that belief. The question of "credibility" must therefore be at the forefront of any discussion of the role of expectations in the transmission of the effects of policy.[13] The claim that price stability is credible as a long-run goal for monetary policy in a way that a merely low inflation rate cannot be is said to follow from the fact that *when long-run costs and benefits alone* are considered, price stability becomes an unequivocal choice.[14] Only when transitional costs and benefits associated with output and employment fluctuations are brought into the picture might some other goal come to look attractive. Hence, the announcement of a low inflation, as opposed to a price stability, target is also an announcement that, in the design and day-to-day execution of their policies, the monetary authorities are concerned with more than price level behavior; it therefore signals that their commitment to a particular inflation target is less than wholehearted.

There are a number of ways of elaborating on this point. It is, for example, well-known that, starting from a current positive inflation rate, a dynamic cost–benefit analysis that considers transition costs will yield a particular long-run target inflation rate above zero, and a time path along which that target will be asymptotically approached. Let us suppose, for the sake of argument, that a policy based upon such a cost–benefit analysis is feasible; but let us also note that inflation's time path is not, as every agent must surely know, just the outcome of monetary policy. It is subject to non-monetary shocks too. Suppose, then, that before a long-run inflation target has been achieved, some such shock moves inflation upward. Unless this shock is transitory, its occurrence will presumably require a recomputation of the subsequent optimal time path for inflation, and delay the date at which the low target inflation rate is ultimately to be achieved, or to be more precise, at which inflation comes within some specified interval above that target. A downward shock, on the other hand, might move the relevant date forward. Also, once the long-run target has been reached, a subsequent shock would put inflation on a path along which transition costs (or benefits) would again become relevant, so that its target value would be restored only gradually.

Moreover, as Marty and Thornton (1995) in particular have stressed, any asymmetry of response to such short-run considerations as we have been discussing here would likely place more emphasis on costs than on gains and could lead to an upward drift in the inflation rate. To the extent that such asymmetry is predictable – and the literature, to which Barro and Gordon (1983) was a seminal contribution, dealing with time-inconsistent policies suggests it will be – a low inflation target loses credibility. As Governor John Crow of the Bank of Canada put it in the 1988 Hanson Lecture (Crow, 1988) which heralded Canada's price stability programme:

> success in what is in effect an attempt to mimic price stability by achieving a stable inflation rate depends on strong public confidence that the authorities would not accept a further acceleration in the rate of inflation. However, if the authorities were unwilling to act to get the rate of inflation down from, for example, 4 percent, why should anyone believe that they would be any more willing to get it back to 4 percent if for one reason or another upward pressures on prices led the inflation rate to rise to 5 percent?

Under a regime in which transition costs are ignored and a price stability goal is set, to be achieved by a certain date and thereafter maintained, non-monetary shocks will not cause that goal to be revised. Rather, in their wake, the authorities will have to take whatever action is necessary to return the price level to its target level (or rather into its target range) as quickly as possible. Expected price level behavior over any particular planning horizon, which is what matters for improving the efficiency of market mechanisms, is thus likely to be subject to less uncertainty when transitional costs are ignored in the setting of long-run targets for price level behavior than when they play a role.

At first sight, the suggestion that the authorities take no account of monetary policy's output and employment effects seems quite unrealistic. As Fischer (1994) in particular has stressed, monetary policy does affect such variables, and it seems unreasonable to pretend otherwise. In fact, however, this is not quite what is involved here. A policy regime that explicitly aims at medium-term price level stability must quantify its target in terms of a range, rather than a precise number, for a particular measure of the price level (or its rate of change) and a time period over which the chosen target variable's value is to be averaged. The wider the range in question, and the longer the period of averaging, the more room will such a target allow for the price level to absorb short-run shocks that might otherwise create fluctuations in output and employment. Thus, a medium-term price stability target, even when it is the sole explicit goal of policy, can be designed to provide a degree of automatic cushioning against such shocks.

What is important to the credibility of such a regime, however, is that its adoption gives a clear signal that the authorities have no intention of trying to optimize policy subject to some short-run output–inflation tradeoff. Earlier, we assumed for the sake of argument that a policy of this type was feasible, but I am aware of no evidence to suggest that traditional monetarist skepticism about this matter is anything other than fully justified. To put it simply, arguments that justify the formal inclusion of output and employment among the targets of monetary policy on the grounds that to do otherwise would be non-optimal are beside the point when the quantitative knowledge necessary for the design and implementation of optimal policies is lacking.[15] A policy regime that explicitly recognizes this will surely be more credible than one which pretends otherwise.

Questions about the public's confidence in its expectations of the future behavior of the price level are also central to the issue of whether, when a policy target is selected, it should specify the pursuit of a given target range for the price level over time, or merely given bounds for the change of the price level, looking forward from any particular moment.[16] At first sight, the latter choice seems preferable. To the extent that non-monetary shocks are capable of shifting the price level upward from time to time, it seems as if it would be unnecessarily costly to insist that monetary policy be used to reverse their effects. And a commitment to do so would introduce extra variability into *short-term* inflation expectations into the bargain. However, a policy regime that did not offset such shocks would cause the price level to follow a random walk over time, and hence introduce greater variability into *long-term* inflationary expectations. If long-run predictability of price level behavior is important, then this property is surely decisively undesirable, and a target path for the price level seems to be called for. Moreover, to set a target path for the price level rather than the inflation rate also reduces the temptation to a central bank to take short-term risks on inflation. If such risks do generate inflation, that is a bygone under an inflation target, but not under a price level target. A bank will be less likely to take inflation risks if it knows that this exposes it to the chance of having to impose a perhaps painful restrictive policy in the future.[17] This point is important, because it suggests that the price level's random walk characteristic under inflation targeting might become significant at time horizons shorter than McCallum (1995) suggests.

In the longer run, we might also expect the credibility of a price level stability regime to help reduce the very nominal stickiness from which some of the transitional costs (benefits) of inflation reduction (increase) derive in the first place, and which underlies many arguments on the side of settling for a low positive inflation rate in the long run. Marty and Thornton (1995) have observed that positive inflation will indeed act as a lubricant to the allocative mechanism in the event of downward stickiness of money wages and prices, as Tobin (1972) argued, but they have also noted that it is hard to see what, other than expectational phenomena, might underpin the institutional rigidities which cause such stickiness, and that perhaps these are malleable in the face of credible policy.

Two important caveats are nevertheless in order here, because economic policy principles are not much use unless they can be translated into practice, and abstract debates about policy credibility can easily take on a somewhat other-worldly character. First, price level measurement issues are crucial when policies are actually implemented, and they can be quite serious enough to blur the distinction between zero and merely low inflation as Fortin's (1990) study of these issues showed. Given the biases inherent in most price indices, price stability in practice probably means a *measured* inflation rate in the 0–2 percent per annum range.[18]

Even more important, there are many other threats to the credibility of monetary policy than the prospect of non-monetary shocks to the price level and its rate of change. Consider the threat of future inflation implicit in chronically imbalanced budgets: For example, in Canada the public debt–GDP ratio, federal and provincial debt combined, currently stands at about 100 percent. Even a quite small probability that some of this debt might be monetarized at some time in the future is damaging to the credibility of that country's inflation control regime. I would hazard a guess that it is, in fact, far more damaging than the fact that an indefinitely long commitment to inflation in the 1–3 percent range has recently replaced a previous promise that, after 1995, a target inflation rate of "clearly less than 2 percent" would be sustained.[19] Here we have a telling example of why the qualitative strength of arguments for the extra credibility of price stability targets that undoubtedly exists in principle sometimes needs to be viewed with a little skepticism in practice.

5 MONETARY POLICY RULES

A target value for a variable that is to be sustained indefinitely into the future is one of the things we might signify when we speak of a "policy rule." Indeed, when Henry Simons (1936) wrote of "Rules versus Authorities in Monetary Policy," a price level rule of just this kind was what he had in mind, and when the phrase "policy rule" is used in this sense, it is easy to attain wide agreement that rule-guided policy is preferable to the alternative.[20] Who, after all, would support a monetary policy that delivered *unstable* and *unpredictable* behavior for a key economic variable such as the general price level? Nevertheless, this whole issue of "rules versus discretion" needs further discussion, because the phrase "monetary policy rule" has taken on a number of meanings over the years, as has its converse "discretionary policy." We have, for example, already touched upon a second sense in which the phrase "monetary policy rule" is used in our earlier discussion of Friedman's (1960) constant money growth rate proposals.

It is still as true as it ever was that the effects of monetary policy are subject to "long and variable lags," and for some observers this observation still implies that, however desirable it might be to aim at price level (or inflation) stability, this target is so far removed along the causative chain that links it to the instruments actually under the authorities' control that it is unwise to anchor monetary policy to a rule for its behavior. If mistakes are made, or if the authorities covertly abandon their target, this will not become apparent, so it is argued, until it is approximately two years too late to do anything about it; better, then, to cast a policy rule in terms of the behavior of some intermediate variable which experience shows to be a leading indicator of the price level. A monetary aggregate is the typical choice here, and Friedman's above-mentioned constant money growth rate regime is the archetype of this version of a monetary rule. However, the proposals of Bennett McCallum (e.g., 1988) and Allan Meltzer (e.g., 1987) to make money growth not a constant, but a lagged function of velocity, represents an important variation on this theme.

When we discuss the issue of "rules versus discretion" in this specific context, there is a good deal to be said in favor of discretion, always provided that we are careful how we use the word. It is surely not arguable, and it ought not to be argued, that discretionary, in the sense of *capricious*, manipulation of some monetary policy instrument might produce a better outcome than adherence to a rule. It is however a defensible position that a policy regime which permits the authorities to use discretion, in the sense of *their best judgment*, in influencing money growth in pursuit of a precisely defined inflation target might be preferable to having it tied down by a rule for its behavior. For example, Friedman's constant growth rate rule is vulnerable to the charge that it ignores questions raised by the fact of ongoing institutional change and its effect on any chosen monetary aggregate. And, although the McCallum–Meltzer variation on the theme is designed to ensure that money growth does indeed respond appropriately to those long-run swings in velocity which one might expect institutional evolution to produce, there still remains the question of how much scope for surreptitious evasion of any rule might be presented by the fact that some institutional developments involve the introduction of new monetary instruments which then need to be attributed to one monetary aggregate or another. A case against even these more sophisticated money growth rules may be mounted along these lines.

The contrast between a money growth rule and a discretionary regime is not in any event quite as clear-cut as it might seem at first sight. No monetary aggregate that includes commercial bank liabilities is under the direct and determinate control of the monetary authorities, and to keep it on a predetermined path must involve manipulation, and discretionary manipulation at that, of policy instruments that are directly under the authority's control. Only a rule for the growth rate of the central bank's own balance sheet is an exception here, which is why some advocates of monetary policy rules have moved in this direction. This latter proposal raises other problems, however, not least that to lay down a rule for the behavior of the quantity of high-powered money would be to deprive the authorities of the flexibility that they might need to perform another of their tasks, namely to act as a lender of last resort. One wonders how the 1987 stock market crash might have evolved in the presence of such constraints on central bank behavior; and one might also question the wisdom of introducing them now, when the effects of the rapid growth of derivatives markets on the robustness of the financial system is still an open question.[21]

Meltzer (1994) has recently proposed a way of dealing with problems of this sort that self-consciously harks back to the discount policy espoused by Walter Bagehot in *Lombard Street* (1873). A rule for the growth rate of unborrowed high-powered money could be combined with a discount window open to borrowers at a penalty interest rate. In normal times, discount facilities would remain unused, but in an emergency they would operate at the discretion of would-be borrowers without the need formally to suspend existing restrictions on central bank behaviour. To say that Meltzer's proposal blurs the distinction between a rule-guided and a discretionary regime is not to criticize it.[22] On the contrary, it comes to grips with a special case of a problem that is quite general with quantitative rules for the behavior of any monetary aggregate: namely, that one can always think of reasons why it might be desirable to suspend them from time to time, and that when such an occasion arises, someone must use their best judgment in bringing that suspension about. In Meltzer's case, the someone is eligible borrowers; but perhaps the authorities would also have to exercise judgment in ensuring that criteria for eligibility kept pace with institutional developments.

Be that as it may, it can be objected that the foregoing discussion fails to address certain components of the case for money growth rules that follow from rational expectations models of monetary policy. In such models, agents who are aware of the parameters determining the time-series behavior of the money supply can and do use that knowledge in forming the expectations upon which they base their own decisions. It might seem, then, that to allow the monetary authorities to use discretion in varying that behavior removes an important source of valuable information, and hence stability, from the economy's structure.

The force of this argument depends once more upon what one means by "discretion." Certainly capricious monetary policy will introduce unnecessary and damaging uncertainty into private sector decision-making. But suppose that the monetary authorities are free to act according to their best judgment in order to aim at a well-defined time path for the price level, and that, as is the case in the above-mentioned rational expectations models, it is the behavior of the price level that agents need to be able to forecast. In such a case, if those making monetary policy were better informed than private sector agents about the variability of the linkages running from the instruments they control to the ultimate price level target, then to tie them down to a money growth rule rather than leaving them free to use their better information would make private sector agents worse off. And if there was nothing to choose between the knowledge of the authorities and the private sector, then the latter would, given knowledge of the ultimate goal of policy, be able to forecast the policies that the authorities' own best judgment would lead them to choose, and a money growth rule would be redundant. Only when the non-bank public knows more about the monetary transmission mechanism than the monetary authorities might a rule be desirable, for in this case the best judgment of ill-informed monetary authorities might well yield inferior policy.

There is, though, a little more to be said about this matter, for in the actual world there will usually be differences in the information available to policymakers and various groups in the private sector, and differences of opinion among them about just what policy measures are appropriate to the maintenance of price stability. It is, moreover, extremely unlikely that informational advantages will always lie with the same group. For example, judgments about whether shocks to the system are permanent or transitory, and if the latter, for just how long they might persist, are, as Brunner and Meltzer (1993) have stressed, particularly difficult to make. In these circumstances, when the interaction between policymakers and the private sector is an ongoing affair, it would surely be helpful to the latter to know how the monetary authorities are likely to behave in each specific instance. Even those who, like myself, are skeptical of the appropriateness of tying them down with a rule, should be willing to concede the desirability of having them adopt and adhere to a widely understood operating procedure, supplemented by frequent and clear public statements about their own interpretation of specific circumstances and their planned response to them.[23]

6 ACCOUNTABILITY AND AUTONOMY

No one would deny that monetary policy can exert enormous power, for good or ill, over the fortunes of those who are subject to it. This simple fact forms the starting point for virtually all arguments for bringing the monetary authorities under democratic control, and these arguments often seem to point to the desirability of a regime whereby discretionary monetary policy is run by a branch of a finance ministry answerable to an elected assembly.[24] Such arrangements are hard to reconcile with rule-based monetary policy; and indeed, when monetary policy is placed in the hands of elected politicians, and the central bank is given the status of just another government department, the likely outcome is widely believed to be higher and less stable inflation than any of the arguments presented earlier in this chapter would lead us to think desirable. That, of course, cannot, in and of itself, be sufficient reason for opposing such arrangements: if the electorate ask for and receive an outcome that the economist would not recommend, then so much the worse for the economist. The crucial point, however, is that this outcome may not be what the electorate wants, and it is precisely this possibility that enables us to reconcile the case for monetary policy rules with the time-honored principle that those who wield power should be accountable to those whom their actions affect.

In representative democracies, agents vote for political programs, not isolated measures, and immediate benefits conferred on relatively small and well-defined groups of agents seem to do more to attract support than small costs widely dispersed across the community at large do to deter it; and if the costs are uncertain in any event, then their deterrent effect on voters is further reduced. The ordinary processes of representative democracy tend to produce an array of government expenditure programs targeted at particular interest groups, financed by taxes levied on the community at large. Furthermore, the likely inflationary consequences of keeping taxes low, resorting to deficit finance, and then to a little monetization of debt, are not widely understood even among sophisticated electorates, so these too become tempting policy options.[25] Add to this the political popularity of promoting high employment, taken in conjunction with inevitable uncertainty about just how hard such policies can be pushed by monetary means before they spill over into inflation, and one has an incentive structure heavily biased, if not toward the deliberate creation of inflation, then certainly toward taking inflationary risks which the electorate, if fully informed and consulted on this issue in isolation, would in all likelihood reject.[26]

This, as the reader will at once recognize, is the basis of the traditional case for taking the conduct of monetary policy out of the political sphere, and for granting what is usually referred to as "independence" to the central bank; but, if the bank is also to be democratically accountable, this word cannot be taken to mean free of all political oversight and control. Nor should it, for the case that I have outlined is against only one particular kind of oversight and control mechanism, namely rendering monetary policy completely subservient to the political processes of representative democracy. That case is quite specific about institutional sources of inflationary bias in monetary policies, and the implied solution to the problems thus generated is therefore just as specific: insulate the act of money creation from the pressures of day-to-day politics. As Louis Rasminsky put it, "the power to print money should be kept clearly separate from the power to spend money."

There is a large middle ground between complete subservience of monetary policy to politics at one extreme, and complete freedom from political oversight on the other. Politically imposed monetary policy rules are located in just that middle ground. They provide a framework within which democratic accountability for the broad strategy of monetary policy may be combined with the insulation of its day-to-day tactics from extraneous and damaging political pressures.[27] In the design of such rules, the central bank's responsibilities should not, of course, be specified in terms so vague as to risk rendering unanswerable in practice the question of whether or not they have been met. If they are to be meaningful, performance criteria must be specified in terms of well-defined and easily measurable variables, such as the price level, or money growth.

The former choice would make the bank accountable for the outcome of policy, and the latter for the behavior of an intermediate target variable. One factor in this choice would be the extent to which failure to meet goals provided an occasion, on the one hand, to punish those responsible, and on the other, to force a change in policy with a view to improving it. If sanctions are to be imposed for failure, there is much to be said for waiting for price level data to reveal that some public harm has been done; if triggering a change in policy is the goal, then holding the central bank responsible for meeting money growth targets at first sight seems more attractive.

There are, however, two problems with politically imposed money growth rules. The first has already been discussed: namely, the difficulty of providing for the influence of institutional change on the effectiveness on any particular rule without simultaneously writing it so vaguely as to render it nugatory as a constraint on policy. The second, probably more important, is that the general public, on whose support the durability of any democratically imposed rule must depend, probably does not understand the relationship between money growth and inflation, and therefore cannot be relied upon to care much about how closely a rule for its behavior is in practice observed. Though the money growth targeting that was much practiced in the 1970s and 1980s stopped far short of being rule-guided in the sense under discussion here, its history does reveal two relevant features: targets were more often overshot than observed, and outside of such specialist groups as the academic community, the financial press, and participants in financial markets who used such information as an input to forecasting the future stance of policy, no one took much notice. A rule that the electorate neither fully understands nor cares much about is unlikely to be imposed democratically in the first place, and, if it were imposed, it would not be binding for very long.

The inflation rate is something which affects the economic welfare of the general public and therefore commands its attention, and which the monetary authorities ultimately control. It is, then, a natural object for a rule-based policy regime which insulates monetary policy from day-to-day pressures while leaving room for accountability, and it is no accident that this is precisely the solution toward which a number of countries have been moving in recent years. Even if the accountability provisions of that regime go no further than requiring the central bank to report regularly and publicly on its performance relative to the goals it has been set, then having them cast in terms of price level behavior at least makes it likely that the audience for that report will be large, attentive, and critical. If the regime goes further, and incorporates the threat of sanctions against policymakers who fail to meet their assigned goals, and if those policymakers are left free to use their best judgment in trying to abide by them, they themselves will have even more incentive to discover the operating procedures most likely to succeed in doing so.

If money growth is indeed crucial to the behavior of the price level, for example, a central banker who is likely to be publicly embarrassed and whose career is likely to suffer if the price level misbehaves will discover this and make use of it without needing to be required to do so by supplementary legislation; and if money growth is not, by itself, a reliable leading indicator of inflation, it would hardly be fair to require a central banker to achieve a time path for it in addition to meeting inflation targets. Here again, however, the desirability of frequent public discussion of central bank operating procedures becomes apparent. Not only is it desirable that the private sector be kept aware of what monetary policy is doing so that its decision-making is improved. It is equally desirable that the central bank remain open to discussion and criticism of its activities so that its chances of discovering the most effective operating procedures are increased.

7 CONCLUDING OBSERVATIONS

The foregoing arguments are easily summarized. Price level behavior is both important to the general public and subject to the control of the monetary authorities; and it is also a legitimate matter for democratic debate. Since low inflation seems to promote economic efficiency in a market economy, there is a strong case to be made for holding the monetary authorities accountable to the electorate for achieving it, or, more controversially, price stability. If those in charge of executing monetary policy are to be held accountable for its outcome, however, they must be left free to exercise discretion, in the sense of their best judgment, in its execution.

The natural way to put such a policy regime in place would be an appropriately drafted central bank law. A goal for price level behavior would be the main, thought not necessarily the only, feature of a clause defining the institution's mandate; while other clauses would lay down rules for the internal governance of the bank, and the terms on which its officers were appointed, designed to ensure them security of tenure in the face of political pressures (always subject to the possibility that they could be removed from office for outright incompetence or malfeasance). The details of such a law would differ from country to country, because it would have to dovetail with other features of political arrangements, but it would be reasonable to use a now considerable body of empirical work, among which Alex Cukierman's (1992) monograph stands out for its thoroughness, as a source of information about just which specific features of central bank laws seem most likely to lead to policy autonomy and the pursuit of low inflation.

Even so, a law, no matter how carefully drafted, is only the starting point for a policy regime. It does not, in and of itself, guarantee a particular outcome, as the above-mentioned empirical work has shown. Though the degree of political autonomy enjoyed by the central bank does seem, on average, to be inversely correlated with inflation, this result is nevertheless heavily conditioned by the experiences of two or three countries – the German Federal Republic, Austria, and Switzerland. It is worth recalling, as Mieno (1995) has noted, that the Bank of Japan, whose success in controlling inflation has been as great as any, operates under a law which, as a result of successive amendments, is unclear to the point of internal inconsistency on this very matter. Moreover and paradoxically, the very vulnerability of the Bank of England to political control, built into the legislation under which it operates, made it much easier for the then recently elected Thatcher government to introduce its stabilization programme in the early 1980s.

As to the question of the influence of the central bank's mandate on its performance, it is well-known that the mandate of the Swiss National Bank is just as much a model of muddle and ambiguity as those of Germany and Austria are paradigms of clarity. In any event, the matter of a bank's mandate has more to do with ensuring its accountability for its actions than anything else. If accountability is to amount to no more than regular public hearings before legislative committees, with the prospect of public embarrassment if performance has been bad, then the type of language usually (and appropriately) found in central bank laws, requiring the preservation of the "stability of the currency" or some such generality may provide a sufficient basis for it. But if accountability involves sanctions, such as dismissal of officials who have failed to meet their goals, then the goals in question surely need to be defined with a degree of quantitative precision about the behavior of a precisely defined statistical series that it would be inappropriate to write into a quasi-constitutional document such as a central bank law. Some supplement to that law, such as the explicit contract that exists between the government of New Zealand and the Reserve Bank, would be called for.[28]

None of this is to argue that a clearly written central bank law is irrelevant. For a political entity starting from scratch with a central bank as is the European Union, a clear law is, on the contrary, probably a necessary condition for successful monetary policy. Necessity and sufficiency are not the same things, however, and as Issing (1993) has emphasized, no monetary policy regime is going to endure in an otherwise liberal democracy without at least the acquiescence, and better the support, of the electorate. For such support to be forthcoming, accountability on the part of the monetary authorities is a *sine qua non.* At the very least the whys and wherefores of current policy must be continuously open to public question, and the possibility that policy, and perhaps policymakers too, can ultimately be changed if those questions are not answered satisfactorily must be guaranteed. The precise means whereby day-to-day autonomy of the monetary authorities can be combined with their longer-run accountability for their actions cannot be discussed in a vacuum. What will work under a Westminster-style parliamentary system is unlikely to be transferred easily to an American presidential–congressional framework; a federal state needs to address the interests of junior governments with measures that will be irrelevant in a unitary state; regionalism is more important in some jurisdictions than others; and so on.[29] Other chapters in this volume will take up these matters on a case-by-case basis, but it is hoped that the general principles set out here will help provide an overall context for their discussion.

Notes

1. I am well-aware that, for nations introducing new currencies, some of those nations themselves, as in Eastern Europe and the Baltic, being new, a fixed exchange rate on some preexisting stable currency, perhaps underpinned by a currency-based arrangement, is an attractive, perhaps even a necessary, means of creating credibility for the new currency (see Selgin, 1994, for a discussion).
2. See Allan Meltzer's (1995) contribution to this conference for an insightful discussion of the international dimension of inflation control issues.

3. Among the studies I have in mind were those of central European hyperinflations (Cagan) and the Confederacy (Lerner) in Friedman (1956), and those of Argentina (Diz), Chile (Deaver), postwar Japan (Keran), South Korea and Brazil (Campbell) in Meiselman (1970).
4. The *locus classicus* for this theoretical framework (without, however, the Phillips curve) were Friedman's essays of the early 1970s, whose most accessible source is R.J. Gordon (1974). I have discussed this material, and the neglect of the Phillips curve in it, though not in Friedman (1968), in Laidler (1995).
5. And, as Allan Meltzer has reminded me, in the 1960s monetary policy was often regarded as capable of contributing to a variety of other goals too – for example, the provision of cheap housing finance, whose pursuit would be interfered with if policy was directed to bringing down inflation.
6. Even before the publication of Friedman's 1969 essay, this line of reasoning was being developed by Harry Johnson (1968, 1969).
7. Tobin's fullest exposition of his views on inflation–unemployment interaction appeared in his 1971 Presidential Address to the American Economic Association (Tobin, 1972). Note that the kind of argument later advanced by monetarists against this position, for example, by Brunner and Meltzer (1993), were already implicit in earlier work by these authors (e.g., 1964, 1971). I have discussed this strand of monetarist analysis in Laidler (1995). See also the next section of this chapter.
8. And, as Brunner and Meltzer (1993) have stressed, it remains an accurate characterization of real business cycle models too.
9. The phrase "shoe-leather costs" seems to derive from Tobin's (1972) discussion of the relatively trivial costs associated with inflation in then conventional analysis. Three of the early papers which questioned this analysis were presented at IEA conferences in 1975 though not published until later: Jaffe and Kleiman (1978), Laidler (1978), and Leijonhufvud (1977). These papers differed in many details and matters of emphasis, and it should be noted that Laidler's in particular built upon Brunner and Meltzer (1971). The UCLA tradition, of which Leijonhufvud's ideas formed a part had, of course, already had influence on Brunner and Meltzer in the 1960s.
10. Phenomena such as these are present in much more acute forms under conditions of what Heymann and Leijonhuvud (1995) call "high inflation." It is an interesting question, requiring much further investigation, whether the conditions they describe are qualitatively different from, or merely more extreme versions of, those obtaining in mild inflations.
11. See, also the contributions to two important conferences sponsored by the Federal Reserve Bank of Cleveland on *Price Stability* (1991) and *Inflation Uncertainty* (1993) for another cross-section of opinions on these issues. These volumes display more agreement about the damaging effects of high and fluctuating inflation than about the desirability of inflation's complete elimination.
12. Inflation expectations were significant in monetarist analysis from the outset, notably as an argument of particular importance in the demand for money function in conditions of rapidly rising prices. In this context, following Cagan (1956), they were usually modeled in terms of the error-learning hypothesis. Even so, before the arrival of the rational expectations hypothesis on the

macroeconomic scene in the early 1970s, monetarist analysis of inflation–output interaction was seldom based on a mechanical application of error learning. For example, in Friedman's (1968) application of the concept to the Phillips curve, explicitly adaptive expectations were conspicuous by their absence, and in other monetarist discussions of the early 1970s this formulation was treated as at best a rough and ready starting point for getting to grips with the role of expectations in the inflationary process, prior to making allowances for other important situation-specific effects, for example in open economies, of devaluations and exchange rate regime shifts. See, for example, Carlson and Parkin (1975) (written in 1971–72) for a telling counter-example to the widespread belief that, before the advent of rational expectations, macroeconomics was content with unthinking applications of mechanical error-learning formulae.

13. As Taylor (1993) noted, there was a consensus on the importance of credibility for the effective work of monetary policy at the 1991 Bank of Japan Conference. Blackburn and Christensen (1989) remains an extremely useful survey of the literature on credibility issues as they arise in the context of monetary policy.
14. This is the conclusion that emerges from Howitt's (1990) survey of these issues. See also Konieczny (1995) and Marty and Thornton (1995). See below, pp. 76–7.
15. Closely related to these considerations are those raised by models in the tradition of Barro and Gordon (1983) in which the more credible the public finds the central bank's commitment to price stability, the greater is the payoff to the bank in terms of output and employment effects from covertly abandoning the commitment in question, with a consequent long-run failure to achieve a socially optimal policy. This literature leads to the insight, associated particularly with Walsh (1995), that contractual mechanisms precommitting the central bank to a more socially desirable policy might be necessary. The argument presented here follows McCallum (1995) in presuming that central banks can follow that desirable policy of their own accord and do not need to be forced to do so as well as in expressing doubts about whether, in practice, any central bank actually has enough quantitative knowledge to be able to execute the type of policies which this literature presumes to be feasible. This is, of course, not to say that contractual mechanisms of the type used in New Zealand, and referred to earlier, are either uninteresting or unhelpful.
16. On this issue, see Scarth (1994), Fillion and Tetlow (1994) and Hendry (1994), who discuss the special case of this issue concerned with the choice between price level stability and zero inflation.
17. I am grateful to Bill Robson for this argument.
18. For this reason, I much prefer McCallum's (1995) term "negligible inflation" to "zero inflation" in this context, since it carries no aura of spurious precision.
19. I am indebted to Chris Green for injecting this note of sanity into my thoughts on policy credibility.
20. The only thing that might be controversial here is the choice of variable to be subjected to a rule. There are still some who advocate the maintenance of a stable and low level of nominal interest rates, or a stable and low unemployment rate. To oppose policy rules such as these is not to oppose rules in

general, but only those that are not technically feasible. We have moved beyond the monetarism of twenty-five years ago, but one aspect of that doctrine still remains valid: namely, that plans for the outcome of monetary policy had better be formulated with respect to the price level or the inflation rate since this is the only variable over which such policy has any systematic long-term influence.

21. It is at this point that the "Free Banking" literature comes into contact with that dealing with monetary rules. On this matter, see Selgin and White (1994).
22. Note that Meltzer's arguments differ from Bagehot's to the extent that the latter also looked to high interest rates to generate gold inflows to bolster the banking system's reserves.
23. I am less enthusiastic about pushing such transparency to the point of having the process of arguing out the pros and cons of particular policy measures itself subject to public scrutiny.
24. See Scott Gordon (1961) for an exposition of the case for subjecting monetary policy to the same degree of democratic control as any other policy.
25. This conclusion probably applies best to economies which have experienced only moderate inflations. There is ample evidence that high inflation and hyperinflation generate strong incentives for ordinary members of the public to acquire enough economic understanding to cope with the phenomenon. The time and effort that must be devoted to this acquisition is one of the many costs which inflation can impose upon the economy. On these issues as they arise in conditions of high inflation, see Heymann and Leijonhufvud (1995).
26. Notice that the argument presented here hinges upon the application of "public choice" analysis to the workings of political processes particularly as they apply to so-called interest groups. The literature referred to earlier, in the tradition of Barro and Gordon (1983), which focuses instead on policy games played between a central bank and the public, and provides the analytic foundations for much contemporary formal analysis of central bank independence, seems to me to pay insufficient attention to these considerations. Eijffinger and de Haan (1995) is an extremely useful survey dealing both with this literature and some of that more firmly rooted in the public choice tradition.
27. One regime that is ruled out by considerations of accountability is an irrevocably fixed exchange rate on some foreign currency. It should be made explicit that this observation does not in any way amount to a case against such emerging arrangements as the single European currency. What it does do is warn that such an arrangement needs to be viewed in the context of an altogether broader movement towards political integration.
28. My own inclination is to think of precisely defined quantitative targets on the New Zealand or Canadian model as desirable features for a policy regime in transition from significant to negligible inflation, when it is important to establish credibility for the monetary authorities. Once negligible inflation has been firmly established, it seems appropriate to induce the general public to ignore the inflation rate in its decision-making. That, it seems to me, can best be done by removing quantitative targets for the variable from centre stage in public discussion. At this point, a clear, but rather general, price stability mandate written to the central bank law seems to be called for.

29. I discussed these issues in a specifically Canadian context in Laidler (1991). Since I have referred to the newly emerging European system of central banks at several points in this chapter, perhaps I should also record my dismay at the lack of attention that has been paid to ensuring its political accountability, and my concern that this will prove to be a serious obstacle to its ultimate success.

References

Bagehot, W. (1873) *Lombard Street, A Description of the Money Market* (London: P.S. King).

Bailey, M.J. (1956) "The Welfare Costs of Inflationary Finance," *Journal of Political Economy*, 64 (February), pp. 93–110.

Bank of Canada (1994) *Economic Behaviour and Policy Choice under Price Stability* (Ottawa: Bank of Canada).

Barro, R.J. and Gordon, D.B. (1983) "A Positive Theory of Monetary Policy in a Natural Rate Model," *Journal of Political Economy*, 91 (August), pp. 589–610.

Blackburn, K. and Christensen, M. (1989) "Monetary Policy and Policy Credibility: Theories and Evidence," *Journal of Economic Literature*, 27 (March), pp. 1–45.

Brunner, K. and Meltzer, A.H. (1964) "Some Further Investigations of Demand and Supply Functions for Money," *Journal of Finance*, 19 (May), pp. 240–83.

Brunner, K. and Meltzer, A.H. (1971) "The Uses of Money: Money in the Theory of an Exchange Economy," *American Economic Review*, 61 (December), pp. 784–805.

Brunner, K. and Meltzer, A.H. (1993) *Money and the Economy: Issues in Monetary Analysis* (Cambridge: Cambridge University Press for the Raffaele Mattioli Foundation).

Cagan, P. (1956) "The Monetary Dynamics of Hyperinflation," in M. Friedman (ed.) (1956).

Carlson, J. and Parkin, J.M. (1975) "Inflation Expectations," *Economica*, NS 42, pp. 123–38.

Crow, J.W. (1988) "The Work of Canadian Monetary Policy," *Bank of Canada Review* (February), pp. 3–17.

Cukierman, A. (1992) *Central Bank Strategy, Credibility and Independence: Theory and Evidence* (Cambridge, Mass.: MIT Press).

Eijffinger, S. and de Haan, J. (1995) "The Political Economy of Central Bank Independence," mimeo, University of Tilburg.

Federal Reserve Bank of Cleveland (1991) *Price Stability* (Special Issue of *Journal of Money, Credit and Banking*, 23 August, pt. 2).

Federal Reserve Bank of Cleveland (1993) *Inflation Uncertainty* (Special Issue of *Journal of Money, Credit and Banking*, 25 August, pt. 2).

Fillion, J.-F. and Tetlow, R. (1994) "Zero Inflation or Price Level Targeting? Some Answers from Stochastic Simulations on a Small Open-Economy Macro Model," in Bank of Canada (1994).

Fischer, S. (1993) "Lessons from Moderate Inflation," in K. Shigehara (ed.), *Price Stabilisation in the 1990s* (London: Macmillan).

Fischer, S. (1994) "Modern Central Banking," in F. Capie, C. Goodhart, S. Fischer

and N. Schmidt, *The Future of Central Banking* (Cambridge: Cambridge University Press).
Fortin, P. (1990) "Do We Measure Inflation Correctly?," in R.G. Lipsey (ed.), *Zero Inflation: The Goal of Price Stability* (Toronto: C.D. Howe Institute).
Friedman, M. (ed.) (1956) *Studies in the Quantity Theory of Money* (Chicago, Ill.: University of Chicago Press).
Friedman, M. (1959) "The Demand for Money – Some Theoretical and Empirical Results," *Journal of Political Economy*, 67, pp. 327–51.
Friedman, M. (1960) *A Program for Monetary Stability* (New York: Fordham University Press).
Friedman, M. (1968) "The Role of Monetary Policy," *American Economic Review*, 68 (March), pp. 1–16.
Friedman, M. (1969) *The Optimum Quantity of Money* (London: Macmillan).
Gordon, H.S. (1961) "The Bank of Canada in a System of Responsible Government," *Canadian Journal of Economics and Political Science*, 27 (February), pp. 1–22.
Gordon, R.J. (ed.) (1974) *Milton Friedman's Monetary Framework* (Chicago, Ill.: University of Chicago Press).
Gray, J. (1978) "On Indexation and Contract Length," *Journal of Political Economy*, 86 (February), pp. 1–18.
Hendry, S. (1994) "Zero Inflation and Price Stability Monetary Policies," UWO mimeo.
Heymann, D. and Leijohnhufvud, A. (1995) *High Inflation* (London: Oxford University Press).
Howitt, P.W. (1990) "Zero Inflation as a Long Run Target for Monetary Policy," in R.G. Lipsey (ed.), *Zero Inflation: The Goal of Price Stability* (Toronto: C.D. Howe Institute).
Issing, O. (1993) *Central Bank Independence and Monetary Stability* (London: IEA).
Jaffe, D. and Kleiman, E. (1978) "Welfare Implications of Uneven Inflation," in E. Lundberg (ed.), *Inflation Theory and Anti-Inflation Policy* (London: Macmillan).
Johnson, H.G. (1968) "Problems of Efficiency in Monetary Management," *Journal of Political Economy*, 76 (September–October), pp. 971–90.
Johnson, H.G. (1969) "Inside Money, Outside Money, Income, Wealth and Welfare in Monetary Theory," *Journal of Money, Credit and Banking*, 1 (February), pp. 30–45.
Konieczny, J. (1994) "The Optimal Rate of Inflation: Competing Theories and Their Relevance to Canada," in Bank of Canada (1994).
Laidler, D. (1978) "The Welfare Costs of Inflation in Neoclassical Theory – Some Unsettled Problems," in E. Lundberg (ed.), *Inflation Theory and Anti-Inflation Policy* (London: Macmillan).
Laidler, D. (1991) *How Shall We Govern the Governor?* (Toronto: C.D. Howe Institute).
Laidler, D. (1995) "Monetarism circa 1970 – a View from 1994," *Kredit und Kapital*, 28, pp. 323–45.
Leijonhufvud, A. (1977) "Costs and Consequences of Inflation," in G.C. Harcourt (ed.), *The Microeconomic Foundations of Macroeconomics* (London: Macmillan).
Lucas, R.E. Jr (1972) "Expectations and the Neutrality of Money," *Journal of Economic Theory*, 4, pp. 103–24.

Marty, A. and Thornton, D. (1995) "Is There a Case for 'Moderate' Inflation?," Federal Reserve Bank of St Louis *Review*, 77 (July/August), pp. 27–37.
Mayer, T. (1978) *The Structure of Monetarism* (New York: W.W. Norton).
McCallum, B.T. (1988) "Robustness Properties of a Rule for Monetary Policy," in K. Brunner and B.T. McCallum (eds), *Money Cycles and Exchange Rates: Essays in Honour of Allan H. Meltzer*, Carnegie–Rochester Conference Series, Vol. 29 (Amsterdam: North Holland).
McCallum, B.T. (1995) "Inflation Targeting in Canada, New Zealand, Sweden, the United Kingdom, and in General," paper presented at Seventh Bank of Japan International Conference (chapter 8, this volume).
Mieno, Y. (1995) "Issues Facing the Japanese Economy and Roles of Central Banks," Bank of Japan *Quarterly Bulletin*, 3 (February), pp. 5–14.
Meiselman, D. (ed.) (1970) *Varieties of Monetary Experience* (Chicago, Ill.: University of Chicago Press).
Meltzer, A.H. (1987) "On Monetary Stability and Monetary Reform," *Bank of Japan Monetary and Economic Studies*, 5 (September), pp. 13–34.
Meltzer, A.H. (1994) "Regulatory Arrangements, Financial Stability and Regulatory Reform," Bank of Japan *Monetary and Economic Studies*, 12 (July), pp. 1–15.
Meltzer, A.H. (1995) "On Making Monetary Policy More Effective Domestically and Internationally," Keynote Address, Seventh Bank of Japan International Conference (chapter 1, this volume).
Menger, C. (1892) "On the Origin of Money," *Economic Journal*, 2 (June), pp. 239–55.
Muth, J.R. (1961) "Rational Expectations and the Theory of Price Movements," *Econometrica*, 29, pp. 315–35.
Phelps, E.H. (1967) "Phillips Curves, Expectations of Inflation and Optimal Unemployment over Time," *Economica*, NS 34 (August), pp. 254–81.
Sargent, T.J. and Wallace, N. (1976) "Rational Expectations and the Theory of Economic Policy," *Journal of Monetary Economics*, 2 (May), pp. 169–83.
Scarth, W. (1994) "Zero Inflation versus Price Stability," in Bank of Canada (1994).
Selgin, G. (1994) "On Ensuring the Acceptability of a New Fiat Money," *Journal of Money, Credit and Banking*, 26 (November), pp. 808–26.
Selgin, G. and White, L.H. (1994) "How Would the Invisible Hand Handle Money?," *Journal of Economic Literature*, 32 (December), pp. 1718–49.
Simons, H. (1936) "Rules versus Authorities in Monetary Policy," *Journal of Political Economy*, 44 (February), pp. 1–30.
Smith, A. (1776) *The Wealth of Nations* (London).
Taylor, J.B. (1993) "Price Stabilisation in the 1990s: An Overview," in K. Shigehara (ed.), *Price Stabilisation in the 1990s* (London: Macmillan).
Tobin, J. (1972) "Inflation and Unemployment," *American Economic Review*, 82 (March), pp. 1–18.
Walsh, C. (1995) "Optimal Contracts for Central Bankers," *American Economic Review*, 85 (March), pp. 150–67.

Comments*

Michael Mussa

I will focus my remarks on two key questions. First, is it reasonable to establish "price stability" or "zero inflation" as the fundamental objective of monetary policy? By "price stability," I mean true price stability in the old-fashioned sense – there is no systematic tendency for the general level of prices to rise or fall over the longer term. Second, if "price stability" or "zero inflation" is not the agreed goal of monetary policy, is it realistic to expect that "low inflation" can be established as a fundamental objective?

In addressing these issues, I will *not* ask what is normatively desirable as a goal for monetary policy, but rather what the facts suggest to be practicably achievable, given the need for monetary policy to sustain adequate popular support.

Turning first to the issue of "price stability," it is important to emphasize two facts from historical experience: (i) monetary policy can deliver true price stability over the longer term; and (ii) the conditions for this to happen do not prevail under modern systems of inconvertible paper monies. Figure 4A.1 is useful in making these points. The two charts show the path of the price level in the United Kingdom and the United States for the past two centuries. In both countries, the price level exhibited long-run stability up to the 1930s. Since the 1930s, however, the price level has been on an inexorable upward trend. It has risen by a factor of about 7 in the United States, and by a factor of about 20 in the United Kingdom.

This inflation of the past fifty to sixty years has occurred across all of the industrial countries, and it is without historical precedent as a world-wide phenomenon. In particular, consider the longer-term inflation experience of England since the pound sterling was introduced as the nominal unit of account in the thirteenth century. When it was introduced, the English pound was worth almost one pound of pure silver. Today, the pound sterling is worth a little more than a quarter of an ounce of silver. Over the course of 700 years, the English pound has been reduced to about 2.5 percent of its original value in terms of silver. Most of this depreciation, however, has occurred recently. In the 1930s, the pound was still worth somewhat more than a third of a pound of silver. Thus, the (compound) average annual inflation rate over six and a third centuries was

* The opinions expressed in these comments are those of the author and do not necessarily represent the views of the International Monetary Fund.

Figure 4A.1 Long price level histories: United Kingdom and United States

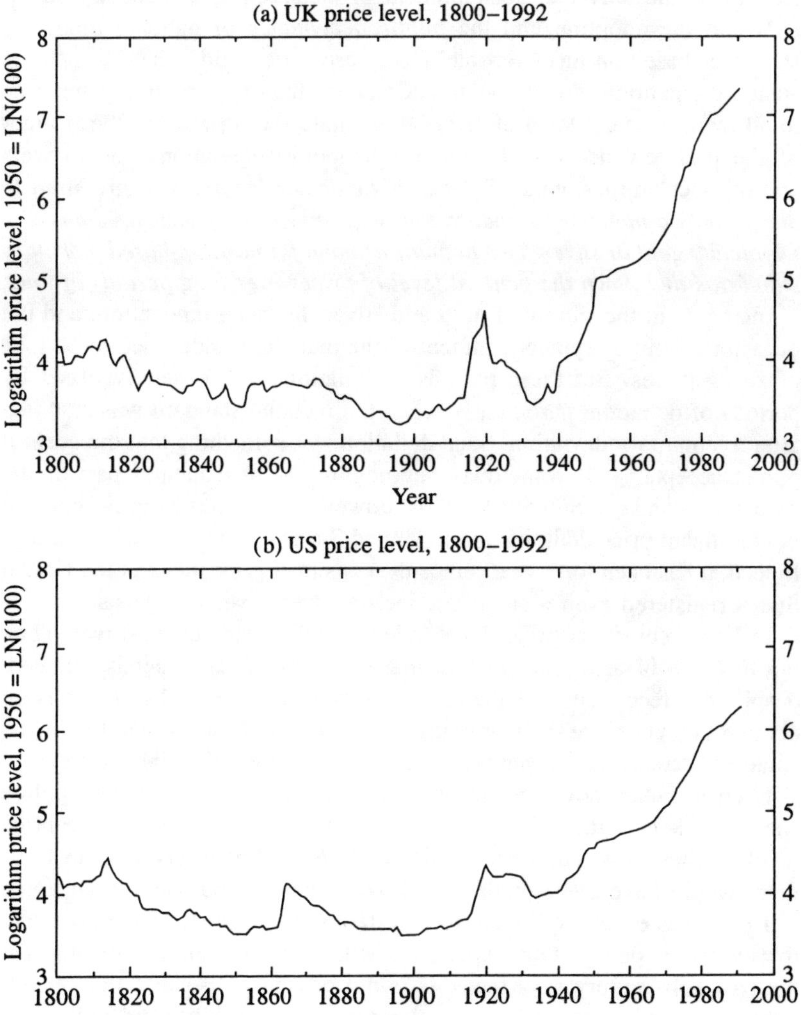

barely one-tenth of 1 percent per year. During the past sixty years, the pound sterling has been reduced to about one-fifteenth of its silver value in the 1930s. Inflation in England during the past sixty years has been very different from anything that preceded it for many centuries. The same is broadly true for inflation in all countries.

The fundamental reason for the upsurge of inflation during the past few decades is the universal abandonment of metallic-based monetary standards and the adoption and the *public acceptance* of national monetary standards based on inconvertible paper currencies. Under the old metallic standards, national governments and central banks were simply not free to allow the general level of prices to escalate ever upward in the manner of the past few decades. Except for temporary deviations due to wars and other calamities, generally *the public demanded and was prepared to accept only a monetary standard that was linked to a physical commodity – typically gold or silver. This popular demand for metallic-based monetary standards tied down the general level of prices over long periods of time.*

Increases in the supply of gold and silver, financial innovation, and the occasional temporary abandonment of the metallic standard led to periods of rising prices. But these periods of inflation were generally offset by periods of deflation, particularly when the metallic standard was resumed after a temporary deviation. Such deflation was something that the general public accepted – if sometimes begrudgingly – as a natural part of the monetary standard. Since the 1930s, however, there has been *no* episode of significant price deflation in the United States – or in any other country. Indeed, it has been forty years since the consumer price index in the United States registered even a small decline on a year-over-year basis.

In Japan, consumer prices have fallen slightly during the past two years; but this is a bizarre phenomenon that is not expected to persist. Indeed, despite this recent small deflation, the consumer price level in Japan is up about 8 percent since the beginning of the current decade – and this is the smallest increase in the general price level in any industrial country.

Even in Japan, however, no one seriously argues that monetary policy should seek to further deflate the economy in order to reduce the price level to where it was at the beginning of 1990. But precisely such an argument would have to be made – and would have to be publicly accepted – if true "price stability" were to be established as the effective objective for monetary policy. Our experience with paper currency standards for the past half-century says that this is not possible – because the general public does not support it. True, long-run price stability did exist and, indeed, was the dominant species when metallic monetary standards held sway over the popular mind. However, metallic monetary standards are, like the dinosaurs, extinct. True, long-run price stability under a discretionary paper standard is, like a unicorn, an entirely mythical beast.

Turning to the second issue, if true "price stability" cannot realistically be the fundamental objective of monetary policy under modern paper currency standards, is there reasonable hope that "low inflation" can be firmly

Table 4A.1 Industrial countries: average inflation rates (CPI)

	1950–9	*1960–9*	*1970–9*	*1980–9*	*1990–4*
United States	1.82	2.33	7.10	5.55	3.64
Canada	2.41	2.53	7.38	6.51	2.78
France	6.16	3.87	8.92	7.34	2.55
Germany	1.13	2.39	4.89	2.90	3.45
Italy	3.02	3.36	12.45	11.37	5.27
Japan	3.04	5.35	9.09	2.53	2.00
United Kingdom	3.51	3.53	12.63	7.43	4.62
Australia	6.51	2.46	9.83	8.41	3.04
Austria	6.77	3.34	6.10	3.84	3.44
Belgium	1.84	2.66	7.13	4.90	2.84
Denmark	3.81	5.34	9.29	6.91	2.08
Finland	6.14	5.05	10.41	7.32	3.20
Ireland	3.86	3.99	12.75	9.35	2.67
Netherlands	3.81	4.12	7.06	2.87	2.83
New Zealand	5.00	3.21	11.46	11.86	2.55
Norway	5.57	3.49	8.37	8.34	2.71
Portugal	0.68	4.02	17.14	17.64	9.08
Spain	6.25	5.75	14.39	10.25	5.57
Sweden	4.42	3.77	8.57	7.94	5.79
Switzerland	1.14	3.12	4.98	3.27	3.89
Unweighted average	3.84	3.68	9.50	7.33	3.70
GDP weighted average	2.79	3.16	8.15	5.71	3.47

established as the primary goal? Here I disagree with those who contend that an inflation rate of zero is the only viable objective for monetary policy and that tolerance of any positive inflation rate implies a serious risk of upward drift. The experience of recent decades provides important support for this position.

Specifically, it is useful to turn to the information provided in Table 4A.1. This table reports the average annual inflation rates for 20 industrial countries for each of the past four decades and for the first five years of the present decade. The following facts are noteworthy:

1. In the 1950s and in the 1960s, the averages of country inflation rates were in the range of 3 to 4 percent.
2. In the 1970s, the averages of country inflation rates more than doubled; and, for every one of the 20 countries, the inflation rate was higher than in the two preceding decades. Common shocks, including oil price increases and the collapse of the Bretton Woods system of pegged

exchange rates, contributed to this general upsurge of inflation. But, the relatively low inflation recorded in some countries, especially Germany and Switzerland, indicates the importance and effectiveness of firm monetary policies in resisting this inflationary upsurge.

3. In the 1980s, the averages of country inflation rates declined from those of the 1970s; and, for individual countries, declines were recorded in 18 out of 20 cases.
4. In the 1990s, the averages of country inflation rates have come down even further and are now back essentially to the averages of the 1950s and 1960s. For individual countries, 18 out of 20 recorded lower inflation in the 1990s than in the 1980s, and the result would be 20 out of 20 with inflation rates now expected for 1995 and 1996.

The important point from all of this is that the widespread and substantial decline of inflation rates since the upsurge of the 1970s is not a fortuitous accident. Good luck may have helped, but the primary cause of much better inflation performance in recent years has undoubtedly been the determined efforts of monetary policy in the industrial countries to deliver relatively low and stable inflation rates. The drive to reduce inflation was often associated with recessions, but the general public appears to have accepted that this was the necessary cost of reducing inflation to tolerable levels. More recently, several countries that are relatively advanced in the present recovery have acted preemptively to tighten monetary policy in order to forestall future inflationary pressures and promote more durable expansions. This also has generally been accepted as necessary and desirable, and has been welcomed in financial markets. Thus, in actual practice, monetary policy in the industrial countries now appears to be oriented toward the fundamental objective of keeping inflation low and stable, and this objective for monetary policy appears to enjoy widespread popular support.

5 Challenges for Monetary Policy in the Evolving Financial Environment

David W. Mullins, Jr

A variety of changes under way in the financial environment will confront monetary policymakers with new challenges in the years ahead. I shall begin by noting the trends in fiscal conditions with which monetary policy will have to coexist.

1 FISCAL TRAJECTORIES OF INDUSTRIALIZED COUNTRIES

Recent decades have seen large increases in government spending relative to GDP. While government revenues have also risen sharply, in recent years revenues have not kept pace with increases in government spending. As illustrated in Table 5.1, the result has been steadily escalating ratios of debt to GDP in most industrialized economies during the past decade and a half. The average gross government debt to GDP ratios of the G-7 countries has risen from 43 percent in 1980 to 74 percent in 1994.

While "on-budget" government spending and liabilities have escalated, so have the "off-budget" government commitments and liabilities. These include off-budget contingent liabilities associated with various government guarantee, insurance and safety net programs, as well as the liabilities of various government-sponsored enterprises. The largest off-balance-sheet government liability consists of the present value of future public pension liabilities. These liabilities arise out of unfunded "pay as you go" pension schemes. As reported in Table 5.2, these future pension net liabilities average 184 percent of GDP for the G-7 countries with a majority of countries with liabilities in excess of 200 percent of GDP. The implicit government liabilities problem looks much worse if one includes government commitments to provide health care benefits. Without difficult policy changes, these off-budget liabilities will produce large future increases in government expenditures, deficits and accelerating on budget

Table 5.1 Industrial countries: general government gross debt (percent of GDP)

	1980	*1985*	*1990*	*1994*
Australia	–	–	–	35.1
Austria	37.2	49.6	56.2	59.0
Belgium	81.6	122.6	128.4	136.0
Canada	44.3	64.7	73.1	95.6
Denmark	33.5	64.1	59.7	68.7
Finland	11.8	16.6	14.5	60.1
France	20.8	31.0	35.4	48.4
Germany*	31.8	41.7	43.4	49.8
Greece	24.2	50.6	73.9	114.1
Italy	57.8	82.3	102.1	129.0
Japan	52.0	68.7	69.8	83.3
Netherlands	46.6	71.5	78.8	79.4
Norway	52.2	40.7	39.2	50.1
Portugal	–	–	67.7	70.5
Spain	17.5	45.1	45.1	62.8
Sweden	44.3	66.7	44.9	92.2
United Kingdom	49.6	52.7	34.4	46.0
United States	43.6	51.5	59.9	68.9

* Data refer to Western Germany through 1990 and to united Germany thereafter.

Source: IMF, World Economic Outlook database.
Mussa and Masson (1995).

debt in the future. In a recent review of fiscal trends, Michael Mussa and Paul Masson of the IMF conclude that "Indeed, it is clear that current trends are unsustainable."[1]

There are a variety of reasons underlying these troubling fiscal trends. The deprivations produced by the Great Depression contributed to a change in the political consensus concerning the role of the government. The entitlement to social benefit spending of the welfare state has become firmly rooted in political constituencies hindering retrenchment.

There are also underlying reasons for the discouraging outlook for the future, in which the imbedded trajectory of government expenditures is expected to outstrip the capacity of governments to generate higher revenues. First, the ageing demographics of industrialized countries, illustrated in Table 5.3, portends rapidly accelerating pension and health care costs and, second, technological change is adversely affecting low-skilled workers resulting in large increases in European long-term unemployment.[2]

The two factors underlying future fiscal trends suggest difficult and troubling social and political confrontations. An intergenerational conflict,

Table 5.2 Estimated net pension liabilities: present value of current and future rights and future contributions (percent of 1990 GDP)

	United States	*Japan*	*Germany*	*France*	*Italy*	*United Kingdom*	*Canada*
A. Gross liabilities	309	496	467	729	742	537	482
Accrued rights	113	162	157	216	259	156	121
New rights	196	334	310	513	483	381	361
B. Assets	265	296	306	513	508	350	231
Existing	23	18	–	–	–	–	–
Future contributions	242	278	306	513	508	350	231
C. Net liabilities (A-B)	43	200	160	216	233	186	250

Source: Van Den Noord and Herd (1993).
Mussa and Masson (1995).

Table 5.3 Percentage of population over 60 years old, 1990–2050*

	1990	*2010*⁺	*2030*⁺	*2050*⁺
OECD	18.2	23.1	30.7	31.2
United States	16.6	19.2	28.2	28.9
Japan	17.3	29.0	33.0	34.4
Germany	20.3	26.5	35.3	32.5
France	18.9	23.1	30.1	31.2
Italy	20.6	27.4	35.9	36.5
United Kingdom	20.8	23.0	29.6	29.5
Canada	15.6	20.4	30.2	30.6

* Regional figures are weighted averages of individual countries.
⁺ Projections.
Source: World Bank (1994).
Mussa and Masson (1995).

pitting the young against the old, is inherent in these demographic patterns. The technology trend produces a widening gap between those in society who are well-off and those who are poor. The potential for societal, generational and, therefore, political discord, underscores the difficulty and importance of putting fiscal positions in balance.

Alan Auerbach (1995) reviews a variety of solutions to the fiscal problems of developed economies. These include budget discipline rules, privatization, federalism, and the need for improved government accounting procedures. His is not a particularly optimistic review. For example, he stresses the inadequacies of simple balanced budget rules in the face of intergenerational fiscal imbalances. Budget surpluses are required to fund liabilities for future spending.

It is encouraging that in many if not most industrialized countries, initiatives are under way to reduce fiscal deficits and move toward more sustainable fiscal trajectories. These initiatives seem to be based on a growing recognition of the problem and an emerging political consensus to confront fiscal unsustainability. However, optimism must be tempered by the difficulty of reversing trends driven by the momentum of underlying demographic and technological trends.

1.1 Implications for Monetary Policy

A number of theoretical studies have argued that high fiscal deficits and government debt can have detrimental effects on the ability of central banks to build credibility and achieve price stability. These studies are reviewed by John Taylor (1995). Deficits financed with money creation are an obvious example of the interaction of fiscal and monetary policy. Overall, central banks seem to have performed well recently despite sharp changes in fiscal positions. During the past decade and a half, fiscal deficits and debt have risen sharply in industrial economies, yet inflation has generally fallen. Central bankers have effectively resisted mounting fiscal pressures.

Nonetheless, the magnitude of the fiscal problem amassing on the horizon suggests central bankers are likely to face increased pressures and difficult choices in the future. Unless arrested, these fiscal trends are likely to produce the traditional pressure to sacrifice inflation to stimulate economic growth in the short term. In theory, these pressures could culminate in attempts to repudiate debt through hyperinflation. The feasibility of inflation-induced debt repudiation is limited by the responsiveness of capital markets. Wary markets can force shorter-term debt maturities and floating rate debt producing rapid escalation of interest costs in response to attempts to repudiate.

While central banks have resisted such pressure in the past, they may be confronted with another difficulty. If the political system fails to bring the fiscal stance into balance, capital market discipline will do so. Faced with apparently unsustainable fiscal trajectories, investors will sharply increase interest rates on government debt, exacerbating the fiscal imbalance. Such a spiral of increased debt financing costs could ultimately lead to a financing crisis, with the market unwilling to finance or roll over government debt.

Clearly, a debt financing crisis would confront monetary authorities with a very difficult environment. In such an environment, money creation may be the only viable form of government finance. The destruction of wealth inherent in the collapse of existing debt values and the sharp contraction of government expenditures would produce a severe economic contraction. More generally, to be effective, monetary policy requires a viable financial system, while debt crises fundamentally undermine financial system viability.

It may seem that discussion of a debt crisis for industrialized economies is highly premature. Projections suggest fiscal burdens are sustainable for many years, perhaps even decades into the future. Nonetheless, forward-looking, fast-moving markets can be expected to accelerate the day of reckoning. Indeed, even in today's capital market environment the highly unlikely prospect of debt crisis in developed countries is already very much on the radar screen.

There is no easy answer to the future fiscal environment confronting central banks. Obviously, monetary authorities must maintain their commitment to price stability and strongly support efforts to bring fiscal positions into balance. However, I hope it is not viewed as overly alarmist to suggest that central bankers need to put on their future research and policy assessment agenda consideration of how to address potential deterioration in conditions and ultimately crisis in government debt markets.

2 THE EVOLVING GLOBAL FINANCIAL SYSTEM

An important development in the financial system is the emergence of global capital markets as a powerful force in the world economy. Not too many years ago financial systems were essentially banking systems with capital markets in a subsidiary role. National financial systems were to a significant degree separate. Information and financial shocks traveled slowly. The forces driving capital market growth include advances in computing, information processing, communications and financial engineering technology which have conspired to reduce dramatically the cost of transacting.

Recent trends will be reinforced by the environment outlined above. First, the trend toward financial liberalization, financial reform or deregulation will be reinforced by the need of the governments to place debt. Countries will need liberal financial systems to compete in the global financial services arena and to support economic growth. Second, the trend toward globalization will accelerate. The logic and economics of international diversification is inescapable and ultimately irresistible. International diversification of both investment and funding will be a major force in global capital flows in the years ahead.

A third trend which will continue, and likely accelerate, is the trend toward the importance of markets as mechanisms of financial intermediation. A corollary is the trend toward markets and financial institutions working in a symbiotic and supportive relationship, not as competitors. Historically, there has been a competition between direct intermediation through financial institutions and market intermediation. Over the past several decades, advances in information technology and telecommunications technology, as well as financial engineering, have increased the importance of markets. Over a wide and increasing range of financial activities, markets have become more important, because of the depth, liquidity, and flexibility afforded by markets. The growth in securitization and in mutual funds; the reshaping of cash flows into products tailored to appeal to specific clienteles; the growth in credit enhancement, where financial institutions split off and sell their liquidity standby capabilities separately from portfolio investment: all of these developments have enhanced the ability of an increasing range of borrowers, issuers, and investors working with financial institutions to tap the depth and liquidity of markets.

In addition, this trend toward the interaction of markets and financial institutions represents a force, steadily eroding the barriers that separate the different segments of the financial services industry. In my view, this interaction of markets and institutions is the unifying force, as financial institutions of all types reach out to interact with markets. Although I shall not address them in this chapter, this has important implications for regulation and supervision, especially with respect to the need to harmonize various regimes.

The final trend which, in my opinion, will continue, is financial innovation. The environment I have described – strong global capital flows, driven by deficits, development, and international diversification – will likely involve a not insignificant degree of volatility; and this is a fertile environment for financial innovation.

Thus, markets and global capital flows have become and will increasingly be a serious force to be reckoned with in most important areas of economic life. Today global capital markets exert an exacting discipline on the policies of governments, firms and other economic agents. This discipline lays bare inconsistent and unsustainable policies. The result of this disciplinary force should be better policies leading to improved economic performance.

These developments have special relevance for central banks because central banks are assigned stewardship of the health of financial systems.

2.1 Financial Innovation

A driving force in the evolving financial system and the growth of markets has been the unprecedented pace and scope of financial innovation during the past several decades. The explosion in financial innovation is rooted in advances in technology that have reduced the cost of transacting. Advances in financial engineering have facilitated the reshuffling and redistribution of risks to tailor financial instruments to appeal to the particular appetites of issuers, borrowers and investors. Merton (1992) argues that financial innovation has not only increased financial efficiency, but also has produced real efficiency gains for the economy.

2.2 The Growth of Derivatives

Perhaps the most notable example of this process has been the rapid emergence of financial derivatives. To many, derivatives epitomize modern global finance – the benefits and the risks and concerns as well. The development and growth of financial derivatives is one of the more remarkable success stories of recent economic history. In the short span of twenty-five years these instruments have sprung from their inception to pervade financial activities throughout the world.

Why have derivatives activities grown so rapidly? Because financial derivatives are simply a superior alternative to more traditional instruments in meeting the needs of many financial practitioners. Derivatives transactions often involve much lower transaction costs compared with equivalent transactions in traditional instruments. Low-cost transacting facilitates investment, issuing and arbitrage approaches that straddle markets, increasing asset substitutability.

Derivatives also improve pricing efficiency. Low-cost transacting translates into superior price discovery as derivatives markets tend to respond more quickly to new information. The unbundling of risks made possible by derivatives allows explicit pricing of distinct sources of risk not easily separable before the development of derivatives. The capacity to unbundle risk and transact at low cost allows the creation of payoff patterns that were not feasible or cost-effective previously. This helps "complete" markets thereby expanding opportunities for trading, hedging, investing and issuing securities.

These characteristics make derivatives efficient vehicles through which businesses can manage risks such as interest rate, foreign exchange, and commodity price risk. By replicating returns on other instruments or markets, derivatives are useful in circumventing institutional rigidities and minimizing administrative costs. As a result, for investors wishing to participate in the returns of particular securities and/or markets, derivatives often provide a lower-cost alternative to direct investment. Because the business of modern financial intermediaries is the transformation of financial flows, derivatives activities are an integral component of their production process.

The fundamental economic attractiveness of derivatives is that they allow one to split up the risks associated with a financial instrument or commodity or business or investment activity. The distinct sources of risks can be segmented, and these separate risks can then be traded around the financial system to those willing and able to bear and manage each risk at minimum cost. This process reduces the cost of risk-bearing for the financial system as a whole thus improving economic efficiency. Derivatives provide a very efficient way through which those who want to take certain risks can do so. For those who do not want to take certain risks, who want to lay off risk, derivatives are a very efficient way to insure against risk. Essentially derivatives have created an efficient, low-cost market for risk that facilitates economic activity. Indeed, many business activities would not be economically viable if one could not hedge risks through derivatives. These economic efficiency gains are the engine propelling the explosive growth of derivatives.

In my view, the emergence of this efficient market for risk insures the continued growth of derivatives activities. The reason is that this market for risk is penetrating the domain of fundamental strategic decision-making. This risk market allows businesses, investors, and financial institutions to isolate and express their strategic expertise. Competition is compelling economic agents to identify and pursue their area of distinctive expertise and insure against other risks. This strategic demand for risk management will likely lead, in developed markets, to new derivatives instruments designed to capture additional sources of risk (e.g., credit derivatives) while emerging markets will develop the basic derivatives instruments analogous to those already well-established in developed markets.

2.3 Effects of Derivatives on Markets

The role of derivatives in reducing frictions, increasing trading and hedging opportunities and creating a low-cost market for risk should contribute to increased financial market efficiency. This is generally supported by empirical results.[3] In general, studies demonstrate the bid–ask spreads on underlying securities are lower in the presence of derivatives (Neal, 1987; Fedenia and Grammatikos, 1989; Damodaran and Lim, 1991a). Moreover, markets with derivatives respond more quickly to new information. Price discovery is improved as information is incorporated more rapidly in prices of underlying securities in the presence of derivatives (Jennings and Stark, 1981; Damodaran and Lim, 1991; Kawaller, Koch and Koch, 1987, 1990; Stoll and Whaley, 1990; Angeloni, Drudi and Majnoni, 1994). Nonetheless, studies have failed to document convincingly any significant increase in trading volumes of underlying assets.

Concurrent with the growth and spread of derivatives activities, recent decades have been characterized by an increase in the volatility of interest rates and foreign exchange rates. While many measures of stock market volatility have fallen, there seems to be an increased incidence of large market movements (Presidential Task Force on Market Mechanisms, 1988). Some have argued that the existence and growth of derivatives has increased financial market volatility in underlying markets. A conceptually more persuasive argument is that because of their efficiency in managing risks, derivatives activities have increased, in part, as a response to increased volatility in underlying markets. In its report on derivatives the BIS Euro-currency Standing Committee of the G-10 central banks argued that "derivatives can be seen more as a consequence than a cause of increased volatility in exchange rates and interest rates."[4]

The empirical evidence to date fails to support the concern that derivatives may increase the volatility in underlying securities prices. To the contrary, in many markets there is evidence that the introduction of derivatives has reduced underlying price volatility. This is true with respect to US stock options (Hayes and Tennenbaum, 1979; Whiteside, Duke and Dunne, 1983; Damodaran and Lim, 1991b). A broad range of studies confirm that futures on bonds either reduced underlying volatility or have no discernible effect. Reduced volatility is documented for Italian government bonds (Esposito and Giraldi, 1994) and either reduced volatility or no significant effect is found in empirical studies of the US government and mortgage bond markets (Froewiss, 1978; Simpson and Ireland, 1982; Bortz, 1984; Edwards, 1988). The rationale is that derivatives, by lowering transaction costs, enhanced liquidity. The evidence on volatility for stock index futures is mixed with some researchers finding reduced volatility (Robinson, 1993) and others, increased volatility (Stoll and Whaley, 1987; Harris, 1989; Damodaran, 1990). In contrast, futures on some commodities have been found to reduce price volatility (Ma, Dare and Donaldson, 1990).

There is also evidence that the existence of derivatives and the associated lower cost of transacting and enhancing hedging opportunities have changed the short-run dynamics of the US yield curve. A study by the Federal Reserve Bank of New York (BIS, 1994b, Annex V argues that in early 1994 the shape of the US yield curve was altered by portfolio realignments and shifts in hedging facilitated by derivatives and the existence of mortgage-backed securities. Since this episode was initiated by the Federal Reserve policy action in February of 1994, the study concludes that financial innovation has likely altered the transmission mechanism of monetary policy from short-term rates through long-term rates to the real economy.

The benefits of derivatives should increase the price level of underlying securities. Lower transaction costs and increased hedging and trading opportunities should enhance liquidity, thereby lowering the returns investors require to hold the underlying security. While the effect may be difficult to confirm empirically, several empirical studies have documented that the introduction of derivatives has increased underlying securities prices. This is true of US stock options (Conrad, 1989; DeTemple and Jorion, 1990) and reduced term premia in the French government bond yield curve were associated with the introduction of bond futures (Citanna and Rovelli, 1991).

It is often argued that derivatives tend to make underlying markets more resilient to shocks due to increased liquidity and better risk distribution. Nonetheless, there continues to be concern about the possibility that in periods of market stress, derivatives could amplify price volatility in underlying securities. The concern is that abrupt market movements could be reinforced by the effects of dynamic hedging, margin and collateral calls, as well as the feedback effects of large moves through derivatives pricing models.

These factors played a role in the 1987 US stock market crash (Report of the Presidential Task Force on Market Mechanisms, 1988; BIS, 1994b, Annex III). In assessing this episode the effects of derivatives in well-functioning markets must be distinguished from market failure. Innovation in derivatives has, in some cases, outpaced the development of infrastructure and market participants' understanding. That this was the case in the 1987 stock market crash is suggested by the paucity of other notable examples of problems of this nature despite the continued growth of derivatives activities. Indeed, it is plausible that increased risk management capabilities produced by derivatives dampened the impact of recent market events such as the breakup of the European exchange rate mechanism in 1992. In any case, there is no comprehensive evidence that derivatives systematically amplify risks in times of market stress.

Overall the empirical evidence suggests that the development and spread of derivatives activities have resulted in better-functioning markets. Derivatives have contributed to improved risk management, lower transaction costs, increased efficiency, and enhanced opportunities for trading, hedging, investing and capital-raising. Because monetary policy works through the financial system, a deeper, more resistant, more efficient and better-functioning financial system should engender benefits that accrue to monetary policymakers as well.

3 IMPACT OF DERIVATIVES ON MONETARY POLICY

There are a number of ways in which the development of derivatives activities may have affected the operation of monetary policy. First, monetary policy works through the financial system and thus a stable well-functioning financial system is important to the efficacy of policy. While there is evidence that derivatives activities have improved the functioning of the financial system, there is also concern that derivatives may have increased its fragility. The concern is that derivatives may have increased the risk of contagious, systemic failure.

3.1 Systemic Risk and Derivatives

As presented, the development of derivatives appears to be an extraordinary success story. But no discussion of derivatives would be complete without addressing the darker side of derivatives. Derivatives disasters, huge losses, failed financial institutions, bankrupt municipalities are reported with surprising frequency. These have inspired many to identify derivatives as a potential source of global systemic risk.

While derivatives activities have been beneficial, they are also quite powerful instruments. The low cost of transacting and potentially high level of leverage allows the archetypical rogue trader to produce massive losses, sufficiently large to threaten the viability of a firm or financial institution. Derivatives' complexity makes internal risk management more difficult; their opaqueness makes market discipline more challenging. Those financial institutions most actively involved in derivatives activities with significant exposures are large institutions. These institutions are also most intimately involved in global markets and payments systems – potential transmission mechanisms for systemic risks. Rapidly growing, new, complex activities near the heart of the global financial system are justifiably of great concern to central bankers.

Nonetheless, in my view, essential safeguards are now well-known and well-articulated in a number of studies. There are two levels of derivatives risk that need to be addressed. First, at the level of the firm, how can the incidence of major derivatives-related losses be reduced? Second, at the level of the financial system, when losses occur at an institution, how can the risk of contagion and systemic crisis be reduced?

Focusing first on the financial system, the most effective antidote to systemic risk is to improve the legal and financial infrastructure. This requires that innovative, complex new instruments, bilateral netting arrangements, and multilateral netting mechanisms and the like, all stand on sound, enforceable legal ground both within a given jurisdiction and across multi-country jurisdictions. This applies to bankruptcy procedures as well. The Brady Commission Study of the 1987 US stock market crash concluded that flaws in market mechanisms, especially clearance and settlement systems,[5] were among the most serious systemic threats. To guard against systemic risk central bankers need also to work to insure important central market mechanisms are well-designed, secured with operational, credit and liquidity backstops sufficient to survive the failure of large participants and that they are well-regulated and robust. These market mechanisms include the microstructures of exchanges, clearing-houses, clearance and settlement systems and payment systems. These are the transmission mechanisms of contagious systemic failure, while derivatives are merely one potential trigger. For example, foreign exchange settlement risk, so-called Herstatt risk, created by the lack of time synchronization of foreign exchange settlement, remains in many observers' view the most serious source of potential systemic risk. Fortunately, there is ample guidance on the principals of sound market mechanisms in various studies including those sponsored by the Group of Thirty and those published by the Bank for International Settlements.[6] It is encouraging that much work is under way to improve important market microstructures in many countries.

Let me turn now to risk at the level of the firm. While improved accounting and disclosure, increased attention to counterparty credit analysis, regulatory supervision and consultation and improved capital standards are all useful in reducing the chances of derivatives disasters, such essentially external remedies have their limits.[7] The necessary and perhaps sufficient remedy at the level of the firm is a sound internal control system and risk-monitoring and management system of the type delineated in the Group of Thirty (1993)-sponsored study on derivatives. Essentially all of the major derivatives problems unearthed in recent years can be traced to inadequacies in risk management and control systems. I believe that one can make the case that these problems would have been prevented or contained with minimum damage had a well-designed risk management system been in place and functioning well. Indeed, in my view, a key job of supervisors is to insure that sound internal control systems are in place and functioning well in regulated institutions.

This invites the following question: If this remedy is so effective and well-known – it has been more than two years since the release of the G-30-sponsored derivatives study – why then do we keep seeing major derivatives losses? Clearly such systems are costly, requiring highly paid expert staff. The costs are viewed as overhead, not generating incremental revenue. This is a tough sell in today's cost-conscious corporate culture and management must give authority to control personnel to constrain the activities of apparently highly profitable derivatives traders, designers and sales people. In my view, it is clear what needs to be done and the responsibility falls squarely on senior management and supervisors to insure that effective risk management systems are implemented.

The problems encountered with derivatives have occurred essentially because financial innovation has, in some cases, outpaced requisite improvement in system-wide and institution-specific infrastructures. The continued growth of derivatives will bring greater benefits but also increased responsibilities for management, regulators and central bankers. There is an encouraging quantum of energy being devoted to dull, but doable work in this area. These important tasks can be summarized as, first, shoring up the financial and legal infrastructure to make it safe for modern financial traffic and robust to an occasional accident and, second, reducing the incidence of accidents though the implementation of well-designed internal risk control systems.

While derivatives have received attention as a potential source of systemic risk, it is worth noting that derivatives are also useful in reducing systemic risk. Derivatives offer market participants including those most vulnerable to risk, increased opportunities for hedging and risk management. Thus, the development of derivatives markets have likely made the financial system better able to absorb shocks, reducing the chances of contagion and systemic failure. Moreover, derivatives' flexibility and design capabilities can be employed to circumvent weak components of the financial infrastructure. An excellent illustration of this is provided by André Perold (1995) who explores the impact of derivatives on payment and clearance and settlement systems. When derivatives substitute in a variety of ways for trading in underlying instruments, the result is often reduced reliance on settlement systems.

Inherent in many derivatives are implicit forms of netting. With such instruments, the amount settled is often far less than the amount that would need to be settled in the equivalent transaction in the underlying asset.

Of course, the implicit netting inherent in derivatives is offset to some extent by transactions in underlying securities used to hedge derivatives. Nonetheless, Perold argues that compared with the equivalent transactions in underlying assets, the use of derivatives reduces the occurrence of large funds and securities transfers and thus can substantially lower the risk of systemic failures. He also presents an example of a derivative explicitly designed to circumvent settlement risk. The Rolling spot currency futures contract on the Chicago Mercantile Exchange was designed to offer an economically equivalent alternative to spot market foreign exchange transactions but without foreign exchange settlement risk (i.e., so-called Herstatt risk).[8]

There are other ways derivatives design can be employed to reduce risk. For example, derivatives facilitate the shifting of the location of settlement. Exposure to foreign bonds or stocks through futures effectively transfers settlement from foreign securities settlement systems to a futures clearing-house. In some cases this allows those wanting to participate in foreign securities returns to avoid less-developed settlement systems in favor of a sounder system. Derivatives design also can be used to reduce legal risk. Regardless of domiciles of counterparties or underlying securities, transactions designed as swaps can specify which legal system (e.g., New York law) applies to disagreements as well as the jurisdiction for adjudication of disputes. This allows transactions in cases where the natural home country legal system entails risk. Therefore, derivatives innovation has the capacity to circumvent weak links in the systemic infrastructure and reduce the effective burden on payments and clearance and settlement systems. This is one of the reasons that derivatives are quite successful competitors in the market for transactions.

3.2 Impact of Derivatives on Policy Indicators

There is general agreement that the growth of derivatives has likely affected traditional quantity indicators of monetary policy such as monetary and credit aggregates (BIS, 1994; Townend, 1995; Deutsche Bundesbank, 1994). First, derivatives have altered the demand for money. It is argued that transactions, precautionary and speculative demands for narrow money have been reduced. The availability of derivatives has reduced transaction costs allowing economic agents to operate with lower transactions balances. Derivatives activities have also provided low-cost risk management alternatives reducing precautionary and speculative money demand. To some extent, these effects might be diminished by an increase in the volume of financial transactions (and, at the margin, an increase economic activity) associated with derivatives activities.

The usefulness of broader monetary aggregates has been adversely affected as derivatives have provided competing alternatives. Low-cost hedging of the price risk of traded assets, for example hedged government bonds, transforms market instruments into lower-risk instruments competing with interest-bearing components of the broad aggregates.

Credit aggregates have also been influenced by the growth of derivatives. Improved risk management capabilities allow banks to offer more flexible, better-tailored credit alternatives on improved terms to borrowers, but by enhancing trading environments derivatives have contributed to the securitization of credit and disintermediation from banks and other traditional financial institutions.

It is not possible or necessary to ferret out the precise net impact of derivatives on traditional monetary indicators. The impact of derivatives is only one component of the broader force of financial innovation such as the growth of money market and bond mutual funds. The force of innovation in a constantly evolving, complex financial system seems to have eroded the stable relationship between aggregates and nominal GDP. For more than a decade, this has been apparent in the USA with respect to narrow aggregates such as M1 and broad aggregates such as total credit (Mullins, 1994). More recently, instability has been noted in the relationship of M2 and GDP in the USA and M3 and relevant economic variables in Germany. Indeed, an article in the Deutsche Bundesbank *Monthly Report* (1994) concedes that "It is true that derivatives impede an empirically meaningful definition of the economically relevant money stock" but concludes that the problem is not new, simply a component of increased complexity in the financial system.[9]

In my view, the erosion of a stable relationship between aggregate indicators and relevant economic variables need not be particularly debilitating to monetary policymakers. It does suggest the importance of examining a wide range of indicators including money and credit flows, price data and forward-looking indicators of economic activity. Indeed, as delineated in a later section of this chapter, derivatives have appreciably augmented the set of available indicators with additions including better-quality indicators as well as truly unique indicators.

While there may be no loss of policy efficacy from problems with aggregates, these developments have eroded the usefulness of aggregates as a tool for communicating the process and progress of policy to the markets, the political system, and the public. The conceptual complexities and empirical instabilities caused by financial innovation also raise doubts concerning the efficacy of monetary policy rules based upon aggregates.

3.3 Derivatives' Impact on Monetary Transmission Mechanisms

While derivatives have likely adversely affected the usefulness of some monetary indicators, the development of derivatives markets should not affect the ability of central banks to establish the desired level of short-term interest rates. The reason is that derivatives do not alter central banks' status as the monopoly supplier of the ultimate means of settlement, central bank reserves. This should insure a non-zero demand for reserves allowing central banks to control short-term rates.

Derivatives have increased the liquidity, depth, flexibility, and transactional efficiency of foreign exchange markets enhancing trading and hedging opportunities. This is likely to have reduced the ability of central banks to influence exchange rates and/or defend a currency exchange rate target through foreign exchange interventions unless such interventions are viewed by market participants as consistent with underlying fundamentals. More efficient and responsive foreign markets should enhance the effectiveness of credible interventions.

Furthermore, researchers argue that derivatives increase the speed with which policy actions are transmitted throughout the financial system. As noted earlier, lower transaction costs and reduced frictions resulting from derivatives activities increase the rate at which new information, including policy actions, is incorporated in asset prices. Derivatives have increased asset substitutability as well. This should increase the speed of transmission of monetary policy actions throughout the maturity spectrum, across different types of assets and exchange rates and into market expectations. This conclusion seems consistent with the rapid response of domestic and foreign financial asset prices to recent monetary policy actions.

While derivatives have undoubtedly increased the speed of transmission of policy actions throughout financial asset prices, there is less agreement concerning the next step in real economic activity and inflation.[10] Analyses of the impact of derivatives on the transmission processes do not produce much in the way of definitive conclusions. Nonetheless, such analyses do share some conclusions concerning the impact of derivatives on monetary policy. Because derivatives allow economic agents to transform their financial exposures cheaply and rapidly, the growth of derivatives might be expected to alter their sensitivity to monetary policy. Even though the incidence of policy is shifted among economic agents, it is argued that in a closed system the impact of monetary policy can not be escaped. Risk might be shifted from some agents to others, but ultimately someone in the economy must bear risk and the incidence of policy. Thus, while the process of policy might be altered, derivatives do not eliminate the control of monetary authorities because the economy as a whole cannot be sheltered by the risk-shifting facilitated by derivatives.

With respect to the interest rate channel, studies conclude that, as noted earlier, monetary authorities' ability to set the desired level of short rates is unaffected by the existence of derivatives, but that the speed of transmissions of policy actions throughout the financial system is enhanced by derivatives. Moreover, derivatives may affect the links between interest rates and aggregate spending through the redistribution of risks. The sensitivity of spending is affected to the extent that derivatives facilitate the shifting of risk, and hence the incidence of policy, in a systematic manner from those with higher to those with lower marginal propensities to spend and invest.

As for the exchange rate mechanism, analyses identify two effects pointing in opposite directions. First, the existence of derivatives would tend to strengthen the exchange rate mechanism due to enhanced asset substitutability. A given change in the difference between domestic and foreign interest rates would be expected to produce larger changes in exchange rates because of derivatives activities. But this effect is counteracted by the enhanced capacity for exchange rate hedging. Through hedging, those most sensitive to exchange rate fluctuations can shift the incidence of such fluctuations to those less sensitive. While currency hedging has long been available through forward markets, derivatives have substantially increased hedging opportunities and reduced the cost of hedging. This is especially true with respect to longer-term hedging through currency swaps. Economic agents whose spending and investment is more sensitive to currency fluctuations can more easily insulate themselves from exchange rate risk, shifting this risk to those less sensitive. This effect would be expected to weaken the exchange rate transmission mechanism at least in the shorter term.[11] Thus, the overall impact of derivatives on the exchange rate mechanism is indeterminate.

There is an interaction between interest rate and exchange rate transmission mechanisms. Because of improved asset substitutability due to derivatives, monetary policy-induced changes in one country's yield curve might be expected to produce more rapid and larger changes in other countries' yield curves. The response of global interest rates to the Federal Reserve's 1994 policy actions seems consistent with this argument. This effect contributes to more rapid and forceful modification of market expectations. Thus, this may reinforce an expectational transmission mechanism through which policy actions alter market expectations and affect real economic decisions.

Analyses of the credit transmission channel reach somewhat more definitive conclusions that derivatives activities have likely weakened this channel of policy transmission. Monetary policy affects spending through the credit channel due to imperfections and constraints which limit firms', consumers' and financial institutions' access to credit.[12] These frictions impeding credit access include information asymmetries, regulatory constraints and other constraints. Such frictions are argued to worsen during tight money periods and ease when policy eases.

Derivatives can potentially reduce such frictions, thereby weakening the credit channel of monetary policy transmission. It is argued that derivatives generally improve the access of firms and others to capital markets. Derivatives can be attached to securities issued, enhancing their marketability and increasing the supply and dissemination of information about the firm. Capital market penetration unleashes market analysts, rating agencies and the like as suppliers of information about the issuer. Moreover, derivatives improve banks' ability to lend through risk-unbundling. This allows banks to focus on risks they are best able to assess and bear and to off-load other risks. It also facilitates portfolio diversification. Non-financial firms also use derivatives, both financial and commodity derivatives, to manage and reduce risks. This too, can improve the creditworthiness of firms and reduce financing constraints. Of course, because of their opaqueness, derivatives could also reduce firms' transparency, limiting some of these benefits.

As is apparent from this brief review, studies of the impact of derivatives on the linkage between policy-induced changes in financial variables and aggregate spending and inflation yield few definitive conclusions. Nonetheless, analysis and an understanding of the nature of derivatives activities do suggest a summary hypothesis – that the existence and growth of derivatives have systematically reduced the forcefulness of monetary policy in the sense that larger policy actions would be required to achieve a given target result for aggregate spending.

There are several characteristics of derivatives activities that suggest this summary hypothesis of reduced policy potency. First, to some significant extent, the potency of monetary policy depends upon the existence of frictions – transactions costs associated with transferring funds into money balances in the simplest inventory transactions money demand models, costs limiting asset substitution and portfolio rebalancing, information asymmetries constraining access to financing and the like. One fundamental engine underlying the growth of derivatives is their efficiency in reducing such frictions. The widespread use of derivatives has systematically and substantially reduced frictions of the type that give monetary policy its leverage. Frictions have been reduced, not eliminated, so policy still retains influence.

The second fundamental engine underlying the success of derivatives is their role in creating an efficient, low-cost market for risk. While it is usually argued that this market risk only allows risk-shifting but no risk reduction for the economic system as a whole, this argument is not sound. Derivatives not only promote risk-shifting but also facilitate diversification which reduces risk. While the risk associated with policy actions is thought of as systematic or undiversifiable risk, this is not strictly true. Domestic US investors with internationally diversified investment portfolios and domestic US firms with access to global funding markets should be less sensitive to US monetary policy actions in their spending and investment decisions. Derivatives substantially enhance the ability of firms and investors to achieve such international diversification. More generally, risk reduction through diversification by reducing economic agents' overall risk can leave them less vulnerable to non-diversifiable policy-induced risk.

The strongest argument for the reduced policy potency comes from examining the underlying process of risk-shifting facilitated by derivatives. Such risk-shifting is arguably the most important force driving derivatives activities. It works because some are more sensitive to risk than others. For the market to clear, those more sensitive to risk are willing to pay a price to shed risk to those less sensitive who are willing to accept risk at the given price. Such a market for risk systematically shifts risk from those more sensitive to those less sensitive. So while total (undiversifiable) risk will be unchanged, this redistribution of risk is by no means random. The economics of this market for risk will systematically shift risk from those most vulnerable to risk to those better able to bear risk. Monetary policy feeds into interest rate risks and foreign exchange risks. Through derivatives, these risks have likely been shifted systematically from economic agents whose real activity is most sensitive to these risks – those most likely to curtail spending and investment, most constrained by financing frictions – to other economic agents better able to bear these risk – less likely to be forced to alter real economic activity.

This systematic redistribution of risks results in real activity less sensitive to risks including those induced by monetary policy. The explosive growth of derivatives is testimony to their capacity to reduce frictions, facilitate risk reduction through diversification, and reduce the system's aggregate sensitivity to risk through risk redistribution. Because the forcefulness of monetary policy depends on such frictions and risk sensitivity, the nature of derivatives activities supports the hypothesis of reduced policy potency.

This does not suggest that derivatives render monetary policy impotent. Nor does it argue that policy is less effective; only that policy actions may need to be recalibrated to reflect the altered responsiveness of the financial and economic environment. Interestingly, this does not suggest larger policy actions would necessarily be observed in practice. Financial innovations and derivatives result in a better-functioning financial system and a sounder economy. Both would be expected to be somewhat more efficient, more self-correcting, more resistant to shocks and perhaps less in need of large policy actions.

Overall, financial innovation and derivatives have substantially changed and improved the functioning of the financial system. Because monetary policy works through the financial system, these innovations have changed the policy transmission process as well. Of course, there is nothing new about change. Policymakers are used to confronting change in the financial and economic environment. The increasing complexity of a rapidly evolving financial system does suggest it might be more difficult to pursue a monetary policy based on simple policy rules. The challenge of change underscores the importance of theoretical and empirical research to provide insight into the nature of the transmission process. It also argues for close attention to a broad range of indicators and for innovation in the process of assessing financial and economic conditions and in policy implementation. As shall be delineated in the next section, derivatives are helpful on this front. The development of derivatives has provided policymakers with new financial indicators and new instruments potentially of use in implementing policy.

4 IMPLICATIONS OF THE EVOLVING FINANCIAL ENVIRONMENT FOR MONETARY POLICY

The evolving financial environment delineated above has a number of implications for monetary policymakers. The growth of markets and their emerging importance to the real economy underscore the need for central banks to build credibility with markets. Credibility with markets is essential if central banks are to be successful in achieving price stability.

Credibility also anchors stabilization policy and enhances the effectiveness of monetary policy as an economic stabilization tool. If markets are convinced monetary policy is committed to price stability, then, when necessary, policy can be eased without engendering inflationary fears and counterproductive movements in long-term interest rates. Absent credibility, the benefits of ease can be offset by the adverse reaction of long-term rates reflecting inflation fears.

In addition, reduced frictions have substantially increased the speed and reach of economic shocks and policy actions throughout global markets. This has reinforced the necessity for close and continuous policy consultations among central bankers throughout the world. In view of the now almost seamless linkages among large markets, this is essential for authorities in countries with well-developed capital markets. The potential speed of contagious systemic crises has also increased. New markets have spawned new risks. As noted earlier, developing the policies and infrastructure to reduce these risks should be a top priority.

4.1 Harness the Technology

The success of financial engineering and the spread of financial technology have expanded the scope and complexity of existing markets and engendered the development and growth of entirely new financial markets. This has broad implications for central banks because monetary policy works through markets. A summary implication is that these developments underscore the importance if not the urgency of central banks dedicating themselves to mastering the technologies of modern finance. As financial innovations continue and markets continue to increase in size, complexity, and in interaction with the real economy, understanding and employing the concepts and techniques of modern finance will become important contributors to central banks' success in pursuit of the traditional objectives of price stability and maintenance of the stability of the financial system.

The creation of new financial instruments, derivatives in particular, warrant special attention. To operate effectively, central banks need to possess the technical and operational expertise to understand these new instruments and markets. The fact that these innovations have altered the environment in which central banks operate creates the necessity for central bank policies rooted in a thorough understanding and consummate technical expertise in these areas. Central banks are unavoidably in the business of finance, and just as unavoidably, these new technologies are now the business of finance. While this no doubt holds challenges for central bankers, it also promises opportunities. Financial innovations have not only produced benefits in improved financial and economic efficiency, but the new financial environment provides central bankers with new sources of information to assess the need for policy actions and new tools for policy implementation.

4.2 New Sources of Information

Financial innovations have expanded both the quality and quantity of indicators useful in policy assessment. Derivatives markets constitute new sources of information useful to central bankers in gauging market sentiment. Futures, forwards, and swap markets can be used to assess the markets' views concerning the expected future values of a wide range of asset prices over various time horizons. Sources of information to assess future short-term interest rates include futures on deposits, futures on short-term government debt, futures on interbank lending rates (e.g., the federal funds rate futures). Longer-term rate expectations can be observed in bond futures and FRAs. Various interest rate swap rates also provide useful information. Over the counter currency forwards provide a deep and liquid market through which market expectations for future spot exchange rates can be observed. Commodity price expectations are available through commodity futures (e.g., various oil-related futures).

In many cases alternative assessments of market expectations have long been available through markets in underlying instruments. In many cases, however, estimates of markets' expectations derived from derivatives markets are superior to traditional estimates. The reason is that in comparison to other markets, derivatives markets are often deeper and more liquid and price discovery is more rapid in the sense that derivatives markets respond more quickly to new information, often leading cash market movements. With any such estimates careful attention must be paid to the obfuscating effects of time-varying risk premia, institutional factors such as taxes, and the like.

Derivatives have also expanded the quantity of indicators providing genuinely new sources of information. An excellent example is the usefulness of derivatives markets information in assessing the dispersion of market participants' expectations of future asset prices. Advances in option pricing theory have made it possible and now routine to derive the implied volatility inherent in an option price. Implied volatility is an estimate of the standard deviation of future price distribution for the underlying asset. Implied volatility derived from options prices thus provides an estimate of the markets' assessment of the future fluctuations of interest rates, exchange rates, stock prices and the like. An increase in implied volatility suggests market participants expect greater fluctuations in the underlying asset price and/or reflect greater uncertainty about future prices.

In addition to deriving a point estimate of volatility, options prices can be used to reveal information concerning the shape of the distribution of expected price changes. Available techniques employ options prices or implied volatilities on a number of options on the same underlying asset. The output can include the expected distribution of the underlying asset price and the evolution of expected distributions through time. Summary measures of the skewness of expected distributions are already widely used by market participants and analysts. A common approach is to compare the prices (or implied volatilities) of puts and calls whose strike prices are spaced symmetrically around the current spot price.[13] If the underlying price distribution is symmetric, the prices and implied volatilities of equally out-of-the-money puts and calls should be identical. Differences in such put–call prices and implied volatilities are interpreted as measures of skewness in market participants' expectations. If call prices or implied volatilities are greater than those for corresponding puts, market participants are perceived to have an upward skewness to underlying price expectations. If puts are more valuable or exhibit higher implied volatilities compared to calls, the market is perceived to be more concerned that underlying asset prices will fall rather than rise.

Policymakers can use implied volatility and other option-derived distributional estimates to judge the level, distribution and evolving path of market expectations as well as to produce probabilistic confidence intervals for future price movements. Well-developed exchange-traded and over-the-counter options markets exist, allowing access to market expectations for short-term and long-term interest rates, exchange rates, stock prices and commodity prices. Quantity indicators such as put–call volume ratios and measures of open interest can be helpful in assessing market sentiment as well. A rich data set is also provided by exotic derivatives for mortgages, various interest rate caps and floors, swaps and swaptions to name a few. Moreover, option pricing techniques can be used to price options imbedded in more traditional instruments such as callable bonds. For example, the implied volatility of very long-dated options on treasury bonds can be estimated by valuing the very long-dated call option imbedded in long-term callable US treasury bonds.

Innovation in securities design further augments the information set. These include bonds with various put, call and conversion options attached, dual currency bonds and the like. Central bankers should take special note of the pricing of inflation index-linked bonds. Such bonds and derivatives such as options based upon these bonds reveal very useful information concerning the markets' expectation of future real interest rates and of future inflation. Such estimates should be most useful not only in assessing the need for policy actions, but more fundamentally in assessing a central bank's success in securing credibility with respect to the objective of price stability.

Clearly there are caveats and practical limitations involved in the use of these data. The quality of such estimates depends importantly on the soundness of analytical pricing models employed and the depth and efficiency of the markets involved. Because expectations are not always accurate predictors, skill and experience is required to interpret and employ this information in policy assessment. Table 5.4 summarizes a number of new indicators produced by financial innovation.

In a recent speech, John Townend of the Bank of England argues that "derivatives are a vast and exciting source of useful new information, and it is incumbent on central banks to study them intensively in order to extract as much information from the data as possible."[14] While there is much work to be done to master these indicators, this work seems to be well under way.

4.3 Operational Use of New Instruments

Just as financial innovation has generated new sources of information, it has also produced a wide variety of instruments that could be useful to central bankers in implementing policy. Central banks' policy implementation often involves intervening in financial markets. Just as private sector financial practitioners have found some derivative instruments superior to traditional instruments, central banks might find it advantageous to intervene using derivatives. For example, central banks could use money market derivatives such as FRAs, futures and/or options to influence money market rates and/or risk premia. An advantage might be that derivatives markets are often larger and more liquid than relevant underlying markets.

Intervention in foreign exchange markets employing derivatives also has advantages. Central bank intervention in the currency forward market is equivalent to sterilized spot intervention.[15] This automatic sterilization occurs because to hedge its exposure, the counterparty institution in the forward transaction undertakes a hedging transaction that is the economic equivalent of a sterilization transaction. Despite this automatic sterilization, the forward transaction has no effect on the central bank's foreign exchange reserves nor on its balance sheet. Such interventions may avoid problems associated with the sterilization of spot currency intervention. Moreover, since forward currency market interventions have no immediate impact on foreign exchange reserves, a central bank could conceivably extend its support of its domestic currency well beyond the current level of foreign exchange reserves. This aspect of derivatives is well-known to private market participants. Derivatives increase the potential scope and forcefulness of financial operations, but the risk of loss is also increased if

Table 5.4 Indicators from derivatives market data

	Market views on future asset prices (forward-type derivatives)	*Expected volatility (option-type derivatives)*	*Distribution of expectations of prices changes*
Exchange rates	Foreign exchange forwards and futures	Impliced volatility of currency options	Call/put price ratios: risk reversals Call/put volume ratios
Short-term interest rates	Futures contracts on e.g., 3-month interest rates FRAs on short-term interest rates Interest rate swaps	Implied volatility of options on 3-month interest rates futures contracts Caps, floors	Call/put price ratios: smile curves Call/put volume ratios
Long-term interest rates	FRAs on long-term interest rates Interest rate swaps	Implied volatility of options on government bond contracts Caps, floors, swaptions	Call/put price ratios smile curves Call/put volume ratios

Source: Adapted from BIS (1994).

currency support is ultimately unsuccessful. Thus, this approach arms central banks with a greater capacity to counter currency pressures not based upon fundamentals. It also allows a central bank to persist longer and more forcefully with increased scope for losses in resisting policy actions that may be warranted by fundamentals. As in many cases, derivatives use in currency interventions promises greater benefits when based upon sound fundamentals and heavier losses when not.

Central banks also have options as a potential policy instrument. Interventions with options can affect volatilities and hedging conditions in financial markets and can be used as signaling mechanisms. Options thus provide specialized tools that could be used to fine-tune interventions. Options hold particular promise to supplement stabilization programs. Many central banks engage in open market interventions to stabilize short-term interest rates at a desired level or to maintain a fixed exchange rate or to defend a foreign exchange rate corridor. Robert Merton (1995) has observed that open market operations of these types are, in the terms of financial economics, dynamic trading strategies. A fundamental result of modern financial engineering is that such dynamic trading strategies can be replicated with options and vice versa. Merton concludes that the process of open market operations used routinely by central banks to stabilize short-term interest rates or exchange rates can be replaced with a policy of selling options (or traditional instruments with options attached) producing economically identical results. For example, a replication policy for open market operations is for the central banks to sell put and call options on short-term money market instruments. If interest rates were to rise, the falling price of money market instruments would result in the exercise of put options. This would require the central bank to buy securities, increasing liquidity and driving interest rates down. If rates fall, the increase in the price of money market instruments would induce the exercise of call options, requiring the central bank to sell money market instruments, draining liquidity and driving up interest rates. Since such an options stabilization policy can be designed to produce actions identical to those with open market operations, why employ the options approach? Merton notes several advantages. First, such a program represents an automatic, preprogrammed, preannounced open market policy. This precommitment to stabilization by the central bank can have signaling advantages that enhance credibility. Moreover, because it is triggered automatically by market fluctuations, such a policy stands guard ready to lean against market movements at all times, including weekends, holidays and domestic non-trading hours. Such a policy steps in to help counter price gaps on market breaks instantly. In addition, private market participants pay for the options at issue, and thus the private sector pays for the stabilization program. Once the stabilization insurance is in the market, it can be repackaged and distributed throughout the system. An analogous approach could be designed to replicate currency support operations. Thus, Merton argues that such an options-based stabilization approach is superior to the traditional approach to open market operations and currency support. Although it can be designed to produce economically identical stabilization results, the options approach is more credible, easier and cheaper to employ in comparison to the traditional approach.[16]

Clearly, the Merton approach represents a stylized, idealized proposal illustrating the potential operational usefulness of options technology. There may be practical or conceptual difficulties that might argue against implementing the approach Merton delineates. Nonetheless, the conceptual equivalence of open market stabilization practices and options is undeniable. This suggests central banks might consider derivatives-based policies to supplement and complement existing practices. Central banks also need to weigh the contamination effects of intervention in derivatives markets.

Such intervention likely entails some loss of information since, if successful, intervention will alter market prices and expectations. This is also true of intervention in traditional markets. Of course, moral hazard is always a risk to be considered in central banks' interventions in markets. Nonetheless, at a minimum it seems plausible that central banks should master the use of derivatives and other financial innovations in many areas of operations. These include the management of foreign exchange and domestic reserves, the design of government securities and the process of the issuance of securities (e.g., efficient auction techniques).[17]

While central banks seem to be pursuing the use of derivatives as sources of information, there appears to be less appetite for the operational use of derivatives by central banks. The often expressed attitude is that new instruments have no convincing advantages over traditional instruments. This would be remarkable if true. The manifest advantages of derivatives have compelled virtually all private sector financial practitioners to employ these instruments. Their unique advantages include low-cost transacting and the ability to isolate precisely and address particular policy needs. They are traded in markets that are often superior price discovery mechanisms. In view of their efficiency and flexibility, most financial practitioners make heavy use of derivatives in pursuing traditional objectives. Indeed, derivatives activities now pervade the global financial system. It would be an interesting result if central banks essentially alone among financial practitioners found these instruments of no operational use. Of course, private financial practitioners have been compelled to use derivatives by the harsh discipline of competition. As public sector entities enjoying a measure of operational and financial autonomy, it is a challenge for central banks to innovate and to pursue efficiency and effectiveness in their operations. If the private sector experience is any guide, such a pursuit will likely lead central banks to use new financial instruments and techniques including derivatives.

5 CONCLUSIONS

During the past decade and a half central banks have achieved much. A remarkable consensus has emerged concerning the objectives of monetary policy – the pursuit of price stability and maintenance of the stability of the financial system. This consensus emerged out of the inflation and economic instability of the 1970s and strengthened despite escalating fiscal deficits in the 1980s.

Nonetheless, the challenges ahead appear formidable. Of course, the key challenge remains unchanged – to frame and implement sound monetary policy. But this must be achieved within an environment transformed by financial innovation. In the past, professional expertise of central banks has been concentrated chiefly in banking and macroeconomics. A review of the challenges and opportunities in the evolving financial environment underscores the importance of financial market expertise in the practice of monetary policy. While financial innovation has increased the complexity of the market environment, these developments have been generally beneficial. Financial innovation has produced better-functioning markets which should be more resilient to shocks. While innovation has likely increased the speed with which financial markets respond to policy action, at the margin the potency of monetary policy may have been diminished. Innovation has also yielded new and better sources of information for policy assessment and new instruments for policy implementation.

The more difficult potential challenge confronting central banks is the worsening of fiscal imbalances in many countries driven by the force of demographics. The risks include the prospect of unsustainable fiscal positions leading to a market crisis resulting in a most difficult policy environment.

While technical financial market expertise will be increasingly required, the success of central banks will continue to depend on establishing credibility with the public, the political system and the markets.

Notes

1. Mussa and Masson (1995), p. 3.
2. Symposium sponsored by the Federal Reserve Bank of Kansas City, Summer 1995.
3. See BIS (1994b), Annex I, for an empirical review and references on recent work.
4. BIS (1994a), p. 1.
5. Report of the President's Task Force on Market Mechanisms (1988).
6. See, for example, Group of Thirty (1993), BIS (1989, 1990, 1992, 1993).
7. I shall not expand on these defiencies here. But one aspect of the inadequacy in such external remedies is the potential for derivatives exposure to escalate to lethal proportions very rapidly often within the inter-review penumbra of periodic credit, accounting and supervisory reviews.
8. Perold (1995), pp. 37–8.
9. Deutsche Bundesbank (1994), p. 56.
10. For an excellent overview of the current state of research on the channels of monetary policy, see Federal Reserve Bank, *Review*, 77 (3), May/June 1995.
11. Of course, theoretically in the longer run one cannot escape the changes in relative prices produced by changes in exchange rates. However, longer-term hedging can provide effective shelter from shorter-term cyclical exchange

rate fluctuations induced by policy. Even for persistent exchange rate changes, longer-term hedging can allow economic agents time to adjust in an orderly and efficient manner.

12. Researchers have posited a narrow credit channel operating through bank lending and a broader balance sheet channel; see Bernanke and Gertler (1995), Kashyap and Stein (1994), Bernanke (1993), Hubbard (1995), Cecchette (1995).
13. These techniques usually employ out-of-the-money European puts and calls. In practice differences in put/call prices, termed "risk reversal" curves, are calculated for currency options while for other options implied volatilities are conventionally employed to produce so-called "smile curves." See BIS (1994b), Annex VI, for a description of several such techniques.
14. Townend (1995), p. 3.
15. See BIS (1994a) for a description of this process.
16. Obviously programs can be modified at any time by repurchasing options, selling other options which alter the parameters of stabilization and/or neutralizing the options though dynamic hedging. Nor would such a policy need to be implemented with options, the markets for which may be thin. Merton presents examples of automatic stabilization programs that replicate open market operations but employ the issuance of instruments such as puttable government bonds and/or government bonds that are convertible from short-term to long-term maturities.
17. See BIS (1994b), Annex VII, for an analysis of the use of derivatives in the management of foreign exchange.

References

Angeloni, I., Drudi, F. and Majnoni, G. (1994) "Intraday Spot-Future Interactions in the Market for Italian Government Bonds."

Auerbach, A. (1995) "Budget Deficits and Debt: Solutions for Developed Economies," Issues and Options Symposium sponsored by the Federal Reserve Bank of Kansas City, Summer 1995.

Bank for International Settlements (BIS) (1989) *Report on Netting Schemes.*

Bank for International Settlements (BIS) (1990) *Report of the Committee on Interbank Netting Schemes of the Central Banks of the Group of Ten Countries.*

Bank for International Settlements (BIS) (1992) *Delivery Versus Payment in Securities Settlement Systems.*

Bank for International Settlements (BIS) (1993) *Payment Systems in the Group of Ten Countries.*

Bank for International Settlements (BIS) (1994a) *Macroeconomic and Monetary Policy Issues Raised by the Growth of Derivatives Markets.*

Bank for International Settlements (BIS) (1994b) Annexes to *Macroeconomic and Monetary Policy Issues Raised by the Growth of Derivatives Markets.*

Bernanke, B.S. (1993) "Credit in the Macroeconomy," Federal Reserve Bank of New York, *Quarterly Review* (Spring), pp. 50–70.

Bernanke, B.S. and Gertler, M. (1995) "Inside the Black Box: the Credit Channel of Monetary Policy Transmission," *Journal of Economic Perspective*, 9, (Fall), pp. 27–48.

Bortz, G.A. (1984) "Does the Treasury Bond Futures Markets Destabilize the Treasury Bond Cash Market?," *Journal of Futures Markets.*

Cecchetti, S.G. (1995) "Distinguishing Theories of the Monetary Transmission Mechanism," *Review*, Federal Reserve Bank of St Louis, May–June, pp. 83–97.

Citanna, A. and Rovelli, R. (1991) "Li'impatto di un nuovo contratto futures sui premi al rischio nella struttura a termine: un'analisi APT per I titoli di Stato francesi," in H. Conti and R. Hamaui (eds), *Operatori e mercati nel processo di liberalizzazione* (Bologna).

Conrad, J. (1989) "The Price Effect of Option Introduction," *Journal of Finance*, 44, pp. 487–98.

Damodaran, A. (1990) "Index Futures and Stock Market Volatility," *Review of Futures Markets*, 9.

Damodaran, A. and Lim, J. (1991a) "The Effects of Option Listing on the Underlying Stocks Return Processes," *Journal of Banking and Finance*, 15, pp. 647–64.

Damodaran, A. and Lim, J. (1991b) "Put Listing, Short Sales and Return Processes," Working Paper, Stern School of Business.

DeTemple, J. and Jorion, D. (1990) "Option Listing and Stock Returns," *Journal of Banking and Finance*, 14, pp. 781–802.

Deutsche Bundesbank (1994) "The Monetary Policy Implications of the Increasing Use of Derivative Financial Instruments," *Monthly Report* (November).

Edwards, R.F. (1988) "Futures Trading and Cash Market Volatility: Stock Index and Interest Rate Futures," *Journal of Futures Markets*, 8, pp. 421–39.

Esposito, M. and Giraldi, C. (1994) "Preliminary Evidence on a New Market: Futures on the Italian Treasury Bonds," *Journal of Futures Markets.*

Fedenia, M. and Grammatikos, T. (1989), "Options Trading and the Bid–Ask Spread of the Underlying Stocks," Working Paper, University of Wisconsin.

Froewiss, K. (1978) "GNMA Futures: Stabilising or Destabilising?," *Federal Reserve Bank of San Francisco Economic Review.*

Group of Thirty (1993) *Derivatives: Practices and Principles* (Washington, DC: Global Derivatives Study Group).

Harris, L. (1989) "The October 1987 S&P 500 Stock Future Basis," *Journal of Finance*, 44, pp. 1155–76.

Hayes, S.I. and Tennenbaum, M.E. (1979) "The Impact of Listed Options on the Underlying Shares," *Financial Management*, pp. 72–6.

Hubbard, R.G. (1995) "Is There a 'Credit Channel' for Monetary Policy?," *Review*, Federal Reserve Bank of St Louis, May–June, pp. 63–74.

Jennings, R.H. and Stark, L.T. (1981) "Earning Announcements, Stock Price Adjustment and the Existence of Options Markets," *Journal of Finance*, 41, pp. 43–61.

Kashyap, A.K. and Stein, J.C. (1994) "Monetary Policy and Bank Lending," in N.G. Mankiw (ed.), *Monetary Policy* (Chicago, Ill.: University of Chicago Press for the National Bureau of Economic Research), pp. 221–61.

Kawaller, I.G., Koch, P.D. and Koch, T.W. (1987) "The Temporal Price Relationship Between S&P 500 Futures and the S&P 500 Index," *Journal of Banking and Finance*, 42 (5).

Kawaller, I.G., Koch, P.D. and Koch, T.W. (1990) "Intraday Relationship Between Volatility in the S&P 500 Futures Prices and Volatility in the S&P 500 Index," *Journal of Banking and Finance*, 14, pp. 373–97.

Ma, C.K., Dare, W.K. and Donaldson, D.R. (1990) "Testing Rationality in Futures Markets," *Journal of Futures Markets*, 10, pp. 137–52.

Merton, R.C. (1992) "Financial Innovation and Economic Performance," *Journal of Applied Corporate Finance*, 4 (4), pp. 12–22.

Merton, R.C. (1995) "Financial Innovation and the Management and Regulation of Financial Institutions," *Journal of Banking and Finance*, 19, pp. 461–81.

Mullins, D.W., Jr (1994) "A Framework for Monetary Stability – A Policy Maker's Perspective," in Wijnholds, Eijffinger and Hoogduin (eds), *A Framework for Monetary Stability*, pp. 5–15.

Mussa, M. and Masson, P. (1995) "Long-term Tendencies in Budget Deficits and Debt," in Symposium sponsored by the Federal Reserve of Bank of Kansas City, Summer 1995.

Neal, R. (1987) "Potential and Actual Competition in Equity Options," *Journal of Finance*, 42, pp. 511–32.

Perold, A.F. (1995) "The Payment System and Derivative Instruments," forthcoming in Chapter 2, *The Global Financial System, a Functional Perspective* (Harvard Business School Press).

Report of the Presidential Task Force on Market Mechanisms (1988) (Washington, DC: US Government Printing Office).

Review, Federal Reserve Bank of St Louis (1995) May–June.

Robinson, G. (1993) "The Effect of Futures Trading on Cash Market Volatility: Evidence from the London Stock Exchange," Working Paper No. 19, Bank of England.

Simpson, W. and Ireland, T. (1982) "The Effects of Futures Trading on the Price Volatility of GNMA Securities," *Journal of Futures Markets*.

Stoll, H.R. and Whaley, R.E. (1990) "The Dynamics of Stock Index Futures Returns," *Journal of Financial and Quantitative Analysis*, 25 (4), pp. 441–67.

Stoll, H.R. and Whaley, R.E. (1987) "Expiration Day Effects of Index Options and Futures," *Financial Analysts Journal*, 43, pp. 16–28.

Taylor, J.B. (1995) "Monetary Policy Implications of Greater Fiscal Discipline," in Symposium sponsored by the Federal Reserve Bank of Kansas City, Summer 1995.

Thornton, D.L. (1994) "Financial Innovation, Deregulation and the 'Credit View' of Monetary Policy," *Review*, Federal Reserve Bank of St Louis (January–February), pp. 31–49.

Townend, J. (1995) "Derivatives and Monetary Policy: A Central Banker's Perspective," Speech at ISDA Tenth Annual Conference in Barcelona, 23 March 1995.

Whiteside, M.M., Dukes, W.P. and Dunne, P.M. (1983) "Short Term Impact of Option Trading on Underlying Securities," *Journal of Financial Research*, 6, pp. 313–21.

Comments
Michael H. Moskow

David Mullins provides a wide-ranging discussion of the profound changes in capital markets over the past fifteen years, and their implications for fiscal, regulatory, and (especially) monetary policy. Mullins looks at these issues from a unique perspective, having had a distinguished and productive career in the academic world, in government, and in the private sector.

Capital markets are characterized by an unprecedented degree of liberalization and globalization. The explosion of derivatives markets is properly regarded as a response to this development. For policymakers, a critical question is whether these developments inhibit the ability of governments to set policy optimally on behalf of its citizens. The question is timely: very recently *The Economist* devoted a special section to this very issue. As a general conclusion, Mullins (echoed by *The Economist*) suggests that the current environment gives policymakers less leeway to pursue unsustainable policies. The market simply reacts too fast. To give an obvious example, suppose investors believe that the fiscal deficit will grow indefinitely at a rate faster than the economy's growth rate. As a matter of simple arithmetic, such a trajectory would leave the government no choice but to repudiate a part of the debt. In practice, governments accomplish partial debt repudiation by generating inflation. In the world of the past, with imperfect capital mobility, many of these investors would have no choice but to hold on to the government debt and hope for the best. In the world of the 1990s, investors could (and doubtless would) sell these bonds in favor of the bonds of another country deemed more creditworthy. The result would be a rapid and deep fall in bond prices, implying soaring interest rates and a dramatic increase in the government's cost of funds. The government could not ignore such a signal from the market. This is certainly the message of the recent debt crisis in Mexico.

As Mullins notes, the decisive implication of this development for policymakers is the extreme importance of credibility. We often talk of a "sustainable fiscal trajectory," as if this trajectory were something real, like the path of a fly ball hit to center field. There is a big difference, however. A major league center fielder can judge the trajectory of a fly ball pretty accurately a few fractions of a second after it leaves the bat. In contrast, neither investors in the market nor anyone else can accurately predict the path of fiscal policy over the next twenty years or so. This "trajectory" describes nothing more than investors' expectations: a fiscal policy trajectory is sustainable if investors regard it as such. Credibility is all.

The Federal Reserve has a critical role in maintaining this credibility. If investors are clear that the Fed will not monetize the debt, then they must be equally clear that fiscal discipline will be maintained in the long run. Perhaps the low interest rates we have seen in the 1990s is evidence that the Fed has this degree of credibility.

Most of the remainder of Mullins's chapter addresses the most dramatic change in global capital markets: the growth of derivatives trading. In Mullins's view, derivatives facilitate gains from specialization. Recall Adam Smith's description of a pin factory. Smith marvels at the increases in productivity from having each craftsman concentrate on those tasks he does best. Derivatives markets apply the logic of Adam Smith's pin factory to the area of risk. For example, an industrial firm can concentrate on production, and transfer undesired risks to investors who (in effect) specialize in risk-bearing. The firm is willing to increase its production level, because it can easily "dispose" of this risk, which is an "unwanted by-product" of the productive process.

According to Mullins, the development of derivatives markets is an essential accompaniment to the globalization and liberalization of the world economy. A closed economy can be predictable, but poor. A world of open economies is far wealthier, as gains from trade are exploited, but also riskier. Derivatives markets allow this risk to be hedged by individual firms, and so facilitate their participation in the global economy.

Mullins provides insightful comments on the implications of derivatives for regulatory and monetary policy. Regulators have tended to be fearful that widespread derivatives activity could be destabilizing to financial markets. Mullins argues that, in contrast, it is likely that derivatives actually reduce systemic risk. First, one of the big potential sources of systemic disruption is payment and settlement risk. This risk increases in the gross cash flows associated with a transaction. In this regard, derivatives contracts are advantageous in that they implicitly net cash flows. For example, it is possible in principle to replicate a swap contract by trading an appropriate portfolio of bonds. However, the actual cash transfers involved in settling a swaps transaction are a fraction of the gross payments required if the replicating portfolio is used. Second, derivatives can replicate within one physical location transactions that otherwise would cross national borders, with attendant legal and settlement risk.

Mullins suggests that if there is a danger in derivatives markets, it is when derivatives are used by firms with inadequate risk management and oversight capabilities. Certainly, recent losses by Orange County, Barings Bank, and Daiwa Bank could all be attributed to these sorts of managerial failures. He suggests that the main challenge presented to regulators by the growth in derivatives activities is to insure that firms have adequate risk management and oversight structures. In fact, Mullins's suggestion is currently the subject of extensive study within the Federal Reserve System. Two proposals are under study for insuring adequate capital against the risks of banks' trading activities: one was put forth by the Basle Committee, and the other grew out of work by the staff of the Board of Governors. In effect, both proposals would require that (before banks could engage in extensive derivatives trading) bank supervisors would have to verify that the banks' risk management systems meet certain well-defined criteria. Two requirements stand out in particular: first, senior management would be directly involved in the risk management process and, second, the back office would be separate from the trading floor. It appears that one or both of these simple criteria were missing in the cases of Barings, Orange County, and Daiwa.

Mullins next addresses the implications of derivatives activity for monetary policy. There is still much disagreement over the monetary transmission mechanism, so it is difficult to speak definitively on the way derivatives might affect the impact of monetary policy. Mullins acknowledges this difficulty, but he hazards a tentative conclusion: that the existence of derivatives reduces the force of monetary policy on real economic activity (that is, a given amount of monetary stimulus would have a smaller effect) and increases the speed with which monetary policy is transmitted through the economy. Without going into details, Mullins's argument is essentially that money is neutral in a frictionless economy, so the sources of monetary nonneutrality must lie in economic frictions, such as informational imperfections and transaction costs. Derivatives markets tend to reduce these sorts of frictions. For example, they provide a more efficient mechanism for price discovery, so they speed up information transmission and reduce informational asymmetries. It follows that, by reducing frictions, derivatives markets reduce the real effects of monetary policy actions. Furthermore, derivatives markets act as a mechanism for spreading shocks across the economy as a whole. One would expect that monetary policy shocks would be transmitted more rapidly through the economy in the presence of derivatives markets.

If this is true, then it appears to represent a dilemma for monetary policymakers: Does this mean that monetary policy will become a weaker tool for counter-cyclical stabilization? Perhaps so, but Mullins offers a counterweight: "Financial innovations and derivatives result in a better-functioning financial system and a sounder economy. Both would be expected to be somewhat more efficient, more self-correcting, more resistant to shocks, and perhaps less in need of large policy actions" (p. 118). In other words, derivatives activity might actually reduce the variability of business cycles themselves, rendering monetary policy less important. While he does not elaborate on this conjecture, one can see why the idea is not entirely implausible. Modern business cycle theory focuses on the impulse that precipitates a downturn, and the propagation mechanism that translates the impulse into a contraction in economic activity lasting months or years. There is much controversy over the nature of the cyclical impulses, but at least some of the more notable economic downturns appear to have been instigated by disturbances to the financial sector. Examples would include the 1929 stock market crash, the high real interest rates in the early 1980s, and perhaps the credit crunch "head winds" in 1990–91. The propagation mechanism may also involve the financial sector in a significant way. To the extent that derivatives markets provide greater resiliency in the financial services industry, better allocation of risks in financial markets, and easier international and cross-market diversification, business cycle disturbances arising from the financial services sector would be less severe. Of course, this is just a conjecture, but an intriguing one. Time will tell whether it proves valid.

Mullins concludes this wide-ranging chapter by looking at ways that the Federal Reserve can actually use derivatives markets in its day-to-day management of monetary policy. One suggestion in particular stands out: that the Fed can supplement its current open market trading procedures with short positions in both puts and calls on short-term treasury securities. Suppose the target interest rate for one-month securities is 6 percent. Under Mullins's suggested procedure, the Fed would sell both calls and puts on one-month treasury securities with a strike price equivalent to a 6 percent interest rate. If the interest rate falls below 6 percent (that is, the price rises), the holders of the calls would exercise their option, obligating the Fed to sell treasuries. But this is precisely the appropriate response of the trading desk to a fall in interest rates: the desk should withdraw reserves by conducting an open market sale. The opposite happens if interest rates rise above 6 percent: the holders of the puts would exercise their option, obligating the Fed to buy treasuries, thus injecting reserves.

According to Mullins, his proposal's advantage is that the appropriate tightening and relaxation of monetary policy happens automatically, via a preannounced structure. The appropriate actions kick in at precisely the right time: there is no need to wait for the next morning's Fed intervention. Furthermore, this approach could, in principle, enhance credibility, since it limits the Fed's discretion: once the options position is put in place, the Fed has no choice whether or not to inject reserves in response to a rise in rates.

Having said this, it is not clear that this proposal is feasible in practice. First, the interest rate elasticity of demand for reserves changes substantially over time. At any particular day, we do not know how big an open market purchase is needed to bring down the federal funds rate by, say, 10 basis points. Each business day, the trading desk in New York, together with the Board of Governors' staff in Washington and one of the regional Federal Reserve Banks, has to reestimate the magnitude of open market operations needed to bring the federal funds rate in line with the target rate. Under Mullins's proposal, this daily recalibration would not be possible: the size of the open market operation would be dictated solely by the number of puts and calls that had been previously sold. In order to hit the Fed's interest rate targets, the trading desk would have to supplement the Mullins procedure with active trading, much as they do now. It is not clear what would be gained by implementing the Mullins procedure.

On a deeper level, investors may be reluctant to take a position in derivatives markets against the Fed. Suppose an investor is considering purchase of a call option written by the Fed on 30-day treasury bills. The investor knows full well that the price of 30-day treasuries can be manipulated by the Fed via open market operations; the Fed could, in principle, extract wealth from this investor by writing the call option, driving the price of 30-day treasuries below the exercise price, and then repurchasing the call at a lower price. Now, I certainly would not suggest that the Federal Reserve engage in such practices. But the theoretical possibility may give investors pause. If it is known that the Fed is an active participant in the market for short-maturity treasury options, this could drive investors away from that market, drying up liquidity, and generating other perverse unintended consequences. Mullins's suggestion bears study, but there clearly are questions that must be addressed.

Part III

Experience with Monetary Policy Guidelines

6 The Rise and Fall of Money Growth Targets as Guidelines for US Monetary Policy*

Benjamin M. Friedman

The practice of central banking seems always to be changing, and the role of money growth targets as guidelines for monetary policy is as good an example as any. With remarkable rapidity – at least in retrospect – quantity targets based on specified monetary aggregates assumed center stage in the conduct of monetary policy, only then to move to the periphery or even fade from the scene altogether. This same evolution, and with about the same timing, has occurred in one central bank after another around the world.

In 1970, the central banks of most of the world's major industrialized economies were carrying out monetary policy primarily in terms of interest rates and/or quantitative credit restrictions. By 1980 the use of money growth targets was an idea whose time had come. Most of the major central banks had put such targets at the core of their monetary policymaking process. By 1990 money growth targets were largely a thing of the past. Today most central banks have either deemphasized their monetary aggregate targets or dropped them altogether, in some cases returning to interest rate-based policy procedures and in others seeking out new organizing principles like direct inflation targets. Now only the Deutsche Bundesbank continues to pledge firm allegiance to money growth targets (and, the Bundesbank's rhetorical claims notwithstanding, German monetary growth has actually fallen within the designated target range only once in the four years since 1990).

The evolution of monetary policymaking in the United States has followed this pattern as well. The Federal Reserve System began to experiment

* I am grateful to Jeff Amato for research assistance; to Stephen Cecchetti, Thomas Jordan, Kenneth Kuttner, David Longworth, Gregory Mankiw, William Poole, Jordan Rappaport, George Rich and James Stock for helpful discussions and comments on an earlier draft; to Donald Kohn and Richard Porter for their cooperation in providing data; and to the G.E. Foundation and the Harvard Program for Financial Research for research support. The complete version of this chapter, including results that are described but not shown here, was circulated as National Bureau of Economic Research Working Paper No. 5465 (February 1996).

with explicit money growth targets in 1970. Beginning in 1975, the US Congress required the Federal Reserve to establish money growth targets and publicly announce them in advance. In 1979 the Federal Reserve publicly declared an intensified dedication to controlling money growth and implemented new day-to-day operating procedures designed to enhance its ability to do so. In 1987 the Federal Reserve gave up setting a target for the narrow money stock but continued to set targets for broader measures of money. In 1993 the Federal Reserve publicly acknowledged that it had "downgraded" even its broad money growth targets – a change that most observers of US monetary policy had already noticed long before.

The question most obviously raised by this about-and-about face is whether monetary policymakers had sound economic reasons for changing their procedures as they did – either in first adopting money growth targets or in subsequently abandoning them, or in both instances. This question is, in large part, empirical. Making money growth an explicit target of monetary policy, or even using money growth in the role of what the literature has called an "information variable," makes no sense unless observed fluctuations in money anticipate movements of prices, or output, or whatever constitutes the ultimate objective that monetary policymakers seek to achieve. (What would it mean to exploit an information variable that contains no relevant information? What would be the point in pursuing an intermediate target that is not observably intermediate between the central bank's actions and the intended consequences?) In either case, whether movements in money anticipate movements in prices and/or output is crucial.[1]

The object of this chapter is to assess the evolving use of money growth targets from the perspective of US monetary policy in particular. Section 1 presents evidence, based on US time-series data, bearing on what Federal Reserve policymakers should have known about the relationship of money to income and prices, and when they should have known it. Section 2 presents evidence showing how the Federal Reserve changed its actual reliance on money growth targets over time. Section 3 addresses the central question of whether the Federal Reserve acted sensibly in this regard, by evaluating the changes in policymaking documented in Section 2 in light of the changes in economic behavior documented in Section 1. Section 4 offers concluding observations.

To anticipate, the chapter's main conclusion is that whatever economic conditions might have warranted reliance on money growth targets in the 1970s and early 1980s had long disappeared by the 1990s, so that the Federal Reserve's "downgrading" of these targets was indeed an appropriate response to changing circumstances. Whether adopting money growth targets in the first place was likewise appropriate is less clear.

1 WHAT DID THEY KNOW, AND WHEN DID THEY KNOW IT?

The Federal Open Market Committee first included a money growth objective in its formal policy directive in February 1970, and money growth appears to have played an on-again/off-again role in steering Federal Reserve actions over the next several years.[2] The main story of the use of money growth targets as guidelines for US monetary policy, however, begins a half-decade later. In 1975 Congress adopted Concurrent Resolution 133 requiring the Federal Reserve System to announce in advance quantitative targets for the growth of key money (and credit) aggregates and, after the fact, to report to the relevant congressional oversight committees on its success or failure in meeting these targets. The Open Market Committee's first published money growth targets specified desired growth rates for the M1, M2 and M3 aggregates – in each case expressed as a target range, rather than a point value – for the one-year period from March 1975 to March 1976.

1.1 Narrow Money

Although the Federal Reserve set targets for the growth of three different monetary aggregates, the center of attention was clearly the narrow money stock M1, which then consisted essentially of currency and demand deposits. The theory of the demand for money for transactions purposes seemed well worked out, especially in comparison to the more open-ended issues involved in demand for money as a means of wealth holding, and as a practical matter it was straightforward that currency and demand deposits were then the two main ways of effecting transactions in the United States. (By contrast, endless debate and ambiguity surrounded any attempt to draw a line separating what was "money" from what was not for portfolio purposes.) Although Friedman and Schwartz's (1963) historical work had used a broader aggregate also including savings deposits at commercial banks (but not thrifts), by the time of Resolution 133 Goldfeld (1973) and others had pointed to M1 as the measure of money exhibiting greatest stability in relation to income in the United States during the post-World War II period. When the Federal Reserve dramatically adopted new operating procedures aimed at achieving targeted rates of money growth, in October 1979, once again M1 was the main focus of attention.

Just what did the evidence of the mid- to late 1970s show about the relationship of M1 to either prices or output? And how has the evidence changed since then?

Figure 6.1 addresses these questions by showing, *for each of a series of*

Figure 6.1 Percentages of output and price variation accounted for by M1 at a two-year horizon for 81 samples

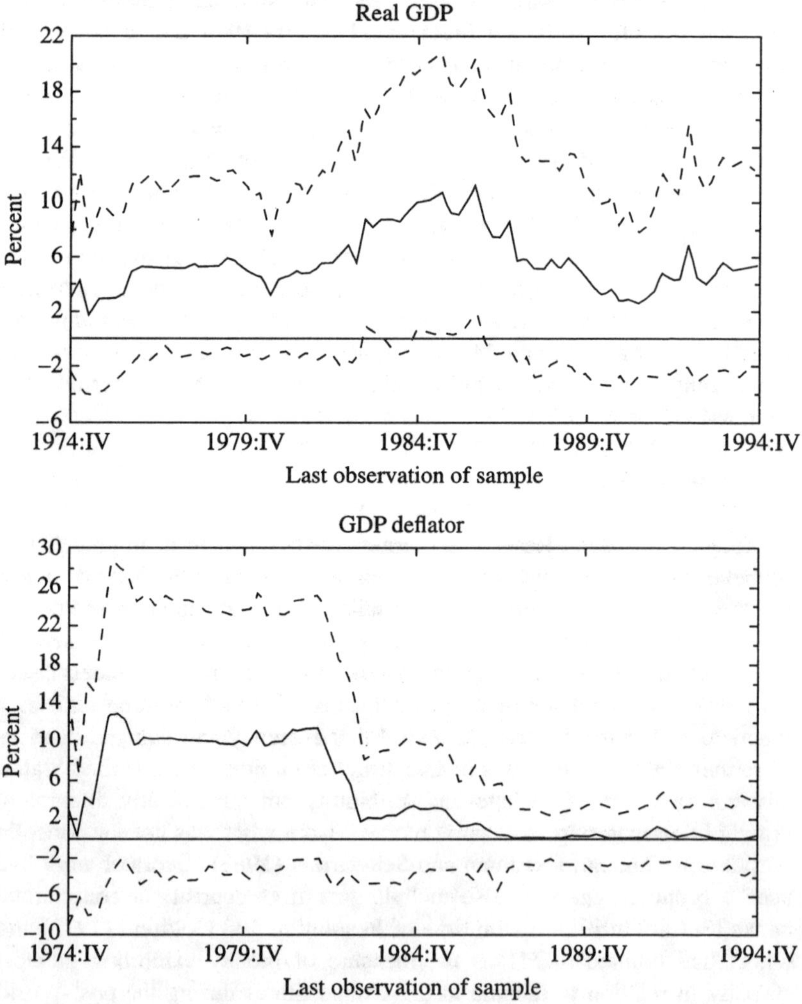

81 different sample periods, the contribution of money to subsequent movements in real output (top panel) and prices (bottom panel) as estimated via the standard vector autoregression methodology. For each of the 81 samples, the figure indicates the respective percentages of output and prices accounted for by money at a two-year horizon. Each such percentage plotted is the product of a variance decomposition based on an underlying three-variable vector autoregression including real gross domestic product, the corresponding price deflator and the M1 money stock (all in logarithms and all seasonally adjusted), with four lags on each variable. The orthogonalization of this system for purposes of the variance decomposition places output first, prices second and money third. In each panel the solid line plots the estimated contribution of money to either output or prices, while the pair of dashed lines indicates the one-standard-error band of uncertainty associated with this estimate.

The initial percentage plotted in each panel of Figure 6.1 refers to the variance decomposition based on the three-variable vector autoregression estimated using quarterly data beginning in 1959:I and ending in 1974: IV. (Because of the four lags on each variable, the regression's first observation is 1960:I and so this initial sample includes 60 observations.) The two initial percentages plotted therefore indicate how someone applying this methodology in early 1975 would have assessed the contribution of the M1 money stock to predicting that part of the subsequent fluctuation of output and prices that is not already predictable from the prior fluctuation of output and prices themselves.[3]

The answer – again, as of 1975 – is that knowing the recent movements of M1 contributes very little to predicting output and prices. At the two-year-ahead horizon considered in Figure 6.1, money accounts for not even 3 percent of the subsequent variation of output, and just over 3 percent of the variation of prices. Neither percentage is significantly different from zero, even at the weak level reflected by the one-standard-error bands.

The other 80 points plotted in each panel of Figure 6.1 indicate the results of analogous variance decompositions based on sample periods ending in 1975:I, 1975:II, and so on through 1994:IV. In each case the question at issue is the same – how much M1 contributes to predicting that part of the subsequent fluctuation of output and prices not already predictable from output and prices themselves – but the vantage point in time from which the question is asked continually moves forward. As the sample end date advances from 1974:IV to 1979:IV, the initial observation remains 1960:I so that the sample size expands (one observation at a time) from 60 to 80 quarters. Thereafter the end date and the beginning date both advance together, so that the sample size remains 80 quarters.

Matters changed somewhat as the end-of-sample vantage point advanced from 1975 to 1995. The contribution of M1 to explaining subsequent *output* fluctuations remained small until the early 1980s, then increased for somewhat more than half a decade (and briefly even became significant by the weak statistical criterion represented by the one-standard-error interval), then declined until 1990, and since then has modestly recovered but has remained insignificant. The contribution of M1 to explaining subsequent *price* fluctuations increased rapidly after 1974, only to decline equally rapidly after 1981, and has since became negligible. It has remained statistically insignificant throughout.

Perhaps even more so than their variation over time, however, what is striking about the percentages plotted in both panels of Figure 6.1 is *how small they are*. At the peak, as seen from the vantage point of late 1986, M1 accounts for just over 11 percent of subsequent output fluctuations. The peak contribution for prices, seen from mid-1976, is just over 13 percent. Moreover, it is not the case that these percentages are so small because two years is too long a time horizon over which to measure the predictive content of money. Results of analogous one-year-ahead variance decompositions (not shown here), based on the same vector autoregressions underlying Figure 6.1, follow roughly similar ups and downs as in the two-year results, but especially for prices the percentage of variance accounted for by money is even smaller.

An alternative way of addressing the contribution of money to predicting the subsequent variation of output or prices is to test explicitly the hypothesis that money has no such predictive power at all. In principle, the 81 vector autoregressions underlying the variance decompositions reported in Figure 6.1 readily admit such a test. Because each of the three variables in these regressions – the respective (log) levels of output, prices and money – is non-stationary, however, standard test statistics based on the normal distribution would be inappropriate for these regressions. Moreover, the distributions of the appropriate test statistics are known only for certain special cases.[4]

The two panels of Figure 6.2 therefore plot p-values for tests of the null hypothesis that all coefficients δ_i are zero in the two *differenced* equations

$$\Delta x_t = \alpha + \sum_{i=1}^{4} \beta_i \Delta x_{t-i} + \sum_{i=1}^{4} \gamma_i \Delta p_{t-i} + \sum_{i=1}^{4} \delta_i \Delta m_{t-i} + u_t \tag{6.1}$$

$$\Delta p_t = \alpha + \sum_{i=1}^{4} \beta_i \Delta x_{t-i} + \sum_{i=1}^{4} \gamma_i \Delta p_{t-i} + \sum_{i=1}^{4} \delta_i \Delta m_{t-i} + u_t \tag{6.2}$$

where x, p and m are, respectively, the logarithms of real gross domestic product, the price deflator and the M1 money stock, u is a disturbance term (different in each equation), and α and the β_i, γ_i, and δ_i (also different in each equation) are all coefficients to be estimated. In parallel with Figure 6.1, the first p-value plotted in each panel of Figure 6.2 gives the result of

Figure 6.2 Significance of M1 in predicting output and prices for 81 samples

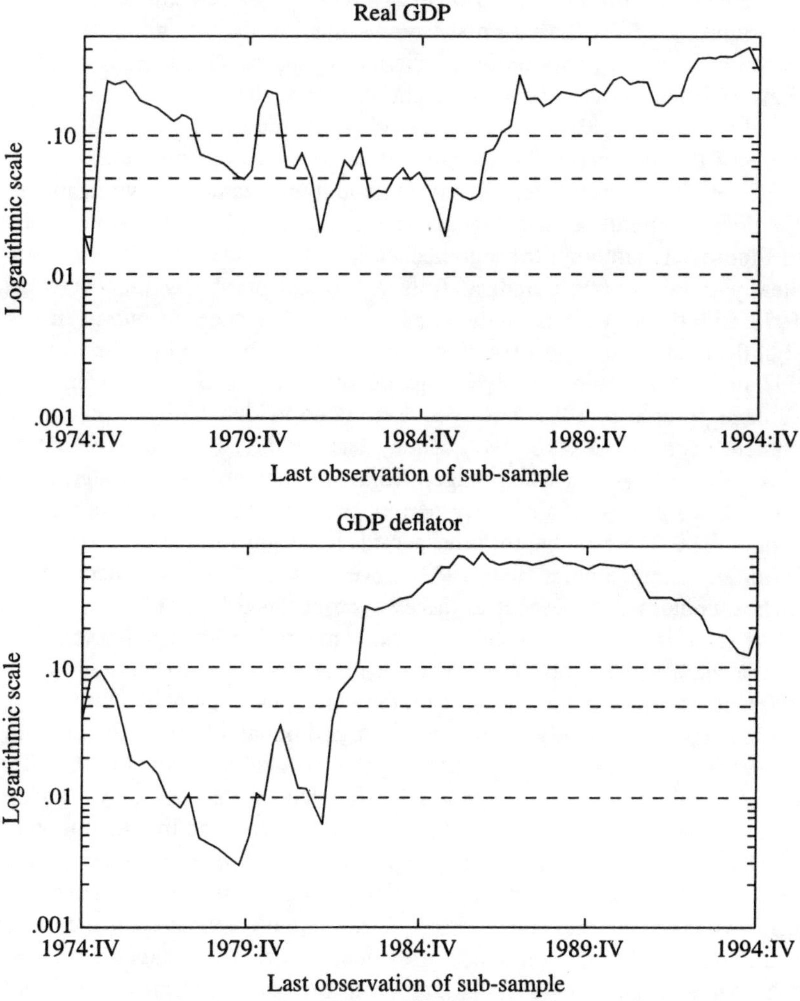

testing the null hypothesis of zero predictive content of money over the sample ending in 1974:IV, and the subsequent 80 values refer to the samples ending in 1975:I, 1975:II, and so on through 1994:IV. The dashed horizontal lines in each panel indicate the 0.01, 0.05 and 0.10 levels.

The results generated by this more explicit hypothesis test differ conceptually from the variance decomposition results shown in Figure 6.1 for several reasons. Most basically, asking the yes-or-no question of whether money has *any* predictive content with respect to output or prices is not the same as asking *how much* predictive content money has. In addition, the significance test based on the regression coefficients refers (by construction) to one-quarter-ahead prediction, while the variance decompositions reported above refer to an eight-quarter horizon. Finally, levels are not the same as growth rates (although it is impossible to evaluate the force of this distinction because of the non-stationarity problem).

Given all of these differences of method, the *p*-values shown in Figure 6.2 do correspond at least roughly to the variance decomposition results in Figure 6.1, although the significance levels indicated in Figure 6.2 are clearly more generous. Judged from a vantage point any time between 1978 and 1987, M1 has predictive content with respect to *output* that is significant at the 0.10 level, and for vantage points between 1981 and 1987 this predictive content is even significant at the 0.05 level. From any vantage point after 1987, however, there is no evidence of any predictive content even at the 0.10 level. Money has significant predictive content with respect to *prices* when judged from any vantage point through early 1983. During most of this early period, this predictive content is significant at the 0.05 level, and for brief periods it is significant at the 0.01 level. From any vantage point since 1983, however, there is no evidence of predictive content with respect to prices even at the 0.10 level.

As is well-known, whether a vector autoregression implies that any particular variable has predictive content with respect to any other, and what variance decompositions ensue from the corresponding coefficient values, can change dramatically when the set of additional variables included in the regression system changes. More specifically in the context of this discussion, Sims (1980) showed that when an interest rate variable was added to a regression system analogous to that used above, and in which money did have predictive content with respect to output, then the interest rate had predictive content with respect to output but money did not.[5] Because central banks are hardly unaware of interest rate movements, it is therefore useful also to evaluate the kinds of evidence presented in Figures 6.1 and 6.2 generated by a regression system that includes an interest rate along with output, prices and money.

Figure 6.3 presents series of two-year-ahead variance decomposition results that are analogous to those shown in Figure 6.1 in every way except that the underlying vector autoregression system includes the level of the federal funds rate as a fourth variable. (Corresponding one-year-ahead results, not shown here, are again highly similar.) Although the time paths traced out as the vantage point moves from 1975 to 1995 look somewhat similar to those in Figure 6.1, especially for the effect of money on prices

Figure 6.3 Percentages of output and price variation accounted for by M1 at a two-year horizon for 81 samples (system also includes federal funds rate)

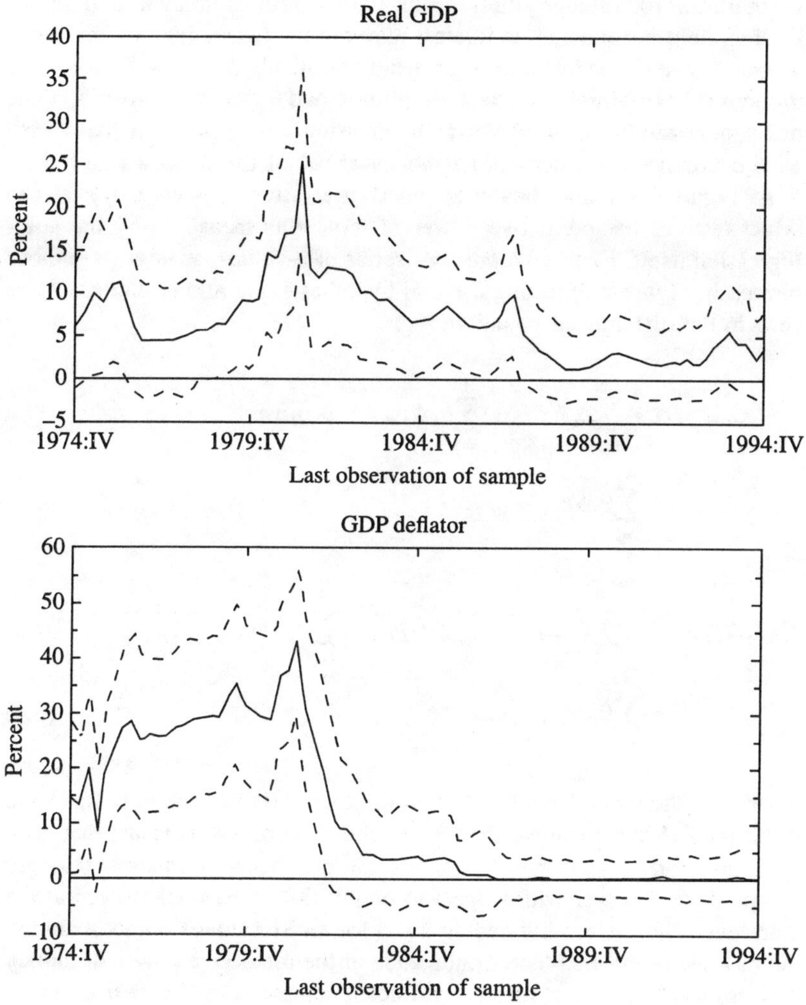

the indicated magnitudes are much larger (note the different vertical scales compared to Figure 6.1). The magnitudes are especially large for the percentage of the variance of prices accounted for by money as seen from vantage points before 1983, and they are also larger for the percentage of output as seen from vantage points between 1979 and 1987. Moreover, in contrast to what Figure 6.1 shows, here the effect of money on output is significant (again in the modest sense implied by the one-standard-error interval) for vantage points throughout 1979–87, and the effect on prices is significant for vantage points during 1976–83. In contradiction to Sims's finding, here introducing an interest rate into the regression system seems to *magnify*, and render more significant statistically, the resulting role of money in explaining subsequent output and price movements. (The orthogonalization of the vector autoregression for purposes of these variance decompositions does order money ahead of the interest rate.)

As Figure 6.4 shows, however, this contradiction does not carry over to direct tests of the predictive power of money as measured by the autoregression itself. Figure 6.4 presents series of p-values, analogous to those plotted in Figure 6.2, testing the null hypothesis that all coefficients δ_i are zero in the differenced equations

$$\Delta x_t = \alpha + \sum_{t=1}^{4}\beta_i \Delta x_{t-i} + \sum_{i=1}^{4}\gamma_i \Delta p_{t-i} + \sum_{i=1}^{4}\delta_i \Delta m_{t-i} + \sum_{t=1}^{4}\theta_i \Delta r_{t-i} + u_t \qquad (6.3)$$

$$\Delta p_t = \alpha + \sum_{i=1}^{4}\beta_i \Delta x_{t-i} + \sum_{i=1}^{4}\gamma_i \Delta p_{t-i} + \sum_{i=1}^{4}\delta_i \Delta m_{t-i} + \sum_{t=1}^{4}\theta_i \Delta r_{t-i} + u_t \qquad (6.4)$$

where r is the federal funds rate and all other variables are as in (6.1) and (6.2). As in Sims's results, the top panel of Figure 6.4 indicates that once the regression system takes the interest rate into account, money no longer has predictive power with respect to output that is significant even at the 0.10 level. Moreover, this finding holds for all 81 vantage points spanning the past twenty years.[6] The significance of the predictive power of money with respect to prices is mostly unaffected compared to Figure 6.2, except for an effect, in the direction corresponding to Sims's finding with respect to output, in the early 1980s.

1.2 Broad Money

M1, of course, is not the only monetary aggregate for which the Federal Reserve has established target rates of growth. Especially in more recent

Figure 6.4 Significance of M1 in predicting output and prices for 81 samples (system also includes federal funds rate)

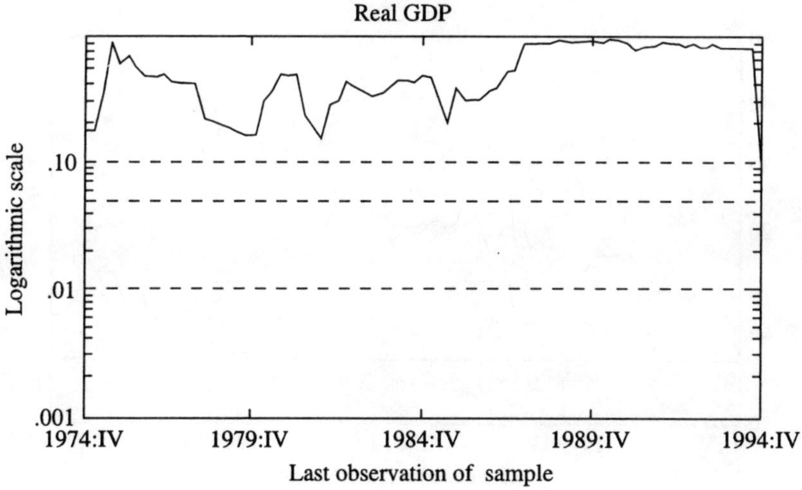

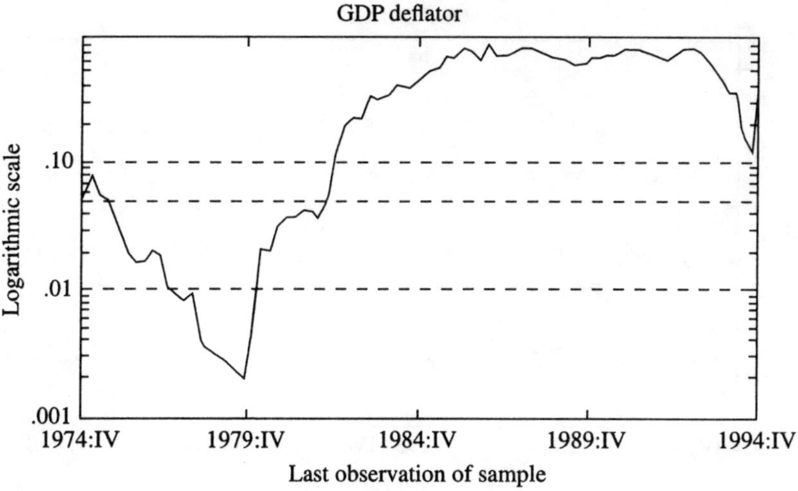

years, M2 has replaced M1 as the main center of attention for monetary policy purposes. Within the Federal Reserve, Feinman and Porter (1992) have argued on empirical grounds that M2 demand not only is more stable than the demand for other standard Ms but also that M2 outperforms potential new candidate measures (for example, what others have called "liquid M2," consisting of currency plus all deposits in M2 that can

Figure 6.5 Percentages of output and price variation accounted for by M2 at a two-year horizon for 81 samples (system also includes federal funds rate)

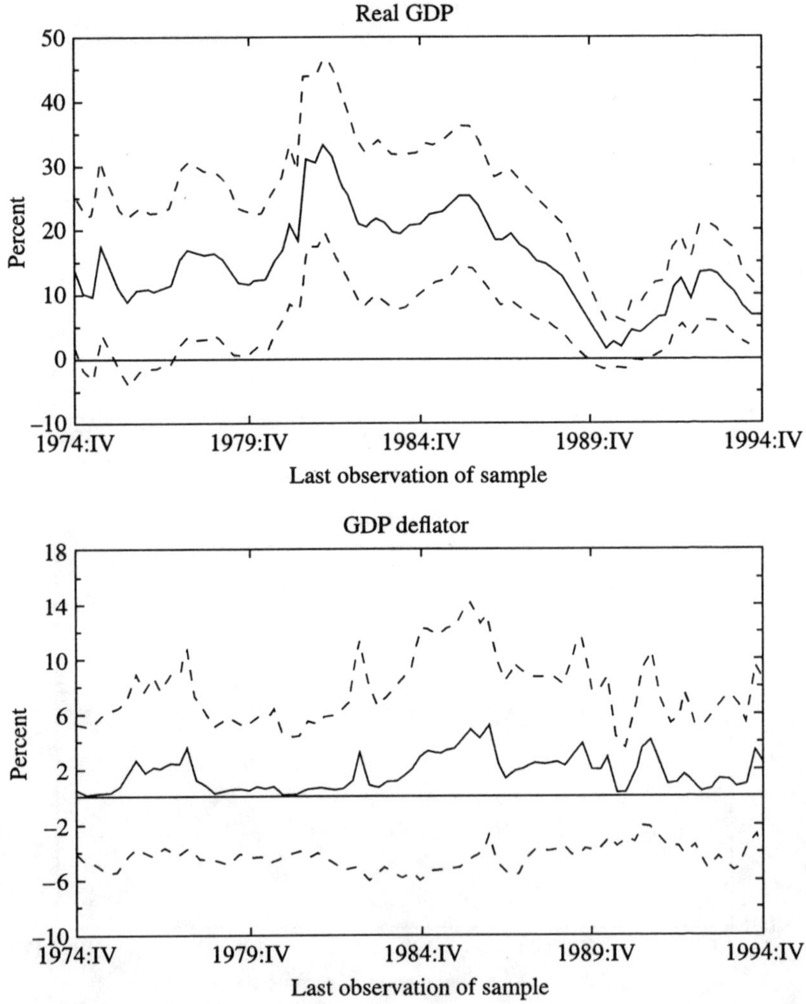

be redeemed at par on demand). Outside the Federal Reserve, Ramey (1993) and Feldstein and Stock (1994) have argued that different forms of error-correction procedures render stable the ratio of M2 to nominal income (or, in reciprocal form, the misnamed M2 "velocity"). Before the 1993 "down-grading," the Federal Reserve's own public statements also attached more importance to M2 than to other aggregates.

Figures 6.5 and 6.6 present evidence for M2 that is analogous to that

Figure 6.6 Significance of M2 in predicting output and prices for 81 samples (system also includes federal funds rate)

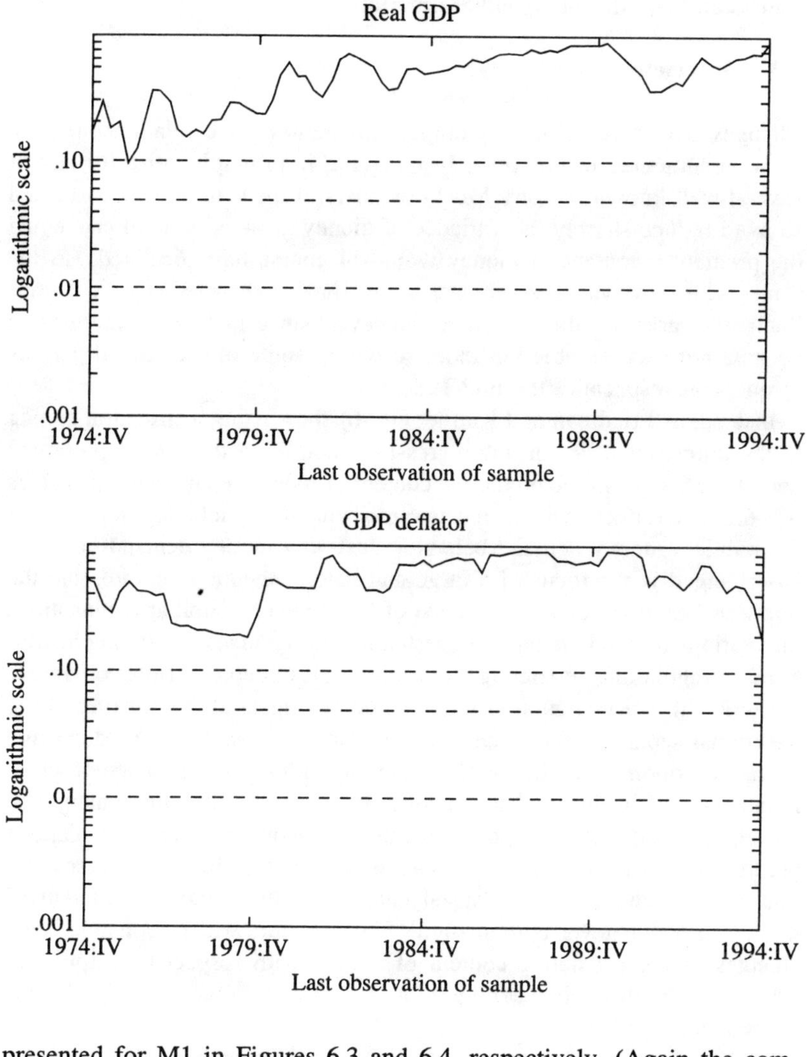

presented for M1 in Figures 6.3 and 6.4, respectively. (Again the comparable one-year-ahead results, not shown here, are highly similar.) As measured by the variance decompositions, the percentage of the variation of *output* attributable to M2 is modestly sizeable and statistically significant as seen from vantage points throughout much of the 1980s, and again briefly (albeit to a lesser extent) during the 1990s. The predictive content of M2 with respect to output as measured directly from the autoregression is (almost) never significant even at the 0.10 level. By contrast, M2 accounts for only a small percentage of the variation of *prices*, and its role is never statistically significant by either criterion.

1.3 Overview

Changes over time in money-output and money-price relationships like those documented in Figures 6.1–6.6 could, in principle, arise for any of several well-known reasons. Most obviously, if the central bank had acted so as to reduce sharply the variance of money growth, with all else equal the predictive content of money would of course have declined. (In the limit, with zero variance, money would have zero predictive content.) Such is clearly not the case here, however, since in fact money growth became not less variable but more so during some of the crucial periods in question (especially the mid-1980s).

Instead, as Friedman and Kuttner (1996) show using a structural analog to the unrestricted vector autoregression underlying the results presented here, the changes in the predictive content of money documented in Tables 6.1–6.6 here reflect changes in economic behavior – including in particular the public's money demand behavior. Just why money demand behavior has changed is the focus of a large and heterogeneous literature, and the question lies well beyond the scope of this chapter. Familiar explanations that various researchers have suggested include changes in banking institutions, in regulations restricting allowable forms of deposits (most obviously the removal of Regulation Q interest rate ceilings and the blurring of the traditional separation between transaction deposits and savings deposits), in macroeconomic conditions (for example, in the pace and persistence of inflation), and in financial technology. It is also possible that changes in the conduct of monetary policy themselves induced changes in deposit holding and other forms of behavior on the part of both businesses and households, which in turn caused changes in the predictive content of money.[7] But whatever combination of such factors was responsible, such changes in the predictive content of money with respect to output and prices clearly affect the usefulness of money growth targets as guidelines for monetary policy.

2 WHAT DID THEY DO, AND WHEN DID THEY DO IT?

Observing what central banks do is usually straightforward. Establishing why they have done it is more problematic. Central bank purchases and sales of securities, the resulting changes in bank reserves, and fluctuations in the relevant short-term interest rate are all known data not long after the fact. But few central banks make clear – genuinely clear – just why they have chosen the actions they have taken.

The usual critics notwithstanding, the problem in this regard reflects more than a mere preference for obfuscation. Under institutional arrangements like those at the Federal Reserve System, where the key decision-making authority rests in a sizeable committee (the Open Market Committee has twelve voting members), different participants in the policy process may have differing reasons for favoring the same action. Requiring them to agree not only on what to do but on a precise statement of why they choose to do it would significantly raise the hurdle facing a policymaking process that must play out in real time. The situation is even more complicated because the Federal Reserve is legally responsible to Congress, which historically has been not only vague and inconsistent in stating its objectives for monetary policy but also slow to alter its formal charges to the Federal Reserve as economic circumstances have changed.

Has the Federal Reserve, then, actually attempted to implement its stated money growth targets? And if so, how would one know?

If there were never any disturbances to the relationships connecting money growth to prices and output, pursuing a money growth target would be indistinguishable from simply varying the interest rate or the quantity of reserves so as to come as close as possible to achieving the desired objectives for prices and output themselves. But in fact these relationships are not unvarying. The approach taken here to inferring whether the Federal Reserve's money growth targets have actually affected its monetary policy actions is therefore to look for *independent* effects of fluctuations in money, relative to the stated growth target, that are not already accounted for by prices and real economic activity. In particular, Taylor (1993) has argued that a simple formula relating the level of the federal funds rate to price inflation and the level of real activity relative to trend has approximately characterized US monetary policy in recent years. The approach taken here is to ask whether, and when – *in addition* – the federal funds rate has also responded to departures of money from the stated target.

2.1 Narrow Money

The first row of Table 6.1 presents estimated coefficient values and t-statistics for the regression

$$r_t = \alpha + \beta\pi_{t-1} + \gamma(U - U^*)_{t-1} + u_t \tag{6.5}$$

Table 6.1 Monetary policy reaction functions allowing for M1 growth targets

End of Sample	α	$\beta\pi$	$\gamma(U - U^*)$	$\theta(1 - D)(m - m^T)$	$\delta \cdot D(m - m^T)$
1975:4	2.201	0.712	−0.866	–	–
	(10.7)	(14.7)	(−8.3)	–	–
1975:12	2.226	0.702	−0.880	–	−0.122
	(11.0)	(15.9)	(−10.0)	–	(−0.1)
1976:12	2.226	0.701	−0.883	−0.123	0.161
	(11.3)	(16.7)	(−11.1)	(−0.1)	(0.2)
1977:12	2.224	0.700	−0.888	0.053	0.459
	(11.6)	(17.2)	(−11.6)	(0.1)	(0.5)
1978:12	2.189	0.718	−0.888	0.163	1.005
	(11.7)	(18.4)	(−12.1)	(0.3)	(1.5)
1979:12	2.139	0.737	−0.894	0.430	0.861
	(11.7)	(19.7)	(−12.3)	(1.1)	(5.2)
1980:12	1.706	0.868	−0.905	0.553	2.191
	(9.0)	(24.7)	(−11.4)	(3.3)	(7.0)
1981:12	1.384	0.997	−0.752	0.622	3.942
	(5.5)	(22.2)	(−7.1)	(3.1)	(4.9)
1982:12	1.398	1.013	−0.644	0.744	2.040
	(5.2)	(21.5)	(−5.9)	(3.6)	(6.5)
1983:12	1.926	0.933	−0.262	1.021	3.299
	(7.2)	(19.7)	(−2.8)	(5.6)	(4.9)
1984:12	2.231	0.893	−0.114	1.076	4.694
	(8.4)	(18.8)	(−1.3)	(5.9)	(4.0)
1985:12	2.353	0.883	−0.071	1.104	0.802
	(8.9)	(18.6)	(−0.8)	(6.1)	(2.2)
1986:12	2.366	0.885	−0.061	1.036	0.102
	(9.2)	(19.1)	(−0.7)	(6.3)	(0.7)

Notes: Numbers in parentheses are *t*-statistics.
Gap between actual and target M1 is measured from the midpoint of the designated target range.

based on *monthly* US data for the sample beginning in 1960:2 and ending in 1975:4 – that is, just before the Federal Reserve had a stated money growth target. Here r is the federal funds rate, π is the inflation rate measured over the preceding twelve months, U is the unemployment rate, and U^* is Gordon's (1993) estimate of the "natural" rate of unemployment.[8] (Taylor's formula instead uses the deviation of real output from trend, but establishing the appropriate output trend is problematic over as long a time period as is ultimately treated here.) All variables are in units corresponding to "percent."

The estimates for (6.5) shown in the first row of Table 6.1 are consistent with standard interpretations of monetary policy behavior.[9] Faster inflation leads the Federal Reserve to set a higher interest rate, although the less-than-unit value of β supports the familiar criticism that in the 1960s and 1970s the magnitude of this response was not sufficient to prevent procyclical fluctuation of the *real* interest rate. Higher unemployment (relative to the "natural" rate) leads to a lower interest rate. The coefficients on both variables are highly significant.

The Federal Reserve's first formally stated money growth targets specified growth ranges for the M1, M2 and M3 aggregates over the one-year period from March 1975 to March 1976. April 1975 was therefore the first month in which the actual value of any given measure of money could be compared to the value implied by the corresponding growth target. With a one-month observation lag, May 1975 was therefore the first month in which success or failure in achieving its money growth target could plausibly have influenced the Federal Reserve's setting of the federal funds rate.

The second row of Table 6.1 presents estimates for the expanded regression

$$r_t = \alpha + \beta\pi_{t-1} + \gamma(U - U^*)_{t-1} + \delta(m - m^T)_{t-1} + u_t \tag{6.6}$$

based on monthly data for the sample beginning in 1960:2 and ending in 1975:12. Here m is the logarithm of the M1 money stock, m^T is the logarithm of the corresponding value constructed by tracing out the growth path implied by the midpoint of the designated target range, and all other variables are as in (6.5). More specifically, both m and m^T refer to the definition of M1 in use in 1975, and the data used for m and used to construct m^T are taken from Federal Reserve sources dated in early 1976. (For purposes of this exercise it is essential to estimate the regression using data that correspond to what policymakers saw and construed as M1 at the time, rather than the standard data available today.[10])

The Federal Reserve did not have a formal money growth target in effect before April 1975 – that is, m^T did not exist – and so for purposes of the regression $(m - m^T)$ simply assumes the value zero for all months in the sample through 1975:3. For 1975:4–1975:5, m^T is defined by tracing out for those two months the growth path implied by the 6¼ percent per annum midpoint of the 5–7½ percent M1 growth target specified for the period running from the first quarter of 1975 to the corresponding quarter of 1976. In June 1975 the Federal Reserve moved forward the base from which it was targeting the monetary aggregates and also shifted to a quarterly computation basis, so that the new targets specified growth ranges for the period 1975:II to 1976:II. For purposes of the regression, therefore, m^T for 1975:6–1975:8 is defined by the monthly values along the path implied by the midpoint of this new M1 growth target (again 5–7½ percent per annum, but from the 1975:II base). Similarly, m^T for 1975:9–1975:11 is defined from the midpoint of the next new target for M1 growth, set in September for the period 1975:III–1976:III (yet again 5–7½ percent per annum, but now from the 1975:III base).

As the second row of Table 6.1 shows, the resulting estimate of δ for the eight months of 1975 in which the Federal Reserve might have reacted to M1 growth in relation to the corresponding target path provides no evidence that the Federal Reserve actually did so. The estimated coefficient is not only small and statistically insignificant but of the wrong sign to reflect behavior consistent with targeting money growth. (If the central bank were actually targeting money, it would presumably *increase* the interest rate when money is above target, not lower it.)

The third row of Table 6.1 presents estimates for the further expanded regression

$$r_t = \alpha + \beta\pi_{t-1} + \gamma(U - U^*)_{t-1} + \delta(m - m^T)_{t-1} \cdot D + \theta(m - m^T)_{t-1} \cdot (1 - D) + u_t \quad (6.7)$$

for the sample beginning in 1960:2 and ending in 1976:12. Here D is a dummy variable equal to 1 in the twelve months of 1976 and zero before, so that the two separate $(m–m^T)$ terms in the regression distinguish the Federal Reserve's attempt to target money growth in 1976 from that earlier on. Subsequent rows present analogous estimates of (6.7) for samples ending in 1977:12, 1978:12, and so on through 1986:12. In each regression D takes on the value 1 in the twelve final months of the sample and zero before.[11] Throughout, values of m correspond to the definition of M1 in use in the particular year in question.[12] For 1976:1–1978:11, values of m^T are defined from the successive midpoints of the rolling annual growth targets that the Federal Reserve established on a quarterly basis. For 1978:12–1986:12, m^T is defined from the midpoint of the successive annual target ranges (in some years called "monitoring ranges") established once per year (and as amended during the year in 1983 and 1985). The Federal Reserve has not designated a formal growth target for M1 since 1986.

For 1976, 1977 and 1978 the estimates shown in successive rows of Table 6.1 provide steadily stronger hints – to say "evidence" would be exaggerating – that the Federal Reserve was taking account of its M1 target in setting the federal funds rate. Unlike the result for 1975, the estimated values of δ are positive and becoming more so year by year – just what would be expected if (6.7) is identified as a monetary policy reaction function, and just the opposite of what would be implied if the equation were instead an inverted money demand function. Although the *t*-statistic steadily increases, however, none of these estimates meets the standard 0.05 significance level.

By contrast, for every year from 1979 through 1984 the estimated value of δ is both large and highly significant.[13] For 1979, for example, the estimated δ implies that, *for given rates of inflation and unemployment*, the Federal Reserve set the interest rate 0.86 of a percentage point (86 basis points) higher for every one percent that M1 was above its target in the preceding month. The estimated response is much larger from 1980 through 1984. For 1985 the estimated δ is smaller but still marginally significant. For 1986 there is no longer any evidence that the Federal Reserve was actually targeting M1 growth.

Although it is not the subject of this chapter, a further notable feature of the results presented in Table 6.1 is the disappearance, after about 1983, of real activity (here measured by unemployment relative to Gordon's natural rate) as a visible influence on monetary policy. This change over time is interesting in its own right and deserves attention in a separate paper. By contrast, inflation on balance increases as an influence on monetary policy during this period.[14]

The regressions reported in Table 6.1 rely on a construction of the key $(m - m^T)$ variable in which m^T is defined from the midpoint of the designated target range for M1. As a result, $(m - m^T)$ is a continuous variable and both (6.6) and (6.7) implicitly assume that the Federal Reserve's response to a deviation of M1 from the midpoint of the target range does not specifically depend on whether observed money is within the range or outside it. Analogous results (not shown here), based on an alternative representation of Federal Reserve behavior that distinguishes discontinuously between values of money that are within or outside the target range – in particular, setting $(m - m^T)$ equal to zero whenever observed money is within the corresponding range, and for observations outside the range setting $(m - m^T)$ equal to the algebraic difference between m and the monthly path implied by either the upper or the lower end of the designated range, whichever is closer – are highly similar.

2.2 Broad Money

Table 6.2 presents results that are directly analogous to those in Table 6.1 but based on values and growth targets for the M2 money stock. (Once

Table 6.2 Monetary policy reaction functions allowing for M2 growth targets

End of Sample	α	$\beta\pi$	$\gamma(U - U^*)$	$\theta(1 - D)(m - m^T)$	$\delta \cdot D(m - m^T)$
1975:4	2.201	0.712	−0.866	–	–
	(10.7)	(14.7)	(−8.3)	–	–
1975:12	2.226	0.702	−0.880	–	−0.164
	(11.0)	(15.9)	(−10.0)	–	(−0.1)
1976:12	2.226	0.701	−0.881	−0.163	−0.148
	(11.3)	(17.0)	(−10.8)	(−0.1)	(−0.2)
1977:12	2.225	0.703	−0.881	−0.163	0.200
	(11.6)	(17.1)	(−11.3)	(−0.2)	(0.2)
1978:12	2.200	0.718	−0.879	−0.169	2.687
	(11.8)	(18.3)	(−11.6)	(−0.3)	(1.7)
1979:12	2.122	0.745	−0.895	0.108	1.561
	(11.5)	(19.7)	(−11.9)	(0.2)	(4.9)
1980:12	1.766	0.843	−0.960	0.933	2.897
	(9.0)	(22.9)	(−11.7)	(2.9)	(5.9)
1981:12	1.537	0.929	−0.880	1.076	4.277
	(6.5)	(21.3)	(−8.8)	(3.2)	(8.5)
1982:12	1.709	0.923	−0.661	1.780	−5.649
	(6.6)	(19.4)	(−6.1)	(5.4)	(−7.3)
1983:12	2.203	0.922	−0.020	0.468	1.250
	(7.7)	(17.5)	(−0.2)	(1.4)	(0.3)
1984:12	2.251	0.918	0.002	0.465	−9.381
	(8.0)	(17.7)	(0.0)	(1.4)	(−4.3)
1985:12	2.353	0.923	0.052	0.214	1.168
	(8.3)	(17.6)	(0.6)	(0.7)	(2.3)
1986:12	2.498	0.899	0.087	0.476	−0.030
	(9.2)	(17.9)	(1.0)	(1.7)	(−0.0)
1987:12	2.488	0.902	0.084	0.420	−0.337
	(9.5)	(18.5)	(0.9)	(1.7)	(−0.7)
1988:12	2.557	0.909	0.066	0.228	−0.565
	(9.9)	(18.9)	(0.8)	(1.1)	(−0.3)
1989:12	2.577	0.910	0.057	0.209	−2.849
	(10.1)	(19.2)	(0.7)	(1.0)	(−3.5)
1990:12	2.647	0.923	0.011	−0.001	0.223
	(10.4)	(19.4)	(0.1)	(−0.0)	(0.1)
1991:12	2.631	0.922	0.008	0.007	1.470
	(10.5)	(19.7)	(0.1)	(0.0)	(1.8)
1992:12	2.566	0.926	−0.013	0.091	1.380
	(10.4)	(19.9)	(−0.2)	(0.5)	(3.0)
1993:12	2.499	0.930	−0.046	0.286	1.721
	(10.2)	(20.1)	(−0.6)	(1.6)	(3.5)
1994:12	2.383	0.941	−0.069	0.433	0.247
	(9.9)	(20.5)	(−0.8)	(2.6)	(0.4)

Notes: Numbers in parentheses are *t*-statistics.
Gap between actual and target M2 is measured from the midpoint of the designated target range.

again, the definitions and observed values for the M2 aggregate for each year are those actually in use at the time.) The Federal Reserve has continued to designate growth targets for M2 through the present day, and so instead of stopping with the 1960:2–1986:12 sample as in Table 6.1, the estimates presented in Table 6.2 continue through the sample ending in 1994:12. Interesting aspects of the results for these later years are the evidence of a continuing strong role of inflation as an influence guiding monetary policy, and the continuing absence of evidence of such a role for real economic activity after 1982.

The results shown in Table 6.2 suggest that the Federal Reserve has actively attempted to target M2 growth during three separate time periods: during 1979–81 (and, more marginally, 1978); in 1985; and during 1992–93 (and, more marginally, 1991). In most of the other years, the estimated value of δ is *negative*, indicating that monetary policy was simply accommodating the demand for M2 (so that (6.6) or (6.7) becomes an inverted money demand equation). For each of 1982, 1984 and 1989, the negative coefficient indicating this kind of accommodative policy is highly significant. As is the case for M1, analogous results (not shown here) based on an alternative representation of the Federal Reserve's response to observed money growth that distinginshes discontinuously between observations of money that are within or outside the designated target range are highly similar.

3 DID THE RISE AND FALL OF MONEY GROWTH TARGETS MAKE SENSE?

How, then, do the changes in the use of money growth targets documented in Tables 6.1 and 6.2 correspond to the changing relationships between money and output and between money and prices traced out in Figures 6.1–6.6? Were these shifts sensible responses to changing economic circumstances?

To be sure, nobody believes that monetary policymakers were necessarily monitoring the evolving results of exercises like those reported in Figures 6.1–6.6 on a continuous basis from 1975 onward. (Indeed, the vector autoregression methodology only came into familiar use in economics in the late 1970s and thereafter.) But empirical relationships that address the key questions at issue here, in one way or another, were central to how policymakers and others in fact conceived the role of monetary aggregates in the monetary policy process. Whether money does or does not have predictive content with respect to output and/or prices is essential to whether the use of money growth targets constitutes a potentially effective strategy under which to carry out monetary policy. Policymakers need not have been tracking estimated relationships of the exact form as those reported here. But to the extent that these relationships, based on data only up through specific points in time, provide an indication of whether there was or was not evidence then that money had such predictive content, that kind of evidence – or the lack of it – at least should have been an important factor in the choice of monetary policy strategy.

3.1 Resolution 133

The empirical case for money growth targets was weak at best when Congress adopted Concurrent Resolution 133 in early 1975. Evidence based on data through yearend 1974 indicated that M1 accounted for only a small percentage of the subsequent variation of either output or prices, and after allowance for the role of interest rates these effects were statistically significant either marginally or not at all. M2 did appear to account for a large and significant share of the subsequent variation of output – though not prices – but this apparent relationship became much smaller and lost its statistical significance after allowance for interest rates.

The Federal Reserve System, however, appears to have acted consistently with this state of affairs. Although the Federal Reserve of course met its new statutory obligation to announce money growth targets, the results presented in Tables 6.1 and 6.2 provide no evidence that these targets actually influenced monetary policy actions in the near-term aftermath of the resolution's adoption. Both M1 and M2 were outside the designated target range most of the time in the latter half of the 1970s, and there is no significant evidence of a response to these departures before 1978. Even for 1978 the estimated response is only marginally significant.

3.2 Volcker Monetarism

Monetary policy looks different beginning in 1979. For 1979–81 there is strong evidence of an effort by the Federal Reserve to target both M1 and M2. Efforts to target M1 growth continued on through 1985 (although the evidence is strong only through 1984). During 1982–4 the Federal Reserve mostly accommodated M2 demand, but there is renewed evidence of an effort to target M2 growth in 1985.

Especially with respect to M1 in 1979 and the first few years thereafter, this change in policy appears in retrospect to have been consistent with changing evidence on key economic relationships. Indeed, from the evidence presented in Figure 6.3 it appears that the Federal Reserve might well have begun earlier to target M1 growth. In the late 1970s evidence was becoming stronger that M1 did account for a sizeable and statistically significant percentage of the subsequent variation of prices (though not output), especially after allowance for interest rates. Given the concern at the time for the upward spiral of inflation, targeting M1 beginning in 1979 seems to have been appropriate, if not late. By contrast, the evidence on M2 is much weaker. M2 did appear to explain a large percentage of the subsequent variation of output (though not prices), but this effect became statistically significant only after 1979. Moreover, the predictive content of M2 measured directly from the autoregression was completely insignificant once interest rates were taken into account.

The main contradiction between policy actions and the underlying economic relationships during this period, however, lies in the Federal Reserve's continuing attempts to target M1 after 1982.[15] With or without interest rates taken into account, the relationship between M1 and prices rapidly lost significance as seen from vantage points beginning in early 1983. To recall, these were years of rapid money growth (8.8 percent in 1982, 10.4 percent in 1983, 12.0 percent in 1985, 15.5 percent in 1986), which – contrary to the public warnings of many advocates of monetary targeting – did *not* result in a renewed increase of inflation rates. Although the fact that money growth was so rapid immediately reveals that the Federal Reserve was not totally committed to its growth targets, the results in Table 6.1 provide evidence that M1 growth remained an independent influence on Federal Reserve policy actions during these years.

3.3 M2 Under Greenspan

After 1986 the Federal Reserve stopped even setting growth targets for M1, and there is no evidence of renewed attention to M2 targets until the early 1990s. Ignoring M1 growth was entirely consistent with the evident relationships – more accurately, the absence of relationships – between M1 and output and prices. Since 1987 there has been no evidence of a significant relationship between M1 and either output or prices, either with or without allowance for interest rates. The picture is more mixed for M2, however, especially after taking interest rates into account. The percentage of the subsequent variation of output attributable to M2 was declining in these years, but it remained significant until 1989. By contrast, the predictive content measured directly from the regression was not significant as judged from these vantage points.

In 1992 and 1993, however, the Federal Reserve returned to actively targeting M2 growth. (As Table 6.2 shows, there is marginally significant evidence for active M2 targeting in 1991 as well.) Judging on the basis of the relationship between M2 and real output shown in Figures 6.5 and 6.6, it is perhaps possible to justify this renewed emphasis on M2 as a response to changing economic conditions. The deterioration in the percentage of output variation attributable to M2 reversed for vantage points beginning in 1990, and by 1992 this effect was again statistically significant with interest rates taken into account (see Figure 6.5). Even at the peak in 1993, however, it was never very large. Moreover, the predictive content of M2 with respect to real output measured directly from the regression was insignificant throughout (see Figure 6.6), as was the connection to prices by both measures. On balance, it is difficult to justify the return to M2 targeting.

3.4 Downgrading

In 1993 the Federal Reserve publicly announced that it had "downgraded" even its M2 target, and Table 6.2 confirms that there is no evidence of an active attempt to target M2 growth in 1994. (M2 was within the target range virtually throughout 1994, but there is no evidence of any influence of M2 on the federal funds rate independent of the influence of inflation and unemployment.) This "downgrading" appears entirely warranted. M2 had never shown any relationship to prices anyway, and what evidence there was of a relationship to output weakened noticeably beginning in 1993 and then disappeared by the end of 1994.

4 CONCLUDING OBSERVATIONS

For the most part, therefore, the Federal Reserve System's use and disuse of money growth targets as guidelines for US monetary policy over the past twenty years appears to have been roughly consistent with what the evidence of the time on money-output and money-price relationships has warranted. With some notable exceptions, money growth targets have been a visible influence on monetary policy actions primarily at times when at least some forms of evidence on these relationships appeared to justify it. More obviously, the Federal Reserve's abandoning money growth targets has been entirely consistent with what the economic evidence has warranted.

In assessing these conclusions, it is useful to keep in mind that the evidence on the key money-output and money-price relationships on which they rely follows from an application (actually, 81 successive applications) of the standard methodology based on vector autoregressions and the associated variance decompositions. More flexible empirical strategies – in particular, methods incorporating error-correction mechanisms – could lead to stronger evidence of a relationship between money and either output or prices, and hence might support a different assessment of what the Federal Reserve has done over these two decades.[16]

But incorporating an error-correction mechanism in the analysis would importantly change the implication for monetary policy of whatever money-output or money-price relationships might emerge. Using money growth as an *intermediate target*, rather than merely as an information variable, means that the central bank consistently acts as if observed deviations of money from the designated growth path constitute signs of undesired movements to come in output and/or prices (or whatever else monetary policy is ultimately seeking to influence). By contrast, the basic idea of an error-correction mechanism rests on the explicit assumption that the underlying relationships do *not* support such an interpretation. Observed deviations of money growth then do not just represent disturbances to output and/or prices, but also systematically reflect aberrant money demand (or money supply) behavior. Depending on the circumstances accounting for that aberrant behavior, money growth could still be a useful tool for monetary policy in the form of an information variable. But evidence of this form would not support the use of money growth as a *target* for monetary policy.

And so money growth targets arrived and, not long after, disappeared. The British historian R.H. Tawney presumably did not have late twentieth-century US monetary policy in mind when he offered this judgment nearly three-quarters of a century ago, but his conclusion aptly summarizes the recent experience with money growth targets nonetheless: "Their practical ineffectiveness prepared the way for their theoretical abandonment. They were abandoned because, on the whole, they deserved to be abandoned."[17]

Notes

1. For discussion of these basics, see, for example, Friedman (1990, 1993).
2. See the evidence provided by DeRosa and Stern (1977).
3. To show more precisely how someone in early 1975 would have answered this question would require using the data (for each of GDP, the deflator and M1) that existed then – not, as here, the revised data for 1959–74 that exist now. The work reported in Section 2 below follows that approach. In this section the emphasis is instead on how the relevant economic behavior has changed over time.
4. See the discussion in Sims *et al.* (1990).

5. Stock and Watson (1989), among others, argued that also including a time trend in the regression restored the predictive content of M1 with respect to output even in the presence of an interest rate, but Friedman and Kuttner (1993) showed that this result depended on the use of a specific interest rate. In line with the discussion above, Stock and Watson's result also disappeared when their 1960–85 sample was extended to 1990.
6. These results highlight the tension in the current literature between use of variance decompositions and use of Granger–Sims "causality" tests, and also between use of levels and use of differenced data. See again the discussion above in connection with Figures 6.1 and 6.2.
7. A further possibility is that the underlying behavior did not actually change, but changes in the conduct of monetary policy – in particular, *prospective* variation of money growth, to offset *anticipated* disturbances to output and/ or prices – caused regression-based methodologies to be unable to discern the continuing relationship between money and these variables (see, for example, Poole (1994) and Friedman (1996)). Friedman and Kuttner (1996) explicitly test this hypothesis and find no evidence to support it. Moreover, the widespread evidence of changes in the public's behavior based on direct tests of money demand behavior strongly contradicts the possibility that this effect could be solely, or even largely, responsible for the changes in predictive content documented in Figures 6.1–6.6. Note also, for example, Cecchetti's (1995) evidence of changes in relationships between inflation and other traditional "inflation indicators."
8. The price index used is "core CPI-U" – that is, the consumer price index for all urban consumers, excluding food and energy items. The inflation rate is calculated as $\pi_{t-1} = p_{t-1} - p_{t-13}$ where p is the logarithm of the price index. The unemployment rate is the rate for the civilian labor force aged sixteen and over. The natural rate is from Gordon (1993), Table A-2, rendered into monthly values and continued at 6.0 percent after 1992. (Gordon's series ends in 1992:II, but it is constant at 6.0 percent throughout 1980–92.)
9. The estimates are, of course, also consistent with other interpretations of interest rate behavior; see Friedman and Kuttner (1996). The discussion below takes up the question of whether an equation analogous to (6.5) can be identified with monetary policy behavior.
10. The problem of *within-year* data revisions still remains. A more precise way to estimate (6.6) would be to use Federal Reserve data sources that were available on a month-by-month basis, but these data are not readily accessible.
11. An alternative procedure would be simply to allow δ in (6.6) to vary over time according to some standard time-varying-parameter specification. Especially for the sample periods with later end dates, such a procedure would avoid the contradiction implicit in holding θ fixed over the entire period from 1975 through the penultimate year of the sample. Friedman and Kuttner (1996) report results for such a procedure, and they are highly similar to those reported here.
12. For 1980 and 1981 the Federal Reserve established separate targets for what were then called M1-A and M1-B. For those two years the regression relies on the M1-B aggregate, which as of 1982 was simply relabeled M1.
13. The reported *t*-statistics somewhat overstate the precision with which the

regression measures δ (as well as the other coefficients) because of serial correlation in the errors. Serially correlated errors could easily result from the Federal Reserve's preference for interest rate smoothing, which the Taylor rule omits. With interest rate smoothing, the Federal Reserve's response to the included variables would assume a partial-adjustment form.

14. It would also be interesting to apply a time-varying-parameter methodology to β and γ (see again note 11), but such an exercise lies beyond the scope of this chapter. Fuhrer (1995) has attempted a form of that experiment, but in a different context and with unsatisfactory results. For purposes of questions like whether the response to inflation is sufficient to make the fluctuation of the *real* interest rate counter- instead of procyclical, it is important to remember that, with $(m - m^T)$ in the regression, what matters is not just β but β plus a term that depends on δ.
15. It is worth pointing out that the finding here of active M1 targeting after 1982 is contrary to the impression of many observers of US monetary policy at the time.
16. For the use of error-correction methods in this context, see again Ramey (1993) and Feldstein and Stock (1994).
17. Tawney (1962), p. 185.

References

Cecchetti, S.G. (1995) "Inflation Indicators and Inflation Policy," *NBER Macroeconomics Annual*, pp. 189–219.

DeRosa, P. and Stern, G.H. (1977) "Monetary Control and the Federal Funds Rate," *Journal of Monetary Economics*, 3, pp. 217–30.

Feinmann, J.N. and Porter, R.D. (1992) "The Continuing Weakness of M2," mimeo, Federal Reserve Board.

Feldstein, M. and Stock, J.H. (1994) "The Use of a Monetary Aggregate to Target Nominal GDP," in N.G. Mankiw (ed.), *Monetary Policy* (Chicago, IL: University of Chicago Press).

Friedman, B.M. (1990) "Targets and Instruments of Monetary Policy," in B.M. Friedman and F.H. Hahn (eds), *Handbook of Monetary Economics*, Vol. 2 (Amsterdam: Elsevier Science Publishers).

Friedman, B.M. (1993) "The Role of Judgment and Discretion in the Conduct of Monetary Policy: Consequences of Changing Financial Markets," in *Changing Capital Markets: Implications for Monetary Policy* (Kansas City, MO: Federal Reserve Bank of Kansas City).

Friedman, B.M. (1996) "Does Monetary Policy Affect Real Economic Activity? Why Do We Still Ask This Question?," in H. Siebert (ed.), *Monetary Policy in an Integrated World Economy* (Tubingen: J.C.B. Mohr, forthcoming).

Friedman, B.M. and Kuttner, K.N. (1993) "Another Look at the Evidence on Money-Income Causality," *Journal of Econometrics*, 57, pp. 189–203.

Friedman, B.M. and Kuttner, K.N. (1996). "A Price Target for US Monetary Policy? Lessons from the Experience with Money Growth Targets," *Brookings Papers on Economic Activity*, pp. 77–146.

Friedman, M. and Schwartz, A.J. (1963) *A Monetary History of the United States 1867–1960* (Princeton, NJ.: Princeton University Press).

Fuhrer, J.C. (1995) "Modeling Long-Term Nominal Interest Rates," mimeo, Federal Reserve Bank of Boston.

Goldfeld, S.M. (1973) "The Demand for Money Revisited," *Brookings Papers on Economic Activity*, pp. 577–638.

Gordon, R.J. (1993) *Macroeconomics*, 6th edn (New York: HarperCollins College Publishers).

Poole, W. (1994) "Monetary Aggregates Targeting in a Low-Inflation Economy," in J.C. Fuhrer (ed.), *Goals, Guidelines, and constraints Facing Monetary Policymakers* (Boston, MA: Federal Reserve Bank of Boston).

Ramey, V. (1993) "How Important Is the Credit Channel in the Transmission of Monetary Policy?," mimeo, University of California, San Diego.

Sims, C.A. (1980) "Comparison of Interwar and Postwar Business Cycles: Monetarism Reconsidered," *American Economic Review*, 70, pp. 250–7.

Sims, C.A., Stock, J.H. and Watson, M.W. (1990) "Inference in Linear Time Series Models with Some Unit Roots," *Econometrica*, 58, pp. 113–44.

Stock, J.H. and Watson, M.W. (1989) "Interpreting the Evidence on Money-Income Causality," *Journal of Econometrics*, 40, pp. 161–82.

Tawney, R.H. (1962) *Religion and the Rise of Capitalism* (Gloucester, MA: Peter Smith).

Taylor, J.B. (1993) "Discretion versus Policy Rules in Practice," *Carnegie–Rochester Conference Series on Public Policy*, 39, pp. 195–214.

Comments*

David Longworth

1 INTRODUCTION

Friedman uses econometric techniques to respond to the questions of whether US monetary policymakers had sound economic reasons for adopting and subsequently downgrading money growth targets. In doing so he provides us with valuable information on what these policymakers knew and when, and what they did and when. I agree with most of what he says, and therefore I would like to pick up on two issues. First, what determines whether one should use money as an intermediate target as opposed to an intermediate indicator? Second, what can Friedman's vector autoregression technique tell us about what monetary policymakers knew, and what would it tell us in the Canadian case? I will illustrate my remarks with reference to both my own country, Canada, and the United States.

2 INTERMEDIATE TARGET VERSUS INTERMEDIATE INDICATOR

Monetary authorities could consider a number of factors in deciding whether or not to elevate a monetary aggregate to the role of intermediate target. Among them are the following:

- does the aggregate have consistent leading information about the ultimate policy target (inflation, output, nominal spending growth)? (Friedman's criterion)
- if there is not much leading information in money, is there contemporaneous information that can be exploited because information on the monetary aggregates becomes known before information on prices and output?
- how tight is the relationship between money and the policy target – for example, what are the standard errors in the relationship and what would they imply about a suitable width for any target band for money growth?

* The views expressed in these Comments are solely those of the author. No responsibility for them should be attributed to the Bank of Canada.

- does money growth, even if it is not a leading indicator, give the monetary authorities a suitable "place to stand" – that is, a suitable nominal anchor to the system – in a country where there is no strong legislative mandate for price stability or some other form of nominal stability?
- does the existence of a monetary target influence the formation of inflationary expectations by the public?
- does having a monetary target provide a rule for setting interest rates?

Viewed from this broader perspective, Friedman's criterion for a monetary target, although highly desirable and perhaps the criterion on which one should place the most weight in most circumstances, is neither necessary nor sufficient for making a monetary aggregate the intermediate target of policy.

Internationally, part of the move away from the use of monetary aggregates as intermediate targets appears to have been motivated by factors other than a worsening in their leading indicator properties for inflation, output, or nominal spending. In fact, in some countries – Canada for one – the monetary authorities are more satisfied with the indicator properties than they were in the past, and yet monetary aggregate targets have been dropped for other reasons and never reinstated. Some of the reasons for dropping intermediate targets and not reinstating them relate to the factors that I have already mentioned:

- although the indicator properties of money for future inflation and output remained good, short-run demand functions relating money to past inflation and output became less stable because of financial innovation, making it more difficult to set appropriate growth targets for the coming year (this is why Canada dropped its M1 targets in 1982);
- price stability as the major goal of a central bank became more generally politically acceptable in many countries, making it possible to define the monetary policy objective, at least in the medium term, as price stability (perhaps with a quantitative definition); as well, in some countries (including Canada), it has been possible to adopt a time path of specific inflation targets and thus monetary targets were not necessary to provide a place to stand;
- in many countries (Germany and Switzerland being important exceptions) it was not clear that the achievement of monetary targets had any effect on inflation expectations (that appears to be the case in Canada and in the United States, at least for most of the period) – the consistent achievement of low inflation seemed to be more what influenced expectations in a big way;

- targets for interest-elastic monetary aggregates were fairly easy to hit and provided rules of thumb for setting interest rates, but proved unsatisfactory in terms of their medium-term performance since interest rates were changed by too little in the short run to have a significant impact on nominal spending (this was a major problem for the Canadian M1 targets);
- methods of forecasting inflation using variables in addition to money, past inflation, and output have increased in sophistication – both in small econometric models with well-specified long-run properties and in vector autoregressive models – and thus central banks are relying on a significant number of "indicators."

To conclude this section of my remarks, I think that monetary policymakers always recognized that there was noise in the monetary aggregates (both in levels and growth rates) that was unrelated to past, current, or future prices and output. But this did not inhibit them, nor do I think it should have, from adopting monetary aggregates as intermediate targets. This being said, however, monetary authorities with a clear ultimate target have every incentive to exploit all the information there is in the monetary aggregates, but not much incentive to have an intermediate monetary target unless it has significant strengths on a number of accounts. In this light I do not predict that there will be an increasing number of countries with intermediate monetary targets.

3 WHAT DO WE KNOW ABOUT WHAT MONETARY POLICYMAKERS KNEW?

In his chapter, Friedman plots *p*-values to test the null hypothesis that all the coefficients on lagged money are zero in the differenced equations for output and prices as a function of lagged output, prices, and money. In this section, I ask what the results would look like in another country. Does it matter whether the authorities care about the CPI or the GDP deflator? And does it matter whether the authorities care about nominal spending, rather than its two components? In each case, I use Canadian data. I also restrict myself to the three-variable systems, the ones without interest rates.

The two Canadian monetary aggregates that I examine are M1 (which consists of currency and demand deposits and is the monetary aggregate we actually targeted from 1975–82) and M2+ (which resembles US M2 plus individual annuities at life insurance companies). (Although the Bank of Canada did not start to look at M2+ until the late 1980s, in growth rate

Figure 6A.1 Canada: M1 in output equation

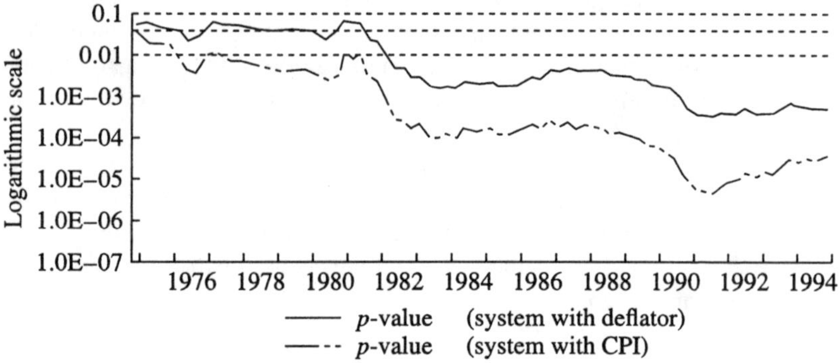

terms it tracks M2 – which it did look at – very closely in the period up to the late 1980s.)

For M1, I use the 1960:I–1974:IV period for the first regression and then add a quarter at a time. The results in the figures are from rolling just the far end of the regression, but it makes little difference empirically whether one rolls the beginning as well.

Figure 6A.1 shows that in the system with the GDP deflator, M1 has been significant in the output equation at the 5 percent level in most quarters – and from 1982 on at the 1 percent level. In the system with the CPI, significance at the 1 percent level was achieved by 1976. It should be noted that because of its Paasche nature and the pronounced terms of trade shocks experienced in a commodity-exporting country like Canada, the GDP deflator can be more volatile in the short run than the CPI.

In the price equation (Figure 6A.2), M1 is rarely significant at the 5 percent level with either price series, but the level of significance is greater in the deflator equation, with the exception of the first year.

Figure 6A.3 plots the significance of M1 in the nominal output equation in a system with lags on real output, the deflator and M1. M1 is always significant at 2 percent and becomes significant at 1 percent after a quarter or two. Recall that there was a very mixed picture for the significance of M1 for both output and prices in the period up to 1982. If the monetary authority were more concerned with nominal spending than with the mix, it would be appropriate to look at the significance in a nominal spending equation directly, and not try to infer significance from the separate equations for output and prices.

M2+ data begin later than that for M1, so the first regression is estimated from 1969:II to 1977:IV. Figure 6A.4 shows that the broad monetary

Figure 6A.2 Canada: M1 in price equation

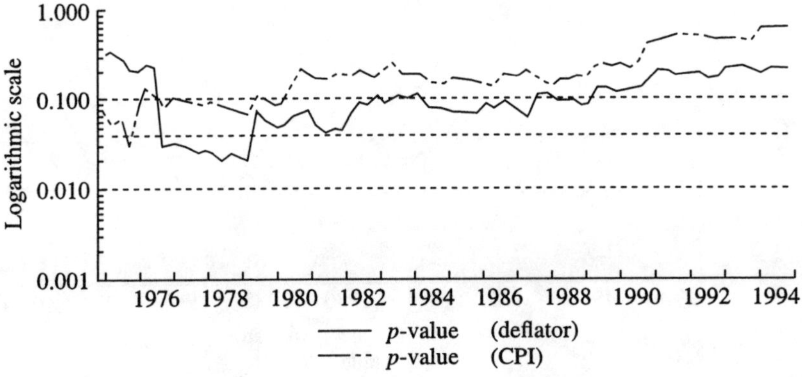

Figure 6A.3 Canada: M1 in nominal output equation

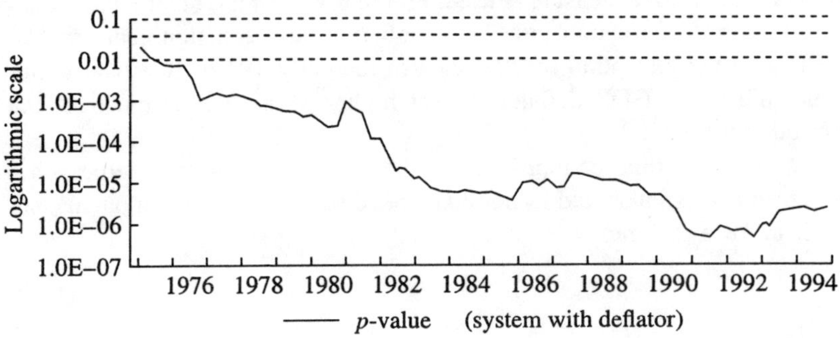

Figure 6A.4 Canada: M2+ in output equation

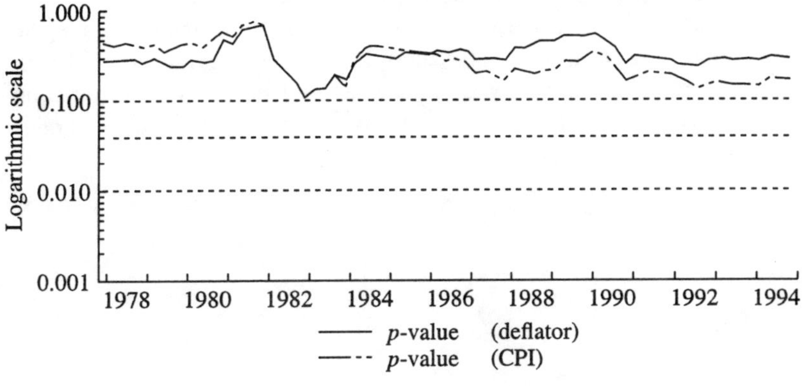

Figure 6A.5 Canada: M2+ in price equation

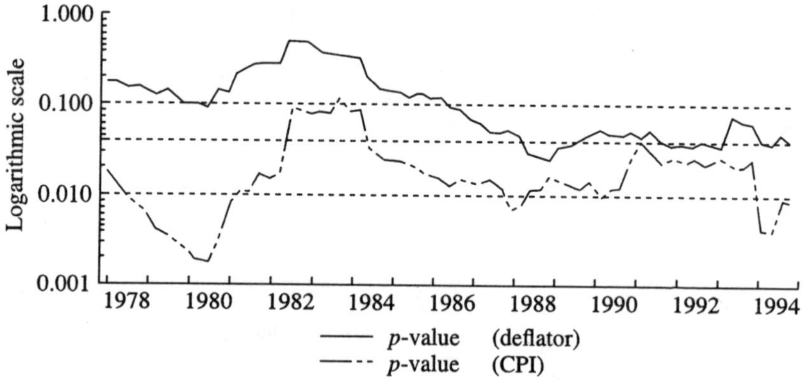

aggregate M2+ has never had significant information about output, no matter which price measure is used. Figure 6A.5, on the other hand, indicates that the information in M2+ for inflation has been significant for the CPI, with the exception of 2½ years in the early 1980s. It was also significant for the GDP deflator, but at higher *p*-values, for much of the period since 1988.

To conclude this section, it seems that differences in price indices and whether one is interested in nominal spending or its two components can both make a difference.

4 CONCLUSION

In conclusion, this chapter raises some thought-provoking results and techniques. Researchers in various countries may wish to undertake parallel studies and to examine the sensitivity to assumptions about the specific goal variables used. In the end, I think that most policymakers will continue to exploit the monetary aggregates as best they can as information variables, but will not be inclined to use them as intermediate targets unless they do so already.

Comments
Georg Rich

1 THE USEFULNESS OF MONEY GROWTH TARGETS

Friedman presents a stimulating analysis of the changing role played by money growth targets in US monetary policy. Although the Federal Reserve System has employed money growth targets since the early 1970s, their significance has varied markedly over the years. Money growth targets assumed center stage in US monetary policy in 1979, but the Federal Reserve's commitment to them turned out to be short-lived. Repeated difficulties with the stability of US money demand prompted the Federal Reserve to abandon targeting narrow money. In 1993 it explicitly confirmed that it was also paying less attention to the broadly defined aggregates.

In his chapter Friedman addresses the question of whether the Federal Reserve's shifts in emphasis on monetary targeting reflected a rational response to the changing nature of the relationship between money and economic activity. To this end, Friedman investigates the impact of changes in the aggregates M1 and M2 on prices and output with the help of a variance decomposition based on a three-variable vector autoregression. The contribution of money to subsequent changes in prices and output is derived for a multitude of samples, with the end date of the sample moving forward continuously from the fourth quarter of 1974 to the fourth quarter of 1994. In this way, Friedman extracts from the data the information on the relationship between money and economic activity that was available to the Federal Reserve at the time of the policy changes. Friedman's results suggests that the contribution of M1 to subsequent movements in economic activity, while small throughout the sample period, became negligible after the mid-1980s. The aggregate M2 fared better than M1, especially with respect to output. But its contribution to subsequent movements in economic activity also declined, notably in the late 1980s and early 1990s.

Friedman then turns to the reaction of the Federal Reserve to changes in the relationship between money and economic activity. He finds that money growth targets, though formally adopted in 1975, only began to influence monetary policy toward the end of the 1970s. For the period from 1979 to the mid-1980s, Friedman uncovers strong evidence of the Federal

Reserve reacting to target misses, notably in the case of M1. This is largely consistent with the changing intensity of the relationship between money and economic activity. Moreover, according to Friedman's estimates, the Federal Reserve temporarily returned to M2 targeting in 1992 and 1993. It is unclear whether the renewed emphasis on M2 targeting – in contrast to the policy shift of 1979 – was justified in the light of the available evidence.

Thus, Friedman concludes that for the most part, the Federal Reserve's shifts in policy strategy constituted a rational response to new information on the link between money and economic activity. As an outside observer of US monetary policy, I do not feel qualified to comment on Friedman's conclusions concerning the rationality of Federal Reserve behavior. Instead, I focus on more general problems arising from Friedman's methodology. In particular, I would caution against drawing policy conclusions from vector autoregressions on the link between money and economic activity. VAR analysis may misleadingly suggest that money only makes a minor contribution to subsequent movements in economic activity even if these movements are caused by monetary disturbances. In the following section, I illustrate this point with the help of Swiss data.

2 EXPLANATORY POWER OF VECTOR AUTOREGRESSIONS

Econometric studies indicate that Swiss demand for the aggregate M2 – defined to include currency, the full array of demand deposits, and savings deposits[1] – is stably related to consumer prices, real GDP and the average yield on government bonds.[2] The stability of that relationship is particularly pronounced after 1976.[3] For the post-1976 period, the estimated elasticities for consumer prices and real GDP are close to and slightly above unity respectively. Moreover, the estimated elasticity for the government bond yield amounts to roughly –0.5, that is, the demand for M2 responds strongly to changes in interest rates. Considering the stability of M2, the Swiss National Bank regards that aggregate as a reliable leading indicator of movements in real GDP and consumer prices.[4]

The leading indicator role of M2 is revealed by Figure 6B.1, displaying year-on-year quarterly rates of change in nominal Swiss GDP and the money stock, with GDP lagged by nine quarters in order to take account of the relatively long lags in the effects of Swiss monetary policy. The chart points to a close relationship between movements in nominal GDP and money growth. However, it also identifies a problem characteristic for highly interest-sensitive monetary aggregates. In three instances (1976,

Figure 6B.1 Growth in the money stock M2 and in nominal gross domestic product

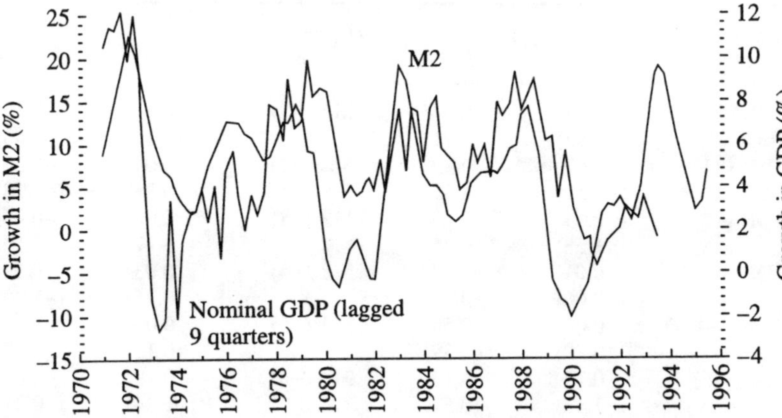

1983 and 1994), M2 growth picked up temporarily, without that increase being followed by an analogous spike in nominal GDP growth. These swings do not reflect instabilities in the relationship between nominal GDP and M2. Rather, they invariably arise in periods of falling inflation and nominal interest rates. Consider, for example, the movements in M2 growth between 1977 and 1984. In late 1977 and 1978, the Swiss National Bank expanded the money supply in an effort to counter a massive real upvaluation of the Swiss franc, imparting a deflationary bias to monetary policy. Although the Swiss National Bank did not expect its policy shift to jeopardize price stability, inflation picked up temporarily, as indicated by the sharp increase in nominal GDP growth about two years later. In 1979 the Swiss National Bank returned to a tight monetary policy, causing nominal GDP growth to slow down again toward the end of 1981. The temporary rise in M2 growth in 1982 and the early part of 1983 mirrored the decline in interest rates, associated with the drop in nominal GDP growth. Since it resulted from the downturn of the economy, it did not impinge on nominal GDP growth, unlike the monetary expansion of 1977–78.[5]

Consequently, depending on the source of the monetary stimulus, a surge in M2 growth may or may not exert an expansionary effect on nominal GDP. This implies that mechanical application of VAR analysis may yield misleading results. Not surprisingly, a bivariate VAR analysis of logarithmic first differences in Swiss nominal GDP and M2 fails to uncover a strong effect of money on economic activity.[6] The sample consists of quarterly data for the period 1978:II to 1994:IV and the regression equation takes account of 8 lags. The variance decomposition suggests that after ninequarters,

Table 6B.1 Bivariate autoregressions in nominal GDP and the money stock M2 (logarithmic first differences)

Dependent variables	*GDP*	*M2*	*Dependent variables*	*GDP*	*M2*
CONST	0.01	0.04	M2 (−1)	−0.11	0.79
	(1.85)	(2.91)		(1.18)	(5.43)
GDP (−1)	−0.07	−0.95	M2 (−2)	0.04	−0.33
	(−0.50)	(−4.35)		(0.33)	(−1.78)
GDP (−2)	0.24	−0.18	M2 (−3)	−0.02	−0.03
	(1.58)	(−0.75)		(−0.17)	(−0.16)
GDP (−3)	−0.01	−0.18	M2 (−4)	0.03	−0.19
	(−0.06)	(−0.73)		(0.25)	(−1.00)
GDP (−4)	0.05	−0.55	M2 (−5)	0.01	0.08
	(0.32)	(−2.39)		(0.12)	(0.47)
GDP (−5)	−0.24	0.13	M2 (−6)	−0.19	−0.04
	(−1.63)	(0.57)		(−1.84)	(−0.21)
GDP (−6)	0.13	−0.14	M2 (−7)	0.10	−0.20
	(0.96)	(−0.61)		(0.99)	(−1.25)
GDP (−7)	0.07	−0.18	M2 (−8)	0.09	0.02
	(0.50)	(−0.83)		(1.10)	(0.17)
GDP (−8)	−0.29	−0.20	*Test*		
	(−2.33)	(−1.01)	*statistics*		
			R^2	0.45	0.78
			Adj. R^2	0.28	0.70
			SE of equ.	0.01	0.01

Sample period: 1978:II–1994:IV. Numbers in parentheses are *t*-statistics.
Source: Swiss National Bank, *Monatsbericht*, Tables B31 and P1.

money explains about 17 percent of the movements in nominal GDP provided M2 ranks first in the ordering of these variables (see Table 6B.1 for the regressions). The results are not changed much if the analysis is extended by increasing the number of lags in the regression equations, by splitting up nominal GDP into production and prices, and by taking account of interest rates.

Aside from the problems caused by the interest-sensitivity of money demand, the VAR analysis of Swiss data raises a further – well-known – difficulty. The movements in nominal GDP are largely explained by their own history, that is, by an autoregressive process. Considering the long monetary policy lags in Switzerland, I doubt that the vector autoregressions correctly capture the influence of money on economic activity.

Let me finish with a comment on Friedman's concluding observations in section 5 of his chapter. He correctly points out that running vector autoregressions on first differences may result in an important loss of information on the link between money and economic activity. Therefore, an error-correction methodology may be more appropriate than Friedman's vector autoregressions in first differences.

According to Friedman, however, application of an error-correction methodology would raise a new problem. If the data were explained by an error-correction process, they would only support the use of money as an information variable, not as a target variable. I do not understand this argument. It is true that the demand for money frequently varies as a result of random shocks. Since many of these shocks are transitory, an error-correction methodology may well be appropriate for modeling money demand. Whether these shocks undermine monetary targeting depends on the speed at which they are reversed. If most unexpected changes in money demand are reversed within the targeting period, they do not undermine the role of money as a target variable. The existence of such random movements merely implies that central banks should not adjust their instruments too rapidly to unexpected shifts in money demand.

Notes

1. The concept of M2 used in these Comments excludes deposits held at banks in Liechtenstein.
2. I draw on an extensive study conducted by Michel Peytrignet at the Swiss National Bank. Employing the Stock and Watson dynamic OLS procedure, he investigates the demand for all the aggregates published by the Swiss National Bank. The money stock M2 turns out to be the most stable aggregate. Peytrignet evaluates the stability of the estimated parameters by shortening successively the sample period. He first drops successive observations at the beginning of the sample period and then repeats that procedure for the observations at the end of the sample period. For the post-1976 period, the estimates for the respective parameters vary within a very small range.
3. There is evidence of instabilities prior to 1977, probably as a result of Switzerland's shift to a floating exchange rate in 1973.
4. The money stock M2, however, is not used as a target variable because it is quite volatile in the short run, due to its high interest-sensitivity. Instead, the Swiss National Bank targets the monetary base, which has been less stable but also less interest-sensitive than the money stock M2.
5. The temporary drop in nominal GDP growth in 1986 stemmed from the fall in the price of oil, rather than from the monetary contraction of 1983/84.
6. I am indebted to my colleague Erich Spörndli for conducting the VAR analysis.

7 Monetary Targeting in Germany*

Manfred J.M. Neumann

1 INTRODUCTION

Monetary targeting was considered an avant-garde experiment when the Deutsche Bundesbank introduced this concept in late 1974 after having been freed of the chains of the Bretton Woods system. Many central banks followed shortly afterward. Today, in contrast, monetary targeting is widely viewed as an outmoded procedure that has lost its pillar, a stable money demand function. For this reason, several countries, like Canada, New Zealand and the UK, have switched to the concept of direct inflation targeting, while other countries have reverted to pure discretion or continue pegging their currency to one of the key currencies or a currency basket. The Bundesbank, in contrast, holds on to its concept steadfastly and advertises monetary targeting as a suitable concept of policy formulation for the future European Central Bank.

In this chapter we examine the Bundesbank's concept of monetary targeting by drawing on and further extending the recent studies by von Hagen (1995) and by Neumann and von Hagen (1993, 1995). The Bank's concept is an intermediate approach to securing the internal value of money. The focus of the concept is on providing the monetary frame for zero or low trend inflation rather than on trying to directly control price movements in the short run. The concept can be summarized by two complementary strategies: (i) the attempt at anchoring the public's expectations as regards medium- to long-run inflation by setting a consistent target rate for monetary growth, and, (ii) systematic short-run deviation from the midpoint target for the purpose of counteracting unanticipated shocks to prices and the exchange rate and for accommodating shocks to money demand.

The following Section 2 considers the quantity-theoretic background of monetary targeting. The Bundesbank's targeting procedure is described in detail in Section 3. An empirical evaluation of the performance record over the period 1979–94 is provided in Section 4. There we present estimates of the conditioning role of the annual monetary targets for inflation

* I would like to thank Jerry Jordan, William R. White and the participants of the conference for valuable suggestions.

and of the Bundesbank's reaction function. Since the trend rate of inflation exceeded the Bank's inflation objective, we also examine the Bank's targeting procedure in search for a built-in bias. It will be shown that rather than the Bundesbank's targets for current money growth the accustomed policy of deviating from target during the course of a year contains an upward bias. Section 5 looks into the issue of money demand stability and examines the impact of German unification on the demand function of the Bundesbank's target aggregate. It will be shown that the unification resulted in a downward shift of the demand function for real M3 balances. Section 6 provides concluding remarks.

2 THE ANALYTICAL BACKGROUND OF MONETARY TARGETING

Monetary policy can serve competing objectives. The literature on the problem of time inconsistency in monetary policy has shown that a central bank will not provide stable money if this objective is put at an equal footing with other objectives, such as stimulating real growth, smoothing the business cycle or stabilizing the exchange rate. The Bundesbank Act provides a clear ranking of objectives. In section 3 the Act requires the Bank to "safeguard the currency" and as late as section 12 the Act stipulates that the Bank shall support the "general economic policy of the government, provided doing so is compatible with the predominant mandate" of section 3.

The Bundesbank's concept of monetary targeting echoes this ranking of objectives by making the objective of zero or low inflation the cornerstone of annual targeting. The basic idea is straightforward. The quantity theory of money implies that providing stable money for the medium to long run requires selecting the appropriate money expansion path for given trends of real growth and velocity. Moreover, by announcing the target path to the public and by explaining its derivation the public's inflation expectations will be anchored, provided the Bank enjoys credibility.

The equation of exchange can be written in first differences of logs as

$$\Delta p_t = \Delta m_t + \Delta v_t - \Delta y_t \tag{7.1}$$

where p denotes the price level, m the money stock, v the income velocity of money, and y real income or output. Using this equation, the Bundesbank determines at the end of year $t - 1$ the average target rate of money expansion for year t, Δm_t^T, as

$$\Delta m_t^T = \pi_t^T + E_{t-1}(\Delta y_t^* - \Delta v_t^*) \tag{7.2}$$

π^T is the Bundesbank's target rate of inflation, Δy^* denotes the growth rate of long-run equilibrium or normal output, Δv^* denotes the percentage rate of change of the long-run equilibrium or trend level of velocity, E is the expectations operator.

Note that the target rate of monetary expansion is based on the Bundesbank's expectations about the rate of change of normal output and of the trend rate of change of velocity rather than on the expected actual changes of output and velocity. This signifies the medium- to long-run orientation of the Bundesbank's targeting concept. Equating actual and target money growth, equations (7.1) and (7.2), yields

$$\Delta p_t = \pi_t^T + (\Delta v - \Delta v^*)_t - (\Delta y - \Delta y^*)_t + f_t^v - f_t^y \tag{7.3}$$

with: $f_t^v = (\Delta v_t^* - E_{t-1}\Delta v_t^*)$
$f_t^y = (\Delta y_t^* - E_{t-1}\Delta y_t^*)$

where the Bank's forecast errors are denoted by f with superscripts v or y.

Thus, if the Bundesbank continously meets her monetary target, $\Delta m = \Delta m^T$, the actual rate of price change will move around the level of the Bank's inflation objective in response to the deviations of output and velocity growth from long-run equilibrium. Faster output growth in the short run tends to reduce actual inflation while faster velocity growth is inflationary. To be sure, the solution equation (7.3) is silent as regards the economic sources of such deviations from long-run equilibrium. They may be due to stochastic shocks to productivity or to money demand. In the case of sluggish price adjustment in the goods markets, those shocks will generate serial correlation in the temporary deviations of output and velocity from the equilibrium rates of change.

The price-gap model of Hallman, Porter and Small (1991) can be used to make the point. The Bundesbank has used this model recently to investigate the empirical relation between money growth and inflation.[1] The price-gap model states that the gap between the equilibrium price level, p^*, and the actual price level, p, equals the difference between the respective gaps for output and velocity. With all variables in logs we have

$$p_t^* - p_t = (y_t - y_t^*) - (v_t - v_t^*) \tag{7.4}$$

Assuming that the actual rate of price change adjusts slowly to the price gap

$$\Delta p_t = \pi_t^* + \alpha(p_t^* - p_t); \quad 0 < \alpha < 1 \tag{7.5}$$

and that the equilibrium rate of inflation has settled at the Bundesbank's inflation target rate, $\pi^* = \pi^T$, yields

$$\Delta p_t = \pi_t^* + \alpha[(y_t - y_t^*) - (v_t - v_t^*)] \tag{7.6}$$

This solution for the short-run rate of price change holds if prices adjust sluggishly while the alternative solution, given by equation (7.3), holds generally. The solutions (7.3) and (7.6) are not in conflict but imply the following "stock" adjustment process

$$(\Delta y_t - \Delta y_t^*) - (\Delta v_t - \Delta v_t^*) = -\alpha[(y_t - y_t^*) - (v_t - v_t^*)] \tag{7.7}$$

Note that the forecast errors have been set at zero. The price-gap model assumes a process of reversion towards long-run equilibrium stretching over time. When the economy is in a boom and/or velocity is suppressed below equilibrium, short-run output growth will slow down, while short-run velocity growth will speed up. As a result, the actual rate of price change may exceed the equilibrium rate of inflation.

For monetary policy this implies that keeping money growth at target secures that actual inflation will not permanently deviate from the desired path. However, departures from equilibrium may last quite some time. If this is unacceptable, monetary policy may deviate from the target path in a stabilizing fashion. Below we will see that the latter strategy is part of the Bundesbank's concept.

3 THE BUNDESBANK'S CONCEPT

The Bundesbank's concept of monetary policy can be characterized by two consecutive steps:

(i) At the end of a year $t-1$ the Bank computes a target rate of average monetary expansion for year t and translates this average target rate into a linear target rate of current money growth, measured from the fourth quarter of year $t-1$ to the fourth quarter of year t. The latter rate is publicly announced.

(ii) During the course of year t the Bank uses the current target rate as a yardstick for steering money growth but the Bank deviates from target in a systematic fashion in response to observations on the short-term evolution of prices, the exchange rate or money demand shocks.

Note that the Bundesbank frequently changed its policy concept during the early years of targeting. For example, the Bank started monetary targeting by announcing for the year 1975 a point target for current money growth. Thereafter the Bundesbank switched to announcing a target rate for average money growth. The concept we describe below is in effect since the late 1970s when the European Monetary System (EMS) came into effect. Therefore, we will concentrate on the period since 1979 in the empirical work of Section 4 below.

3.1 Deriving the Monetary Target

As has been mentioned before, the Bundesbank uses the following equation for computing first a target rate of annual average money growth, Δm_t^T,

$$\Delta m_t^T = \pi_t^T + E_{t-1}(\Delta y_t^* - \Delta v_t^*) \tag{7.8}$$

Table 7.1 provides the Bank's numerical inputs for each year since 1979.

The inflation objective, π_t^T, applies to the deflator of GDP. It is a normative rate that signals the level of inflation the Bundesbank is willing to tolerate over the medium to long run. The Bank argues that a measured inflation rate of up to 2 percent is roughly compatible with an underlying true rate of inflation of zero because price indices cannot properly take into account the improving quality of goods in the basket or the occurrence of new goods.[2] In line with this reasoning, the inflation objective has been set at 2 percent since 1986; see Table 7.1. But note that the inflation objective served a different purpose during the early 1980s when the Bundesbank tried to sqeeze out the inflation inherited from the 1970s. During those years, the Bundesbank refered to the inflation objective as "the rate of unavoidable inflation" and used it as a signal of her intention to gradually reduce actual inflation. This was achieved by announcing each year an inflation objective somewhat below the most recent rate of actual inflation.

The Bundesbank approximates the expected equilibrium growth rate of output, $E_{t-1}\Delta y_t^*$, by the expected growth rate of potential output. The Bundesbank refers to it as "production potential." Potential output is estimated by a CES production function that takes estimates of the capital stock and of the natural rate of employment into account.[3] As can be read from Table 7.1, the expected growth rates have ranged between 1.75 and 3 percent.

Not much is known of how the Bundesbank forms its expectations

Table 7.1 Targeting average expansion (percent p.a.)

Year	*Inflation objective* (1)	*Expected growth of potential output* (2)	*Expected growth of trend velocity* (3)	*Average target* (4)	*Actual growth* (5)
1979	3.5	3.0	>0	6.5	9.1
1980	~4	3.0	1.0	6.0	4.8
1981	3.75	2.5	1.0	5.25	4.4
1982	3.5	1.75	0	5.25	4.9
1983	3.5	1.75	0	5.25	7.3
1984	3.0	2.0	0	5.0	4.8
1985	2.25	2.25	0	4.5	4.6
1986	2.0	2.5	0	4.5	6.4
1987	2.0	2.5	0	4.5	8.1
1988	2.0	2.0	−0.5	4.5	6.4
1989	2.0	2.25	−0.5	4.75	5.7
1990	2.0	2.5	−0.5	5.0	4.5
1991	2.0	2.5	−0.5	5.0	4.8*
1992	2.0	2.75	−0.5	5.0†	8.2
1993	2.0	3.0	−1.0	6.0	7.9
1994	2.0	2.5	−1.0	5.5	9.0
Mean	2.6	2.4	−0.15	5.15	6.3

* Corrected for unification effect: 14.6 percent.
† Downward adjustment by 0.25 percent "in view of high liquidity."

about the equilibrium rate of change of the velocity of money, $E_{t-1}\Delta v_t^*$. Though it seems obvious that forecasts of the trend rate need to be based on estimates of a money demand or velocity function, it is not clear whether the Bank went to such pains in the early years of monetary targeting. Table 7.1 shows that the expected rate was set at zero for most of the early 1980s, while later the declining trend of the velocity of the target aggregate was taken into account. We will come back to this question in Section 4 below.

As regards the target aggregate, it is to be noted that the Bundesbank switched to the money stock M3 in 1987. Until then the annual target had been set for an aggregate called "central bank money stock," M_{CB}. It was defined as

$$M_{CB,t} = C_t + r_{1974}^D D_t + r_{1974}^T T_t + r_{1974}^S S_t \qquad (7.9)$$

where C denotes the currency holdings outside the banking system, D denotes demand deposits, T denotes time deposits with maturities below four years, and S denotes savings deposits at statutory notice all held by domestic non-banks. The deposits were weighted with constant coefficients, denoted by r; the coefficients were set at the 1974 values of the respective minimum reserve ratios.

Since 1988 the Bank's targets refer to the broad money stock M3:

$$M_{3,t} = C_t + D_t + T_t + S_t \tag{7.10}$$

Comparing equations (7.9) and (7.10), we see that the alternative aggregates sum the same components though with differential weights. While currency in circulation enters both aggregates with an absolute weight of unity, the deposits are counted in the central bank money stock with weights way below unity. When in late 1974 the Bundesbank introduced monetary targeting, the Bank rated the central bank money stock a target aggregate superior to any other monetary aggregate. In its Report for 1975, for example, the Bank emphasized that the weighting of deposits with constant minimum reserve ratios "tends to take better account of the money-like character of these deposits than single addition does."[4]

This perception was put aside when in 1987 a political debate about introducing a withholding tax induced a flight from deposits into currency; the resulting large shift in asset demand was accommodated by the Bundesbank. As a result, the currency component grew much faster than deposits, blowing up the growth rate of the central bank money stock by much more than the growth rate of money stock M3 (by 8.1 percent compared to 6.6 percent). This feature made the M3 aggregate more attractive to the Bank: "the main reason for abandoning the central bank money stock . . . was that currency carries a smaller (relative) weight in the money stock M3, which shows a less marked response to interest-rate-and exchange-rate-induced disruptions and extreme situations (such as had been seen in 1987 and were also expected for 1988) than does the central bank money stock."[5] As a matter of fact, the switch from central bank money to M3 bore fruit immediately, as the differential growth of both aggregates continued through 1988 until the tax project was given up by the government.

At this point it is important to note that the focal point of the Bundesbank's concept is not the target rate of average money growth, Δm_t^T, as given by equation (7.8), but rather the target rate of current money growth. The latter is defined by the Bank as the rate of planned money growth from the fourth quarter of year $t-1$ to the fourth quarter of year t. Denote this rate by $\Delta m_{t,44}^{T}$. This target rate figures prominently in all policy discussions. The Bundesbank does not explain how the target for current money growth is derived from the average target rate though there is a mathematical relationship between both rates. Given that the current target rate equals the annualized quarter-to-quarter growth rate, $\Delta m_{t,\tau}^{T}$,

$$\Delta m_{t,44} = (1 + \Delta m_{t,\tau})^4 - 1 \tag{7.11}$$

it can be derived by the following formula

$$\sum_{\tau=1}^{4} (1 + \Delta m_{t,\tau}^{T})^{\tau} = \frac{1 + \Delta m_{t}^{T}}{1 + \Delta m_{t-1,44}} \sum_{\tau=1}^{4} (1 + \Delta m_{t-1,\tau})^{\tau} \tag{7.12}$$

The formula relates the targeted quarter-to-quarter growth rate $\Delta m_{t,\tau}^{T}$, to the planned average target rate, Δm_{t}^{T}, and the previous actual growth rates, $\Delta m_{t-1,44}$ and $\Delta m_{t-1,\tau}$.

Finally, the Bundesbank specifies a target range for current money growth

$$c + \Delta m_{t,44}^{T} > \Delta m_{t,44}^{T} > \Delta m_{t,44}^{T} - c \tag{7.13}$$

Table 7.2 informs about the target range and the midpoint target rate for each year since 1979. As column 1 of Table 7.2 indicates, the coefficient c was set at 1.5 percentage points during the early 1980s and at 1 percentage point for most years thereafter. Given that the money stock M3 can only indirectly be controlled by changing non-borrowed reserves and administrative interest rates, a target range is indispensable though it does not serve just this purpose, as we will see below.

3.2 Reacting to Short-Term Events

While the basic idea of the Bundesbank's targeting approach is to influence the public's inflation expectations as well as actual inflation over the medium to long run by setting the appropriate target path for money growth, this does not restrict the Bank from deviating from the midpoint target rate by a large margin. On the contrary, the Bundesbank has repeatedly explained that it may have to deviate from the midpoint target rate to account for short-run events, such as sharp changes in the external value of the D-Mark, an unexpected strong rise in the price level or shifts in money demand.

In the Report for 1980 the Bank explained this strategy as follows: "the flexibility with which the Bundesbank responds in the short run to unusual disturbances owes much to the fact that in the last analysis the monetary

Table 7.2 Announced targets for current money growth* (percent p.a.)

Year	Target range (1)	Midpoint target: Actual (2)	Midpoint target: Corrected (3)	Midpoint target: Difference (4)	Actual growth (5)
1979	6–9	7.5	3.3	4.2	6.4
1980	5–8	6.5	5.8	0.7	4.9
1981	4–7	5.5	5.5	0	3.6
1982	4–7	5.5	6.3	–0.8	6.1
1983	4–7	5.5	4.7	0.8	6.9
1984	4–6	5.0	3.9	1.1	4.6
1985	3–5	4.0	4.4	–0.4	4.5
1986	3.5–5.5	4.5	4.5	0	7.8
1987	3–6	4.5	2.6	1.9	8.0
1988	3–6	4.5	3.3	1.2	6.8
1989	~5	5.0	3.6	1.4	4.6
1990	4–6	5.0	5.2	–0.2	5.3
1991	4–6	5.0	4.8	0.2	4.8
1992	3.5–5.5	4.5	4.9	–0.4	9.6
1993	4.5–6.5	5.5	4.0	1.5	7.7
1994	4–6	5.0	4.3	0.8	5.7
Mean		5.2	4.4	0.8	6.1

* Measured from the previous fourth quarter to the current fourth quarter.

growth target is only an 'intermediate target variable,' the final objective . . . being to safeguard the currency. Although the longer-term curbing of the expansion of the money stock is essential for this purpose . . . it may become necessary to take short-term measures which in themselves could be regarded as a temporary departure from the path of medium-term expansion."[6] Specifically, the Bank considered an expansionary deviation from the midpoint target rate appropriate "if 'home-made' price and cost increases slackened, the exchange rate of the D-Mark steadied and external disequilibrium lessened."[7] As regards the appropriateness of accommodating money demand shocks, the Report for 1991 states: "The Bundesbank tolerated this 'undershooting' of monetary growth, which was attributable to a shift in the demand for money in eastern Germany . . . as being consistent with its monetary policy objectives."[8]

Surprising as it may be to foreign observers, the Bundesbank does not lend its policy to activist stabilization of the business cycle. As a rule, this is not very clearly stated. For example, in the Report for 1982 the Bank writes, "The Bundesbank's aim was to improve the monetary conditions for an economic recovery," but goes on, "without overstepping the limits set to monetary policy or increasing the money supply to a greater extent than stabilization policy requirements warranted. The Bundesbank made this objective clear by announcing the monetary target for 1982."[9]

Two years later the Bundesbank clarified its principal position by stating that monetary targeting was to be equated with the mandate of having to support the general economic policy of the government. To quote from the Report for 1984:

> In all the years in which monetary targeting has been practised, the economic data on which the Bundesbank has based its formulation of the monetary target have invariably been consistent with the macroeconomic objectives outlined in the Federal Government's Annual Economic Report. Conversely, the Federal Government for its part has invariably accepted the annual monetary target as a fitting contribution by monetary policy to the implementation of the official annual forecast. This practice can be regarded as the fulfilment of the mandate assigned to the Bundesbank by law (section 12 of the Bundesbank Act).[10]

Summing up, the strategy of deviating from target in the shorter run can be summarized by the following reaction function (Neumann and von Hagen, 1993):

$$\Delta m_{t,\tau} - \Delta m^T_{t,\tau} = -\beta_1(\Delta p - \pi^T)_{t,\tau} + \beta_2(\Delta q - E_{t-1}\Delta q^*)_{t,\tau} + \beta_3\mu_{t,\tau} \tag{7.14}$$

where q denotes the (log of the) real exchange rate of the D-Mark and μ is a perceived shock to money demand. The reaction function implies that the Bundesbank counteracts excessive inflation, leans against the wind of real exchange rate appreciation and accommodates perceived shocks to money demand.

This concludes the description of the Bundesbank's policy concept.

4 THE BUNDESBANK'S PERFORMANCE

In this section we examine the policy record. The sample period is 1979 to 1994 and includes the eastern part of Germany from 1991. All time series have been adjusted for the unification effect.[11] Subsection 4.1 describes the characteristics of the money growth process, provides estimates of the Bundesbank's reaction function and checks on the conditioning role of monetary targets for inflation. Given that inflation has been higher on average than the Bundesbank's inflation objective implied, subsection 4.2, finally, examines if the actual money targets were biased upwards.

4.1 The Bundesbank's Reaction Function and the Impact of Target Announcement on Inflation

We begin with a few regressions that describe the properties of annual money growth, measured as percentage rates of change between the fourth quarters of adjacent years.

As a first observation we note that money growth is serially uncorrelated:

$$\Delta m_{t,44} = \underset{(2.7)}{3.84} + \underset{(1.4)}{0.32}\Delta m_{t-1,44} + \underset{(2.9)}{4.2}D_{92} \tag{7.15}$$

$$\overline{R}^2 = 0.34 \quad DW = 1.72 \quad Q_4 = 7.68$$

Numbers in parentheses are t-ratios and Q_4 is the Ljung-Box Q-statistic for fourth-order residual autocorrelation. The respective 5 percent significance levels are 2.2 and 9.48. Neither the t-statistic for lagged money growth nor the Q-statistic is significant at the 5 percent level. Note that the regression includes a dummy variable for the year 1992 when the Bundesbank was forced by an extreme wave of speculation against major EMS currencies to let money growth go.

A second observation is that money growth is not correlated with the current midpoint target rate:

$$\Delta m_{t,44} = \underset{(2.7)}{6.23} - \underset{(-0.2)}{0.07}\Delta m^T_{t,44} + \underset{(2.5)}{3.67}D_{92} \tag{7.16}$$

$$\overline{R}^2 = 0.33 \quad DW = 1.65 \quad Q_4 = 7.48$$

Finally, we observe that the target rates are correlated:

$$\Delta m^T_{t,44} = \underset{(3.5)}{2.34} + \underset{(4.1)}{0.52}\Delta m^T_{t-1,44} \tag{7.17}$$

$$\overline{R}^2 = 0.53 \quad DW = 2.43 \quad Q_4 = 1.23$$

In sum, we find that the midpoint target rate has no predictive value for actual money growth in the short run and that the latter is serially uncorrelated.

These observations on the characteristics of money growth suggest that indeed the Bundesbank flexibly deviates from the midpoint target rate in response to short-run events. Therefore, we estimate reaction function (7.14) in a first step as follows:

$$(\Delta m - \Delta m^T)_{t,44} = \underset{(3.6)}{1.02} - \underset{(-3.3)}{0.65} (\Delta p - \pi^T)_{t,44} + \underset{(2.7)}{0.21} \Delta q_{t,44}$$

$$- \underset{(1.2)}{0.19} (\Delta y - \Delta y^*)_{t,44} + \underset{(2.6)}{3.39} D_{92} \tag{7.18}$$

$\bar{R}^2 = 0.71 \quad DW = 1.29 \quad Q_4 = 2.53$

In this estimate the price level is represented by the CPI, the real exchange rate by an index of the weighted real exchange rate of the D-Mark *vis-à-vis* 18 industrialized countries, and output by real GDP.[12]

The estimate supports the conjecture that the Bundesbank deviates from the announced target growth in order to fight excess inflation and to lean against the wind of exchange rate appreciation. The size of the estimated coefficients suggests that the Bundesbank's response to such events is moderate. To test for the specific conjecture that the Bank does not respond to the business cycle, the regression includes the deviation of GDP growth from normal. The estimated coefficient is not significant at conventional significance levels, confirming our conjecture.

The estimate of the reaction function still misses a potentially important element, namely the hypothesized accommodation of perceived shocks to money demand, denoted in equation (7.14) by μ_t. Since those shocks are not directly observable, we approximate them by the residuals from log-linear estimates of the velocity of central bank money (sample period 1970–87) and of the velocity of money stock M3 (sample period 1970–94).[13] Of the first estimate we use the residuals for the period 1979–87, of the second estimate the residuals for the period 1988–94.[14] Reestimating the reaction function with this additional regressor and eliminating the insignificant business cycle variable yields

$$(\Delta m - \Delta m^T)_{t,44} = \underset{(5.6)}{0.94} - \underset{(-5.4)}{0.60} (\Delta p - \pi^T)_{t,44} + \underset{(3.5)}{0.16} \Delta q_{t,44}$$

$$+ \underset{(6.8)}{5.93} D_{92} + \underset{(5.1)}{0.59} my_t \tag{7.19}$$

$\bar{R}^2 = 0.90 \quad DW = 1.99 \quad Q_4 = 2.25$

Thus, we find that adding the proxy for money demand shocks as a regressor improves the estimate considerably. The adjusted R^2 rises from 0.71 to 0.90

Figure 7.1 Target range and money growth

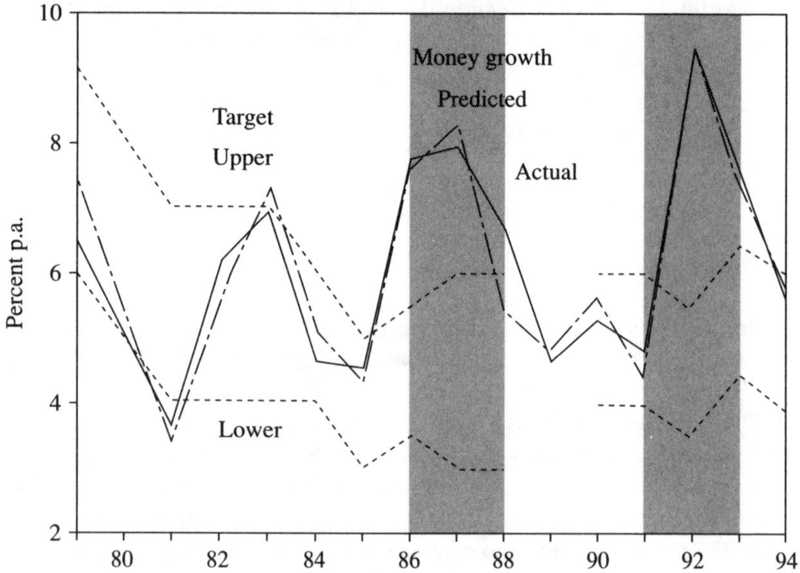

and the residuals of the regression remain well-behaved. Also note that the estimated coefficients as regards the response to excess inflation and changes in the real exchange rate do not change significantly, while the significant coefficient multiplying the proxy variable for money demand shocks has the expected positive sign and is significantly smaller than unity. This suggests that money demand shocks are not fully accommodated.[15]

Figure 7.1 shows how actual and predicted money growth, $\Delta m_{t,44}$, developed relative to the target range. The predicted values were computed from regression (7.19). They track quite well. Since 1982 money growth moves in the upper half of the target range. The two occurrences of an overshooting of the target range lasted for two to three years. The 1986–88 episode is of particular interest. As has already been mentioned, the overshooting of 1987/88 was largely due to an accommodation of shifting asset demand from deposits into currency. The preceeding dramatic jump of money growth in 1986 from 4.5 to 7.8 percent, in contrast, entirely reflects a leaning against the wind of exchange rate appreciation. The appreciation of the D-Mark in 1986 was extreme, amounting to 6.4 percent to be compared to 0.3 percent on average over the 1979–94 period. The second overshoot of 1992–93 was largely due to the Bundesbank's response to the crisis, if not breakdown, of the European Monetary System (EMS).

It remains to check on whether the announced monetary targets play the strategic role the Bundesbank ascribes to them. A basic tenet of the Bank's concept is that the target announcement provides information that impacts on the inflation expectations of the public. We test for this information effect in an indirect fashion by regressing the rate of price change alternatively on actual money growth and on the target rate of money growth. To rule out spurious regression, the money growth rates will be lagged by one year. This gives

$$\Delta p_{t,44} = \underset{(0.6)}{0.11}\Delta m_{t-1,44} \quad \overline{R}^2 = 0.42 \quad \rho = \underset{(6.4)}{0.83} \tag{7.20}$$

and

$$\Delta p_{t,44} = \underset{(2.9)}{0.55}\Delta m^T_{t-1,44} \quad \overline{R}^2 = 0.50 \quad \rho = \underset{(2.8)}{0.63} \tag{7.21}$$

where ρ is the coefficient of the AR(1)-term. The estimates indicate that in contrast to actual money growth the midpoint target rate contributes to explaining the rate of price change. Alternatively, we may regress the rate of price change on its own lag

$$\Delta p_{t,44} = \underset{(1.5)}{1.05} + \underset{(3.4)}{0.67}\Delta p_{t-1,44} \tag{7.22}$$

$$\overline{R}^2 = 0.42 \quad DW = 1.47 \quad Q_4 = 2.52$$

and add the midpoint target rate

$$\Delta p_{t,44} = \underset{(-1.9)}{-3.82} + \underset{(2.5)}{0.48}\Delta p_{t-1,44} + \underset{(2.6)}{1.05}\Delta m^T_{t,44} \tag{7.23}$$

$$\overline{R}^2 = 0.58 \quad DW = 2.11 \quad Q_4 = 0.50$$

Again we find that the midpoint target rate significantly contributes to the explanation of the rate of price change. Thus, the estimates lend support to the Bundesbank's view on the importance of target announcements.

4.2 Excess Inflation and Monetary Targets

Though inflation has been lower in Germany than in most other countries, it has been higher than the Bundesbank had desired. Measured over the sample period 1979–94, inflation averaged close to 3.2 percent, while the Bundesbank's inflation objective had been set by 0.6 percentage points lower, at 2.6 percent on average.[16] Excess inflation in the short run can be due to many factors; excess inflation in the long run, however, presupposes an excessive trend growth of the money supply.

Why has this happened? Did the excessive trend growth of money result from an upward bias in the Bundesbank's monetary target rates? To check for this, we investigate the Bank's forecast errors as regards potential output growth and the velocity trend as well as whether the current money targets were in line with the underlying average target rates.

Suppose the Bundesbank had committed no forecast errors as regards the growth rate of long-run equilibrium or normal output, Δy_t^*, and the long-run equilibrium or trend rate of change of velocity, Δv_t^*. Call the implied average target rate of money growth the full information target, $\Delta m_t^{T,FI}$. This gives

$$\Delta m_t^{T,FI} = \pi_t^T + \Delta y_t^* - \Delta v_t^* \tag{7.24}$$

or, since the trend rate of change of velocity depends on the real income elasticity of money demand, η, and the equilibrium growth rate of income,

$$\Delta m_t^{T,FI} = \pi_t^T + \eta \Delta y_t^* \tag{7.25}$$

Subtracting the full information target for average money growth from the Bundesbank's actual average target, Δm_t^T, gives the forecast error.

Table 7.3 provides the full information target rates in column 2 and the total forecast errors in column 3. The full information target rates were calculated using equation (7.25). The equilibrium rates of change of output are approximated by the actual growth rates of potential output, recently published by the Bundesbank.[17] The income elasticity of money demand was reestimated for each year from a conventional money demand function, letting the sample period run from 1960 until two years before the target year. The procedure serves to allow for gradual changes in the estimated income elasticity and for the availability of this information at the time when the Bundesbank chose a particular target rate.

The calculated total forecast errors are negative for most years, averaging –0.7 percentage points over the sample period 1979–94. Thus, we find that the average target rates were not biased upward but downward. The dominant source of the errors is a systematic underestimation of the trend decline in the velocity of money. It accounts for about 80 percent of the total forecast error, on average; see columns 4 and 5 of Table 7.3.

Next we check if the Bundesbank's midpoint target rates for current money growth, as given by column 2 of Table 7.2, were set in line with average target rates, printed in column 4 of Table 7.1. This is done by applying formula (7.12). Column 3 of Table 7.2 provides the corrected

Table 7.3 Errors in average money targets (percent p.a.)

Year	*Actual target* (1)	*Full information target* (2)	*Total error* (3) = (1)–(2)	*of which: Underestimate of* *Potential growth* (+) (4)	*Fall in velocity* (–) (5)
1979	6.5	6.7	–0.2	0.0	–0.2
1980	6.0	7.5	–1.5	–0.2	–1.3
1981	5.25	7.0	–1.7	–0.4	–1.3
1982	5.25	6.4	–1.1	–0.9	–0.2
1983	5.25	5.7	–0.5	–0.3	–0.2
1984	5.0	5.2	–0.2	0.0	–0.2
1985	4.5	4.4	0.1	0.3	–0.2
1986	4.5	4.5	–0.0	0.2	–0.2
1987	4.5	4.2	0.3	0.5	–0.2
1988	4.5	5.8	–1.3	–0.5	–0.8
1989	4.75	5.2	–0.5	0.1	–0.6
1990	5.0	6.2	–1.2	–0.3	–0.9
1991	5.0	6.5	–1.5	–0.5	–1.0
1992	5.0	6.7	–1.7	–0.5	–1.2
1993	6.0	5.8	0.2	0.5	–0.3
1994	5.5	5.6	–0.1	0.1	–0.2
Mean	5.15	5.85	–0.69	–0.13	–0.56

midpoint target rates. For most years we find that the announced target rate for current money growth did not adequately reflect the Bundesbank's average target rate. In ten out of sixteen years the announced current target rate was set too high relative to what the Bundesbank had planned for average money growth. On average over the sample period 1979–94 the upward bias amounts to 0.8 percentage points; see column 4 of Table 7.2.

In sum, we find that the two types of error almost cancel each other out over the sample period. While the average target rate was set too low, by 0.7 percentage points per year, this was compensated for by setting the announced target rate of current money growth too high, by 0.8 percentage points per year. It follows that the excess inflation mentioned above of 0.6 percentage points per year was not enforced by excessive targets for current money growth.

Given that the targets for current money growth were about right on average, the excess inflation must be have been fueled by faster money growth than was targeted. As a matter of fact, average annual money growth, as given by column 5 of Table 7.1, exceeded the average full information target (5.85 percent) by 0.45 percentage points per year. The excess of current (fourth quarter to fourth quarter) money growth over the current midpoint target, for comparison, amounted to 0.9 percentage points per year; see columns 2 and 5 of Table 7.2. Finally, note that the respective estimate of the constant in the reaction function (7.19) does not significantly differ from the annual excess inflation of 0.6 percentage points.

5 IS THE DEMAND FUNCTION OF THE TARGET AGGREGATE STABLE?

Monetary targeting requires a stable money demand function for the target aggregate. Early studies of German money demand concluded that the demand for money functions of money stocks M1 and M3 were stable, except for the possibility of a break in 1973.[18] More recent studies with data that include the German unification of 1990 present conflicting results. For example, von Hagen (1993) finds that the stability of the money demand function must be rejected for money stock M3 but not for M1, while Hansen and Kim (1995) find a break for both aggregates in 1990.

Since the Bundesbank used the central bank money stock CBM as a target aggregate until 1987 and money stock M3 thereafter, we estimate with annual data log-linear error-correction models (ECM) for the real demand of both aggregates as functions of real GDP, y, and a long-term public bond yield, r. By means of Augmented Dickey–Fuller tests it can be shown for both monetary aggregates, deflated by the GDP deflator, that they are integrated variables of order one with real GDP.

For the (log of the) real central bank money stock, denoted by cbm, we estimate with data of 1960–87

$$\begin{aligned}(1 - \underset{(2.0)}{0.40}L^1)\Delta cbm_t &= \underset{(2.1)}{0.01} + \underset{(2.7)}{0.59}(1 - \underset{(2.6)}{0.71}L^1)\Delta y_t - \underset{(2.6)}{0.010}\Delta r_t \\ &\quad - \underset{(-4.5)}{0.93}\,[cbm_{t-1} + \underset{(28.0)}{2.92} - \underset{(75.6)}{1.12}\,y_{t-1} \\ &\quad + \underset{(6.4)}{0.019}r_{t-1}] + v_t \qquad (7.26)\end{aligned}$$

$\overline{R}^2 = 0.58 \quad DW = 1.73 \quad Q_4 = 2.67$

Breaktest 1973: $F = 5.27^*$ Log likelihood = 30.73*
1978: $F = 0.53$ Log likelihood = 5.32

We first note that the adjustment coefficient multiplying the error-correction term is rather high due to the use of annual data. The null hypothesis of no cointegration is rejected at the 5 percent significance level according to the critical values of McKinnon's table (critical t-value: –4.07). Applying the Chow break test, we find that a break cannot be rejected at the 5 percent level of significance for 1973, confirming the results of the early literature.

Next we estimate an ECM for the real demand for M3. The sample period is 1970–94. The time series for M3 and GDP include East Germany from 1990. To account for unification-induced shifts we use two dummies in the cointegration equation denoted by D_{90} and D_{91-94}; the dummies have value one in the years indicated and zero otherwise. This gives

$$\begin{aligned}\Delta m_{3,t} = {} & \underset{(3.1)}{0.01} + \underset{(9.1)}{0.97}\Delta y_t - \underset{(3.1)}{0.009}\Delta r + u_t - \underset{(4.9)}{0.95}\,[m_{3,t-1} + \underset{(18.1)}{5.07} \\ & - \underset{(44.9)}{1.59}\,y_{t-1} + \underset{(3.8)}{0.012}r_{t-1} + \underset{(3.3)}{0.08}D_{90} + \underset{(6.5)}{0.11}D_{91-94}]\end{aligned} \tag{7.27}$$

$\overline{R}^2 = 0.81 \quad DW = 1.94 \quad Q_4 = 4.04$

Breaktest 1978: $F = 0.17$ Log likelihood = 1.00
1990: $F = 2.93^*$ Log likelihood = 13.21*

Again we find a high adjustment coefficient. In this case the null of no cointegration is rejected at the 10 percent level of significance only (critical value: –4.6). The Chow break test rejects a break for 1978. However, not unexpectedly we cannot reject a break at the 5 percent level of significance for the unification year 1990.

Thus, our estimates with annual data support the results of von Hagen (1993) and of Hansen and Kim (1995) who used quarterly data. Apparently, the German unification induced a shift in the money demand function for M3. The two dummies used in regression (7.27) above already indicate that the stock demand for M3 has shifted downward by a sizeable amount. To further investigate this shift, we replace the two dummies by a structural break variable. The variable is defined as the product of GDP of total Germany times a dummy D_{90-94}; the dummy is set at value one for the years indicated and at zero otherwise. Reestimating the cointegration equation for the sample period 1970–94 gives

$$m_{3,t} = \underset{(-17.6)}{-5.10} + \underset{(43.4)}{1.59}\,y_t - \underset{(-3.4)}{0.01}r - \underset{(-6.1)}{0.01}(y_t * D_{90-94}) \tag{7.28}$$

$\overline{R}^2 = 0.99 \quad DW = 2.49 \quad Q_4 = 9.37$

Figure 7.2 Actual and predicted real balances M3

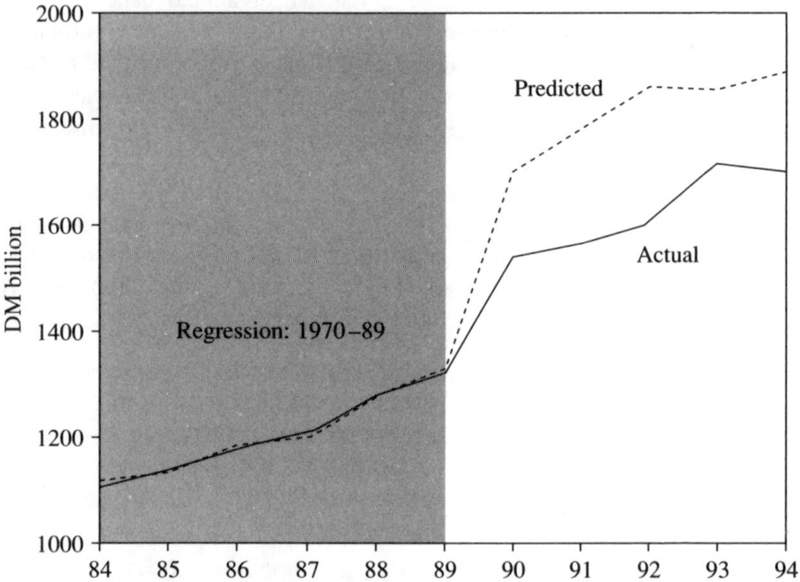

The estimate shows that the income elasticity of stock demand is significantly lower since German unification. Note that a similar check for a significant change in the interest elasticity is negative.

The size of the downward shift is given by the product of the structural break variable times the estimated coefficient. Averaging over the years 1990–94, we find that the downward shift amounts to 9.7 percent.

An alternative approach for estimating the size of the shift is estimating regression (7.28) for the shorter sample period 1970–89 and computing the out-of-sample predictions with the GDP data for united Germany. Figure 7.2 shows that since 1990 real M3 balances are "missing" and Figure 7.3 indicates that the downward shift amounts to about 10 percent.

The question is what this large shift does reflect. To some extent it may result from biased national accounting. According to national accounts, East German GDP equals about 8 percent of West German GDP. If the true relative size is 2 instead of 8 percent, the estimated downward shift of money demand vanishes. However, East German GDP cannot be that small. Therefore, we conclude that the observed downward shift of the stock demand for real M3 balances reflects a lower income elasticity of East German money demand.[19] This conjecture is in line with estimate

Figure 7.3 Prediction errors of the real demand for M3

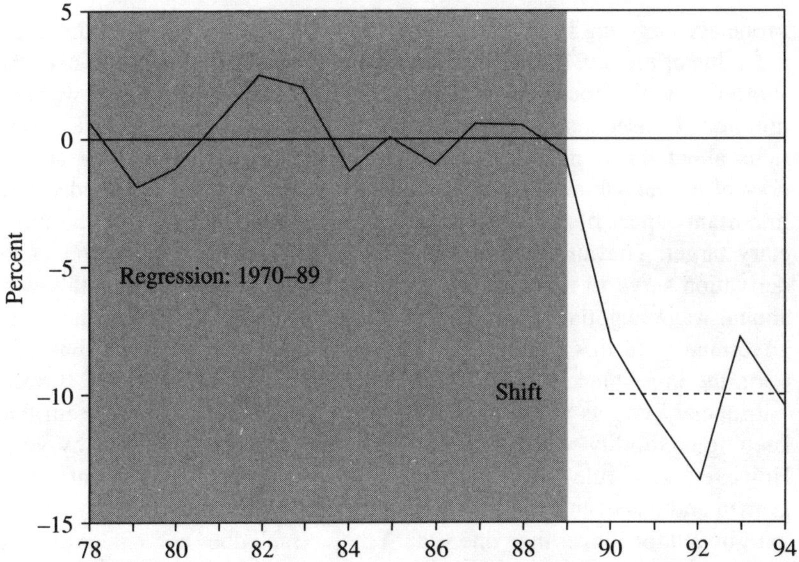

(7.28). Finally, it may be noted that the stock demand function for the more narrow aggregate M1 has shifted too since unification, though in the opposite direction. To be sure, an upward shift of the demand function for M1 is compatible with a downward shift of the demand function for the more broadly defined M3. All it needs is the following rank order of income elasticities of money demand, where superscripts *W* and *E* denote West and East Germany, respectively:

$$\varepsilon(m_1, y)^W < \varepsilon(m_1, y)^E \leq \varepsilon(m_3, y)^E < \varepsilon(m_3, y)^W$$

It reflects the fact that in comparison to West Germans East Germans still find cash and demand deposits more attractive than time deposits.

The apparently different allocation of balances between M1 and the additional components of M3 in the eastern region of Germany will not stay for ever but vanish over time, though presumably very slowly as it is likely to depend on the level of wealth. Consequently, the estimated downward shift of M3 demand for united Germany will decline gradually. This leads us to conclude that the reliability of the Bundesbank's annual monetary targeting of M3 has not seriously been impaired by the German unification.

6 CONCLUDING REMARKS

Monetary targeting is an intermediate approach toward securing the internal value of money. Rather than promising the control of inflation over the shorter run, the focus is on setting the monetary frame for low trend inflation. Consequently, the monetary targets are derived from assumptions about the trend rates of change of the velocity of money and of normal output while changes of capacity utilization are disregarded. An important aspect of the concept is the public announcement of the monetary target. The information about the target and the explanation of its derivation serve to influence the public's inflation expectations, this way annual wage negotiations as well as budget planning at different levels of government. In this chapter, we have provided some evidence that supports the importance of target announcement as an informational device.

Monetary targets are useless if they are not credible. It may seem that keeping credibility requires meeting the announced targets year by year. However, as a rule the Bundesbank deviates from the midpoint target growth and has even overshot the target range twice since 1979 by a large margin and for longer than one year. Yet the Bank does not appear to have lost its credibility, either domestically or internationally. This may be puzzling. The explanation, we believe, is twofold.

First, in the short run the Bundesbank does not follow a policy of unpredictable pure discretion but a policy of rule-based discretion. Since the early 1980s the Bundesbank has explained to the public that its concept of monetary targeting includes deviating from the midpoint target in response to excess inflation, appreciation of the D-Mark and perceived shocks to money demand. We have estimated a reaction function that reflects this "systematic discretion." Second, by legal set-up the Bundesbank is a relatively independent central bank and the public perceives that the central bankers are eager to keep this independence from government. There is a continous flow of confirming evidence as the Bundesbank comments in public on budget policies as well as on issues of the government's general economic policies. Of course, what counts in the last analysis is keeping trend inflation low.

All in all, this has been achieved. It does not mean that the Bundesbank has made no mistakes, or that the practice of monetary targeting cannot be improved upon. We have presented some evidence that the targets for monetary growth have not always been adequate. Yet, it is to be acknowledged that our investigation bypasses any psychological consideration that may have played a conditioning role at the time when a specific target had to be set. In actual policymaking such considerations may be justified provided they do not serve as an excuse for letting money growth getting out of hand in the long run.

Notes

1. See Deutsche Bundesbank (1992).
2. See Deutsche Bundesbank, *Report for the Year 1984*, p. 40.
3. For details see Deutsche Bundesbank (1995).
4. Deutsche Bundesbank, *Report for the Year 1975*, p. 11. For an early critique of this weighting scheme see Neumann (1975).
5. Deutsche Bundesbank, *Report for the Year 1988*, p. 37. A detailed discussion of target aggregate M3 is provided by Deutsche Bundesbank (1988).
6. Deutsche Bundesbank, *Report for the Year 1980*, p. 32.
7. Deutsche Bundesbank, *Report for the Year 1980*, p. 31.
8. Deutsche Bundesbank, *Report for the Year 1991*, p. 45.
9. Deutsche Bundesbank, *Report for the Year 1982*, p. 30.
10. Deutsche Bundesbank, *Report for the Year 1984*, p. 39.
11. Extending the currency area to East Germany raised the money stock M3 by 14.6 percent in 1990.
12. Note that the expected equilibrium rate of change of the real exchange rate has been set at zero. The sample mean of the actual rate of change is –0.3 percent.
13. Denoting the long-term yield of government bonds by r, the log of GDP by y, the log of the velocity of central bank money by v^{CBM}, and the log of the velocity of M3 by v^{M3}, the following estimates served for deriving the proxy variable of money demand shocks:

    1970–1987:

    $$v_t^{CBM} = \underset{(12.3)}{3.73} - \underset{(-5.7)}{0.22y_t} + \underset{(4.1)}{0.013r}$$

    $$\overline{R}^2 = 0.83 \quad DW = 2.16 \quad Q_4 = 5.63$$

    1970–1994:

    $$v_t^{M3} = \underset{(18.2)}{5.09} - \underset{(-16.7)}{0.59y} + \underset{(3.8)}{0.012r} + \underset{(3.3)}{0.08D_{90}} + \underset{(6.5)}{0.11D_{91-94}}$$

    $$\overline{R}^2 = 0.97 \quad DW = 2.39 \quad Q_4 = 5.47$$

    D_{90} and D_{91-94} are dummy variables to account for a unification-induced change in the level of velocity.
14. Note that the residuals have been multiplied by –1.
15. As a note of caution, our proxy variable is likely to mix in an unknown fashion shocks to money demand and innovations in the money supply.
16. As it happens, the result is the same for the CPI as well as for the GNP deflator.
17. See Deutsche Bundesbank, *Monthly Report*, August 1995, p. 42.
18. See OECD (1979), Boughton (1981), Neumann (1983), Buscher (1984), Neumann and von Hagen (1987).

19. Given the relative size of the East German GDP, an elasticity of 1.5 is consistent with estimate (7.28).

References

Boughton, J.M. (1981) "Recent Instability of the Demand for Money: An International Perspective," *Southern Economic Journal*, 47, pp. 579–97.

Buscher, H.S. (1984) "The Stability of the West German Demand for Money: 1965–82," *Weltwirtschaftliches Archiv*, 120, pp. 256–78.

Deutsche Bundesbank, *Annual Report*, various.

Deutsche Bundesbank (1988) "Methodological Notes on the Monetary Target Variable 'M3'," *Monthly Reports*, 40 (March), pp. 18–24.

Deutsche Bundesbank (1992) "The Correlation Between Monetary Growth and Price Movements in the Federal Republic of Germany," *Monthly Reports*, 44 (January), pp. 20–8.

Deutsche Bundesbank (1995) "Production Potential in Germany and Its Determinants," *Monthly Reports*, 47 (August), pp. 39–54.

Hagen, J. von (1993) "Monetary Union, Money Demand and Money Supply," *European Economic Review*, 37, pp. 803–27.

Hagen, J. von (1995) "Inflation and Monetary Targeting in Germany," in L. Leiderman and L.E.O. Svensson (eds), *Inflation Targeting* (London: CEPR).

Hagen, J. von and Neumann, M.J.M. (1988) "Instability versus Dynamics: A Study in West German Demand for Money," *Journal of Macroeconomics*, 10, pp. 327–49.

Hallman, J.J., Porter, R.D. and Small, D. (1991) "Is the Price Level Tied to the M2 Monetary Aggregate in the Long Run?," *American Economic Review*, 81, pp. 841–58.

Hansen, G. and Kim, J.R. (1995) "The Stability of German Money Demand: Tests of the Cointegration Relation," *Weltwirtschaftliches Archiv*, 131, pp. 286–301.

Neumann, M.J.M. (1975) "Konstrukte der Zentralbankgeldmenge," *Kredit und Kapital*, 8, pp. 317–45.

Neumann, M.J.M. (1983) "Stabilität von Geldnachfrage und Geldpolitik," *Wirtschaftsdienst*, 63, pp. 415–20.

Neumann, M.J.M. and Hagen, J. von (1993) "Monetary Policy in Germany," in M.U. Fratianni and D. Salvatore (eds), *Monetary Policy in Developed Economies* (Westport, Conn.: Greenwood Press), pp. 299–334.

Neumann, M.J.M. and Hagen, J. von (1995) "The Strategy of Monetary Targeting: Can the German Experience Provide a Model for the ECB?," paper presented at the CEPR conference "What Monetary Policy for the European Central Bank?," Frankfurt.

OECD (1983) "Demand for Money in Major OECD Countries," *OECD Economic Outlook*, Occasional Studies.

Comments*

William R. White

Neumann's chapter is a very nice combination of both sophisticated and simple econometric work, well blended with theory, institutional knowledge, and a nice recap of the historical experience of monetary targeting in Germany. Moreover, he arrives at some neat and controversial conclusions. Over the past decade, the Bundesbank has systematically allowed a higher rate of inflation than its targeted rate (3.2 versus 2.6 percent). Moreover, this overshoot has not been a result of technical or economic misjudgments leading the Bundesbank systematically to set monetary targets too high to be compatible with its inflation target. There were such misjudgments, but luckily they were offsetting. Rather, the deviation has been entirely a consequence of the Bundesbank missing the monetary targets it has set for itself. And finally, in spite of missing both its inflation objective and its monetary objective, Neumann contends that the Bundesbank has nevertheless managed to retain its credibility, in the sense that the "target announcement provides information that impacts on the inflation expectations of the public" (p. 189). In short, the Neumann chapter provides the framework for a lively discussion of recent German monetary policy.

To say that I found the chapter stimulating is not to say that I agreed with all parts of it. Let me begin with a quibble before moving on to more substantial issues. At the beginning of his chapter, Neumann contrasts countries pursuing direct inflation targeting with those which have reverted to pure discretion. This is not a proper contrast, because the first statement has to do with the choice of objectives and the second has to do with the choice of means or instruments. I would contend that the past decade has been characterized by more and more central banks signing on to the idea that domestic price stability should be the primary objective of monetary policy. I would also contend that the past decade or so has been characterized by a growing eclecticism as to how that single objective should be best achieved; an eclecticism arising from ongoing shifts in the demand for money function in many countries and increasing difficulties in maintaining fixed exchange rate relationships given developments in international financial markets. Paradoxically, the conduct of monetary policy now depends more on rules *and* discretion than it ever did before.

* I would like to thank Renato Filosa, Gabriele Galati and especially Stefan Gerlach for their comments.

In raising issues concerning the analytical background of monetary targeting, I am conscious that Neumann may be attempting simply to describe the analytical framework which has historically underpinned German monetary targeting. While I am not expert enough to debate the facts of German monetary history, I must say that I find the traditional equation of exchange a very unsatisfactory framework for expounding the advantages of monetary targeting. On the one hand, it does indicate an important attribute of such targeting; namely, that there will be no long-run inflationary bias provided that the central bank has no longer-run bias in its calculations of economic potential or velocity and that the central bank succeeds in hitting its monetary targets. On the other hand, another important advantage of monetary targeting is not highlighted by the equation of exchange; namely, the way in which such targeting provides an automatic counter-cyclical movement of interest rates in the face of demand shocks. This point was made forcefully by John Taylor in chapter 2 of this volume. In effect, when the *IS* curve moves, controlling *M* means sliding up or down the *LM* curve to resist that movement. This is not an inconsequential omission. Central banks who pursue the objective of price stability are commonly accused of neglecting the cycle and of not caring about unemployment. This is absolutely not the case, even if fine-tuning of the unemployment rate has been replaced by a kind of automatic pilot. It would be nice if the analytic framework underlying monetary targeting made all the advantages clear.[1]

Turning to the section on deriving the monetary target, one is struck first by the alleged willingness of the Bundesbank to accept that there is a 2-percentage-point bias in the annual growth rate of the CPI. This strikes me as a large number in light of Canadian estimates that the bias is of the order of one half of 1 percent in that country. Surely German statisticians are as accurate as Canadian ones! But more seriously, if it is agreed that there is an initial bias in sampling procedures, would one not expect this to be either corrected over time or some kind of adjustment put in place? After all, given the indexing of social and other programs, the failure to make such adjustments is very costly to the government. The upshot of this line of thought is that one must be increasingly careful over time not to assume an element of bias which is not there.

It is also worth noting another question pertaining to the derivation of monetary targets which is nowhere discussed in this chapter; namely, how the German authorities decided on the pace with which the rate of growth of monetary aggregates would be brought down over time (from 4.5 percent to 2 percent). If inflation is at desired levels, then the desired rate of money growth can be worked out rather mechanically given assumptions about velocity and potential growth. However, if inflation is not initially at desired levels, then deciding on how fast the rate of growth of money should decelerate demands answers to all the nasty questions that monetary targeting is supposed to avoid. David Laidler made a similar point in chapter 4 of this volume: monetary targeting does not provide a very useful policy framework when one is initially far away from equilibrium.

In the section on reacting to short-term events, Neumann states that the Bundesbank "may have to deviate from the midpoint target range to account for short-term events." However, this assertion immediately raises a question: at what point do the deviations become so great that it is no longer appropriate to call it monetary targeting? Indeed, it is interesting to note in this regard that, in his equation (7.16), Neumann fails to find any relationship between actual and target growth rates of money in Germany. Since this evidence is by no means conclusive,[2] I return to this issue below.

Most of the remainder of this section, as well as the following one, has to do with the Bundesbank's reaction function which is specified such that movements in certain independent variables cause the Bundesbank to allow (generate) deviations in money growth from the specified target growth rate. I have concerns at both the conceptual and empirical level. Dealing first with conceptual issues, how can the money stock be the dependent variable when the Bundesbank does not control it directly? Neumann notes this, but in my view does not take the point to its logical conclusion. The dependent variable under the Bundesbank's control is the level of short-term interest rates, which may or may not respond to deviations in money growth rates from target. Indeed, viewed from this perspective, it is not at all clear that the Bundesbank could achieve close control over the quantity of money even if it wanted to do so. Renormalizing equation (7.24), a demand function for real money, implies very large interest rate movements indeed to compensate for even relatively small movements in the other independent variables.[3]

I also question the structural specification of equation (7.14), his basic reaction function. What it says is that when inflation exceeds the target, the rate of growth of the money stock will be reduced below the target. Why? The whole purpose of having a monetary target is that when inflation rises above target there will be an automatic counter-cyclical movement in interest rates (and potentially the exchange rate), the magnitude of which will depend on the interest elasticity of the monetary aggregate being targeted. If the elasticity is so large that the resulting interest rate movements are judged inadequate, then one might countenance specifying a counter-cyclical monetary target as well. However, in Germany, the problem seems more likely to be too little elasticity of demand rather than too much, as I noted just a moment ago. At the very least, one might ask the Bundesbank how it decided on the size of the parameters it chooses to put in the operating version of equation (7.14), if indeed it is the reaction function it is using.

I also have some concerns about the estimated version of this reaction function (equation (7.18)), the elucidation of which will bring us back to the question of which variable the Bundesbank is targeting. The first point to note about equation (7.18) is that it imposes an implicit constraint of one on the target money growth rate. Reestimating the equation (my equation (1); see Appendix) indicates that the constraint is far from being satisfied (0.23 is significantly different from one but not significantly different from zero) and that the monetary target should be removed from the equation (my equation (2)). The indications from this latter equation is that the Bundesbank responds to excess demand of whatever sort, but not to the quantity of money as such.

Given my stated concern about using a monetary aggregate as the dependent variable in the reaction function, I replaced it with a short-term interest rate. My equation (3) shows that there is no reaction to deviations of money growth from the specified target growth rate. However, my equation (4) indicates that the Bundesbank reacts very strongly to deviations of inflation from the target inflation rate; indeed, given that the parameter of this variable is greater than one, it seems clear that the Bundesbank is prepared to raise real rates quite sharply in such conditions. Equation (5) is a variation on equation (4) and includes the "gap" term in levels rather than growth rates. This gives a specification which is very similar to the "Taylor rule" which has been used by John Taylor of Stanford to predict the Fed's short-term behavior. Equation (5) indicates that the Bundesbank's reaction function can indeed be described quite well in this fashion, further supporting the other econometric evidence above which implies that "targeting" may be a rather strong term to describe the Bundesbank's approach to broad money.

Turning now to the impact of the target announcement on inflation, Neumann's equation (7.20) is interpreted by him as indicating that the announcement of a monetary target affects inflationary expectations because it affects actual inflation in the following year. Again, there are some conceptual and empirical problems. At the conceptual level, Neumann admits that his use of *actual* inflation is a long way away from testing the maintained hypothesis that inflationary *expectations* are influenced by announcement effects about the money supply. Indeed this proposition could only be tested given direct measures of inflationary expectations, say drawn from indexed bond yields as in the United Kingdom.

What should also be a testable proposition is that announcement effects about monetary targets have effects on inflationary expectations in addition to the announcement effects implicit in inflation targets. The Bundesbank seems to assert that this is so, and it may very well be right in spite of David Laidler's assertions to the contrary (chapter 4, this volume). There is no question that the ongoing and regular need to comment on the behavior of the targeted money supply keeps the vigilance of the Bundesbank constantly in the public eye. However, one problem with having both a final objective and an intermediate objective is the danger of confusing the public when the latter has to be sacrificed to the former, say given a shift in the demand for money. When countries have an announced exchange rate target, in addition to announced targets for both inflation and money growth, the scope for compromise and confusion is likely to be greater still.

At the empirical level, it is also worth noting that equation (7.20) is not very robust. Adding in a constant term renders insignificant the target money growth variable, while adding the lagged rate of inflation makes both actual and targeted money growth insignificant (see my equation (6)). Given the very indirect nature of the test being conducted, this is perhaps not very surprising.

The decomposition carried out in the section on excess inflation and monetary targets was very neatly done and leads to some conclusions that are not very flattering to the Bundesbank. In effect, Neumann asserts that the Bundesbank has apparently made systematic technical errors, which happily have turned out to be offsetting. Moreover, the Bundesbank has also systematically missed its monetary targets with the expected implications for inflation. While I have no technical reason to dispute these results, I hope you will understand if I say that I have no wish to endorse them either.

Finally, Neumann asks whether the demand function of the target aggregate is stable, and in response he notes a sharp downward shift in 1990. I found this puzzling because I thought the suggested break was in an upward direction. I also found puzzling the suggestion that the identified break might reflect an East German preference for M1, given that M1 is internal to M3. However, what I did welcome was Neumann's suggestion that a once-and-for-all shift in the demand for money need not prevent that function from being used again for purposes of monetary targeting. And I would add a further, related point. Just because the demand function for a monetary aggregate is *statistically* stable, it may still not be a suitable candidate for monetary targeting. Given a badly fitting function, which is *instability* in a different sense, it may be practically impossible to reject the hypothesis of parametric stability. However, that same bad fit will imply that movements in the aggregate contain little or no reliable information as to whether changing spending patterns call for (i.e. indicate) a change in interest rates. While an aggregate possessing such variability should not be used as an indicator for setting policy instruments in the short term, it may nevertheless have a useful role to play in both anchoring monetary policy and explaining policy over the longer run. As I understand it, these latter two objectives figure prominently in the successful conduct of monetary targeting in Germany.

Appendix: Annual Data, 1979–94

$$\Delta m_t = \underset{(4.5)}{5.01} + \underset{(1.1)}{0.23}\Delta m_t^T - \underset{(2.3)}{0.38}(\Delta p - \pi^T)_i - \underset{(1.6)}{0.16}(\Delta y - \Delta y^*)_t$$
$$+ \underset{(4.6)}{0.22}\Delta q_t + \underset{(3.7)}{3.00}D_{92} \qquad (1)$$

$\overline{R}^2 = 0.82 \quad DW = 1.96$

$$\Delta m_t = \underset{(33.2)}{6.17} - \underset{(2.0)}{0.32}(\Delta p - \pi^T)_t - \underset{(1.7)}{0.16}(\Delta y - \Delta y^*)_t + \underset{(4.6)}{0.22}\Delta q_t + \underset{(3.6)}{2.77}D_{92} \qquad (2)$$

$\overline{R}^2 = 0.81 \quad DW = 1.76$

$$r_t = \underset{(13.4)}{6.30} - \underset{(0.6)}{0.13}(\Delta m - \Delta m^T)_t + \underset{(4.1)}{1.31}(\Delta p - \pi^T)_t + \underset{(1.8)}{0.37}(\Delta y - \Delta y^*)_t \qquad (3)$$

$\overline{R}^2 = 0.59 \quad DW = 1.67$

$$r_t = \underset{(16.6)}{6.12} + \underset{(5.1)}{1.41}(\Delta p - \pi^T)_t + \underset{(2.2)}{0.41}(\Delta y - \Delta y^*)_t \qquad (4)$$

$\overline{R}^2 = 0.61 \quad DW = 1.58$

$$r_t = \underset{(17.8)}{7.10} + \underset{(2.8)}{0.66}(\Delta p - \pi^T)_t + \underset{(3.7)}{0.43}(y - y^*)_t \qquad (5)$$

$\overline{R}^2 = 0.74 \quad DW = 1.42$

$$\Delta p_t = \underset{(0.1)}{-0.25} + \underset{(0.6)}{0.12}\Delta m_{t-1} + \underset{(4.3)}{0.82}\Delta p_{t-1} \qquad (6)$$

$\overline{R}^2 = 0.57 \quad DW = 1.14$

Note: *t*-statistics in parentheses.
Sources: All data from von Hagen (1995), except r_t (day-to-day money, average for December), *y* (real GDP) and *y** (production potential) from Deutsche Bundesbank, *Monthly Report*, August 1995.

Notes

1. The equation of exchange approach implies that demand shocks lead to deflation rather than inflation. The increased demand for real balances induced by the needs of trade can be met only by price decreases if both the money stock and velocity are constant. In the real world of course, a demand shock would be met by an increase in velocity reflecting both increased income and higher interest rates. Indeed, in the limit, the increase would likely be so great as to imply increases in prices in the short term given unchanged money. Perhaps the fundamental point here is that the equation of exchange is not a good starting point for analysing short-run phenomena simply because velocity varies so much in the short run.
2. Milton Friedman most famously noted that an absence of correlation does not imply a lack of causation when he described the empirical relationship between inflation (subject to random shocks) and targeted money. In the same vein, James Tobin noted that correlation does not necessarily imply causation (*post hoc, ergo propter hoc*).
3. Note that the interest rate enters only with a lag and that it is a long-term interest rate which, of course, is outside the control of the central bank. On the basis of traditional relationships, the short rate would have to move twice as much as the needed change in the long rate to effect desired changes in the growth rate of money.

Reference

Hagen, J. von (1995) "Inflation and Money Targeting in Germany," in L. Leiderman and L.E.O. Svensson (eds), *Inflation Targeting* (London: CEPR).

Comments

Jerry L. Jordan

Neumann describes in a thorough, yet succinct, manner how monetary targeting is practiced by the Bundesbank. Namely, the Bundesbank's concept is an "intermediate approach to securing the internal value of money." Because the Bundesbank is renowned for its success in safeguarding the D-mark, it is a valuable exercise to analyze the procedure underlying this success. Neumann has done this both precisely and effectively.

What, then, are the conditions that explain the Bundesbank's success? Is it monetary targeting *per se*? Some readers of Neumann's chapter might reasonably infer that because monetary targeting has been a successful approach in Germany, other central banks can secure the value of their own currencies if they too adopt monetary targeting. One might thus conclude that monetary targeting is a sufficient, and perhaps necessary, condition for maintaining the purchasing power of money.

Two important and probably more fundamental conditions have characterized the German monetary policy regime over the past two decades, however. First, the Bundesbank's relative success has been associated with a *genuine, well-defined, and widely supported* commitment to the *primary objective* of price stability. One implicit hypothesis is the necessity of this commitment to the primacy of the price objective. If you don't know where you are going, it clearly doesn't matter how you get there.

Second, the Bundesbank's commitment to monetary targeting was an internally generated decision. Does the success of monetary targeting depend on whether a central bank chooses it or, as was the case in the United States, has it imposed? In a similar vein, would an internally generated objective of price stability be sufficient for its own success? If you do know where you are going, it may not matter how you get there.

At the heart of these matters is the issue of credibility. Neumann suggests that credibility arises from a practice that is ultimately consistent with price stability, yet is flexible enough to respond to short-run events that do not interfere with achieving the primary objective. What are the key features that account for the credibility enjoyed by the Bundesbank? Is monetary targeting the defining ingredient? Or is it the mandate of section 12 of the Bundesbank Act?

To address these questions, it is useful to compare and contrast the Bundesbank's monetary targeting experience with that of the Federal

Reserve. Interestingly, the target formulation process and associated problems Neumann describes are in many ways strikingly similar to the practice and experience of the Federal Reserve from the early 1970s until 1993. Analyzing the different ways that monetary targeting evolved in the two countries provides some valuable lessons – particularly for the success of monetary union in Europe.

1 THE MONETARY TARGETING EXPERIENCE

Monetary targeting began in Germany around the same time it did in the United States – the mid-1970s. In Germany, monetary targeting was initiated *internally* by the Bundesbank. Neumann highlights a critical role of the language in the Bundesbank Act, which stipulates that the Bundesbank shall support the "general economic policy of the government, *provided that doing so is compatible with the predominate mandate*," that is, to "*safeguard the currency*" (italics added). Thus, the Bundesbank Act leaves no doubt about the priority of policy objectives.

Although the Federal Reserve monitored money growth in the early 1970s, US monetary targeting was not formalized until 1975, when Congress passed a Concurrent Resolution on Monetary Policy (CR 133) requiring "numerical target ranges with respect to rates of growth of monetary and credit aggregates." According to one analyst, then Fed Chairman Arthur Burns resisted this course, claiming "such targets would be a straitjacket, and we could damage our country" (Wells, 1994, p. 155). Thus, unlike the case in Germany, monetary targeting was initially mandated by the legislature and opposed by the central bank. Furthermore, neither the Federal Reserve nor Congress was willing to identify the protection of the purchasing power of money as the primary objective of monetary policy.

Despite an inflation rate of about 7 percent, the primary concern of US economic policy in the mid-1970s was "stimulating growth and reducing unemployment." The notion of a tradeoff between inflation and output was widely accepted – even in the long run, according to some. One might argue that as long as there is a perceived tradeoff, no credible commitment to price stability is possible. Thus, it seems clear that the apparent failure of monetary targeting in the United States in the 1970s was ultimately due to a lack of commitment on the part of both the public and policymakers to maintain the purchasing power of the dollar.

The predominance of the tradeoff paradigm in US policy deliberations still persists. It accounts for the poor rhetoric associated with explanations of US monetary policy decisions. In contrast, the Bundesbank neither explains its actions in terms of sacrificed output nor indicates that standards of living need to be depressed for a greater good. Neither does the Bundesbank's rhetoric imply that the unemployment rate must rise in order to reduce inflation, suggesting that there are too many people working, earning an income, and supporting their families.

Moreover, the Bundesbank's Minister of Finance did not publicly advocate reducing the external value of the currency, as was the case in the United States in the late 1970s. This situation, of course, was followed (happily) by strong support for increasing the external value of currency and reducing domestic inflation in the early 1980s and then by a well-publicized policy to reduce the external value of the currency in 1985.

2 ISSUES OF CREDIBILITY

One aspect of Neumann's chapter that deserves more emphasis is how well the Bundesbank has dealt with credibility. Neumann indicates that "the basic idea of the Bundesbank's targeting approach is to influence the public's inflation expectations" (p. 183). Although he argues that the Bundesbank's targeting approach does not restrict the Bank from deviating from the midpoint target rate, Neumann stresses that the longer-term curbing of the money stock expansion is essential for safeguarding the currency. The idea is not explicitly stated, but we are left with the impression that the Bundesbank's credibility could not have been achieved without an announced monetary target consistent with price stability.

One might conjecture that monetary targeting is more successful in Germany because money demand is more stable there. This is clearly not true. Historically, the experiences with monetary aggregates in Germany and the United States are strikingly similar. For example, both central banks initially placed emphasis on narrow measures of money (the base in Germany and M1 in the United States) only to move to broader measures in the face of velocity shifts. But the broader measures also present problems of interpretation regarding velocity.

Dealing with "shifts in velocity" gets at the heart of the credibility issue. As Neumann illustrates in his Figure 7.3, unification had a substantial impact on estimated M3 demand.[1] He suggests this was essentially a problem of choosing the right scale variable. In principle, M3 demand is determined by wealth (that is, permanent income). Presumably, as wealth rises in Germany's eastern regions, the effects on both estimated M3 demand and measured velocity will vanish.

All of this seems reasonable. However, an alternative conjecture seems equally plausible. Suppose unification posed a threat to the credibility of the Bundesbank's commitment to a non-inflationary monetary policy. Might not holders of M3 in the former West Germany have reduced desired levels of M3 balances in anticipation of higher inflation? That is, an increase in inflation expectations would have reduced M3 demand and raised M3 velocity. Under this scenario, any attempt to maintain M3 growth at its previous rates would clearly be inflationary. What is more, even a slowdown in M3 growth could accommodate an acceleration in the price level. This is the obverse of the well-known paradox identified by Michael Parkin.[2]

The point here is that a central bank must be careful when attributing shifts in velocity to simple changes in money demand. The implications for velocity also depend on the credibility of the policy. These implications can be important.

Although Neumann presents evidence that German monetary targets have not always been attained, his analysis maintains that the targets are important for credibility. One might question whether the source of this credibility is monetary targeting *per se*. The evidence embodied in his estimates of the Bundesbank's reaction function indicate that Bundesbank policy actions are not affected by the state of the business cycle. That is, there is little or no evidence that the Bundesbank systematically reacts to short-run movements in output growth.

3 IMPLICATIONS FOR MONETARY UNION

The issues I have been discussing are particularly relevant for monetary union. One might question whether the conditions that fostered successful monetary targeting in Germany will prevail in the post-unification period. Can monetary union survive without a mandate for a price stability objective such as that specified in Section 12 of the Bundesbank Act? How would the new monetary authority integrate money demand? The problem of specifying a monetary target for a single currency would pale in comparison to the Bundesbank's problem of specifying a target for the mark immediately after unification. The analysis above suggests that without a clear and unambiguous objective, it is questionable that monetary targeting alone would produce the price stability enjoyed in Germany in recent decades.

4 CONCLUDING COMMENTS

Neumann's chapter provides a constructive summary of the German experience with monetary targeting. My remarks have attempted to round out his discussion by focusing on an intangible yet critical component of monetary policy: credibility. The experiences of the United States and Germany during the past few decades indicate that credibility is an important ingredient to the successful attainment of price stability.

A credible policy, however, requires a commitment to a well-defined objective. In Germany, the Bundesbank Act clearly specifies that safeguarding the currency is the predominant objective. One might reasonably question whether the Bundesbank would have enjoyed as much success in monetary targeting or as much credibility without this mandate.

Recent experiences also suggest that successful monetary policy is more likely to be durable when the commitment is embraced by the public and the monetary authority than when it is merely imposed in an indirect and unclear fashion. Since the early 1980s, central banks around the world have increasingly adopted behavior that recognizes the primacy of the price stability objective. In cases where a mandate has been imposed by legislative act, that objective has been direct and clear.

Notes

1. It is interesting to note that around the same time, the United States experienced a large, and apparently permanent, increase in the velocity of its M2. Some have argued that this shift in M2 velocity was largely a consequence of financial innovations that reduced transaction costs and gave a large segment of households access to bond markets. The unique financial environment characterized by an extremely steep yield curve acted as a catalyst for households to learn about bond mutual funds. It now appears that bond funds are a permanent and significant form of household wealth.
2. Michael Parkin identifies a paradox that arises when a central bank engineers a credible disinflation. Since a credible disinflation will likely be associated with an increase in money demand and a decline in velocity, a central bank may need to increase money growth to above-trend levels during the transition to lower inflation. Indeed, failure to accommodate the increased money growth may have adverse effects.

Reference

Wells, W. (1994) *Economist in an Uncertain World* (New York: Columbia University Press).

8 Inflation Targeting in Canada, New Zealand, Sweden, the United Kingdom, and in General*

Bennett T. McCallum

1 INTRODUCTION

One major objective of this chapter is to discuss arrangements and experiences in four countries that have recently adopted explicit inflation targets as guides for the conduct of monetary policy. The countries in question are Canada, New Zealand, Sweden, and the United Kingdom, all of which adopted official inflation targets between 1990 and 1993.[1] As these countries instituted their inflation targets with substantially different legislative provisions and targeting procedures, their experiences should eventually provide useful information concerning the design of effective central bank arrangements. But too little time has passed to date for such conclusions to be drawn with any confidence, so in the meantime it will be necessary to base tentative evaluations of inflation targeting on theoretical analysis and more generalized historical experiences. The second major objective of this chapter, accordingly, is to provide an analytical discussion of this type of the more important strengths and weaknesses of inflation targeting schemes.

The organization of the chapter is as follows. Section 2 consists of a description of the inflation targeting procedures currently in place in the four countries, with Section 3 reviewing the limited record of experiences to date. Then Sections 4 and 5 consider two alternative rationalizations for inflation rate targets, one stemming from the technical literature on dynamic inconsistency in monetary policy and the other based on more pragmatic considerations. Then in Section 6 it is asked whether some other nominal variable, rather than the inflation rate, might be preferable as a

* I am indebted to Krister Andersson, Jack Beebe, Marvin Goodfriend, Mervyn King, David Mayes, Allan Meltzer, Edward Nelson, and Lars Svensson for helpful comments and to the Bank of England and the Reserve Bank of New Zealand for informative visits involving useful discussions with many individuals.

target. Section 7 considers the issue of inflation versus price level (or growth rate versus growing-level) specifications of the target path, and Section 8 concludes.

2 INFLATION TARGETING ARRANGEMENTS

We begin in this section with a description of the inflation targeting arrangements now in place in Canada, New Zealand, Sweden, and the United Kingdom.[2] In this discussion and elsewhere in the chapter the countries will be treated in alphabetical sequence. Somewhat more attention will be devoted to New Zealand than to the other countries, however, the reason being that the New Zealand set-up is significantly more ambitious than elsewhere. This greater ambition has two distinct dimensions. First, the chosen numerical target values for inflation rates are somewhat lower – closer to zero – in New Zealand than elsewhere. But more important is the second dimension: New Zealand has gone much farther than elsewhere in terms of legislation and formal governmental arrangements that are intended to enhance credibility and give a degree of permanence to the anti-inflationary undertaking.

2.1 Canada

The ultimate achievement of price level stability became the centerpiece of Bank of Canada monetary policy in 1988 when then Governor John Crow delivered that year's Eric J. Hanson Memorial Lecture at the University of Alberta. Canada's formal and explicit inflation target scheme began only in February 1991, however, when the Bank of Canada and the Minister of Finance jointly announced a series of targets. Participation by the latter was significant because it signaled "that the government was supportive of the price stability goal" (Freedman, 1995, p. 21). The Minister of Finance cannot dismiss the Governor, it should be noted, but can issue a "policy directive." Such an action has as yet never been taken, however.

The series of targets announced in 1991 called for target bands, with a width of 2 percentage points. The band's midpoint was specified to fall to 3 percent at the end of 1992, then to 2.5 percent as of mid-1994, and finally to 2.0 percent at the end of 1995. Subsequently, in December 1993, the government and the Bank agreed to maintain the latter target – a 1–3 percent band – intact to the end of 1998, with some possible further reduction in the midpoint value to be chosen in late 1995.

The specific price index utilized in the Bank of Canada's target scheme is the Consumer Price Index (CPI) excluding food, energy, and the contribution from changes in indirect taxes. The rationale for these exclusions is that the components in question are frequently subject to sharp temporary movements that, because of their transitory nature, should not be responded to by monetary policy.

An important component of any monetary policy targeting arrangement is the feedback procedure that is used in selecting instrument settings. Apparently the Bank of Canada's procedure is basically to use an econometric model to calculate, given experts' assessments regarding future values of exogenous variables, the time path of a "monetary conditions" index that will be required to achieve an inflation path near the midpoint of the target range. The monetary conditions index is defined so that its changes reflect changes in exchange rates s_t and interest rates R_t, both nominal, with three times as much weight given to ΔR_t as to Δs_t. When the monetary conditions index needs to be increased in value, the Bank of Canada "would act to adjust the level of liquidity in the system through adjustments to settlement balances of direct-clearing financial institutions thereby producing an appropriate rise in interest rates" (Duguay and Poloz, 1994, p. 196).[3]

The possibility of enhancing commitment to the inflation targeting arrangement was alive in early 1992, after the government proposed amendments to the Bank of Canada Act that would have changed the Bank's mandate so as to focus exclusively on price stability. But although the proposal was supported by the Governor of the Bank, it was rejected by a parliamentary committee. Testimony to this committee by academic economists was, according to Laidler and Robson (1993), almost unanimously opposed to the proposed changes.

2.2 New Zealand

As was mentioned above, by far the most ambitious of the four arrangements is that of New Zealand, which features a target range of only 0–2 percent and a degree of formal institutionalization that goes well beyond the extent found elsewhere. In this regard there are two notable features. The first is the Reserve Bank of New Zealand Act 1989, enacted by Parliament, which specifies that "stability of the general level of prices" shall be the overriding objective of monetary policy – indeed, it is the only objective mentioned. This Act requires the Bank's Governor and the Minister of Finance to make periodic Policy Targets Agreements (PTAs) regarding the price index to be targeted and its allowable range. A second notable feature is the provision whereby the Governor, who must report on inflation performance twice each year, may be dismissed prior to the end of his five-year term if the inflation rate falls outside its specified target band.[4]

As of October 1995, three PTAs had so far been in force. The first, dating from March 1990, mentioned the 0–2 percent inflation band as the eventual target but specified a less ambitious range for a transition period, since the inflation rate at the time was above 6 percent. This transition range was also specified in the second PTA, which was put in place in December 1990 after an election which changed the governing party in Parliament. Then in December 1992, after inflation had reached the 0–2 percent range, the PTA was revised to reflect that fact, with the objective becoming that of maintaining (rather than achieving and maintaining) inflation within the target band.

The current PTA specifies that the Reserve Bank of New Zealand (RBNZ) will monitor a number of price indices but that "the formal price stability target will be defined in terms of the All Groups Consumers Price Index (CPI), [that] being the measure that is monitored most closely by the public." But whereas the basic requirement is to keep 12-month increases in the CPI in the 0–2 percent range, there are some important exceptions or "caveats." Specifically, the PTA recognizes that "there is a range of possible price shocks arising from external sources, certain government policy changes, or a natural crisis which are quite outside the direct influence of monetary policy." Consequently, "the CPI inflation rate can [occasionally] be expected to move outside the 0–2 percent range in response to particular shocks" without it being concluded that the RBNZ is failing to meet the requirements of the PTA. Specific types of listed shocks include changes in the terms of trade or indirect tax rates, natural disasters or livestock disease outbreaks, and changes in the interest-cost component of the CPI.[5]

Although such caveats are sensible, the way in which they are being handled in practice, as of July 1995, warrants some discussion. Specifically, the RBNZ's semi-annual Monetary Policy Statements are being written so as to focus attention on the "underlying inflation rate," which is measured by changes in a modified version of the CPI that excludes the interest cost component and also "one-off effects on the CPI of aggregate price level shocks." The result, then, is that periods in which the basic CPI inflation rate exceeds 2 percent, but does so because of caveatable shocks, are described not in those words, but instead as being periods in which the *underlying* inflation rate lies *within* the 0–2 percent band.

There are evidently some problems with this practice, as the RBNZ has itself recognized. One of these is that accountability, which the Act emphasizes, is compromised by a process that in effect has the RBNZ constructing measures by which its own performance will be evaluated. This is the case for the underlying inflation rate since it is not directly obtainable from price index series or components developed and published by Statistics New Zealand. Instead, some of the adjustments involve estimated effects necessarily based on response coefficients obtained from econometric models or by other disputable methods. A second problem is that such adjustments to the basic CPI are adopted only when the effects of the shocks in question attain a "significant" magnitude. But smaller (and downward!) shocks of the same type are not recognized in the adjusted series, so it does not possess full definitional consistency or conceptual coherence over time. In addition, there is an element of ambiguity introduced to the RBNZ's review process by the use of the underlying inflation index with its incorporation of adjustments related to the PTA caveats. In particular, the question arises of whether other caveats are also permitted in addition to those built into the index.

For these reasons, a better method of managing the caveats, one might think, would be to adopt officially (as the PTA's formal price stability measure) some CPI index that is adjusted only in indisputable ways that are based entirely on numbers published by Statistics New Zealand. Such adjustments would exclude the interest cost component and perhaps indirect tax effects, but would not reflect all of the adjustments now used by RBNZ. Preferably the index would be calculated and given prominence by Statistics New Zealand. Then the effects of other caveatable shocks – which should not be frequent – would be handled by explicit discussion of the relevant circumstances.

In terms of its policy feedback procedure for achieving the inflation rate targets, the RBNZ adjusts monetary conditions in response to discrepancies between expected future inflation rates and the target midpoint. If the inflation rate forecast for a period two to six quarters in the future is above 2 percent, for example, the RBNZ will tighten monetary conditions. The main indicator variable used in gauging monetary conditions is the (trade-weighted) exchange rate, which is among quickly responding variables the one that is believed to have the greatest predictive and explanatory power for the inflation rate. When forecasted inflation exceeds the target range, then monetary conditions are tightened until the exchange rate appreciates enough to drive the forecasted future inflation rate back into its target range. Short-term interest rates also serve in this indicator capacity, but to a substantially lesser extent. In terms of money market operating procedures, the main instrument of direct control is the RBNZ's target level of commercial bank settlement balances at the RBNZ. Desired adjustments in conditions are usually achieved, however, without any actual change in this variable (or any other variable directly controlled by the RBNZ) by means of relatively clear communication to the financial markets of the RBNZ's desires and intentions.[6]

The volume of information provided to the public by the RBNZ is quite large. In addition to the semiannual Monetary Policy Statements, the RBNZ publishes semiannual forecasts and expository articles regarding monetary policy in its quarterly *Bulletin*. In addition, the Governor gives numerous talks regarding fundamental policy issues, and some of these are available from the RBNZ in printed form.

It should be mentioned that although the exchange rate plays a central role in the RBNZ's feedback procedure, it does not have the status of an intermediate target. Its chosen values are merely those that are needed, in the judgment of the RBNZ, to achieve the inflation targets.[7] A rather striking fact is that there have been no foreign exchange market interventions by the RBNZ since the dollar was floated in 1985 – no purchases or sales of foreign exchange.

2.3 Sweden

Sweden's adoption of inflation targets was announced by the Riksbank in January 1993, following the breakdown in November 1992 of the krona's exchange rate peg to the ECU. The target rate was set at 2 percent, with a tolerance band from 1 to 3 percent. This target was scheduled to apply to the 12-month inflation rate of the CPI excluding effects of indirect taxes and subsidies, but beginning only in 1995 because outcomes in 1993 and 1994 were viewed as already determined to a large extent. The inflation targeting scheme in Sweden is not highly institutionalized, in comparison with Canada and New Zealand. In particular, the Riksbank's 1993 announcement was made by its governing board without any accompanying statement from the government. Consequently, there is little to prevent the board from altering or eliminating the inflation targets unilaterally (Svensson, 1995a). The board's composition is therefore of importance. In that regard seven of its eight members are appointed by the parliament, with terms that coincide with parliament's, and the eighth member – the Governor – is appointed by these seven. The Governor's term is five years but his position is not a dominating one. Indeed, one of the seven board members appointed by parliament is designated chairman, and his position is decisive in the event of a tie vote. Another relevant feature is that parliament's ruling party (or coalition) has control over four of the seven board appointments, including the chairman. There is, accordingly, room for concern that the Riksbank's policies could be sensitive to political forces.

The Riksbank now publishes an inflation report, *Inflation and Inflation Expectations in Sweden*, three times per year. Svensson argues that "there is some ambiguity to what extent the governor and the board stand behind the document. Furthermore, the document has been devoid of monetary policy conclusions and clear policy recommendations . . . an explicit inflation forecast is conspicuously absent" (1995a, p. 83). Nevertheless, the introduction of this document represents an "improvement in the quality of monetary policy discussion" (1995a, p. 83).[8] It should in this context be mentioned that the traditional channel of information in the form of speeches and lectures by the Governor and staff members "has been very actively used in the period since the krona began to float" (Andersson and Berg, 1995, p. 12) and that in 1994 the Riksbank Governor participated – for the first time ever – in a public hearing before parliament's Finance Committee.

2.4 United Kingdom

The United Kingdom, like Sweden, turned to inflation targets after its exchange rate peg to the ECU collapsed (the month in this case being September 1992). There was more governmental involvement, however, since the Bank of England has had very little independence *vis-à-vis* the Treasury. Thus the initial announcement in October 1992 of inflation targets was made by the Chancellor of the Exchequer, rather than the Governor of the Bank of England. The target band specified for the retail price index excluding its mortgage interest component (RPIX) was 1 to 4 percent, with the rate to be below 2.5 percent by "the end of the present Parliament" (i.e., by spring 1997 at the latest). In addition, since September 1992 there have been four significant institutional changes, as follows:[9]

(i) Monthly meetings between the Chancellor and Governor now provide the forum in which decisions on interest rates are made – but the Chancellor continues to make decisions after hearing the Governor's views.
(ii) The Bank now publishes a quarterly *Inflation Report* that presents analysis and views of its staff and officers.
(iii) In April 1994 the Chancellor agreed to publish minutes of his monthly meetings with the Governor, the publication date being two weeks after the subsequent meeting. Also, when interest rates are changed, a press notice outlining the rationale is issued.
(iv) The Bank has been given control over the precise timing of interest rate changes, provided that any change chosen by the Chancellor will be effected before the next monthly meeting.

In the view of some analysts, item (iii) is of major importance, since decisions by the Chancellor that go against the recommendations of the Bank will quickly be identified as such. Also, the *Inflation Report* clearly gives the Bank an opportunity to put forth and explain its views.

The policy feedback procedure used by the Bank of England is quite similar to the ones prevailing in Canada and New Zealand. In particular, money market conditions are adjusted so as to keep the expected inflation rate – the Bank's forecast for 1–2 years in the future – within the target band, if possible. Money market conditions are measured, however, in terms of short-term interest rates alone (rather than in combination with exchange rates, as in Canada and especially New Zealand).

A striking feature of the four arrangements described is the similarity of the feedback procedures used by the central banks of the three English-speaking nations.[10] In all of these, money market conditions are tightened or loosened when inflation forecasts for (approximately) a year ahead lie outside the target range, whose width is 2 percent. The manner in which the inflation targets are formally institutionalized is quite different across these nations, however, with New Zealand's arrangement featuring more legislation and more explicitness than those of Canada and Britain.

3 EXPERIENCES TO DATE

Here the task at hand is to present a brief review of the relevant experiences of the four nations since adoption of their inflation targets. The most basic question to ask, of course, is whether actual inflation performance has been favorable – with rates close to the target-band midpoints and therefore reasonably close to zero. In that regard, figures reflecting annual observations on the basic CPI inflation rates are reported in Table 8.1. For comparison, values are also reported for the (unweighted) average of CPI inflation rates across 23 industrialized nations, as compiled and calculated by the International Monetary Fund (IMF).

In one regard, the figures reported in Table 8.1 are rather striking. Specifically, over the reported years prior to 1990, when the first of these inflation targets was introduced, the four countries all had inflation rates that were higher than the 23-country average. In contrast, during each of the recent years 1992, 1993, and 1994, three of the four inflation targeting nations experienced less inflation than the 23-country average. Whether or not this outcome is a result of the inflation targeting schemes *per se*, as

Table 8.1 CPI inflation rates, percentage change from previous year

	Average, 1977–86	*1987*	*1988*	*1989*	*1990*	*1991*	*1992*	*1993*	*1994*
Canada	7.5	4.4	4.0	5.0	4.8	5.6*	1.5	1.8	0.2
New Zealand	13.1	15.7	6.4	5.7	6.1*	2.6	1.0	1.3	1.7
Sweden	9.2	4.2	5.8	6.4	10.5	9.3	2.3*	4.6	2.2
United Kingdom	9.5	4.1	4.9	7.8	9.5	5.9	3.7*	1.6	2.5
Industrial countries	7.3	3.1	3.4	4.4	5.0	4.5	3.3	3.0	2.4

* Year during which inflation targets were introduced.
Source: IMF (*International Financial Statistics* and *World Economic Outlook*).

opposed to national desires for sharply reduced inflation, it would seem to be the case that behavior has in fact altered in these four countries.

The inflation rates reported in Table 8.1 pertain to basic CPI index numbers, not the adjusted series that are used as the actual target variables. Accordingly, relevant quarterly observations (of annual inflation rates) for the four nations' targeted variables are given in Table 8.2. These numbers are somewhat different, of course, but the basic message is much the same as with the raw CPI measures reflected in Table 8.1.

Table 8.3 reports real GDP growth rates on an annual basis for the four inflation targeting nations and also, as above, the average value for 23 industrial countries. In these figures one can find some evidence suggesting that undesirable real effects were generated by the adoption of stern anti-inflationary measures, especially when it is recognized that such measures were actually introduced a few years prior to the formal targeting arrangements.[11] But there has been an encouraging revival of growth recently: during 1993 and 1994, output growth rates above the 23-nation average were recorded in Canada, New Zealand, and the United Kingdom.

Also relevant is performance in terms of unemployment rates. Table 8.4 presents a picture that is less favorable than that of Table 8.3, in the sense that unemployment rates in New Zealand and Sweden were still, as of 1994, much higher than in the years prior to 1988 or 1991, respectively. In the case of New Zealand, there have been many other major structural reforms – for example, involving government finance and labor market arrangements – that have taken place during the relevant period. Nevertheless, by March 1995, the rate had fallen to 6.6 percent.[12]

A highly relevant consideration is whether the expectations of market

Table 8.2 Target variable inflation rates, percentage change from one year earlier

	*Canada**	*New Zealand*†	*Sweden*‡	*UK*§
1989:I	4.8	3.8	6.6	–
:II	4.9	3.6	6.6	–
:III	5.0	3.9	6.4	–
:IV	4.7	3.4	6.6	–
1990:I	4.3	3.5	9.6	–
:II	3.8	4.0	10.0	–
:III	3.7	3.7	11.1	–
:IV	3.8	3.4	11.2	–
1991:I	4.4	3.5	11.5	8.4
:II	4.0	2.6	10.5	6.7
:III	3.4	2.1	8.7	6.2
:IV	2.7	1.7	8.1	5.6
1992:I	1.6	1.3	3.6	5.7
:II	1.7	1.4	2.3	5.3
:III	1.4	1.5	2.4	4.2
:IV	1.5	1.8	2.0	3.8
1993:I	1.9	1.8	4.9	3.4
:II	1.4	1.6	5.0	2.8
:III	1.8	1.5	4.6	3.0
:IV	1.8	1.3	4.4	3.4
1994:I	1.6	1.1	1.9	2.6
:II	1.7	1.1	2.2	2.4
:III	1.7	1.2	2.8	2.2
:IV	1.6	1.5	2.5	2.2
1995:I	2.0	1.9	2.9	2.9
:II	2.5	2.2	3.2	2.8

* CPI excluding food, energy, and indirect taxes.
† Underlying inflation rate as calculated by Reserve Bank.
‡ CPI excluding indirect taxes and subsidies.
§ RPI excluding mortgage interest charges, reported by NISER.

participants concerning future inflation rates have fallen together with recent actual rates. Although there exist published figures pertaining to expectations as reflected in various surveys, these have various weaknesses including non-homogeneity across countries and over time as well as the inherently dubious nature of unofficial survey data. A better indicator, perhaps, is provided by interest rate differentials across countries. There may be different average values of long-term real rates of interest in different nations because of economy-specific risk characteristics, but if these are approximately constant over time then movements in nominal interest differentials

Table 8.3 Real GDP growth rates, percentage change from previous year

	Average, 1977–86	*1987*	*1988*	*1989*	*1990*	*1991*	*1992*	*1993*	*1994*
Canada	3.1	4.2	5.0	2.4	−0.2	−1.8	0.6	2.2	4.5
New Zealand	1.6	−1.7	3.0	−0.5	−0.1	−2.1	−0.2	4.1	4.8
Sweden	1.7	3.1	2.3	2.4	1.4	−1.1	−1.9	−2.1	2.2
United Kingdom	2.1	4.8	5.0	2.2	0.4	−2.0	−0.5	2.2	3.8
Industrial countries	2.7	3.2	4.4	3.3	2.4	0.8	1.5	1.2	3.0

Source: IMF (*International Financial Statistics* and *World Economic Outlook*).

Table 8.4 Unemployment rates, percentages

	Average, 1977–86	*1987*	*1988*	*1989*	*1990*	*1991*	*1992*	*1993*	*1994*
Canada	9.3	8.8	7.8	7.5	8.1	10.4	11.3	11.2	10.4
New Zealand	4.3	4.4	6.8	7.3	9.2	10.8	10.4	9.4	8.2
Sweden	2.6	1.9	1.6	1.4	1.5	2.9	5.3	8.2	7.9
United Kingdom	7.8	10.0	8.0	6.3	5.8	8.1	9.7	10.3	9.3
Industrial countries	6.7	7.3	6.8	6.2	6.0	6.8	7.7	8.1	8.1

Source: IMF (*International Financial Statistics* and *World Economic Outlook*).

should reflect movements in expected inflation rates reasonably well. Consequently, long-term bond rate differentials relative to Switzerland (a low-inflation nation) are reported in Table 8.5 for the years 1987–94. For all four of our inflation targeting nations the differentials have fallen significantly, with the most spectacular decrease occurring for New Zealand. As of 1994, the differential was smallest for New Zealand and largest (among the four nations) for Sweden.

There are various statistical investigations that could be conducted in an attempt to determine whether the inflation targets are credible and effective in the various nations. An interesting example of such a study is provided by Debelle (1996), for example, who has compared the anti-inflationary arrangements of Canada, New Zealand, and Australia by examining expected

Table 8.5 Long-term government bond yields, percentage points above yield in Switzerland

	1987	*1988*	*1989*	*1990*	*1991*	*1992*	*1993*	*1994*
Canada	5.8	6.1	4.7	4.8	3.4	3.3	3.8	3.4
New Zealand	12.2	9.3	7.6	5.8	3.6	2.4	2.6	2.2
Sweden	7.6	7.2	6.0	6.4	4.3	4.5	4.5	4.1
United Kingdom	5.4	5.2	4.4	4.4	3.6	3.7	3.8	2.8

Source: IMF (*International Financial Statistics* and *World Economic Outlook*).

inflation series and sacrifice ratios (as well as interest rate differentials). There are, however, two major difficulties with such studies. One is the questionable nature of some of the comparisons themselves. The calculation of sacrifice ratios is in that regard especially plagued by conceptual weaknesses involving measurement of capacity output and the economics profession's poor understanding of Phillips-type relationships (short-run wage–price–output dynamics).[13] Second is the limited observation period available at present.

With regard to this last consideration, I would argue that it is much too early yet to be attempting evaluations of the inflation targeting arrangements in our four nations. New Zealand's has been in place about twice as long as those in Sweden and the United Kingdom, and even for New Zealand the time span is less than six years – less, arguably, than the duration of a single typical business cycle. But the issues at hand concern institutional arrangements that should be judged on the basis of their effects on the operating characteristics of economies over long spans of time – the average performance, that is, over a number of cycles. Indeed, although the cost of a transition period is certainly relevant for any nation contemplating the introduction of a new monetary policy regime, the questions of greatest interest concern behavior after the transition period has been completed. And from that perspective it will be another decade or two before the potential advantages or disadvantages of the institutional arrangements will be clearly evident. Consequently, it is my contention that it is far too early for a predominantly empirical evaluation to be made of the inflation targeting arrangements in Canada, New Zealand, Sweden, and the United Kingdom.

Nevertheless, policy-oriented economists are rightly very interested in questions concerning the attractiveness of inflation targeting schemes. So it is necessary to try to develop a tentative and preliminary evaluation – which will consequently have to be based primarily on theoretical reasoning together with empirical evidence of a more generalized sort. To attempt such an evaluation will be the object of the next four sections.

4 THE PRAGMATIC CASE FOR AN INFLATION TARGET

In considering the desirability of an inflation target, there are two distinct ways of framing the question. One is whether adherence to an inflation targeting scheme is the best possible way of conducting monetary policy, whereas a second is whether inflation targeting is more desirable than the typical manner in which policy is currently conducted by actual central banks. We shall attempt to make some headway on both of these issues, but will initially limit our inquiry to the second of them, saving the first (and more ambitious) for Section 6.

Currently, there are two ways of conducting monetary policy that are quite common among actual central banks. One is to maintain a fixed value for some foreign exchange rate – an objective that requires monetary policy to be dedicated primarily to that task.[14] Whether such an objective is desirable is basically a question of whether the microeconomic (i.e., resource allocation) advantages of a fixed rate are greater than the macroeconomic (i.e., stabilization policy) disadvantages. For small economies in which a large fraction of market exchanges are conducted with foreigners, and which tend to experience the same macroeconomic shocks as their trading partners, it may well be advantageous to maintain a fixed exchange rate.[15] But for a substantial number of economies, including those of some small nations, the macroeconomic disadvantages – that is, the inability to use monetary policy for objectives other than maintaining a fixed exchange rate – outweigh the advantages. From this point onward, accordingly, it will be presumed that the discussion is concerned with economies of that type, that is, ones with floating exchange rates.

For this type of economy, the most common way of conducting monetary policy is to tighten or loosen monetary conditions each decision period so as to achieve an appropriate balance between the competing objectives of a low inflation rate and a low unemployment rate (or, almost equivalently, a high rate of output relative to capacity). A few central banks, such as those of Germany and Switzerland, utilize targets relating to monetary aggregates in this process, but most do not. Our objective, then, is to compare inflation targeting with this conventional way of conducting monetary policy – that is, choosing instrument settings period by period so as to achieve a chosen degree of stimulus in light of inflation and unemployment objectives. In this context, there are basically two different lines of argument that have been used to justify adoption of inflation targeting. One of these builds on the academic literature concerning dynamic inconsistency in monetary policy while the second is a less formalized, more pragmatic argument. Let us concern ourselves initially, and for the remainder of this section, with the latter.

The pragmatic argument for inflation targeting begins with the proposition that, from a long-run (i.e., steady state) perspective, monetary policy has a dominating influence on an economy's (average) inflation rate and a negligible influence on its rate of unemployment or output relative to capacity. This proposition has wide support among central bankers and also within the academic community, where a version of it is often termed the "natural rate hypothesis." It should be noted that the proposition as here stated does not entirely rule out the possibility that monetary policy may affect the steady state path of *capacity* output – that is, it does not require that there is no influence on capital intensity. The claim is rather that departures of output from "capacity" or its "normal" level cannot be permanently effected by any monetary means (Lucas, 1972). But there is also a presumption that non-superneutrality effects on capacity are not very large.

What about monetary effects on the (steady state) rate of *growth* of output? Until recently it was taken for granted by most analysts that monetary policy could not have *any* permanent effect on the average rate of output growth. In the past decade, however, the endogenous growth literature (see Romer, 1986; or Rebelo, 1991) has suggested that level effects may be converted into rate-of-growth effects if the returns to human and non-human capital together are not diminishing – that is, if all production functions have elasticities with respect to human and non-human capital that sum to 1.0 exactly. Also, there has been some cross-section empirical work that purports to find a negative effect of inflation on long-term growth rates.[16] Now, if a causal relationship of this type actually existed, it would of course provide an extremely powerful stimulus to the position that inflation should be kept at negligible (or perhaps negative) levels, for even small changes in maintained growth rates will yield enormous income level effects when cumulated over time. It is my judgment, however, that there is at present not nearly enough persuasive analysis of either type – theoretical or empirical – to justify the position that inflation affects sustained growth rates. Accordingly, since such a position is not necessary to justify the conclusion that a near-zero inflation rate is desirable, it would seem prudent not to adopt it.

This last-mentioned presumption, that near-zero inflation is desirable, itself stems from various analytical and practical considerations. First, that even fully anticipated inflation is costly, due to the "shoe-leather" effects of failing to satiate agents with the transaction-facilitating services of money balances (which require no resources to produce), is indisputable and has received a stimulating recent restatement by Lucas (1994).[17] Second, it is the case that all actual tax systems are specified (at least partially) in nominal terms. Thus inflation is apt to reduce the steady state level of capital intensity and also to induce a wasteful allocation of valuable human resources (e.g., accountants, lawyers, financial market participants) into activities that produce no utility-generating goods or services. Third, although there is no necessary theoretical connection between average rates of inflation and prevailing levels of inflation variability and uncertainty, in practice it is evidently true that more variability occurs at higher rates – and the resulting uncertainty is presumably both harmful and unnecessary. Finally, it is probably true that a substantial fraction of actual individuals are confused by non-zero inflation, and so make suboptimal choices of various types.[18]

It is of course quite widely agreed that monetary policy also has important *short-run* effects, that is, effects on fluctuations away from steady state paths. When monetary conditions are tightened (or loosened), there is a tendency for output relative to capacity to fall (or rise). These effects are only temporary in duration but are long-lasting enough to have major consequences for human welfare. As a result, it is the case that central banks have a legitimate basis for their manifest concern with cyclical conditions. But while there is considerable professional agreement that such effects are important, their exact nature is very poorly understood. It is not just that the economics profession does not have a well-tested quantitative model of the quarter-to-quarter dynamics. The situation is much worse than that: we do not even have any basic agreement about the qualitative nature of the mechanism. This point can be made by mentioning some of the leading theoretical categories, which include: real business cycle models; monetary misperception models; semi-classical price adjustment models; models with overlapping nominal contracts of the Taylor variety or of the Fischer variety; models with nominal contracts set as in the recent work of Fuhrer and Moore; NAIRU models; Lucas supply function models; MPS-style markup pricing models; and so on.[19] Not only do we have all of these basic modeling approaches, but to be made operational each of them has to be combined with some measure of capacity output – a step that itself involves competing approaches – and with several critical assumptions regarding the nature of different types of unobservable shocks and the time-series processes generating them.[20] Thus there are dozens or perhaps hundreds of competing specifications regarding the precise nature of the connection between monetary policy actions and their real short-term consequences. And there is little empirical basis for much narrowing of the range of contenders.

Accordingly, a rather natural conclusion would seem to be that central banks' monetary policy strategies should be designed in a manner that is primarily concerned with their long-run effects – those that result on average over time and about which we have considerable knowledge – rather than the short-run or temporary effects about which we know comparatively little. But the long-run effects are principally price level or inflation rate effects. Consequently, since we know that inflation is socially undesirable (and also unpopular), it seems rather sensible to dedicate monetary policy to the goal of achieving an inflation rate close to zero – one that is of negligible importance from the perspective of most economic actors.[21] Making inflation prevention the *sole* objective might then be justified on the grounds that monetary policy can effectively be directed at only one target, since all a central bank can do, essentially, is to tighten or loosen monetary conditions.[22] But since a single weighted average of inflation and output growth components could be targeted, a better argument might be that it would be difficult to obtain public understanding of, and support for, such a target variable (or even an unweighted sum).

It is interesting to compare the foregoing argument, which is expressed in my own words,[23] with a rationale for the New Zealand framework as expressed by the RBNZ (1993, p. 21), as follows:

> Experience both here and abroad has shown that the only beneficial economic outcome that monetary policy can deliver assuredly and sustainably is price stability. Monetary policy has a short-term impact on the real economy, but this impact is not sustained. Growth and employment gains or losses are mostly replaced by changes in prices and wages, while most initial competiveness changes generated by movements in the nominal exchange rate are similarly eroded. Monetary policy cannot therefore be used to raise the trend in growth or employment, or sustainably influence the real exchange rate.
>
> Nor does the short-term impact of monetary policy actions on growth and employment provide a reliable avenue for the use of monetary policy in smoothing out fluctuations in real economic activity. Successful counter-cyclical monetary policy would require that the nature and timing of the peaks and troughs of activity, *and* of monetary policy's impact, be well understood. Unfortunately, monetary policy is a relatively blunt instrument, and our state of knowledge is not precise enough for us to be confident of being right significantly more often than wrong.

Pursuing real economy fine-tuning objectives would thus risk diverting monetary policy down paths where it has no sustained beneficial impact, and often down paths that turn out to lead in directions opposite to those anticipated. At the same time as reducing the chances of achieving what monetary policy is best at – maintaining price stability – this approach would add a drag to economic performance by generating uncertainty and pushing up real interest rates.

Additionally, because it is typically easier to relax policy to stimulate activity than to tighten policy to offset overly rapid, inflationary, growth, monetary policy aimed at smoothing activity is likely to have a bias that leads to higher overall inflation. The costs of a more inflationary environment are thereby added to the costs resulting from higher risk and uncertainty.

Here the last paragraph relies upon an argument that one might interpret as essentially political in nature. Specifically, the phrase "it is . . . easier to relax . . . than to tighten policy" evidently refers to political pressures on central banks, since there is no greater *technical* difficulty in tightening. Furthermore, one might see the source of the problem as involving the tendency of political processes in today's democratic nations to exhibit impatience and short-sightedness. This tendency would lead to an inflationary bias because the desirable effects of a policy loosening (i.e., its output stimulus) occur more quickly than the longer-lasting undesirable effects (i.e., its inflation stimulus), whereas the desirable effects are the slower to occur in the case of a tightening.

The foregoing line of argument suggests that it is sensible to strive for a negligible inflation rate, and also that short-run activist attempts to smooth out cyclical fluctuations are unlikely to be successful. Thus it suggests that inflation targeting is apt to be preferable to the usual way in which central banks conduct monetary policy. But nevertheless the argument does not literally imply that it is best to aim for some constant inflation rate each monthly (or quarterly) decision period.[24] Consequently, some other possibilities will be discussed in Section 6. But first it will be useful to discuss an alternative way of making the case for an inflation target.

5 THE DYNAMIC INCONSISTENCY CASE FOR AN INFLATION TARGET

There is a large amount of literature that uses a second – related but distinct – line of argument in developing the case for inflation targeting.

Specifically, several academic writers[25] and a few from central banks[26] have for this purpose drawn upon results on dynamic inconsistency of monetary policy, results that were developed by Kydland and Prescott (1977) and Barro and Gordon (1983a). Since these results are well-known, the present review can be very brief. The analysis presumes that aggregate output (relative to capacity) depends upon the *unexpected* component of monetary policy and that the central bank's objectives are to keep both inflation and output close to target values – values which accurately reflect society's preferences but with an externality-induced excess of target output over its capacity (or natural rate) value. At any point of time, so the argument goes, expectations regarding policy will be "given" (i.e., predetermined), so monetary conditions easier than previously expected would yield an output bonus whereas conditions tighter than expected would result in an output shortfall. Consequently, the optimal choice by the central bank will be a policy setting that reflects a compromise between the value that would yield the inflation objective and some other (looser) setting that would be preferable because of its stimulating effect on output. But this same type of "discretionary" choice procedure will be repeated period after period, so rational agents will come to expect it. Thus on average monetary conditions will be easy but not easier than expected and consequently there will be no output bonus realized – even though a greater-than-desired inflation rate is generated. The central bank realizes that it is behaving suboptimally, according to this analysis, but can do nothing about it because it has no ability to precommit its future policy actions – there exists no "precommitment technology." In order to eliminate the inflationary bias and generate superior outcomes, it is necessary for external constraints to be placed on the central bank[27] – and inflation targets provide one convenient vehicle for imposing such constraints. Now, the foregoing line of argument certainly identifies one important pressure on central bank behavior, a pressure that in principle tends to induce an inflationary bias to policy choices. It is questionable, however, whether this was actually the main pressure that led many central banks to behave in an inflationary manner during the 1970s.[28] Since most central bank analysts and decision-makers had not yet embraced the idea of rational expectations or perhaps even the expectations-augmented Phillips curve, it seems likely that a belief in the existence of a long-run tradeoff between inflation and unemployment may have been of greater actual importance.

In any event, it is the contention of McCallum (1995a) that an independent central bank is not inevitably destined to behave in the manner described above. While the pressure from dynamic inconsistency exists, there is no necessity for a central bank to succumb to it. Despite the absence of any precommitment technology, a central bank can nevertheless achieve better results in terms of its own preferences (which will tend to mirror society's) by abstaining from the temptation to exploit each period's expectations regarding monetary conditions, instead choosing policy settings that would be optimal if expected inflation were equal to the target rate. If the central bank consistently abstains in this way, the resulting monetary conditions will not be easier than required for the desired inflation rate, so the latter will be achieved on average. But as in the "discretionary" equilibrium, there will be no expectational errors on average, so the average rate of output (relative to capacity) and unemployment will be the same. Thus, since there will be no inflationary bias, the outcomes will on average be superior. And there is nothing tangible to prevent an actual central bank from behaving in this "committed" or "rule-like" fashion, so it is my contention that some forward-looking central banks will in fact do so. Analytical results that *presume* non-committed or discretionary behavior may therefore be misleading.

Contributors to the literature understand, of course, that outcomes would be preferable from the central bank's own point of view if it were to behave in the committed fashion. Why, then, do they presume that such behavior will not be adopted by actual central banks? The usual argument is that despite the superiority on average of committed behavior (that abstains from exploitation of expectations), it remains true that *within* each period expectations *are* given, so a superior outcome *for that period* can be achieved by monetary conditions easier than the committed setting. Furthermore, the public is assumed to understand this and therefore to expect the discretionary inflation rate – which makes easy conditions necessary to avoid depressed output levels. Thus the public will expect the discretionary inflation rate, according to the usual argument, *even if* the central bank is behaving in a non-inflationary (committed) manner. My contention, by contrast, is that if the central bank behaves in a committed manner, then the public will observe that behavior pattern and will soon come to expect such behavior.[29] That is what is usually implied by the assumption of rational expectations – that expectations conform (except for random errors) to actuality.

The foregoing argument is similar in some respects to that of Taylor (1983, p. 125), who concluded his discussion of Barro and Gordon (1983b) with the statement that it is "difficult to see why the [optimal] zero-inflation policy would not be adopted" by a central bank. The literature's main response to Taylor is provided by Canzoneri (1985), who first acknowledges "that Taylor would probably be right were it not for private information" (1985, p. 1060) but then goes on to say that if "the Fed's forecast of money demand is private information, a resolution of the precommitment problem is much more difficult to come by . . . [because] . . . direct verification of the Fed's adherence to the ideal policy rule is not possible" (1985, p. 1061). The alleged problem in this case still results, however, from the presumption that the central bank attempts to exploit existing expectations. The present argument is that a competent central bank may see that such a strategy is fruitless (on average) and therefore abandons it. If it does so it will be free to adopt the policy that Canzoneri finds "ideal" even in the private information setting.

There is also a second aspect of the standard literature on dynamic inconsistency and central bank behavior that seems misleading. This aspect concerns a result developed by Walsh (1995), and utilized by Persson and Tabellini (1993), concerning contracts between a nation's government and its central bank. Specifically, the result indicates that if a nation's government provides its central bank with an incentive arrangement (i.e., a "contract") that makes the latter's rewards negatively dependent upon the inflation rate, then it is possible to induce optimal monetary performance even though the central bank's decision calculus is of the discretionary type that would lead to an inflationary bias in the absence of this inducement.

The misleading feature of the Walsh and Persson–Tabellini result is that such an arrangement does not actually eliminate the motivation for dynamic inconsistency, it merely locates it in a different place. Thus, under the proposed arrangement the government would have to enforce the contract – say, by reducing the central bank's budget when inflation is high – but the government has exactly the same incentive not to do so as the central bank has to be too easy in its monetary stance in the first place. To put the point in other words, if the absence of a precommitment technology is actually a crucial problem, then it will still apply to a consolidated entity consisting of the government and central bank together, just as it would to an independent central bank. Furthermore, this weakness of the literature's position cannot be overcome by suggesting that the monetary authority's objective function can be specified at the "constitutional stage" of the political process – for constitutions must be enforced and the enforcing party will be subject to the same temptation as an independent central bank.

The foregoing argument does not imply, it should be said, that government–central bank contracts or explicit mandates are undesirable. But it suggests that the pragmatic line of analysis outlined in Section 4 provides a more persuasive basis for such arrangements than does the literature on dynamic inconsistency. In addition, it suggests that the more important function of mandates or contracts may be in constraining the government, rather than the central bank.

The rationale for this last suggestion is as follows. The arguments of both this section and the one before suggest that a key requirement for good monetary policy is patience or far-sightedness. It is desirable, that is, that policy decisions not be dominated by short-run considerations that would induce an inflationary bias. But governments (i.e., treasuries and other executive agencies) are typically more closely involved in political processes than central banks, and the political processes of today's democracies tend to be short-sighted and impatient in their emphasis. Consequently, governments are less likely than central banks to exercise the patience that is required to behave in a committed manner, as discussed above. But the existence of mandates or contracts that emphasize inflation prevention makes it more difficult for governments to bring pressure to bear on central banks to tilt their policies toward short-run payoffs. Such arrangements thereby provide central banks with enhanced opportunities to behave in a rule-like or committed fashion that avoids any inflationary bias. Doing so does not necessarily entail any failure to respond to current shocks, however, since such responses carry no necessary implications for the average rate of inflation; there is no inescapable tradeoff between "flexibility and commitment." Implicit recognition of this point is a strength of the Walsh and Persson–Tabellini analysis.[30]

6 CHOICE OF TARGET VARIABLE

It has been argued that inflation targeting can be useful because it helps to focus a central bank's attention toward the objective that is most relevant from a long-run perspective and because it helps to deflect political pressures that tend to be short-sighted and excessively inflationary. It is not entirely clear, however, that some other nominal variable would not function as well or better in this capacity. In my own studies, for example, I have usually worked under the presumption that it would be preferable to express quarterly targets in terms of a nominal spending variable – such as nominal GDP – rather than inflation itself, even if the principal (but not sole) objective of monetary policy is the prevention of inflation.

The rationale for a nominal spending target, formulated perhaps in growth rate form,[31] begins with the idea that it would entail little if any deterioration in terms of long-run average inflation performance. If, for example, nominal GDP growth rates were kept close to a target value equal to the expected long-term average growth rate of real GDP, then inflation (in terms of the GDP deflator) would be kept close to its desired value. This is so because long-run output growth rates are virtually independent of monetary conditions and are predictable with relatively high accuracy (say, within ±0.5 percent per year) over long spans of time. The same would not be true for targets in terms of monetary aggregates, such as M1 or M2 growth rates, because of velocity changes that may be sizeable and are difficult to predict.

But the relevant issue here is nominal GDP growth versus inflation, not money growth rates. In that regard it seems obvious that an inflation target would, if successful, provide tighter short-run control over the inflation rate. But it is nevertheless arguable that nominal GDP targeting would be preferable, especially if inflation control is not the sole concern of monetary policy, for three reasons. First, because the prices of goods and services are widely believed to react more slowly than output in response to monetary actions,[32] cycling and dynamic instability are more likely to occur with a price level or inflation target. In other words, the problem of "instrument instability," which would render the targeting attempt entirely unsuccessful, is intensified. Second, the output-stabilizing properties of a smoothed path for nominal GDP are likely to be better than with a smoothed path for the price level. About this one cannot be certain, because – as emphasized above – the economics profession has a very poor understanding of the dynamic interaction between nominal and real variables, as well as the magnitude and serial correlation properties of various types of shocks. But, furthermore, this poor understanding leads to a third reason. It does so by suggesting that it is more difficult to devise a policy rule for hitting inflation targets than nominal GDP targets, because the former requires an understanding of the forces that determine the split of nominal GDP growth into its inflation and real growth components.[33] When a central bank takes stimulative policy actions, it can predict with more accuracy when (and by how much) nominal GDP will respond than it can for the price level.[34]

An often expressed objection to GDP targeting is that national income statistics are not produced often enough or quickly enough, and are significantly revised after their first release. But the essence of the approach is to use some reasonably comprehensive measure of nominal spending; it does not need to be GDP or GNP *per se*. Other measures could readily be developed on the basis of price and quantity indices that are reported more often and more promptly.[35] It might even be possible to devise a monthly measure that is conceptually more attractive than GDP, by making the price index more closely tailored to public perceptions of inflation and/or by using a quantity measure that treats government output more appropriately. In any event, if policy adjustments are based on expected future target discrepancies, rather than past misses, then this issue is not directly relevant.

The possibility of instrument instability, mentioned above, is related to the width of the target band employed, whatever the identity of the target variable. Thus if the target band is excessively narrow, then attempts to keep the targeted variable within its limits could generate ever-increasing cycles in the setting of the instrument variable, with the consequence being explosive oscillations in other variables as well as the one targeted. The point is that speedy responses to instrument changes are helpful in promoting stability. So if it is true, as suggested above, that nominal spending responds more quickly than the price level to altered monetary conditions, it may be possible to keep nominal spending growth but not inflation within a given percentage bandwidth.

In this regard, some relevant evidence for Canada and the United Kingdom has recently been developed in studies by Fillion and Tetlow (1993) and Haldane and Salmon (1995). In both cases, simulations with quantitative models were conducted to determine how tightly inflation rates could be controlled by policy feedback procedures of the general type used by the Bank of Canada and the Bank of England. Fillion and Tetlow estimate that a ± two standard deviation bandwidth is about seven percentage points in Canada whereas the Haldane and Salmon results for the United Kingdom imply a width of about 12 percentage points (that is, the standard deviation of the inflation rate with feedback control is about three percentage points).[36] The Canadian study uses a calibrated model in which time periods are interpreted as years whereas the British results pertain to an estimated econometric model with quarterly time periods. Both studies suggest that a 0 to 2 percent band would be violated a large fraction of the time.

An analogous study for Australia conducted by Debelle and Stevens (1995) indicates, by contrast, the possibility of much tighter inflation control. Specifically, results based on simulations with an estimated quarterly model include inflation rate standard deviations as low as 0.64 percentage points, implying a ± two standard deviation bandwidth of just 2.56 percentage points (see Debelle and Stevens, p. 24). This value is so much smaller than in the Haldane and Salmon paper that one is led to wonder what aspects of these studies are responsible for the difference. In that regard it is true that the residual variances in the model's estimated relationships are somewhat smaller in the Debelle–Stevens study, but there is another difference that may also be of major importance. This difference involves the specification of the policy feedback rule postulated for the central bank. Whereas Haldane and Salmon used simple feedback rules with nominal interest rate settings in response to inflation and other realizations from previous periods, Debelle and Stevens use *optimal* feedback rules for real interest rates based on the minimization of a forward-looking loss function.[37] The latter would imply, I would guess, a much more complex feedback rule. But since simple rules often work (in simulations) nearly as well as complex ones, there may be another significant difference. Specifically, I am inclined to conjecture that the Debelle–Stevens analysis assumes that the central bank has knowledge of *current-period* values of real output and the price level when selecting its instrument setting. If so, then I would argue that the exercise is seriously unrealistic in its assumption about information available to the central bank. McCallum (1994) more fully develops this argument, which involves the contention that current-period values should be treated as elements of the central bank's information set only for asset prices. In the case of real income and inflation rates, only lagged values should be treated as known.

It might be noted that the UK study by Haldane and Salmon (1995) contains some rather striking results pertaining to the possible desirability of a nominal GDP target. In particular, their Table 5 indicates that the root–mean–square (RMS) targeting errors for annual inflation rates are smaller when nominal GDP growth is the target variable than when inflation itself plays that role. With a feedback rule coefficient of 0.25, for example, the RMS errors are 2.9 and 3.5 percent, respectively, with the GDP growth and inflation targets. These results are not fully applicable to actual arrangements in Canada, New Zealand, or the United Kingdom, even if we neglect econometric model issues, because the policy rules simulated involve responses to previous-quarter target misses, rather than discrepancies between expected future magnitudes and target values. But the results do illustrate in a general way one type of consideration that leads some analysts to believe that nominal spending targets are worthy of serious consideration. On the other hand, such targets would be more difficult to explain and justify to the public, so their most useful role might be in terms of central bank decision-making rather than public pronouncements. Also, it must be recognized that, as mentioned in note 34, there may in practice be strong similarities between nominal income and inflation targeting. The references cited in note 23, as providing earlier statements of the case for inflation targeting, were actually put forth as proposals for nominal income targeting.

7 GROWTH RATES VERSUS LEVELS

In this section we briefly consider the question of whether it is preferable to have a growth rate target or one of the growing-levels type, that is, one in which the (log of the) basic variable is difference-stationary or is trend-stationary. This topic is often discussed under the heading of "inflation versus price level targets," but the same considerations would apply if the target variable were nominal GDP or some other nominal aggregate.[38] In particular, the weakness of the growth rate choice is that it will – by treating past target misses as bygones – introduce a random walk or "unit root" component into the time-series processes for all nominal variables, including the price level (whatever index is chosen) or more precisely its logarithm. Thus there will be a possibility that the price level will drift arbitrarily far away from any given value (or path) as time passes, implying considerable uncertainty as to the value that will obtain in the distant future (e.g., 50 years from the present).

By contrast, the principal disadvantage with a levels-type target path is that the target variable will be forced back toward the preset path after any disturbance has driven it away, even if the effect of the disturbance itself is of a permanent nature. Since any such action entails general macroeconomic stimulus or restraint, this type of targeting procedure would apparently induce extra cyclical variation in demand conditions which will imply extra variability in real output if price level stickiness prevails. And variability in output and other real aggregative variables is probably more costly to society (in terms of human welfare) than variability in the price level about a constant or slowly growing path. Now, it is not entirely clear that fully permanent shocks are predominant, but most time-series analysis seems to suggest that the effects of shocks are typically quite long-lasting – indeed, virtually indistinguishable from permanent. Consequently, it would seem preferable not to drive any nominal target variable back to a preset path – or at least not to do so quickly. In other words, it seems preferable to adopt a nominal target of the growth rate type, rather than the levels type.

One reason for reaching the foregoing conclusion is that very few economic transactions are based on 50-year planning horizons. A typical "long-lasting" arrangement might be more like twenty years in duration. But price level uncertainty twenty years into the future would not be terribly large even if the log of the price level were to behave as a pure random walk with zero drift. Assuming that the random, unpredictable component at the quarterly frequency has a standard deviation of 0.0045 – roughly the value for the United States over 1954–91 – then a 95 percent confidence interval for the log price level twenty years ahead would be within 8 percent (plus or minus) of the current value.[39] This, I would suggest, represents a small degree of uncertainty in comparison with the magnitudes that have prevailed over the 1960s, 1970s, and 1980s, essentially because the drift or trend rate has been non-zero and uncertain.

Even so, it might be possible to do even better by adoption of a target that is a weighted average of the growth rate and growing-levels type. In my study of targeting procedures for Japan, I found that a weighted average target that gives a weight of 80 percent to a growth rate path and 20 percent to a growing levels value yields quite desirable results. Specifically, in the relevant simulations typical deviations from the growth rate target path are almost as small as when growth rate targets are aimed for, and the deviations from a growing-levels path are also reasonably small. In particular, there is a distinct tendency for the simulated nominal values to return to the growing-levels path, rather than drifting away arbitrarily as when pure growth rate targeting is adopted.

8 CONCLUSIONS

In this concluding section, I will attempt to summarize the foregoing arguments very briefly and in a manner designed to bring together various threads of the argument so as to yield some highly tentative judgments concerning the desirability of inflation targeting. In terms of general attractiveness, this chapter suggests that inflation targeting is likely to yield results that are superior, when averaged over long spans of time, to those provided by the typical discretionary mode of monetary policymaking that is prevalent today. The reason is that the discretionary mode possesses an inflationary bias, which results from the short-sighted nature of pressures that bear upon central banks. It is crucial to understand that elimination of this inflationary bias does not entail any necessary suboptimality in terms of policy responses to shocks of a cyclical nature. The bias stems from the tendency for the desirable effects of a monetary loosening to occur more promptly than the undesirable effects.

The dynamic inconsistency literature suggests that the discretionary mode of policymaking is inevitable, in the absence of external constraints on the central bank, but that suggestion is here disputed. Central banks can abstain from attempts to exploit inflationary expectations, and thereby avoid the inflationary bias, if they are far-sighted and resolute. It is nevertheless desirable to have an anti-inflationary target expressed in some formal, institutionalized agreement or mandate because such a target will help to ward off short-sighted, inflationary pressures from branches of government more closely involved in the political process.

It is arguable that some nominal variable other than inflation might be technically superior as a target for monetary policy, the growth rate of nominal spending being a leading contender. Use of such a target variable might yield superior cyclical behavior in terms of output and employment along with inflation performance that is not significantly worse, over long time spans, than with inflation targets. Current knowledge in macroeconomics does not permit any firm conclusion in this regard, however, and in terms of facilitating communication between a central bank and its nation's citizens, inflation would appear to be the preferable target. In any event, there are evidently some fairly strong operational similarities between nominal income growth targets and inflation targets with supply-shock caveats as implemented by, for example, the Reserve Bank of New Zealand. The discussion presented in Section 6 probably overemphasizes the distinction.

Notes

1. There are also some other nations, including Finland, which have adopted official inflation targets. They have been excluded from my assignment in order to keep the study to a manageable size.
2. More extensive descriptions have recently been published in Leiderman and Svensson (1995).
3. The specification of the monetary conditions index is theoretically rather unappealing, as it combines a variable expressed in monetary units with one whose units involve only time. A related point is that, from a long-run perspective, the level of R_t is negatively related to monetary stringency.
4. Note that dismissal is not automatic. The Act's provision is that "The Governor-General may . . . on the advice of the [Finance] Minister, remove the Governor from office . . . if the Minister is satisfied . . . That the performance of the Governor in ensuring that the Bank achieves the policy targets fixed under . . . this Act has been inadequate."
5. This paragraph and the next three are adapted from McCallum (1995b), as are portions of Sections 4, 5, and 6.
6. On this topic, see Archer (1995) and Hansen and Margaritis (1993).
7. The same is true, of course, of short-term interest rates.
8. Furthermore, in June 1995, the Inflation Report featured a summary by the Governor with policy conclusions that had been cleared with the board.
9. This account is adapted from King (1995).
10. I think it best not to classify Sweden as an English-speaking nation, despite the great proficiency of many of its citizens.
11. In the Swedish and UK cases, the previous anti-inflationary measures involved exchange rate pegs to the ECU.
12. It has been pointed out to me by David Gruen that the fraction of the New Zealand population that is recorded as participating in the workforce has also fallen since the beginning of reforms. This seems at first glance to be an undesirable outcome. But if some of the jobs in the pre-reform era were actually non-productive, the long-run consequences may be positive even in this respect.
13. On the latter topic, see Section 4 below. Mayes and Chapple (1995) also expresses skepticism regarding the reliability of calculated sacrifice ratios.
14. That the maintenance of a fixed (nominal) exchange rate requires the dedication of monetary policy – that is, that fiscal policy cannot be used for this

purpose on a long-run basis – is argued by McCallum (1996, pp. 135–6 and 144–5).

15. In this case, it will also be advantageous to go one step farther and have a common currency with the other nation or nations, so as to eliminate currency exchanges that use up valuable resources.
16. Some of these findings are discussed by Fischer (1995) and Okina (1995).
17. Incidentally, it is incorrect to claim (as in Laidler, 1995) that the societal nature of money is not reflected in the shoe-leather cost calculus. To the contrary, it is precisely that nature that justifies the analytical modeling features that lead to shoe-leather costs; without the societal, transaction-facilitating, medium-of-exchange features of money, models would properly be specified in such a way that no shoe-leather cost would result from anticipated inflation.
18. There is no inconsistency in believing this and also believing that it is best to assume rational expectations for most analytical purposes. One does not want to design policy in a way that attempts to exploit systematic expectational errors of any particular type.
19. In this list I have not included "menu cost" models, which have attracted much attention, because they have not been developed fully enough to be operational, that is, estimated with quarterly data.
20. Which could be white noise or autoregressive or moving average or some combination.
21. "Negligible" inflation is one way of expressing succinctly Alan Greenspan's concept of price level stability, namely, as a condition in which "price levels [are] sufficiently stable so that expectations of change do not become major factors in key economic decisions."
22. I am inclined to say that all a central bank can do is to create base money at a slow or rapid rate. But many analysts would prefer alternative indicators.
23. Earlier versions appear in McCallum (1988, 1993).
24. The New Zealand framework calls, of course, for departures from a constant inflation rate in periods with sizeable supply shocks.
25. A few leading references are listed in McCallum (1995a). Also see Debelle and Fischer (1995).
26. Examples include King (1995) and (to some extent) Archer (1995, pp. 4–5).
27. See, for example, Blanchard and Fischer (1989, pp. 596–614), Debelle and Fischer (1995), and Persson and Tabellini (1994).
28. In the case of the United States, the late 1960s was a crucial inflationary period but other nations' central banks were constrained by the Bretton Woods arrangement until 1971.
29. This sentence says "will soon come to" because it is very unlikely that expectations would adjust immediately following a *change* in policy behavior.
30. The same statement applies to Svensson (1995b). All of these authors presume, however, that central banks will behave in a discretionary manner, attempting to exploit expectations – which I dispute.
31. The issue of whether it is preferable to formulate nominal targets in growth rate (difference-stationary) or growing-level (trend-stationary) form will be taken up below in Section 7.
32. This is suggested by a very large member of empirical studies. A notable recent contribution is Christiano, Eichenbaum, and Evans (1994).

33. The policy rule proposed by Meltzer (1987), to set base money growth at the average (over the previous three years) value of output growth minus base velocity growth, does not require knowledge of the period-by-period effect of money on real variables. But Meltzer's rule, like mine (McCallum, 1988), is designed to achieve a desired inflation rate on average, not on a period-by-period basis. It should therefore be regarded as a nominal income growth rule in which the target value changes as the (implicitly) forecasted rate of average real growth changes.
34. David Archer has argued that this third suggestion of mine fails to recognize that actual inflation targeting schemes, such as New Zealand's, respond to discrepancies between target values and inflation rates expected to prevail a year or so in the future, not past discrepancies. In practice, such discrepancies may be highly correlated with recent GDP target misses.
35. In the United States, for instance, one could in principle use the product of the CPI and the Fed's Industrial Production Index, both of which are published monthly. Monthly availability is also a feature of the Bureau of Economic Analysis nominal series entitled "Personal Income."
36. It should be noted that these standard deviations pertain not to forecast errors, but to control errors in simulations that assume rational expectations.
37. These rules are optimal, of course, only for the particular model used. My own work presumes that, in light of our ignorance regarding nominal-to-real dynamics, it is more sensible to look for a simple rule that performs reasonably well in a variety of models.
38. Alternative analyses have been presented by Fischer (1995) and Fillion and Tetlow (1994), among others.
39. Note that there is no contradiction between this figure and the Haldane–Salmon and Fillion–Tetlow results reported in Section 6, even abstracting from any possible difference between the United States and the other countries. Specifically, the present figures pertain to a one-period ahead *forecast error* whereas the Section 6 values pertain to variability around a constant target value.

References

Andersson, K. and Berg, C. (1995) "The Inflation Target in Sweden," Working Paper, Sveriges Riksbank.

Archer, D. (1995) "Rules for Monetary Policy: The Rationale Underlying the New Zealand Approach," Working Paper (March).

Barro, R.J. and Gordon, D.B. (1983a) "A Positive Theory of Monetary Policy in a Natural Rate Model," *Journal of Political Economy*, 19 (August), pp. 589–610.

Barro, R.J. and Gordon, D.B. (1983b) "Rules, Discretion, and Reputation in a Model of Monetary Policy," *Journal of Monetary Economics*, 12 (July), pp. 101–21.

Blanchard, O.J. and Fischer, S. (1989) *Lectures in Macroeconomics* (Cambridge, Mass.: MIT Press).

Canzoneri, M.B. (1985) "Monetary Policy Games and the Role of Private Information," *American Economic Review*, 75 (December), pp. 1056–70.

Christiano, L.J., Eichenbaum, M. and Evans, C. (1994) "The Effects of Monetary Policy Shocks: Some Evidence from The Flow of Funds," NBER Working Paper 4699.

Crow, J.W. (1988) "The Work of Canadian Monetary Policy," Bank of Canada *Review* (February), pp. 3–17.

Debelle, G. (1996) "The Ends of Three Small Inflations: Australia, New Zealand, and Canada," *Canadian Public Policy*, 22 (March), pp. 56–78.

Debelle, G. and Fischer, S. (1995) "How Independent Should a Central Bank Be?," in J.C. Fuhrer (ed.), *Goals, Guidelines, and Constraints Facing Monetary Policymakers* (Boston, Mass.: Federal Reserve Bank of Boston), pp. 195–221.

Debelle, G. and Stevens, G. (1995) "Monetary Policy Goals for Inflation in Australia," Research Discussion Paper 9503, Reserve Bank of Australia.

Duguay, P. and Poloz, S. (1994) "The Role of Economic Projections in Canadian Monetary Policy Formulation," *Canadian Public Policy*, 20 (2), pp. 189–99.

Fillion, J.F. and Tetlow, R. (1993) "Zero Inflation or Price Level Targeting? Some Answers from Stochastic Simulations on a Small Open-Economy Macro Model," in *Economic Behavior and Policy Choice Under Price Stability* (Ottawa: Bank of Canada), pp. 129–66.

Fischer, S. (1995) "Modern Central Banking," in F. Capie, S. Fisher, C. Goodhart and N. Schnadt (eds), *The Future of Central Banking* (Cambridge: Cambridge University Press), pp. 262–308.

Freedman, C. (1995) "The Canadian Experience with Targets for Reducing and Controlling Inflation," in L. Leiderman and L.E.O. Svensson (eds), *Inflation Targets* (London: Centre for Economic Policy Research), pp. 19–31.

Haldane, A. and Salmon, C. (1995) "Three Issues on Inflation Targets," Working Paper, Bank of England.

Hansen, E. and Margaritis, E. (1993) "Financial Liberalization and Monetary Policy in New Zealand," *Australian Economic Review* (November), pp. 28–36.

King, M. (1995) "Changes in UK Monetary Policy: Rules and Discretion in Practice," Working Paper, Bank of England.

Kydland, F.E. and Prescott, E.C. (1977) "Rules Rather than Discretion: The Inconsistency of Optimal Plans," *Journal of Political Economy*, 88 (June), pp. 473–92.

Laidler, D. (1996) "Inflation Control and Monetary Policy Rules," in this volume.

Laidler, D. and Robson, W.B.P. (1993) *The Great Canadian Disinflation: The Economics and Politics of Monetary Policy in Canada, 1989–1993* (Toronto: C.D. Howe Institute).

Leiderman, L. and Svensson, L.E.O. (1995) *Inflation Targets* (London: Centre for Economic Policy Research).

Lucas, R.E., Jr (1972) "Econometric Testing of the Natural Rate Hypothesis," in O. Eckstein (ed.), *The Econometric of Price Determination* (Washington, DC: Board of Governors of the Federal Reserve System), pp. 50–9.

Lucas, R.E., Jr (1994) "On the Welfare Cost of Inflation," Working Paper, University of Chicago.

Mayes, D. and Chapple, B. (1995) "The Costs and Benefits of Disinflation: A Critique of the Sacrifice Ratio," Reserve Bank of New Zealand *Bulletin*, 58 (March), pp. 9–21.

McCallum, B.T. (1988) "Robustness Properties of a Rule for Monetary Policy," Carnegie–Rochester Conference Series on Public Policy, 29 (Autumn), pp. 173–203.

McCallum, B.T. (1993) "Specification and Analysis of a Monetary Policy Rule for Japan," Bank of Japan *Monetary and Economic Studies*, 11 (November), pp. 1–45.

McCallum, B.T. (1994) "Specification of Policy Rules and Performance Measures in Multicountry Simulation Studies," *Journal of International Money and Finance*, 13 (June), pp. 259–75.

McCallum, B.T. (1995a) "Two Fallacies Concerning Central Bank Independence," *American Economic Review Papers and Proceedings*, 85 (May), pp. 207–11.

McCallum, B.T. (1995b) "New Zealand's Monetary Policy Arrangements: Some Critical Issues," Reserve Bank of New Zealand Discussion Paper G95/4.

McCallum, B.T. (1996) *International Monetary Economics* (New York: Oxford University Press).

Meltzer, A.H. (1987) "Limits of Short-Run Stabilization Policy," *Economic Inquiry*, 25 (January), pp. 1–14.

Okina, K. (1996) "The Policy Objectives and the Optimal Institutional Framework of a Central Bank," in this volume.

Persson, T. and Tabellini, G. (1993) "Designing Institutions for Monetary Stability," *Carnegie–Rochester Conference Series on Public Policy*, 39 (December), pp. 53–84.

Persson, T. and Tabellini, G. (1994) *Monetary and Fiscal Policy – Volume I: Credibility* (Cambridge, Mass.: MIT Press).

Rebelo, S. (1991) "Long-Run Policy Analysis and Long-Run Growth," *Journal of Political Economy*, 99 (October), pp. 500–21.

Reserve Bank of New Zealand (1993) *Post Election Briefing Paper.*

Romer, P. (1986) "Increasing Returns and Long-Run Growth," *Journal of Political Economy*, 94 (October), pp. 1002–39.

Svensson, L.E.O. (1995a) "The Swedish Experience of an Inflation Target," in L. Leiderman and L.E.O. Svensson (eds), *Inflation Targets* (London: Centre for Economic Policy Research).

Svensson, L.E.O. (1995b) "Optimal Inflation Targets, 'Conservative' Central Banks, and Linear Inflation Contracts," Working Paper, Stockholm University.

Taylor, J.B. (1983) "Comments," *Journal of Monetary Economics*, 12 (July), pp. 123–5.

Walsh, C.E. (1995) "Optimal Contracts for Central Bankers," *American Economics Review*, 85 (March), pp. 150–67.

Comments
David Mayes

It is not surprising to learn that the Reserve Bank of New Zealand is thoroughly convinced of the advantages of inflation targeting and of our particular approach to it. However, it is clear that others can manage to achieve considerable price stability through different regimes. To appreciate our particular design of system it has to be seen in the context of needing to counteract a history of poor inflation performance over a couple of decades, with Ministers of Finance who were prepared to intervene very substantially and run large deficits. A system with a clear target was needed so that the expectations of price setters throughout the economy could be affected. A definition of a target for inflation, which would be as close to price stability as possible was wanted, with a firm incentive structure for the Bank to resist the temptations to miss the target. The design also sought to keep short-run political interference out of the implementation of monetary policy, which accounts for the five-year Policy Targets Agreement (PTA). (The current PTA is shown as an Appendix.)

No system is perfect, and we are alert to how ours could be improved. However, we are concerned that any changes which might be made increase and do not damage credibility. For that reason I find it hard to believe that there would be much enthusiasm for changing the target of keeping inflation between zero and 2 percent on a continuing 12 month basis. But I can see scope for changing the exact price series that we target or for altering the caveats if such changes represented clear improvements.

Let me therefore begin these remarks by following up an area where change might be possible. In his chapter McCallum suggests that it would be a good idea if someone other than the Reserve Bank computed the target. As things stand at present the Reserve Bank publishes a series labeled "Underlying Inflation," which is its own interpretation of the target as spelt out in the Policy Targets Agreement. This has received general acceptance from government and parliament as a fair representation of the objective. However, accountability might appear more robust if an outside authority computed the target. Our approach has been to see if the statistical authority – Statistics New Zealand – could undertake the task. Unfortunately there are some substantial obstacles to achieving this. Clearly the integrity of existing series, especially the CPI, should not be compromised. The consumer price series are not revised, they do not have a list of components which may vary from time to time, nor do they involve an element of econometric computation. Mimicking the terms of the Policy Targets Agreement involves doing all of these, because certain items are caveated in the PTA, allowing their exception from the constraint of inflation being within the zero to 2 percent range. (These are set out in the Appendix.)

Excluding interest and credit costs, which is the principal caveat, does not provide a problem because they are not revised, the caveat applies all the time, and no econometric estimation is required. Indeed as a result we use the Statistics New Zealand computation of it. They publish the series labeled "CPI ex-interest and credit charges" along with the CPI itself each quarter. However, I should say in passing that life would be a great deal easier for us if the normal headline CPI excluded interest as it does in many countries. It is not, after all, a consumer price but a reflection of how people choose to finance their purchases. It would only rarely be necessary to invoke any other caveat. The first problem with the other caveats, which relate changes in government charges (i.e., non-market prices), indirect taxes and terms of trade shocks, is that they use the word "significant," a word which is undefined in the PTA. We have announced that we interpret significant to mean "more than 0.25 percent on the CPI over any 12 month period." This, of course, is arbitrary but setting a fairly coarse limit like this means that items rarely have to be removed from the headline CPI and our underlying measure represents over 90 percent of consumers' expenditure all the time. The problem described here would apply whatever non-zero exclusion was decided upon, whether fixed or variable.

It is difficult to judge in advance whether a particular shock will amount to 0.25 percent on the CPI over a 12-month period – prices may rise slowly and only breach the 0.25 percent level in the fourth quarter. Nevertheless, the whole shock needs to be removed to avoid a blip in the series. Thus the underlying inflation series needs to be revised retrospectively to remove the first effects of the shock from earlier periods.

Similarly, if we take, say, an oil price shock, it is quite a complex matter to say how it feeds through into consumer prices. There could readily be a problem in distinguishing the initial shock from second-round effects. We have produced a little manual explaining how we do these calculations and some private sector analysts usually get the outcome right to within one decimal place before we publish the number. (We only receive the new price data when they are published by Statistics New Zealand and normally spend an hour computing and checking the numbers before publishing the estimate of underlying inflation ourselves.)

This whole process is not the simple, transparent one we would prefer.

There are a number of alternatives. Some are "mechanical" approaches to estimating a series for underlying inflation from the components of the CPI such as a weighted median or the trimmed mean (omitting the extreme 10 percent of price changes, for example), others involve simplifying the caveats. We have been publishing the weighted median from the maximum level of detail available on the CPI components for a while now but had been worried by the degree of downward drift in the series (caused substantially by the impact of the continuing adjustment of government charges to market prices and the "user pays" principle). Having noticeable downward drift compared with the actual CPI in a series used for accountability could harm credibility, as it might appear that we were choosing a measure that made our job easier. However, we have more recently discovered, in some work with the Reserve Bank of Australia, that using a lower level of disaggregation reduces the drift in the median measure.

This may seem a rather trivial issue to focus on in the context of all the aspects of an inflation targeting regime but we have succeeded in keeping inflation within zero to 2 percent every quarter since 1991 with one exception when it was 2.2 percent. We are therefore not at present actively looking for an alternative regime. This is not to say that we have not made mistakes nor that there are no problems with our approach. Interest rates were clearly too low in late 1993 and early 1994. We were wrongly worried about undershooting the range and, despite tightening earlier than most people expected in 1994, did not do so fast enough to avoid going outside the band in the June 1995 quarter. We were unlucky to go outside the band as fresh vegetable prices rose by 40 percent as the result of a dry summer and wet winter and that alone took us outside the band. This has taught us two lessons:

1. It is important not to *aim* too close to the edge of the band as random shocks can take you through the edge of the band, and
2. When one reaches the edge of the band it becomes much more difficult to operate policy and there is a temptation to be more active.

However, more important than this, we have come to recognize both from empirical estimation and from experience that there are asymmetries in the system (Mayes and Riches, 1995). Thus we have been able to estimate a short-run Phillips curve that is not only nonlinear but asymmetric (the approach is similar to that in Clark, Laxton and Rose, 1995). The implication from this is that it is important to be more vigilant about inflation taking off than it is to guard against deflation. The costs of a downward shock are apparently substantially lower than those of an upward one and errors can be corrected more readily. But, as McCallum points out, these conclusions are model-dependent and we are going on to test their robustness across specifications.

We clearly need to be more alert and forward-looking than most central banks because of the narrowness of our target range and this places a very considerable emphasis on the quality of forecasting. While it is true that forecasting becomes more uncertain the further ahead one looks, it is important to remember that policy is endogenous. Our record in forecasting inflation eight quarters ahead is no worse than that four quarters ahead because policy has time to respond to help keep the eight-quarter variance low. With the zero to 2 percent target the inflation forecast any distance ahead is in effect a bounded variable. Since the bulk of the impact of policy occurs three to six quarters ahead we have less impact on the four-quarter ahead figure. Our modeling incorporates this endogeneity of policy.

I do want to counter one statement in McCallum's chapter. The Reserve Bank does not normally *set* monetary conditions as he writes. We produce a forecast four times a year, we explain what monetary conditions will need to be like in order to achieve inflation between zero and 2 percent and, in particular, spell out how it will be necessary to change conditions if events do not pan out as we outline. The market then normally delivers outcomes for interest rates and the exchange rate which are consistent with that outlook for policy. If it does not we will say so. But it is unusual for us to act. We do not set an interest rate, we do not intervene in the foreign exchange market. However, we can act readily and effectively by controlling the amount of cash available for settlement in the overnight markets. The market is fully aware that we can and will act if it is necessary. However, we have only acted twice in the past four years or so despite a halving and then doubling of short rates over that period. On each occasion the action has come near the turning point of monetary conditions to prevent the change occurring as early as the market wanted. In late 1993 we acted to prevent inflation going below zero and in August 1995 we acted to prevent a premature easing.

In setting monetary conditions we have regard to both interest rates and the exchange rate and their transmission through to inflation. While we have from time to time hightlighted the short-run direct impact of the exchange rate, we do not operate an exchange rate target. Indeed, as for any small open economy, we cannot affect the mix of monetary conditions, only the level.

A second small point concerns the remark on page 216 that we communicate a great deal with the market in public statements. Although the Governor does indeed make a lot of speeches they are almost entirely off the record and represent an attempt to explain our policy to as large a section of the population and overseas investors as possible. Our statements normally have one of two purposes: to indicate that monetary conditions are in danger of becoming inconsistent with maintaining price stability and, second, to say that we have changed our view of the future. Official statements to show changes in view are fairly few between forecasts as economic events do not usually move that rapidly. It was only in 1995 that we had to make somewhat more statements because we were at the edge of the target range and near a turning point in the economic cycle. There were no communications with the market except the quarterly forecasts between November 1995 and the time of writing in June 1996.

The final area I want to mention is nominal income targeting. McCallum argues that there may be a case for targeting some nominal variable rather than prices directly. This relies on sustainable growth being predictable and indeed on data on the nominal variables being available. Unfortunately we have no income measures of GDP and our output and expenditure measures have substantial and enduring discrepancies. The statistics are produced around three months later than price figures.

However, to base the argument on the practical considerations is ducking the issue. The interesting question is whether a nominal target filters out shocks appropriately. Clearly it will tend to act firmly against demand shocks as in those cases real and price movements will be positively correlated. Supply shocks on the other hand will tend to be accommodated. However, with a similar narrow bandwidth the constraints imposed by such a policy would be much harsher and hence for an equivalent policy stance the bands would have to be wider.

Even if one is just targeting inflation, a large element of the assessment of future inflationary pressures is likely to resort to estimates of output gaps. This in turn requires a view of sustainable output. Thus one cannot avoid the judgment of sustainable growth whether one is nominal income or inflation targeting. The nature of the difference between the two measures in practice will depend on the lags between the output and inflation cycles. I also suspect that the concept is weaker in its appeal to the man in the street than is a direct inflation target. It would need rather greater credibility in the country to be a serious alternative at present.

Appendix: Reserve Bank of New Zealand Policy Targets Agreement

This agreement replaces that signed under section 9(4) of the Reserve Bank of New Zealand Act 1989 (the Act) between the Minister of Finance (the Minister) and the Governor of the Reserve Bank of New Zealand (the Governor) on 19 December 1990.

It is made under section 9(4) of the Act, and also under section 9(1) of the Act, so that it shall also apply during the Governor's next term of office.

In terms of section 9 of the Act, the Minister and the Governor agree as follows:

1. **Price Stability Target**

   Consistent with section 8 of the Act and with the provisions of this agreement, the Reserve Bank shall formulate and implement monetary policy with the intention of maintaining a stable general level of prices.

2. **Measurement of Price Stability**

   (a) In pursuing the objective of a stable general level of prices, the Bank will monitor prices as measured by a range of price indices. The formal price stability target will be defined in terms of the All Groups Consumers Price Index (CPI), being the measure that is monitored most closely by the public.

   (b) For the purposes of this agreement, 12-monthly increases in the CPI of between 0 and 2 percent will be considered consistent with price stability.

3. **Deviations from the Targets**

   (a) There is a range of possible price shocks arising from external sources, certain government policy changes, or a natural crisis which are quite outside the direct influence of monetary policy. The Bank shall generally react to such shifts in relative prices in a manner which prevents general inflationary pressures emerging.

   (b) This approach means that the CPI inflation rate can be expected to move outside the 0–2 percent range in response to particular shocks. The principal shocks are considered to be:

   - significant changes in the terms of trade arising from an increase or decrease in either import or export prices;
   - an increase or decrease in the rate of GST, or a significant change in other indirect tax rates;
   - a crisis such as a natural disaster or a major disease-induced fall in livestock numbers which is expected to have a significant impact on the price level;
   - a significant price level impact arising from changes to government or local authority levies; and
   - a movement in interest rates that causes significant divergence between the change in the CPI and the change in the CPI excluding the interest costs component.

(c) In the event of such shocks, the Reserve Bank shall be fully accountable for its handling of the price effects, and, in particular, for any movements outside the 0–2 percent band. In each Policy Statement made under section 15 of the Act, the Bank shall detail fully its estimate of the direct price impact of any such shock and the impact on the Bank's achievement of the price stability target. The Bank shall also detail what measures it has taken, or proposes to take, to ensure that the effects of such shocks on the inflation rate are transitory.

4. **Renegotiation of the Targets**

The policy targets are established on the understanding that the monetary policy instruments available to the Bank are adequate to achieve the objective. The Governor shall inform the Minister if he considers that any changes in the availability or effectiveness of these policy instruments impair the conduct of monetary policy. The Minister and the Governor may then set new policy targets.

5. **Implementation**

(a) The Bank shall implement monetary Policy in a sustainable, consistent and transparent manner.

(b) Each Policy Statement released by the Bank under section 15 of the Act shall contain a statement of how the Bank proposes to formulate and implement monetary policy to ensure that price stability is maintained over the succeeding five years.

Signed by:

Ruth Richardson
Minister of Finance

Donald T Brash
Governor
Reserve Bank of New Zealand

16 December 1992

References

Clark, P., Laxton, D. and Rose, D. (1995) "Asymmetry in the US Output–Inflation Nexus: Issues and Evidence," IMF Working Paper No. WP/95/(July) (Washington, DC: International Monetary Fund).

Mayes, D. and Riches, B. (1995) "Effectiveness of Monetary Policy in New Zealand," Conference on Effective Monetary Policy, Sydney, October 1995.

Comments

Jack H. Beebe

I agree strongly with McCallum's overall analysis and conclusions. However, I want to expand on a few points. I also want to draw a clear distinction between explicit *goals* or *objectives* on the one hand and explicit (rule-based) operating procedures on the other. My own preference is to make a public commitment to monetary policy goals, but not necessarily to the operating procedures, a position that differs from the work of McCallum, Allan Meltzer, and John Taylor. I want to make it clear, however, that I favor their work, and prefer *internal* use of rules as an important input to discretionary monetary policy. If used in this way, I would expect the implications of these rules to be discussed publicly. However, the external public *commitment* would be to an inflation goal, not to any specific operating rule. I will break my comments into several points.

First, McCallum presents data on inflation expectations in four countries that target inflation, as measured by spreads of their long-term bond rates over those in Switzerland, a consistently low-inflation country. As McCallum notes, in three of the four countries, his measure of inflation expectations has fallen by much less than inflation itself. This result is consistent with comparisons of actual inflation and inflation-expectations surveys, as discussed in a separate paper by two economists at the Federal Reserve Board, John Ammer and Dick Freeman.[1] The apparent lag of inflation expectations behind actual inflation in these countries supports the idea that credibility is gained mainly by results rather than by the independent effects of the public targets themselves.

While I strongly believe that governments and central banks should jointly set explicit public inflation targets, I do not base this position on a claim of enhanced credibility, or a lower "sacrifice ratio," in the transition to a new inflation regime. I base it on the fact that such a target would help constrain the central bank toward achieving and maintaining a single, consistent, and predictable inflation regime over a very long period of time.

Second, McCallum points out that the most common approach traditionally used by central banks is to achieve an appropriate *balance* between *competing* objectives of low inflation and high output. He then asks whether inflation targeting would be an improvement. McCallum answers yes, for two main reasons. First, he notes several reasons why inflation is detrimental to the long-run level or growth of economic capacity. Second, he notes that, in the long run, monetary policy has a dominating influence on prices, but a negligible influence on output relative to capacity.

I agree with these points. However, I think McCallum might overstate the distinction between aiming at an appropriate balance between inflation and output goals on the one hand, and maintaining an inflation target on the other. *Modest* (relatively passive) counter-cyclical policy adjustments in the short run can still be consistent with achieving an inflation target over the long run. This point has been made by John Taylor, Bill White, and others in this volume, and is illustrated by the policy feedback rules proposed by McCallum and John Taylor. Under Taylor's rule, for example, the short-term interest rate is adjusted each period according to gaps between real GDP and its trend and between inflation and its target, where the weights on these two gaps are *equal.* Thus, in the short run, stabilization policy plays an important role. (In fact, one could argue it is as important as the inflation target.) In the long run, however, real GDP growth equals its trend, so all of the weight goes to inflation.[2] A similar point applies to nominal GDP rules like McCallum's, which implicitly put equal weight on real GDP and price changes in the very short run, but full weight on prices in the long run. I might add that, through the link from money to nominal income, the monetarist rule of constant money growth also puts some implicit weight on real output in the short run.

Third, McCallum raises the issue of whether targets should be established in terms of the *rate* of inflation or the price *level*, and points out some disadvantages of both. An inflation target "forgives" past misses and permits the price level to drift. A price level target, however, even one with a positive trend, requires periods of sharp monetary response that would increase volatility in real GDP.

I was impressed by McCallum's calculation that, *based upon past disturbances to the US price level*, the amount of *drift* that we could expect under an inflation target would be modest. While his calculation can be faulted by the Lucas critique, he concludes, correctly I believe, that greater volatility in real GDP would be a more serious problem than price level drift relative to target, and therefore supports inflation targets over price level targets.[3]

Finally, McCallum asks whether the target should be for inflation or nominal GDP growth. On this issue, and the related issue of rule-based operating procedures, the chapter does not always maintain a clear distinction between ultimate goals and operating procedures. In the chapter's conclusion, McCallum argues for a public *inflation* target because of its clarity. But in discussing the operational aspects of inflation targeting, he presents a favorable case for a nominal GDP or income target over an inflation target. Our staff work argues similarly.[4] McCallum concludes correctly, I believe, that hitting an operational target for nominal GDP growth would entail little deterioration in terms of the performance of long-run average inflation. Furthermore, he cites a number of reasons why nominal GDP targets *operationally* would be preferable to inflation targets. For example, since nominal GDP reacts more quickly than inflation to monetary actions, instrument instability is less likely to be a problem and the path for real GDP is likely to be smoother.[5] Work by Judd and Motley on our staff has reached similar conclusions.[6] But I think Ben would agree that these considerations pertain more to rule-based procedures than to public commitments to ultimate goals.

In highlighting the distinction between goals and procedures, I would like also to distinguish between the roles of the government and the central bank. It seems to me that the government's role is to instruct the central bank about its ultimate goals, or to decide on these goals jointly with the bank, while the central bank's role is to achieve the goals. It seems reasonable for the government to have a central role in deciding the inflation target, since inflation and its variability affect welfare, and regime shifts in inflation can have large distributional effects. However, I do not think the government should get involved with nominal GDP or operating procedures, especially since no single set of operating procedures could be guaranteed to work well in all future circumstances.

The issue of US inflation targets recently has been raised by the introduction of legislation by Senator Mack of Florida. His proposed bill would supersede the Humphrey–Hawkins Act, which currently governs the relationship between the government and the Federal Reserve and contains both ambiguities and inconsistencies.

Senator Mack's proposal would remove the requirement to establish and report on ranges for the monetary aggregates. More importantly, it would clarify the Fed's goals, placing primary emphasis on "price stability." It would require the Fed to define a numerical inflation target that it deems consistent with price stability and to state the time frame for achieving it. The Fed also would choose the specific inflation index to target, which in effect would let the Fed decide which kinds of shocks to exclude. Finally, the Fed would be required (as it is now) to report to Congress twice a year on its progress in achieving the goal and its plans for the future.

I believe the Mack bill would be a dramatic improvement on the Humphrey–Hawkins Act. Moreover, I would take what I am sure is a minority position at the Fed in suggesting it could be improved by *not* allowing the Fed to set the numerical target and index unilaterally. Actually, I would favor the New Zealand or Canadian approach of requiring that these important goal parameters be *jointly* agreed upon between government and the central bank, while the operating procedures be left to the central bank.

In closing let me say that I focused on only a portion of the thoughtful and pertinent issues in McCallum's interesting chapter.

Notes

1. John Ammer and Richard T. Freeman (1994) "Inflation Targeting in the 1990s: The Experiences of New Zealand, Canada, and the United Kingdom," Board of Governors of the Federal Reserve System, *International Finance Discussion Papers*, No. 473.
2. If the GDP gap is interpreted as a predictor of the future change in inflation, one could argue that the weight is shifted toward inflation targeting.
3. McCallum also argues that it might be even better to target a weighted average of a level and a growth rate. However, some research has found that his approach is only slightly less likely to lead to instrument instability than a straight level target in models of the US economy (John P. Judd and Brian Motley (1992) "Controlling Inflation with an Interest Rate Instrument," FRBSF *Economic Review*, 1992: 3, pp. 3–22).
4. John Judd and Brian Motley (1993) "Using a Nominal GDP Rule to Guide Discretionary Monetary Policy," FRBSF *Economic Review*, 1993:3, pp. 3–11.
5. McCallum also argues that we know more about forecasting growth in nominal GDP (aggregate demand) than about how that gets divided into inflation and real GDP growth. This point is correct if a stable monetary or credit aggregate is available, but is less clear in a case like the USA where no such aggregate exists.
6. John Judd and Brian Motley (1991) "Nominal Feedback Rules for Monetary Policy," FRBSF *Economic Review*, 1991:3, pp. 3–17.

9 Japanese Monetary Policy, Rules or Discretion? A Reconsideration

Kazuo Ueda

1 INTRODUCTION

The two major objectives of a central bank are the maintenance of the stability of prices and that of the financial system. To use harsh language, the Bank of Japan (henceforth, the BOJ) has failed to meet each of the two objectives once during the past two and a half decades. In the early 1970s the rate of inflation rose to levels above 20 percent. Since 1992 the economy has been suffering from the most serious instability in the financial system since the 1920s. The purpose of this chapter is to review the BOJ's conduct of monetary policy over the past two to three decades and discuss the relationship between the two mistakes and the way monetary policy has been carried out.

I emphasize the contrast between a textbook-type central bank which sets the money supply to control inflation and/or GDP and central banks in the real world which pursue a variety of policy objectives using mostly interest rates as instruments. Based on some recent literature which describes the behavior of central banks in industrialized countries, especially the Fed, I analyze the behavior of the BOJ in some detail. I show that despite the diversity of the objectives pursued by the BOJ, some distinct patterns can be observed in its behavior. These behavioral patterns of the BOJ are related to the two major monetary problems Japan has faced since 1970.

A brief discussion of the nature of the two monetary problems is in order. The inflation of 1973 and 1974 in Japan was clearly a monetary phenomenon. During the expansion of the economy which started in early 1972, the rate of inflation quickly increased to crisis levels; the rate of increase in the GDP deflator was already 7.4 percent in 1972:IV, went up to 17.2 percent in 1973:III right before the oil price increases and to levels above 20 percent in 1974. Correspondingly, the monetary base was expanding at rates above 15 percent already in 1971 and at 25 percent in 1973:II. Clearly, the BOJ had failed to fulfill its responsibility.

The monetary expansion which started in 1986 was a very powerful one with six consecutive decreases in the official discount rate. The monetary base increased at a rate of 13.6 percent in 1987:III against a real GDP growth rate of 4.1 percent. The rate of inflation, however, stayed at around 0 percent. What was inflated were stock and land prices. The Nikkei 225 shot up to 39000 in December 1989 from about 13000 in early 1986. The BOJ turned to tightening in May 1989 with an inflation rate of only 2 percent, bringing the Nikkei 225 down in the summer of 1992 to around 14000, the level of 1986.

In the early 1990s most people regarded the volatile asset price movements as the formation and collapse of a bubble with no serious real consequences, and praised the BOJ for successful control of the prices of goods. The economy, however, has not fully recovered from the recession which started in mid-1991, despite statements to the contrary by the EPA (Economic Planning Agency). The financial system is suffering from bad loans amounting to about 10 percent of GDP. The GDP deflator has been growing at negative rates since 1994:II. People have now realized the connection between the speculative boom in the assets markets in the late 1980s, its collapse in the 1990s, the bad debt problem and the volatile movements in monetary policy. The criticism of the BOJ is based on the realization that a more stable monetary policy could have prevented both the speculative boom and the bad debt problem.

In the next section, I analyze the BOJ's monetary policy, especially its policy targets and the response of policy instruments to target variables, in a variety of ways. In Section 3 I point out that each of the two mistakes of the BOJ led to an interesting debate between academics and the BOJ on the desirability of money growth targets. In Section 4, some results of the simulation of the performance of money growth target-oriented monetary policy are presented. The last section offers some concluding remarks.

2 THE BOJ's POLICY TARGETS AND ITS REACTION FUNCTION

In analyzing the behavior of the BOJ it is useful to compare it with that of other central banks. A useful reference point is offered by Bernanke and Mishkin (1992). Some of their conclusions that relate to my analysis are offered here for later reference:

(B–M1) Central bankers have multiple objectives and a crisis mentality.
(B–M2) When central bankers' concern about inflation is strong, they are likely to adopt money growth targets, but they do not adhere to

the targets strictly. Short-run adherence to money growth targets does not seem to be necessary for inflation control.

(B–M3) The outcome of monetary policy does not appear to depend much on the operating procedure or the choice of instruments.

2.1 The BOJ's Policy Instruments and Operating Procedure

This chapter will not discuss the BOJ's policy instruments and operating procedure in detail. A brief discussion, however, is offered by way of introduction.[1]

The major policy instrument of the BOJ has long been short-term interest rates, especially the official discount rate. In a simple model of monetary policy, changes in the discount rate would have no significant effects on the economy if discount window lendings are rationed by the central bank, as is the case in Japan.[2] The BOJ, however, has generally moved interbank interest rates such as the call rate and the bills discount rate in line with the official discount rate, and has changed the official discount rate only if a change in interbank rates is of a long-term nature. In this sense, the BOJ's policy stance has been most clearly represented by the official discount rate.

In addition to short-term interest rates, the BOJ relied until 1991 on the so-called "window guidance," that is, restrictions on lendings of major financial institutions, to supplement its main policy instruments. Window guidance perhaps made the effects of a discount rate change more effective and rapid in the environment of less-than-perfect flexibility of interest rates. Thus, with most interest rates now free to move, it is no longer used. The BOJ also used changes in the official reserve requirement ratios for monetary control purposes until the early 1980s.

The BOJ's operating procedure is one of interest rate targeting. Basically, it has supplied as much high-powered money or, more narrowly, reserves as the private sector has demanded at the going interest rate. In other words, in the short run the BOJ has paid attention to interest rate stability. It has never adopted monetary base targeting or money supply targeting. I offer some evidence on this point in subsection 2.4 below.

In what follows I let short-term interest rates, the official discount rate and the call rate represent the BOJ's monetary policy stance.

2.2 Cyclical Changes in the Stance of Monetary Policy

Among the many targets of central banks, perhaps the most important in normal times has been the state of the economy, or more specifically, the GDP gap. The BOJ is no exception.

Table 9.1 The discount and call rates in recessions

	Quarter after peak	*June 1957*	*Dec. 1961*	*Oct. 1964*	*July 1970*	*Nov. 1973*	*Jan. 1977*	*Feb. 1980*	*June 1985*	*April 1991*
IK	1	0.297	0	−0.333	−0.177	1.783	−1.191	2.038	0	0
	2	0	0	−0.409	−0.27	0	−0.41	−0.342	0	−0.5
	3	0	0	−0.353	−0.201	0	−0.538	−1.017	−0.461	−0.272
	4	−0.104	−0.401	0	−0.279	0		−0.547	−0.929	−0.728
	5				−0.089	0		−0.844	−0.11	−0.75
	6							0	−0.332	−0.359
Total		0.193	−0.401	−1.095	−1.016	1.783	−2.139	−0.712	−1.832	−2.609
IC	1	1.88667	0	−2.55	−0.5	2.63367	−1.388	3.2961	0.18546	−0.04887
	2	−1.83	0	−1.22	−0.66667	0.09666	−0.04666	−0.40784	1.0278	−0.77093
	3	0	0	−0.73	−0.75	0.86367	−0.613	−2.05566	−1.22883	−0.80586
	4	−0.73	0.12333	−0.61	−0.33333	−0.16767		−1.49287	−1.61727	−0.91154
	5				−0.724	−0.00466		−1.39527	0.1268	−0.86304
	6							0.13087	−0.4418	−0.47877
Toal		−0.67333	0.12333	−5.11	−2.974	3.42167	−2.04766	−1.92467	−1.94784	−3.87901

IK: the discount rate.
IC: the call rate.
Entries are interest rate changes over a quarter.

Romer and Romer (1994) have shown that the Fed has responded to the US business cycle very consistently. That is, the federal funds rate decreases quickly and significantly once the economy passes its peak. Conversely, after a trough in the economy the Fed tightens without too much delay.

Table 9.1 presents the same analysis as Romer and Romer for the downturns of the Japanese economy during the past forty years. The entries in the table are changes in the official discount rate and the call rate in each quarter. The top row of the table shows the date of the peak of each cycle.

With only a few exceptions the rates decline once the economy passes its peak. Some differences between the USA and Japan are: In the USA interest rates have declined without exception during recessions, while this is not the case in Japan. The size of the decline in rates is larger for the USA; the average decline in the federal funds rate between the peak and trough is 3.4 percentage points, while the corresponding figure is –0.9 percentage points for the discount rate and –1.7 percentage points for the call rate. The BOJ also responds with some lag to downturns, while the Fed's response is immediate.[3] It is ironic to observe that one of the few exceptions to the declining pattern of interest rates during recessions is the period after the peak of 1973. Despite the maintenance of interest rates at high levels, the rate of inflation went up. This implies that policy was too expansionary before the peak.

Table 9.2 does the same for recovery periods. Here, no distinct patterns emerge. Unlike in the USA, interest rates do not seem to rise as the economy passes its trough. If anything, the rates seem to keep declining for a while after the trough. The most significant is the current period. Almost two years have passed since the last trough; but the discount rate is still being cut. This indicates the seriousness of the current recession.[4]

The analysis shows that the BOJ responds consistently to movements in real GDP, lowering rates in recessions and increasing them in recoveries. But the rates increases seem to come fairly late during recoveries. Thus, (B–M1), that is, the hypothesis that central banks respond to variables in crisis situations, does not seem to apply to the case of real GDP.

2.3 Motivations for the BOJ's Policy Changes

The last section has shown that the BOJ carries out a counter-cyclical policy to a certain extent. I now show that this has in fact been the BOJ's intention by reference to statements by the chairman of the BOJ's policy committee at the time of policy changes.

In Table 9.3 I have summarized the statements to highlight the

Table 9.2 The discount and call rates in recoveries

	Quarter after trough	*June 1958*	*Oct. 1962*	*Oct. 1965*	*Dec. 1971*	*Mar. 1975*	*Oct. 1977*	*Feb. 1983*	*Nov. 1986*	*Nov. 1993*
IK	1	−0.729	−0.378	0	−0.484	−0.55	−0.133	0	−0.374	0
	2	−0.262	−0.606	0	−0.038	−0.716	−0.617	0	−0.294	0
	3	−0.166	−0.075	0	−0.462	−0.984	0	−0.217	0	0
	4	−0.199	0	0	0	−0.25	0	−0.283	0	0
	5	0	0.112	0	0	0	0	0	0	0
	6	0.119	0.618	0	0.918	0	0.618	0	0	−0.75
Total		−1.237	−0.329	0	−0.066	−2.5	−0.132	−0.5	−0.668	−0.75
IC	1	−0.85	−0.73	0	−0.40067	−1.598	−0.11234	−0.44474	−0.1227	−0.22255
	2	−1.15333	−0.97333	0	−0.31033	−0.81367	−0.635	0.26784	−0.71626	−0.14933
	3	0.12	0.12	0	−0.35033	−2.352	0.25967	−0.1751	−0.03284	0.02359
	4	0	0.24333	0	0.022	−1.00667	−0.13567	−0.1019	0.27604	0.13312
	5	0.06333	0.67	0.12333	0.70233	−0.293	0.19867	−0.33747	−0.0364	−0.0483
	6	0	1.52334	0	0.94033	0.327	0.68973	0.30847	−0.1562	−0.835
Total		−1.82	0.85334	0.12333	0.60333	−5.73634	−0.26506	−0.4829	−0.78836	−1.09847

Table 9.3 Motivations for discount rate changes

	Direction	*Y*	*P*	*NX*	*e*	*Money*	*Stability*
1967:9–1968:1	Up	*X*(*NX*)		*A*			
1968:8	Down			*R*(*A*)			
1968:9	Up	*X*(*P*)	*A*				
1970:5–1972:6	Down	*A*			*X*(*Y*)		
1973:4–1973:12	Up		*A*				
1975:4–1978:3	Down	*A*	*R*(*A*)	*A*	*X*(*Y*)		
1979:4–1980:3	Up	*X*(*P*)	*A*	*X*(*e*)	*A*', *X*(*P*)	*B*	
1980:8–1981:12	Down		*R*(*A*)				
1983:10–1987:12	Down	*A*		*A*	*A*		
1989:5–1990:8	Up		*A*			*B*	*A*
1991:7–1993:9	Down	*A*	*R*(*A*)	*B*	*B*		*A*', *B*

Direction: direction of the discount rate change.
Y: GDP.
P: inflation.
NX: the current account.
e: the exchange rate.
Money: the money supply.
Stability: the stability of the financial system.

Entries mean:
A, major motivations; *B*, important factors;
X(*Z*), the variable is of concern because it affects *Z*;
R(*A*), reversal of previous move.

Figure 9.1 Monetary policy and macro-fluctuations

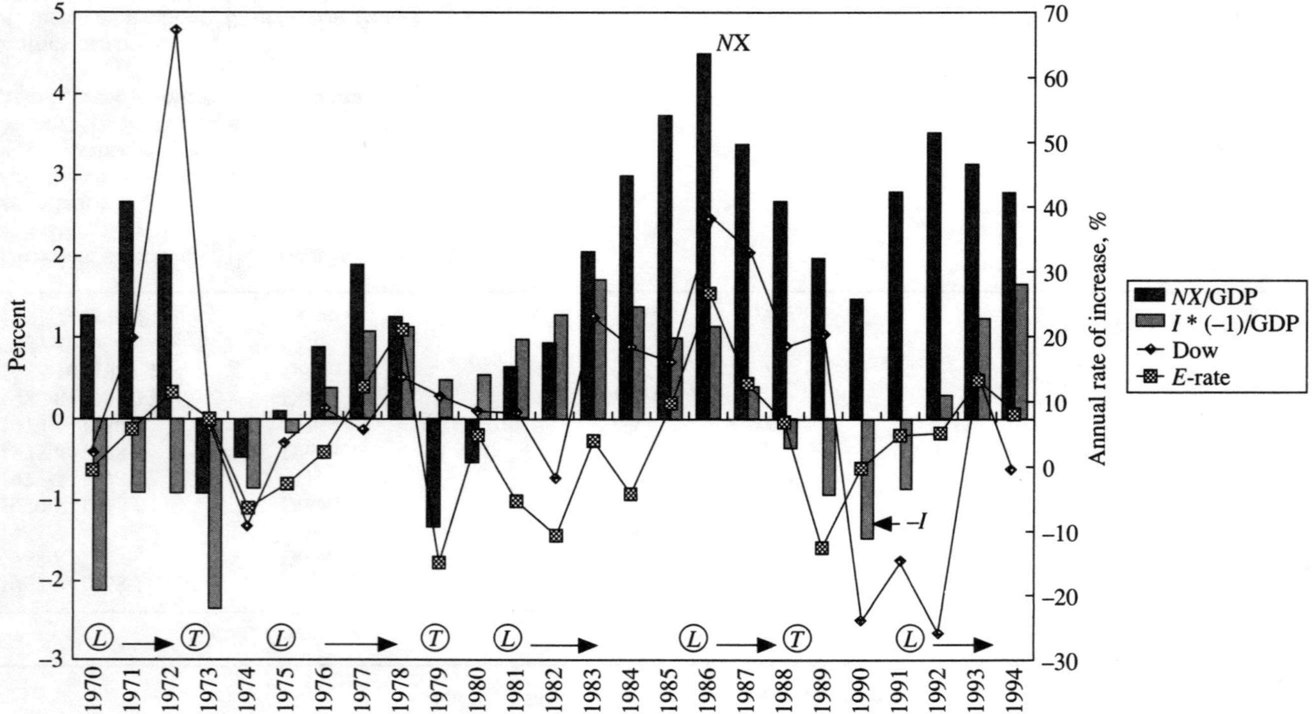

motivations for discount rate changes. The first column represents periods of consecutive changes in the discount rate in one direction. The direction of change is shown in the second column. For each of the target variables, *A* means that it was the major concern of the BOJ at the time of the rate change. *B* means that it was mentioned as a motivation for policy change. *A*' is in between *A* and *B*. *X*(*Z*) is meant to imply that the variable was regarded as important as a cause of the movement in *Z*. *R*(*Z*) means that the policy in the previous period is reversed because the BOJ has successfully controlled movements in *Z*. I have used many judgments and discretion to arrive at this table. For example, some of the statements have been ignored either because the logic presented was not clear-cut or because the variable did not seem to be as important as other variables.

The table shows a number of interesting things about the BOJ's behavior. First, as with other central banks, the BOJ's policy depends much on real GDP and inflation. Second, it has also paid attention to the current account and the exchange rate. Third, there is some evidence that the money supply has been watched since the late 1970s. Fourth, consideration of the stability of the financial system has been an important motivation for policy changes since 1989.

More specifically, the first two rows represent the typical BOJ behavior during the 1950s and 1960s. The major target of policy was the current account. The BOJ tightened when the current account recorded a deficit and loosened as the current account improved.

Since 1970, most of the interest rate reductions have been partly motivated by a concern for GDP, an observation consistent with the analysis of the last section, and most of the upturns by a concern for inflation. Importantly, most of the reductions in rates since 1970 have been motivated also by exchange rate and/or current account movements. It may be seen from Figure 9.1 (see page 260) that these are the periods of a current account surplus and a sharp appreciation of the yen. An interpretation of the BOJ's behavior is offered below.

2.4 The BOJ's Policy Reaction Function

A more formal approach to identifying policy targets of a central bank is to estimate the bank's reaction functions. This approach involves an inherent difficulty, that is, target variables themselves are dependent on policy decisions, thus creating simultaneous equations bias when a policy variable is regressed on targets. Here, I offer a brief survey of the literature and present estimation results of several BOJ policy reaction functions, without pretending that these are the best equations one can find.

Table 9.4 The BOJ's reaction function

	DP	*GAP*	*BOJ*	*E*	*NX*	*DM–DM**		*IC*(–1)	R^2	*DW*
(1) 1956:3–1974:4	11.9	–9.4			–73.6				0.525	0.346
	2.47	*–2.02*			*–5.55*					
(2) 1975:1–1995:1	37.3	25.80			–90.1				0.686	0.315
	5.51	*4.39*			*–7.99*					
(3) 1970:4–1995:1	6.63		0.0144	0.293	–29.6			0.682	0.95	1.99
	2.09		*4.55*	*0.848*	*–3.65*			*10*		
(4) 1979:3–1995:1	–13		0.0138	1.346	–35.8	0.0492		0.638	0.949	1.88
	–1.16		*3.53*	*2.68*	*–4.29*	*0.386*		*5.34*		
	DP+	*DP–*	*BOJ1*	*BOJ2*	*BOJ3*	*BOJ4*	*NX*	*IC*(–1)	R^2	*DW*
(5) 1970:4–1995:1	7.27	4.05	0.0163	0.0151	0.131	0.009	–28.8	0.708	0.95	1.99
	2.27	0.183	2.48	1.91	1.98	1.15	–3.37	10		

Notes:

1. *DP*: GDP deflator inflation rate, relative to one year before.
   GAP: GDP gap, with full-employment GDP estimated to be exponentially linear with a kink in time trend at the end of 1973.
   BOJ: Business conditions, favorable–unfavorable, from the BOJ's *Short-Term Economic Survey*.
   E: Log of the yen price of the dollar.
   NX: Current account/GDP.
   *DM–DM**: One-year growth rate of M2 minus its forecast.
   DP+: *DP* if annual inflation rate is above 5%, otherwise 0.
   DP–: *DP–DP+*.
   BOJ1: *BOJ* if *BOJ* is above zero and is increasing, otherwise zero.
   BOJ2: *BOJ* if it is above zero and decreasing, otherwise zero.
   BOJ3: *BOJ* if it is below zero and decreasing, otherwise zero.
   BOJ4: *BOJ* if it is below zero and increasing, otherwise zero.
2. The dependent variable is the call rate, *IC*. All equations include a constant. Equations (3)–(5) are estimated with correction for first-order serial correction.
3. Number in italics are *t*-statistics.

Among recent attempts at estimating the BOJ's reaction functions, Hutchison (1988) finds that the call rate responds significantly to the exchange rate and to some extent nominal income (as proxied by retail sales), but not to the difference between the actual money supply growth and the BOJ's forecasts for the period of 1973–85. The last result shows that the forecasts are not a policy target. Okabe (1992) finds that the determinants of the call rate are inflation, the exchange rate, and the current account for the period of 1975–90. In the following I update these results and offer some new insights.

In Table 9.4 some estimates of the BOJ's policy reaction functions are presented. The equations are not derived from the maximization of an objective function of the BOJ, but are more or less in line with previous analyses of the reaction functions. In all cases the stance of policy is assumed to be represented by the call rate. All the independent variables are lagged by one period to alleviate the problem of simultaneous equation bias.

Equations (1) and (2) compare the policy stance before and after the first "oil shock." This division also roughly corresponds to the division between the fixed exchange rate and flexible exchange rate periods. The GDP gap variable has a wrong sign in equation (1). The current account has a strong effect on the call rate, as expected from the discussion in the previous section. For the post first "oil shock" period, all the three-variables are significant and have correct signs. Thus, before 1974, monetary policy, as a first approximation, responded only to the current account, while since then it has responded also to inflation and GDP developments. The effect of the current account on monetary policy, however, remains surprisingly strong even after the adoption of the flexible rate.

Equation (3) uses a result of the BOJ's short-term survey of major enterprises as a proxy for GDP gap. This variable is carefully watched by the BOJ and may be a better indicator of the state of the economy. The equation includes the exchange rate as well. The result is not very different from equation (2), with the exchange rate being insignificant. This could be a result of high correlation between the exchange rate and the current account. In equation (4), we add the forecast errors of the money supply, calculated by using the BOJ's forecast of the money supply. If the forecasts are in fact policy targets, the call rate should respond positively to the error. The response is positive, but insignificant. Thus, we find no evidence for a target-like role for the money supply forecasts.

Finally, in equation (5), we do something more precise. That is, the response of the call rate to inflation and the business cycle is assumed to be non-linear, or piecewise linear. The estimation result shows that the BOJ does not respond to inflation unless the rate of inflation exceeds 5 percent.[5] This is consistent with the hypothesis (B–M1) that central banks respond to some of the target variables only at crisis levels. The result also shows that the call rate does not respond significantly to *BOJ*3, that is, it does not go up in the early stage of a recovery, although at other times it moves procyclically. This accords exactly with the finding in subsection 2.1 that, unlike the Fed, the BOJ does not raise interest rates quickly after the trough of the business cycle. Given that the BOJ has succeeded in controlling inflation since the mid-1970s, this finding probably implies that a quick move to monetary tightening in economic recoveries is not a necessary condition for inflation control.

2.5 Summary and Interpretation

The foregoing analysis of the BOJ's policy targets and the pattern of response to the state of the economy can be summarized as follows. The BOJ carries out a feedback type policy in the sense that it increases (decreases) interest rates as the GDP gap shrinks (widens) and the rate of inflation rises (declines). The response, however, is non-linear in that short-term interest rates rise only when the inflation rate is very high and or in the later stages of economic recovery. The BOJ also watches the exchange rate and the current account carefully, but does not seem to have any money growth targets.

These findings roughly match the B–M hypotheses. As with (B–M1), the BOJ pursues many targets. It has a crisis mentality especially with respect to inflation. Although the BOJ has not adopted money growth targets as in (B–M2), it has started to pay attention to money growth since the inflation of the early 1970s. The BOJ, however, seems to respond to the state of the business cycle continuously with the exception of the early stages of a recovery, as does the Fed.

What can we make of the BOJ's significant response to the current account and the exchange rate after the mid-1970s? The following interpretation was offered in Ueda (1993b), and I still believe that it is not far off the mark. The interpretation is succinctly summarized in Figure 9.1. It presents the current account relative to GDP, (–1) times the share of investment in GDP,[6] the rate of change in yen per dollar, the rate of change in the Nikkei 225 and the timing of shifts in monetary policy. *L* stands for the first lowering of the discount rate after a period of tight monetary policy. *T* stands for the first increase in the discount rate after a period of loose monetary policy. An exception is early 1986, when *L* appears after *L*, because there was no tightening in between.

The chart reveals clearly that all these variables are closely related. The interpretation of the relationships offered in Ueda (1993b) is as follows. A current account surplus causes an appreciation of the yen. It also worsens trade conflicts. The presumption has been that an appreciation of the yen exerts a strong deflationary impact on the economy. The public calls for measures to increase aggregate demand and reverse the trend of the exchange rate. Foreign governments also ask for an expansionary macro-policy. For these reasons, interest rates are lowered, leading to increases in asset prices and, with a lag, to a rise in investment and a worsening of the current account. There is, of course, the question why the BOJ wants to expand if one of the policy targets is to create a worsening of the current account. It could be that a monetary expansion leads to a worsening of the current account through expansion of domestic demand, which outweighs the effect of exchange rate depreciation.

The figure shows that the above pattern has been repeated four times in the past twenty-five years, the early 1970s, the late 1970s, the mid- to late 1980s and the mid-1990s. The only deviation from the pattern is that in the mid-1990s we did not see an increase in stock prices. This interpretation of the variables in the figure will prove important in evaluating the performance of the BOJ's monetary policy.

3 THE BOJ's MISTAKES AND MONEY SUPPLY CONTROVERSIES IN JAPAN

3.1 Causes of the Failure of Monetary Policy

During the past three decades, the BOJ has made two major mistakes. First, it allowed the rate of inflation to surge to levels above 20 percent in the early 1970s. Second, it sat back and watched the Nikkei Dow go up to near 40000 in 1989. The rise in land and stock prices looked all right for a while, apart from the arbitrary reallocation of wealth. But the monetary tightening in the early 1990s led to a sharp collapse of what was perhaps a bubble and has thrown the Japanese financial system into the worst crisis in the postwar period. Thus, the BOJ has made two most serious mistakes, creating inflation and creating financial instability.

The source of the mistakes can be inferred from the interpretation of the correlation between the exchange rate, the current account and monetary policy offered in the last section.[7] Most easing of monetary policy during the past two and a half decades was prompted by a large current account surplus and exchange rate appreciation. The BOJ was worried about the deflationary impact of the yen appreciation on the economy and concerned about trade conflicts brought about by large surpluses. These considerations

Figure 9.2 Underestimates of business conditions by the BOJ survey

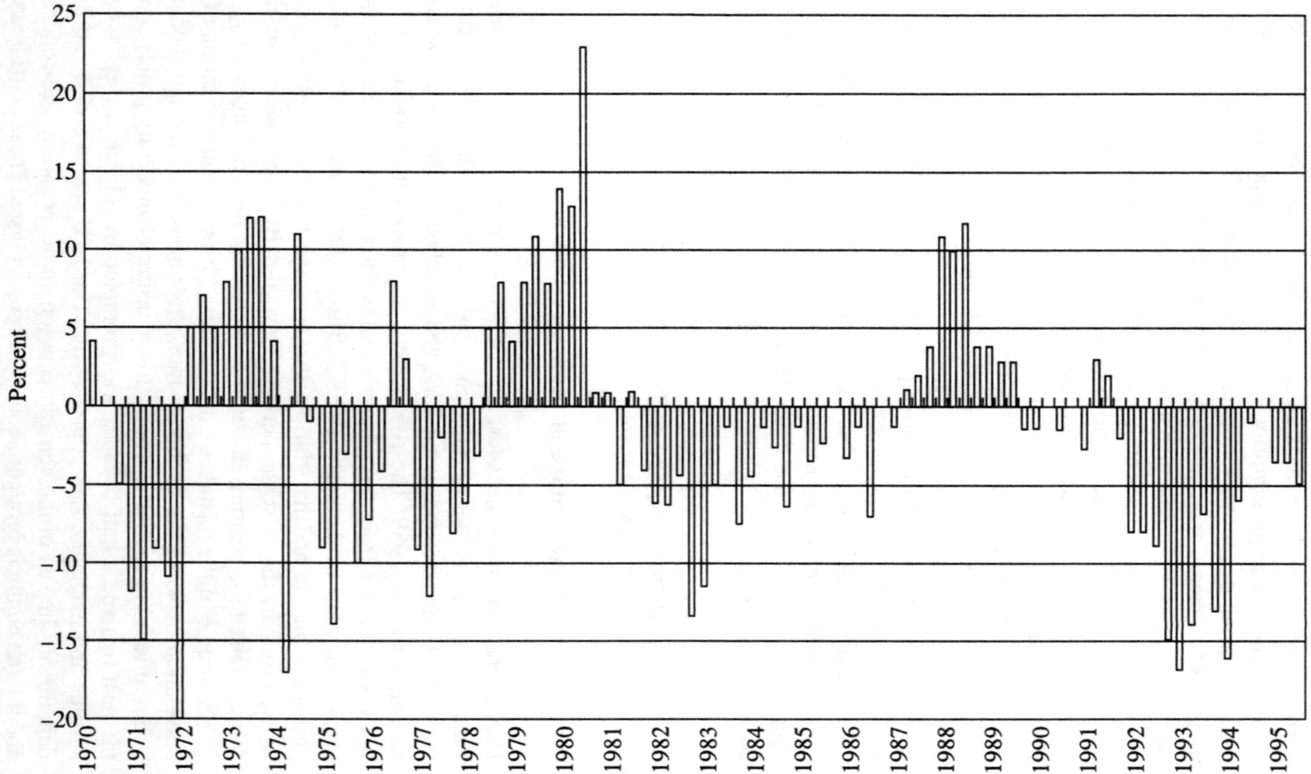

led to the adoption of excessively loose monetary policy in the early 1970s and the mid-1980s.

One of the sources of the mistakes is that the BOJ, or whoever put pressure on the BOJ, overestimated the deflationary impact of the appreciation of the yen. In the last section some evidence was presented for the BOJ's reliance on its short-term survey of enterprises for its policy decisions. The survey asks the enterprises to report their estimates of business conditions in the next quarter as well as their judgment of business conditions in the current quarter. This allows the calculation of expectational errors of business conditions. Figure 9.2 shows that underestimates were large in the three periods of loose monetary policy between 1970 and 1990. Each period of underestimation of business conditions came immediately after a sharp appreciation of the yen. In all three periods interest rates were lowered. In the late 1970s, however, the second round of oil price increases had forced the BOJ to tighten relatively early.

In each case, a move to tighter monetary policy was delayed by political interventions. In the early 1970s pressures to maintain an expansionary stance came from the then Prime Minister Tanaka. In the late 1980s international policy coordination and the existence of large fiscal deficits put strong pressures on the BOJ to expand.

The above consideration suggests that the two mistakes of the BOJ are typical of the problems inherent in a discretionary approach to policymaking. Policymakers can misjudge the state of the economy. Under discretion, politicians and others find it easy to intervene in a central bank's policymaking.

A short comment on the current situation is in order. Since 1991, the current account surplus has increased. The yen has gone up. And the BOJ turned to loosening in the middle of 1991. All much the same as before. Land and stock prices, however, have stayed stagnant; and the economy has not shown a strong recovery. The pace of reductions in the current account surplus has been slow. Underlying these deviations from the previous pattern has been the bad debt problem of the Japanese financial system.

3.2 Money Supply Controversies in Japan

The assertion that money growth targets are necessary is a recurrent theme in monetary economics. It is interesting to observe that this assertion has surfaced in Japan each time the BOJ's policy has gotten into trouble.

The inflation in the early 1970s naturally gave rise to a series of papers attempting to analyze its causes. Kanemitsu and Komiya (1974) criticized the BOJ's policy most clearly. They asserted that the inflation was caused by excessive money supply growth, which was in turn a result of the BOJ's decision to increase the growth rate of high-powered money. They did not go so far as to propose a money growth target. The implication, however, was clear that more attention to indicators such as the money supply or monetary base was desirable. In his paper (1980), Toyama of the BOJ criticized Kanemitsu and Komiya, claiming that monetary base is an endogenous variable. Therefore, according to him, the high growth of monetary base was a result, not a cause, of inflation.

Given the operating procedure of the BOJ, Toyama was partly right in that at least part of the monetary base was endogenous and its high growth was a result of inflation. This does not mean, however, that the BOJ was not responsible for the inflation of the period. The BOJ could have increased interest rates earlier than it did. Kanemitsu and Komiya might have agreed with this, but they went further and pointed to the usefulness of paying more attention to the money supply.

In the aftermath of the bursting of the bubble of the late 1980s, the recession which started in 1991 has been characterized by very low growth rates of the money supply. For example, the growth rate of M2+CD in 1991 was 2.6 percent against 6.3 percent growth of nominal GNP, and in 1992 money growth decreased to 0.1 percent while GNP grew at 2.6 percent. Iwata (1992) criticized the BOJ for allowing the money supply to grow at such low rates and proposed that the BOJ set money or high-powered money growth targets. McCallum (1993) also advocated use of base money targeting, showing that such a policy would have enhanced the stability of nominal GNP. Okina's reaction (1992) was in a sense similar to that of Toyama. He argued that given the BOJ'S current operating procedure, monetary base was an endogenous variable rather than a policy instrument. The BOJ can set interest rates so as to hit money supply targets, if this is desirable.

The debates involve two issues: first, whether or not a money growth target is a good thing; second, whether, given a money supply target, use of interest rates or the monetary base would be the optimal operating procedure. If (B–M3) is correct, the second question is rather unimportant. I would like to stop here and in the next section look at the performance of a version of base money targeting.

4 WOULD MONEY GROWTH TARGETS HAVE PREVENTED THE BOJ's MISTAKES?

Given the two serious mistakes committed by the BOJ and the ensuing claim that the adoption of a money growth target was appropriate, an interesting question is whether a money growth target would have prevented the BOJ from making the mistakes.

As far as I know, the only study that comes even remotely close to addressing this question is McCallum (1993). He advocates using the monetary base for nominal income growth targeting. McCallum supports the use of the monetary base not for meeting money supply targets, but for meeting nominal income targets.

More specifically, he considers the effect on nominal income stability of the adoption of a rule that dictates that base money grow at a constant rate with adjustments for changes in the demand for monetary base and for deviations of actual income from target income. Based on a simple time-series analysis, he concludes that such a rule would have increased the stability of income.

In what follows I use a variation on the McCallum approach to address a more specific question of what would have happened in the two periods of monetary instability, the early 1970s and the period since the late 1980s. The method of analysis is a simple one. Given that the variables we are interested in are inflation and stock prices, I run a simple three-variable VAR, real GDP, GDP deflator and an index of stock prices, with monetary base added as an exogenous variable to the system. Then, a policy reaction function which entails base targeting is introduced and its effect on the paths of the three variables is analyzed.[8] In the simulation, the system is shocked by the residuals of the estimated VAR system.

More specifically, the data used are seasonally adjusted real GDP, GDP deflator, Nikkei 225 and seasonally adjusted monetary base. Monetary base is currency in circulation plus bank deposits at the BOJ with the latter adjusted for changes in the official reserve requirement ratio by the same method as used by McCallum.[9] Estimation is carried out using quarterly data for the period 1967:I to 1995:I. Each variable is first differenced after being logarithmically transformed.

The results of the estimation are shown in Table 9.5. The right-hand-side variables are two lags of the three variables and the current value of and two lags of the monetary base. The specification is similar to that of McCallum with the exception of the choice of variables. The monetary base is significant only at very high levels of significance with the exception of the stock price equation. The inclusion of the current value of the monetary base raises some doubt about possible simultaneous equation biases. Such biases could be especially serious given the partial lagged reserve accounting system used in Japan. In fact, when only lagged values are included, the monetary base was not even significant in the stock price equation. I choose, however, to work with the system in Table 9.5. My major

Table 9.5 Real GDP, GDP deflator and stock price equations

	dy(−1)	*dy*(−2)	*dp*(−1)	*dp*(−2)	*ds*(−1)	*ds*(−2)	*db*	*db*(−1)	*db*(−2)	R^2
dy	0.0841	0.305	−0.167	−0.0601	0.0401	−0.00752	0.0948	0.00793	0.0656	0.334
	0.901	*3.18*	*−1.25*	*0.469*	*2.77*	*−0.527*	*1.62*	*0.133*	*1.09*	
dp	−0.0952	0.143	0.474	0.272	0.00752	0.00173	0.0578	0.0154	0.0583	0.686
	−1.45	*2.11*	*5.06*	*3.01*	*0.738*	*0.172*	*1.41*	*0.366*	*1.38*	
ds	−0.975	0.355	−1.31	−0.151	0.363	−0.188	1.08	0.689	−0.323	0.236
	−1.49	*0.528*	*−1.41*	*−0.168*	*3.58*	*−1.88*	*2.63*	*1.65*	*−0.769*	

Notes:
1. Notations are *y*, real GDP; *p*, GDP deflator; *s*, Nikkei 225; *b*, the monetary base, and *d*( ) is the log difference operator.
2. The numbers in italics are *t*-statistics.
3. The equations include a constant term not shown in the table.
4. The sample period is 1967:III to 1995:I.

conclusion will be that monetary base targeting is not as ideal as one would like it to be. Consequently, the use of a system like the one in Table 9.5 which shows strong effects of the monetary base would reinforce my conclusion.

The next step is to simulate the model with the McCallum-type base money supply rule. The rule is:

$$db = a + c^*(b(-1)/y(-1) - b(-17)/y(-17))/16 + d^*(y^* - y) \qquad (9.1)$$

where b is the monetary base, y is GDP and y^* is the target GDP. The first term on the right-hand side of equation (9.1) represents a target growth rate for nominal GDP and monetary base. The second term is adjustment for changes in money demand, and the third term is the response of the base to deviations of GDP from the target level. The target GDP, y^*, is assumed to grow at a constant rate.

The first exercise I carry out is to determine whether the above rule would have allowed the BOJ to avoid the inflation of the early 1970s. I simulate for the period 1969:I to 1975:IV using the model. What matters is the setting of the initial date and the target growth rate. I have chosen the starting date well in advance of the inflation of the 1970s in order not to miss the effects of shocks on the inflation rate that took place before the inflationary period.

Even under a money supply growth rule, it would be unrealistic to assume that the target growth rate stays constant for decades. The target rate would be adjusted to changes in the expected growth rate of potential output and the target rate of inflation. As a proxy for the expected medium-term growth rate of the economy, I use a survey carried out by the EPA. The survey asks corporate executives at what rate they think the economy will grow for the next three years. Unfortunately, the survey started in 1974. But there is one observation for 1966, which is 10.7 percent. I thus assume that the target nominal GDP growth rate is 13.7 percent, which is 10.7 percent plus a 3 percent rate of inflation. The target inflation rate could instead be 2 percent or 4 percent, but it does not make much difference.

The simulated inflation rate is shown in Figure 9.3 with a tag of 13.7 percent. Clearly, the inflation rate is lower along the simulated path. But the difference is not as large as one would have hoped. At the peak the simulated inflation rate is around 18 percent, while the actual rate is about 22 percent. This rather disappointing result comes from the third term of equation (9.1). Actual GDP did not grow as fast as 13.7 percent, creating a large gap between actual and target GDP.[10] This raises the obvious point

Figure 9.3 Simulated inflation rates, 1971–5

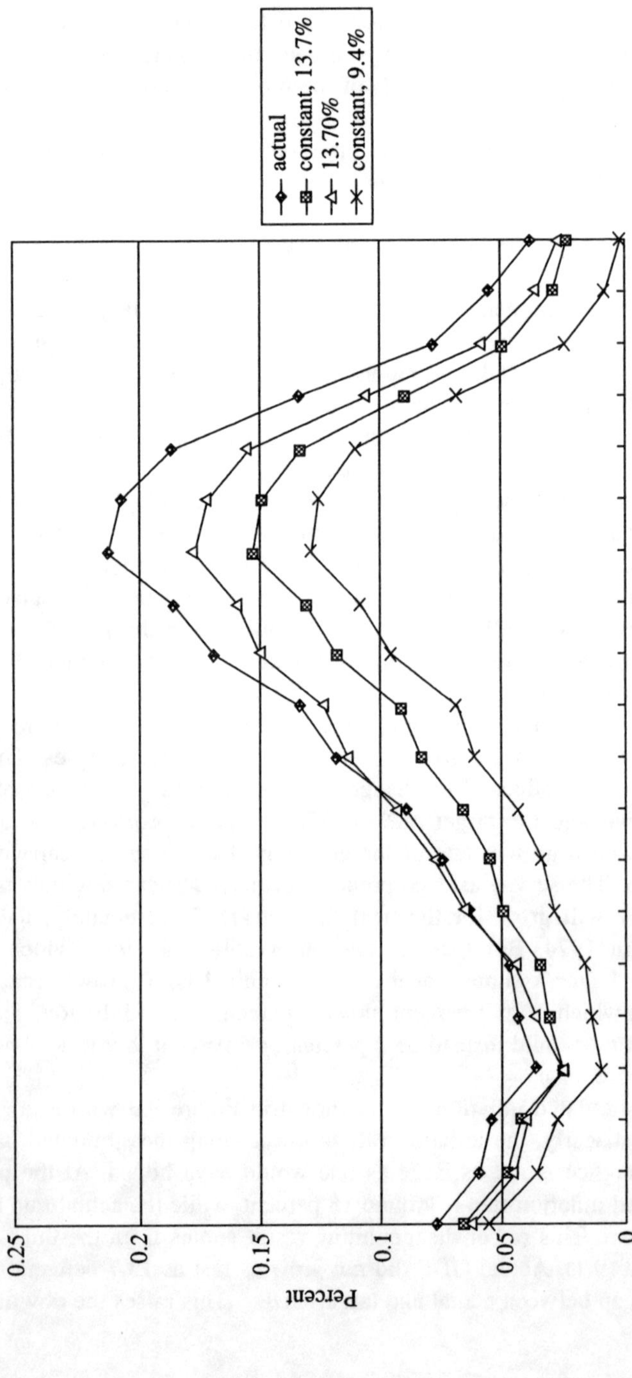

that the performance of a rule like (9.1) depends much on the assumed medium-term growth rate of the economy.

One alternative is to make the base money rule literally of a constant growth rate type, by assuming that *c* and *d* of (9.1) are zero. The simulation result with this assumption is shown in the same figure with a tag of "constant, 13.7 percent." The difference between the actual and simulated paths is now much larger. Moreover, the difference is more striking for the pre-"oil shock" years. That is, until the third quarter of 1973, the "constant, 13.7 percent" path stays below 10 percent, but the actual and the "13.7 percent" paths are above 10 percent already in the second quarter of 1973. The chart also presents the result of the application of the strict constant base growth rule with a growth target of 9.4 percent for nominal GDP and monetary base with a tag of "constant, 9.4 percent." This rate corresponds to a 6.4 percent estimate of the three-year growth rate of real GDP at the beginning of 1974 in the EPA survey, plus a 3 percent rate of inflation. The entire path shifts downward by about two to three percentage points. Inflation is very much under control until 1973:III, but not in 1974, the year of oil price increases.[11]

Obviously, any decreases in the rate of inflation on the simulated path do not come without costs. In Figure 9.4 the paths of real GDP growth are shown. With some exceptions, the growth rate of GDP is much lower for the simulated paths. Probably the large negative growth rates for the simulated paths would have been politically unbearable.

To summarize, the strict constant base money growth rule would have prevented the demand-pull inflation until late 1973, but not the inflation created by the oil price increases. Allowance for adjustment of base growth to GDP gap seems to deprive the base money rule of the ability to prevent even the demand-pull inflation of 1973, depending on the assumed growth rate. In addition, real GDP growth rates would have been lower than the actual ones under any version of the base money rule that has been analyzed here.

Next, I carry out the same type of simulation for the period 1985:I to 1995:I. The target growth is again assumed to equal the expectation of corporate managers as surveyed by the EPA. As of 1985 the expected growth rate was 4.4 percent. I add an inflation rate of 2 percent to arrive at 6.4 percent for the target growth rate for nominal GDP and monetary base. Given the possible relationship between volatile asset price movements and the instability of the financial system in the 1990s, the variable which is of interest in our context is stock prices. A more stable path for stock prices would have probably meant a more stable financial system.

As can be seen from Figure 9.5, the base supply rule as represented by

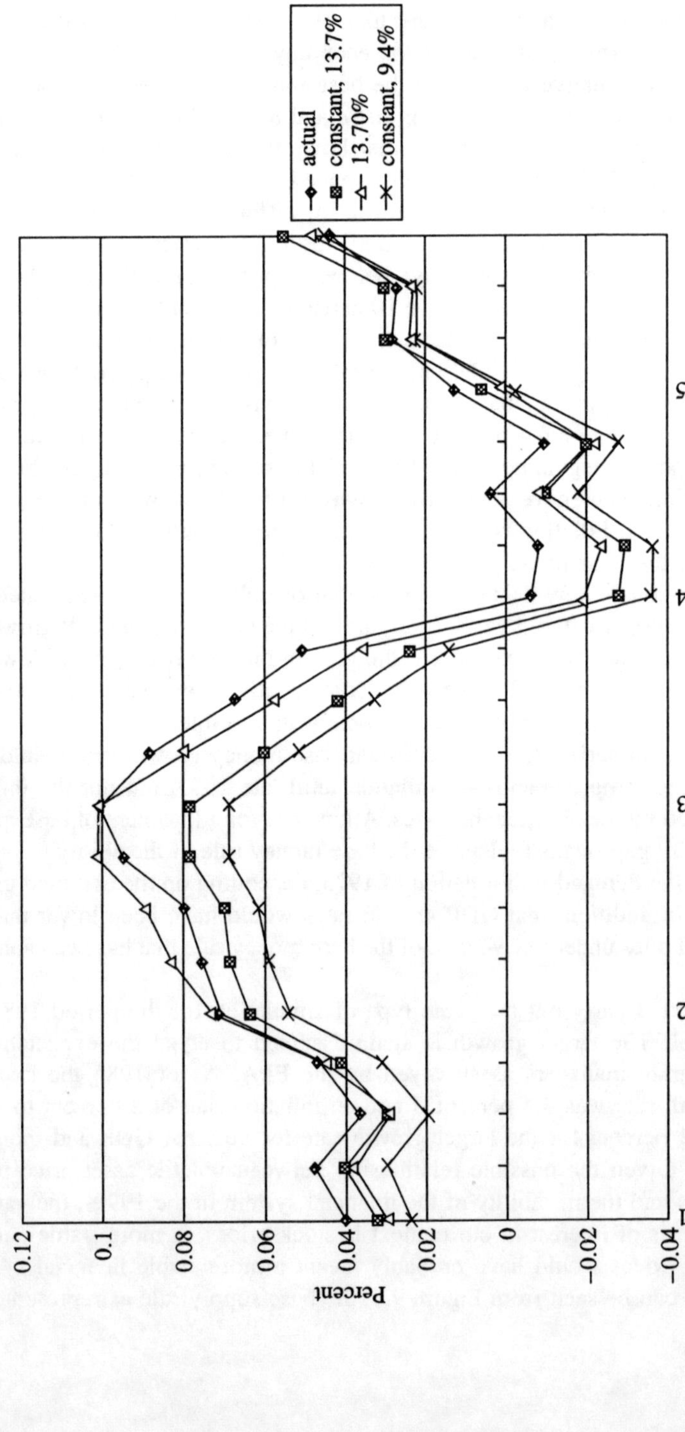

Figure 9.4 Simulated GDP growth rates, 1971–5

Figure 9.5 Simulated Nikkei 225, 1986–95

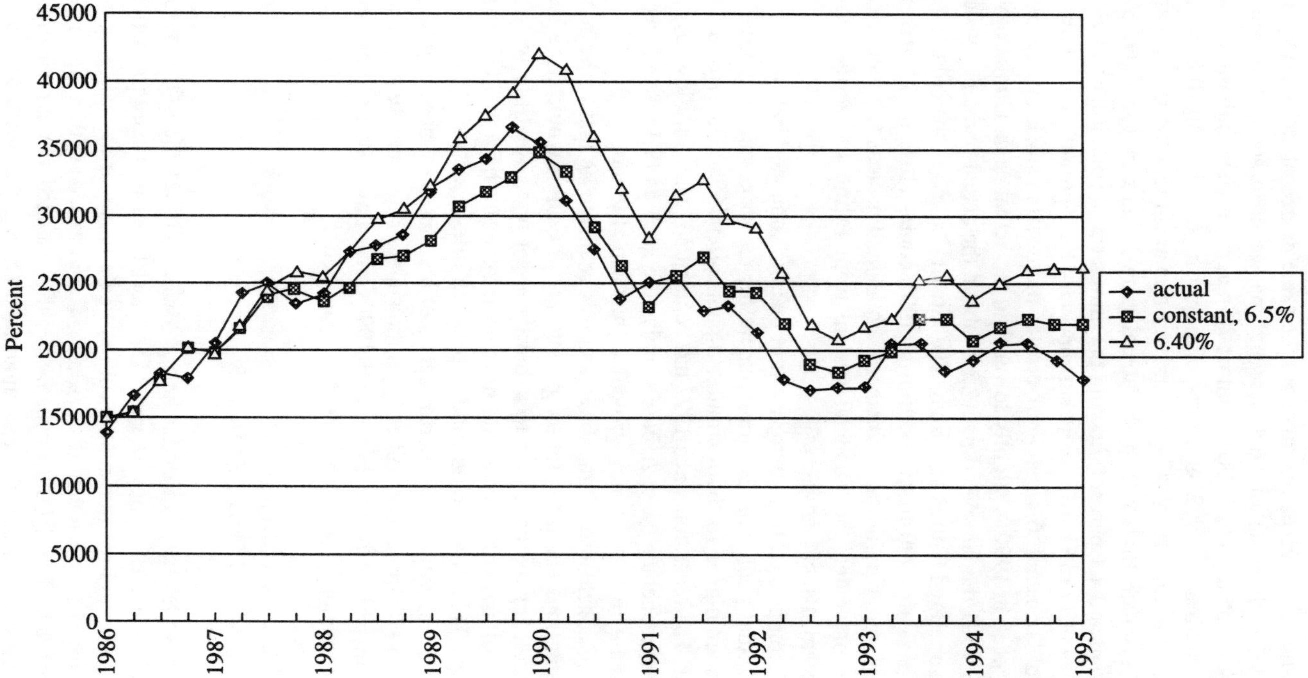

equation (9.1) gives rise to about the same degree of stock price volatility, shown with a tag of "6.4 percent," as we have seen. The peak in the Nikkei 225 around 1990 is almost 20 percent higher than the actual peak. The bottom in 1992 is correspondingly higher, leaving the volatility at about the same level. The major reason is again that the 6.4 percent target rate is much higher than the actual growth rates in 1986 and 1987, 4.4 percent and 4.1 percent, making the third term of equation (9.1) very large.

The use of the strict constant monetary base growth rule, shown with a tag of "constant, 6.4 percent," creates more stable stock price movements. The peak in 1990 is slightly lower than the actual peak. On the other hand, after 1991 the simulated path stays above the actual path. The volatility of the simulated path is still high. The rate of decline in the Nikkei 225 from the peak in 1990 to the bottom in 1992 comes close to 50 percent. Naturally, one would doubt whether such a small decrease in volatility would have prevented the financial system from facing the serious instability problem it faces now.

Turning to GDP growth, we find that the simulated paths do better than the actual path. This is more evident for the strict rule. The GDP growth rates are higher for both simulated paths after 1992. The reason for this is clear. The recession since 1992 has "coincided" with very low growth rates of the monetary base. A base supply rule such as (9.1) avoids as sharp a decrease in base money growth as has actually happened.

The conclusion of the above analysis seems to be that under reasonable assumptions about the target growth rate of GDP it would have been very difficult for the base rule to avoid the asset price volatility we observed, although the volatility would have been lower for both real GDP and asset prices. This gives some mild support to rule-based policy.

The less satisfactory performance of the monetary base targeting in the early 1970s probably comes from the supply shock nature of the inflation. The instability of the 1980s and 1990s may have been a more monetary phenomenon. Thus, the base rule does better.

5 CONCLUDING REMARKS

Using the language of Bernanke and Mishkin (1982), the BOJ has responded to a number of policy targets. The most consistent pattern in the BOJ's behavior, and for that matter, in the Fed's behavior as well, has been that interest rates are lowered in recessions and raised, with a lag in Japan, in recoveries. The BOJ has also carefully watched the movements in the current account and the exchange rate. During the downturn since 1970,

Figure 9.6 Simulated GDP growth rates, 1986–95

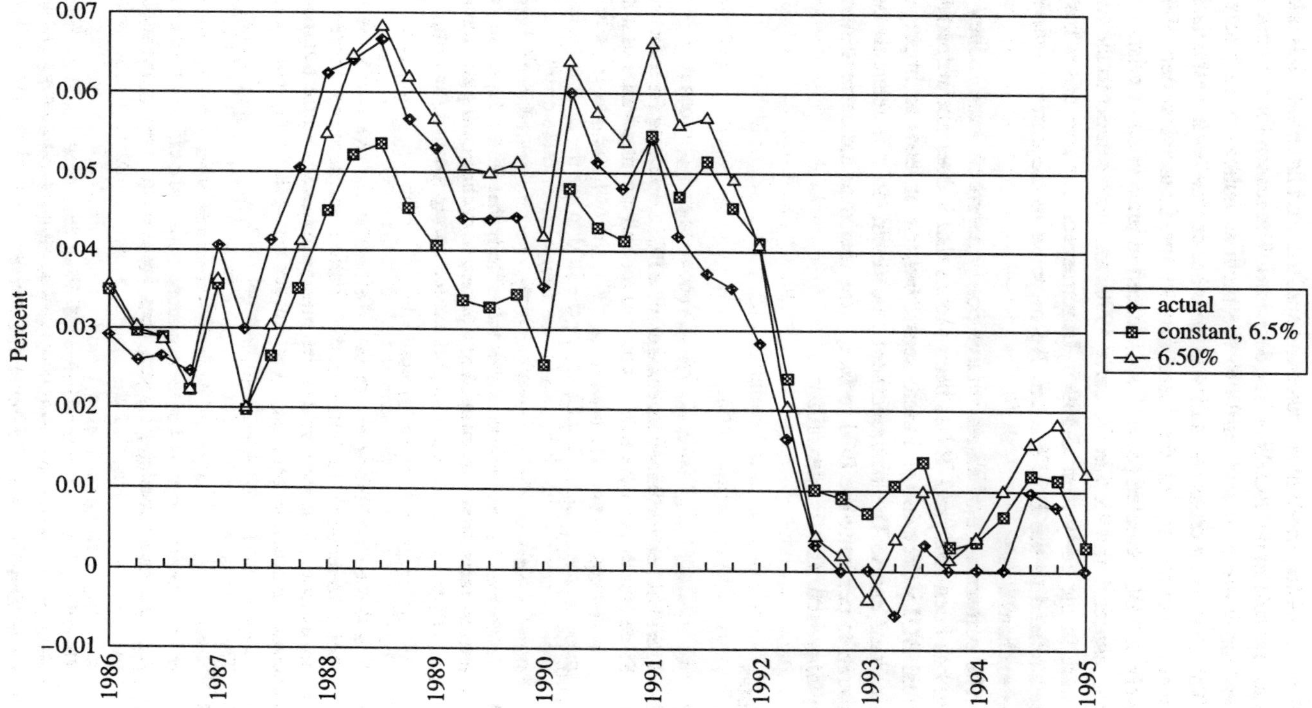

the concern for the current account and the exchange rate has played a dominant role in the BOJ's policy decisions. The reason for the concern has been partly political and partly to use them as indicators of future GDP.

The BOJ has a crisis mentality as do other central banks, especially with respect to inflation and the instability of the financial system. Unfortunately, the BOJ created (or did not succeed in preventing) a crisis situation with respect to inflation in the early 1970s and with respect to the financial system in the early to mid-1990s. In retrospect, the two crises may have been related to the BOJ's excessive response to the current account and the exchange rate.

The performance of an alternative policy approach, base money targeting, has been analyzed. It has been shown that it does not outperform the actual BOJ policy in the Pareto sense, but that it leads to improvements in certain cases. The improvements, however, do not seem to be large enough to persuade the BOJ to forego the merits of the current discretionary approach, that is, flexibility.

Notes

1. For detailed discussions, see Okina (1993) and Ueda (1993a).
2. There has been an important change in the BOJ's operating procedure recently. Since March 1995 the BOJ has moved the call rate in advance of a discount rate change. Moreover, since July 1995, the call rate has been below the discount rate, making it difficult for the BOJ to use the discount window for base money control. It remains to be seen whether these changes in the relative importance of instruments and in the operating procedure are permanent.
3. Another difference not shown in the table is that in the Japanese case real interest rates do not show as clear a pattern of decline during downturns. This is perhaps due to regulations that existed during most of the sample period which had limited the flexibility of interest rates.
4. The USA experienced a similar period in the early 1990s.
5. It would be interesting to estimate the threshold above which the BOJ responds to inflation. Here the threshold value is just assumed. Some preliminary estimations using a grid search method indicated that the threshold value could be much larger than 5 percent, for example 8.5 percent.
6. The average has been adjusted to equal zero.
7. The discussion which follows is more fully developed in Ueda (1993b).
8. Needless to say, a more desirable approach would be to use a large macroeconometric model of the economy to study the effects of policy change. An ideal macromodel, however, does not seem to exist at the moment. A more serious criticism of the approach used would be that a switch to a monetary base growth rule would change the VAR system significantly. Therefore, the coefficients estimated using past data would be useless for simulation. I accept this criticism but present the results of the above simple simulation for want of a better alternative.

9. Monetary base is the average of monthly data. The monthly series is for end of month, seasonally adjusted at the monthly level. Use of the average of daily data was also attempted. The VAR coefficients changed significantly. The simulation results, however, did not change much.
10. More precisely, the estimated negative shocks to GDP in the VAR system hold down the levels of GDP in the simulated path as well.
11. Application of equation (9.1) with a 9.4 percent target growth rate creates a path that falls roughly between the constant 13.4 percent and the constant 9.4 percent cases for both inflation and real GDP.

References

Bernanke, B. and Mishkin, F. (1992) "Central Bank Behavior and the Strategy of Monetary Policy: Observations from Six Industrialized Countries," NBER Working Paper No. 4082.

Hutchison, M. (1988) "Monetary Control with an Exchange Rate Objective: The Bank of Japan, 1973–86," *Journal of International Money & Finance*, 7, pp. 261–72.

Iwata, K. (1992) "Throw Away the BOJ Theory" (in Japanese), *Weekly Toyo Keizai*, 12 September.

Kanemitsu and Komiya (1974) "Japan's Foreign Exchange Policy under the Floating System: A Critical Analysis," a paper presented at the Williamsburg Conference on the Experience of Greater Exchange Rate Flexibility, Williamsburg, Virginia, May 1974.

McCallum, B.T. (1993) "Specification and Analysis of a Monetary Policy Rule for Japan," *Monetary and Economic Studies*, Bank of Japan, 11 (2) pp. 1–45.

Okabe, M. (1992) "Developments of Japanese Monetary Policy" (in Japanese), in K. Shigehara (ed.), *New Developments in Monetary Theory and Policy* (Tokyo: Yuhikaku).

Okina, K. (1992) "The BOJ Theory is Correct" (in Japanese), *Weekly Toyo Keizai*, 10 October.

Okina, K. (1993) "Market Operations in Japan: Theory and Practice," in K. Singleton (ed.), *Japanese Monetary Policy* (Chicago, Ill.: University of Chicago Press).

Romer, C.D. and Romer, D.H. (1994) "What Ends Recessions?," NBER Working Paper No. 4765.

Toyama, S. (1980) *Twenty One Misunderstandings in Monetary Economics* (in Japanese) (Tokyo: Toyo Keizai.)

Ueda, K. (1993a) "A Comparative Perspective on Japanese Monetary Policy: Short-Run Monetary Control and the Transmission Mechanism," in K. Singleton (ed.), *Japanese Monetary Policy* (Chicago, Ill.: University of Chicago Press).

Ueda, K. (1993b) "Japanese Monetary Policy from 1970 to 1990: Rules or Discretion?," in K. Shigehara (ed.), *Price Stabilization in the 1990s* (London: Macmillan).

Comments*

Frederic S. Mishkin

In the first part of his chapter, Ueda characterizes the behavior of the Bank of Japan and finds that it is consistent with many propositions in my paper with Ben Bernanke (1992) that Ueda refers to. First, central banks have multiple objectives. In the case of the Bank of Japan these include the inflation rate, the gap between actual and potential GDP, the foreign exchange rate and the current account. Second, central banks have a crisis mentality, that is, they focus on the problem that is currently most pressing. The Bank of Japan has focused on price stability when inflation is high, the current account when the current account surplus reached high levels and the exchange rate when it appreciated sharply. Third, although central banks have used monetary targets in the past as part of their strategy for conducting monetary policy, they have not adhered to these targets closely. This also characterizes the Bank of Japan's behavior.

Since Ueda's chapter provides support for the analysis in Bernanke's and my chapter, I am put in the uncomfortable position for a discussant of not being able to find much that I disagree with in the first part of his chapter. Thus, I will focus more of my comments on the second part of his chapter which looks at the question of what would have been an appropriate monetary policy stance for the Bank of Japan since the 1970s.

1 ASSESSING JAPANESE MONETARY POLICY

Ueda outlines two past "mistakes" of monetary policy: the first was the run-up of inflation around the first oil shock in the 1970s and the second was the bubble economy of the late 1980s. Ueda points out that the high inflation rate in Japan in the early to mid-1970s was the result of overly expansionary monetary policy due to excessive money supply growth which started at the beginning of the 1970s. When combined with the 1973 oil shock, this led to inflation rates which climbed to around the 20 percent level.

Ueda blames the Bank of Japan for the failure to rein in money growth

* Any opinions expressed in this chapter are those of the author, not those of the Federal Reserve Bank of New York or the Federal Reserve System, Columbia University or the National Bureau of Economic Research.

during this period. However, it is not fair to only point out a central bank's failures; it is also important to give credit where credit is due. The Bank of Japan had major successes in its conduct of monetary policy after the 1971–5 period. Tighter control of the monetary aggregates by the Bank of Japan helped produce a highly desirable economic environment for Japan after 1975 which was the envy of many developed countries, one with low inflation and low inflation variability while the Japanese economy was experiencing very high rates of growth.

The second "mistake" that Ueda points out is his proposition that the bubble economy in the late 1980s was due to overly expansionary monetary policy by the Bank of Japan. Although there may be some truth to this proposition, the evidence for it is by no means strong. Even Ueda's evidence in his counterfactual simulations of the economy that examine what would have happened if monetary growth had been lower during this period suggests that only quite a small part of the bubble in stock prices could be attributed to overly expansionary monetary policy.

The experience in the United States also casts some doubt on the view that the bubble can primarily be attributed to monetary policy. Much evidence with US stock price data indicates that it is very hard to explain many sharp movements in stock prices with fundamentals. For example, the stock market boom in 1927–9 or in 1987, both of which burst dramatically, are not easily explained by fundamentals, and in both these periods it is hard to ascribe these "bubbles" to overly expansionary monetary policy. Evidence of this type should make us cautious in pinning the blame for the bubble in Japanese asset prices on the behavior of the Bank of Japan.

The bottom line is that asset prices seem to have a life of their own and, although influenced by monetary policy, are not completely controlled by it.

2 LESSONS FROM THE JAPANESE MONETARY POLICY EXPERIENCE

Ueda's chapter has stimulated me to think about what lessons we can learn from the Japanese monetary experience to help guide central banks in their conduct of monetary policy. There are five basic lessons that I would like to point out here.

1. *Large swings in growth of monetary aggregates are useful guides for monetary policy* When monetary base growth exceeded 15 percent annual

rates in the 1971–3 period, leading to very high M2+CDs growth in Japan, it is very clear that high inflation would be the result. Paying more attention to monetary aggregates growth would have mitigated the first monetary policy mistake Ueda pointed out in his chapter. Indeed, this lesson was learned by the Bank of Japan after the first oil shock episode: when the second oil shock occurred in 1979, the Bank of Japan kept much tighter control over money growth and as a result Japan had a far better inflation performance than most other developed countries.

2. *However, monetary aggregates may be less useful as a guide for monetary policy when swings in their growth are smaller in magnitude* The problem with monetary aggregates as a guide to monetary policy is that there frequently are unanticipated shifts in velocity that alter the relationship between money growth and nominal spending. When swings in money growth rates are large, velocity shifts are usually small relative to the large swings in money growth rates, thus enabling money growth rates to provide useful information about the path of nominal spending. Another way of describing this situation is to think of velocity shocks as the noise that obscures the signal from monetary aggregates, and thus, in the case of large swings in money growth rates, the signal-to-noise ratio is high. On the other hand, when swings in money growth are smaller, then noise from velocity shocks may dominate the signal from the monetary aggregates, thus making monetary aggregates a poor indicator of the path of nominal spending. In this case, the signal-to-noise ratio is low, making monetary aggregates a poor guide for monetary policy. This seems to be the current situation in the United States and many other countries where inflation and money growth rates are quite low, and this is why many central banks in these countries have been deemphasizing monetary aggregates in their conduct of monetary policy.

In the context of the Japanese experience, Ueda's chapter presents some evidence on the usefulness of a monetary base rule *à la* McCallum and finds that it would not have led to substantially improved performance. I do not find Ueda's evidence convincing, first because it makes use of a VAR-like methodology that suffers from the usual identification problems inherent in this approach. Second, given the recent Nobel prize to Robert Lucas, it is important to acknowledge that Ueda's analysis is highly subject to the Lucas critique. The reason a monetary aggregate rule is desirable is because it affects expectations in a way that can improve inflation performance. Therefore, putting a new monetary rule into operation affects expectations, thereby changing the parameters of equations like those estimated by Ueda, making it highly likely that the estimated equation using past historical data will not provide reliable information on how the adoption of the rule will affect the economy.

Even though I find Ueda's evidence unconvincing, I have my doubts about the efficacy of a monetary base rule. The demand for the monetary base can change dramatically because the demand for currency, a large component of the base, is subject to substantial shocks. Similarly, the demand for reserves, the other component of the base, is subject to substantial changes in a world where our payments system is undergoing dramatic change. Velocity shocks are therefore likely to be large in the equation of exchange linking the monetary base to nominal spending, thus creating the problem of a low signal-to-noise ratio for the monetary base as a guide to nominal spending. Thus the problems which I have described above for using monetary aggregates as a guide for monetary policy are particularly relevant for the monetary base, especially in situations in which the swings in growth rates of the monetary base are not large.

3. *It is very dangerous to always associate monetary policy easing or tightening with a fall or a rise in short-term nominal interest rates* Because most central banks use short-term nominal interest rates, typically the interbank rate, as the key operating instrument for monetary policy, there is a danger that central banks and the public will focus too much on short-term nominal interest rates as an indicator of the stance of monetary policy. Ueda falls into this mode of thinking in his chapter by always describing a fall in short-term interest rates as an easing of monetary policy by the Bank of Japan and a rise as a tightening of policy. This view is highly problematic because movements in nominal interest rates do not always correspond to movements in real interest rates. For example, during the late 1970s in the United States, short-term nominal interest rates were high, but real interest rates were extremely low, even negative. Similarly, during the contraction phase of the Great Depression in the United States, short-term interest rates fell to near zero and yet real interest rates were extremely high. This is a highly relevant issue for Japan currently (October 1985). Short-term interest rates which are near zero do not indicate that monetary policy is easy if the economy is undergoing deflation as is the case for Japan: then real interest rates may actually be quite high despite the low nominal interest rates.

4. *Other asset prices besides those on short-term debt instruments contain important information about the stance of monetary policy because they are important channels of the monetary policy transmission mechanism* Research in monetary economics has come a long way in understanding

that other asset prices besides interest rates have major effects on aggregate demand. Since research also shows that monetary policy has important effects on these other asset prices, they are important channels of the monetary transmission mechanism. The view that other asset prices such as stock prices, foreign exchange rates and land prices are an important part of the monetary transmission mechanism is held by monetarists, Keynesians and neo-Keynesians. An example of this can be seen in the papers appearing in a symposium on the monetary transmission mechanism I have organized which will be appearing soon in the *Journal of Economic Perspectives* and which includes papers by the two Honorary Advisers to the Bank of Japan, Allan Meltzer and John Taylor. Although there are strong disagreements between the authors about some elements of the monetary transmission mechanism – not surprising given that economists, particularly academic economists, always like to disagree – all of them stress how important other asset price effects are to the way monetary policy affects the economy.

The view that other asset prices besides short-term interest rates matter has important implications for monetary policy. When we try to assess the stance of policy, it is critical that we look at other asset prices besides short-term interest rates. For example, if short-term interest rates are low or even zero and yet stock prices are low, land prices are low and the value of the domestic currency is high, then monetary policy is tight, not easy.

5. *Monetary policy can be highly effective in reviving a weak economy even if short-term interest rates are already near zero* One common view is that when a central bank has driven down short-term nominal interest rates to near zero, there is nothing more that monetary policy can do to stimulate the economy. Both monetary theory and empirical research on the US experience during the Great Depression when interest rates on short-term Treasury bills were near a floor of zero indicate that this view is demonstrably false. Expansionary monetary policy to increase liquidity in the economy can be conducted with open market purchases which do not have to be solely in short-term government securities. This increased liquidity helps to revive and reflate the economy by raising price level expectations and by reflating other asset prices which then stimulate aggregate demand. Therefore monetary policy can be a potent force for reviving economies which are undergoing deflation and have short-term interest rates near a floor of zero. Indeed, because of the lags inherent in fiscal policy and the political constraints on its use, expansionary monetary policy is the key policy action that is required to revive an economy experiencing deflation.

Comments

Krister Andersson

Ueda's very interesting chapter covers many important issues for monetary policy and gives an especially insightsful analysis of the workings of monetary policy in Japan.

The chapter discusses the important subjects of the responsibility and accountability of central banks. Furthermore, it addresses the practical questions for implementing monetary policy of which indicators central banks should use; what central banks can achieve; the extent to which targeting monetary aggregates helps in achieving price stability; and the role which asset prices should play in the formulation of monetary policy.

Without a doubt it is important to have a clear objective for monetary policy. It is generally agreed that price stability is the obvious objective for monetary policy. The major task of central banks then is to persistently pursue a policy to achieve and maintain price stability. Ueda's chapter discusses the use of various indicators of real economic activity and inflationary pressures and highlights the importance of these indicators.

I will limit myself to three issues which allow me to share some of the experiences which we have at Sveriges Riksbank, the central bank of Sweden: first, the role of the exchange rate in the transmission mechanism; second, the role of the current account in the formulation of monetary policy; and third, the role of asset prices in the formulation of monetary policy.

1 THE ROLE OF THE EXCHANGE RATE IN THE TRANSMISSION MECHANISM

I would like to concentrate on Ueda's discussion of the role of exchange rates and current account movements for achieving price stability because it is an important matter for most central banks.

Clearly, the real effective exchange rate plays an important role in assessing monetary conditions as do real interest rates. As a matter of fact, the effect of interest rate changes on the exchange rate is an important factor in achieving price stability in an open economy with flexible exchange rates. The experience in both Canada and in Sweden has been that interest rate changes become particularly effective in curbing inflationary pressures if they also have an impact on the exchange rate. It is typically the case that a move in the exchange rate is, at least in the short to medium term, as important as the direct effect achieved on inflationary pressures from higher interest rate levels. The short-term dampening effect on inflation is sometimes predominantly a result of decreasing inflation expectations and the pass-through of cost decreases on imports to consumer prices through a stronger currency. On the other hand, the direct impact on the inflation rate of an interest rate change, although delayed, is longer-lasting than the immediate effect on the inflation rate from exchange rate movements.

To summarize, I would therefore like to strongly support the view that it is appropriate to pay attention to the exchange rate.

2 WHAT ROLE SHOULD DEVELOPMENTS IN THE CURRENT ACCOUNT PLAY IN THE FORMULATION OF MONETARY POLICY?

The current as well as the expected future exchange rate clearly has an impact on the savings–investment balance of any country. The value of the currency is also influenced by the credibility of economic policies and whether favourable growth with price stability is expected to be achieved and maintained. While all of these aspects clearly are relevant for the formulation of monetary policy it does not follow, however, that the current account should play a major role when conducting monetary policy. Persistent savings imbalances are often a result of structural problems in the economy rather than the stance of monetary policy.

The tendency for an appreciation of the currency at times of a surplus in the current account may give room for lower interest rates without jeopardizing price stability, but there are limits to the extent to which monetary conditions may be eased. Instead, other parts of economic policy, in particular structural policies, will have to address persistent imbalances in the trade balance and in the current account.

Developments in Sweden during the past ten to fifteen years illustrate this view. During the latter half of the 1980s, Sweden exhibited a low or even negative savings rate in the household sector despite a tightening of monetary conditions. A reason for this was the tax code which favored debt financing and caused after-tax real interest rates to be low or even negative. After a major overhaul of the tax system, the household savings rate increased sharply.

3 THE ROLE OF ASSET PRICES IN MONETARY POLICY

It is important to assess the inflation pressure in the economy and it is, therefore, necessary to pay close attention to asset prices when formulating monetary policies since they enter into consumption and investment decisions.

Having said that, I think that Ueda perhaps is a little too harsh in blaming the Bank of Japan and monetary policy for asset price developments. I question whether a more stable monetary policy could have prevented the bubble. I also question the statement in the chapter that monetary policy is responsible for the bubble bursting.

First of all, once a bubble has developed, you might as well let it burst as soon as possible. The total loss in welfare is probably lower the earlier asset prices are corrected in line with underlying fundamentals. Second, one should recognize the difficulties in evaluating to what extent asset prices are leading indicators for consumer price developments and an inflationary development. In my own country, Sweden, asset prices picked up when inflation had been high for some time, and regulated markets coupled with limited investment opportunities abroad for households and insurance companies contributed to inflated real estate prices.

Structural policies are essential to avoid asset price bubbles. In Sweden, restrictions on the financial markets and restricted access to international diversification, as well as the tax system, all played an important role in inflating real estate prices. In Sweden, as in a large number of countries, debt financing received a more favorable tax treatment than equity financing, and the deductibility of interest payments when calculating taxable income made increases in leverage attractive with adverse consequences for the real estate market and eventually the banking sector. Furthermore, fiscal policy in general should have played a stronger role in dampening price developments, in particular because Sweden employed a fixed exchange rate.

In the case of Japan, Ueda suggests that the lower growth rates of the economy would have been politically unfeasible and therefore it would not have possible to use money growth targets to mitigate the effects of the asset price bubble.

I actually draw the opposite conclusion – that a monetary policy directed solely toward price stability, whether through money growth rates or an inflation target, is helpful precisely because it would have demonstrated the costs in terms of lower growth, thereby putting the spotlight on necessary changes in the economy. For instance, the high interest rates connected with maintaining the fixed exchange rate at the beginning of the

1990s forced politicians to combat the fiscal imbalances plaguing Sweden earlier than they might otherwise have done. A clear-cut mandate for price stability may very well facilitate and speed up structural changes by making costs in terms of lower growth rates more visible at an earlier stage in the cycle. Needless to say, the limitations in conducting monetary policy in accordance with this principle have to be recognized and assessed for each country.

To conclude, it is a very interesting chapter and a similar analysis for other countries would be most useful in the policy debate. As a matter of fact, it is clearly in the interest of central banks to carry out this kind of analysis in order to enhance the understanding of the limitations of what monetary policy can achieve under given conditions. We are indebted to Ueda for such a good start along this path.

Comments*

Marvin Goodfriend

Ueda asks in his chapter how much better (if at all) Japanese monetary policy would have been in two episodes: the high inflation period 1972–4 leading up to and following the 1973 oil price shock, and the 1986–9 asset price "bubble" period, if the Bank of Japan (BOJ) had followed a McCallum-like rule for targeting nominal GDP.

On the whole, Ueda finds that following such a rule would have made relatively little difference. For instance, Ueda argues that a rule would not have prevented inflation in the aftermath of the oil price shock very well. He does believe that a rule would have prevented some of the boom in nominal GDP associated with the asset price bubble in the late 1980s; but he argues that it would have had a relatively small effect on asset prices themselves. In short, the chapter's bottom line is to "damn the nominal GDP rule with faint praise," to use an expression popular in the United States.

In some ways I agree with Ueda's conclusions, but in other ways I do not. In any case, my views are motivated by a somewhat different interpretation of developments than presented in Ueda's chapter.

1 INFLATIONARY POLICY IN THE 1970S AND ITS AFTERMATH

My reading of events in the early 1970s is that the collapsing Bretton Woods fixed exchange rate system in 1972–3 left the BOJ without a nominal anchor for monetary policy and with little credibility for low inflation. Japanese monetary policy continued to focus in large part on stabilizing the yen–dollar exchange rate – by resisting yen appreciation with excessive Japanese money growth. The result, even before the oil price shock, was rising inflation.

The situation was made worse by the fact that the collapse of Bretton Woods left US monetary policy, too, without a nominal anchor. So the attempt by Japanese authorities to stabilize the yen's value against the dollar was, to use another expression popular in the United States, like

* The views expressed here are mine alone and not necessarily those of the Federal Reserve Bank of Richmond or the Federal Reserve System.

"the blind leading the blind." When the oil price shock hit in 1973, monetary policy in both the United States and Japan was particularly susceptible to creating more inflation than it would have if a credible commitment to price stability had been in place.

The lesson learned from the early 1970s is that acquiring and maintaining a reputation for low inflation is the key to effective monetary policy. It took the Fed until 1979 to consistently take tough actions necessary to achieve its low-inflation objective. Japanese authorities too took the lesson learned in the early 1970s – what Ueda refers to as the first mistake – to heart. And they did so perhaps a little earlier than US authorities, so that Japan handled the oil shock at the end of the 1970s well, much better than did the United States. Inflation as measured by the GDP deflator in Japan rose from about 5 percent in 1972 to more than 20 percent after the first oil shock. But Japanese inflation moved little above 5 percent in the late 1970s and early 1980s in the aftermath of the second oil shock. Measured by the GDP deflator, US inflation moved above 10 percent after both the first and the second oil price shocks.[1]

By the mid-1980s both the Fed and the BOJ were well along in acquiring credibility for low inflation through policy actions that held inflation in check – actions that I would characterize as rule-like behavior enforced by reputational considerations. The authorities had learned to tighten policy decisively in a business upturn before pressure on capacity caused a rise in actual inflation and inflation expectations. Roughly speaking, policy had come to approximate a nominal GDP targeting rule somewhat like McCallum proposes. Monetary policy is not constrained by an explicit legislative mandate for price stability in either Japan or the United States. Policy is discretionary. Yet the BOJ and the Fed have found from experience that it is best (for the most part) to behave as if they are committed to a rule. Hence, there is now less difference than one might expect between a rule and voluntary self-restraint learned from experience.[2] So I agree with Ueda's main conclusion that following an explicit rule would not make much difference; but as I see it, that is only because the behavior of the BOJ and the Fed has by now come a long way toward approximating one.

2 GO–STOP POLICY IN THE LATE 1980S

I agree with Ueda on a second point too – that one cannot have expected a nominal GDP target to have prevented much of the asset price bubble after 1986. Real GDP growth averaged 4 percent per year from 1987 until 1991 in the recovery and expansion following the 1985–86 recession. The strong growth during those years took the real GDP output gap as measured by the Organization of Economic Cooperation and Development (OECD) from –4 percent to +4 percent.[3]

Closer adherence to the nominal GDP target prescribed in a rule clearly would have restrained the rise in inflation during this period (assuming the GDP target was chosen to reflect sustainable productivity growth rates). And such restraint would probably have calmed the euphoric atmosphere somewhat. But I do not think that a rule would have directly restrained the asset price appreciation very much. After all, bullish sentiment about the Japanese economy at the time was truly extraordinary.

Nevertheless I believe as Ueda does that there was, to use his words, a second monetary policy mistake in the late 1980s. I see it this way. According to the 1994 OECD survey of Japan, real short rates fell from a range of 2.5 percent in mid-1986 to 1 percent in early 1989 – with a drop of nearly 1.5 percentage points in late 1988 – even though real GDP growth was then very strong and the real GDP output gap was narrowing rapidly. The BOJ began to bring real short rates up in the second half of 1989 only after the real GDP gap had disappeared.[4]

The delay created doubts in the markets about the BOJ's commitment to low inflation which began to unhinge the CPI inflation rate. CPI inflation moved up from below 1 percent in early 1989 to nearly 4 percent by mid-1990. More spectacularly, the growth of manufacturing unit labor costs in Japan went from 2 percent in 1989 to over 7 percent by 1992. Also, an inflation scare probably contributed significantly to moving long-term bond rates up from around 4 percent in the first half of 1989 to 9 percent by mid-1990. In the meantime, the Nikkei Stock Average rose from just above 20000 at the start of 1988 to nearly 40000 in early 1990; the Nikkei was to fall sharply to the 25000 range by the end of 1990, and below 20000 by 1992.[5]

The BOJ moved to restore credibility for low inflation first by raising real short rates to 4 percent in late 1989 and then by raising real rates from 4 percent to 6 percent in 1990, keeping them near their peak through the first half of 1991. I identify the go–stop sequence, beginning with the delay in raising rates in 1989 and ending with the sharp tightening in 1990, as the second policy mistake.

Looked at from this perspective, one must ask what could have caused the BOJ to depart from the rule-like behavior in support of low inflation that had evolved during the previous ten years or so. In part, the reluctance to take more decisive action to tighten policy sooner may have been due to the effort to stabilize the yen against the dollar.[6] The yen–dollar rate fell from around 155 in early 1987 to 125 in the spring of 1988. It held in that range in 1988, and then rose again throughout 1989 to peak at around 160 in the spring of 1990. Japanese authorities may have been willing to tighten monetary policy only after the significant yen depreciation in 1989 and 1990. If that is the case, then the lesson from the second mistake is the same as that from the first: Japanese monetary policy may have been distracted once again from pursuing domestic objectives by an exchange rate objective.

3 RECESSION AND RECOVERY IN THE 1990S

In keeping with the theme of Ueda's chapter, I would like to consider the response of the BOJ to the recession that began in 1991, and ask whether one can identify actual or potential policy mistakes in the most recent period. The recovery from the 1991–3 recession has been much slower than expected for a number of reasons. One is that the BOJ may have eased policy relatively slowly at first to be sure to restore its credibility for low inflation. Unfortunately, one of the costs of compromising credibility is that it usually takes some overcompensation to restore it. This is the lesson from US policy in the late 1970s and 1980s.[7] So I would not count slowness in easing policy as a third mistake; to my mind it is a consequence of the second.

The slow recovery is probably partly the result of the excessive boom in the 1980s for two other reasons. First, overbuilding needed to be worked off. Second, the asset price bubble and collapse first raised bank capital, and bank lending with it – then the collapse hurt collateral values, caused loan defaults, depleted bank capital, and cut into banks' ability and willingness to lend. Nonetheless, loan demand has been weak enough that the reluctance of banks to lend is probably responsible for relatively little of the weak economic recovery, at least to date.

There could, however, be a "chicken and egg problem" with regard to bank lending. A strong expansion would be the simplest means of resolving the banking system's difficulties. Yet doubts about the banking system's ability to support sustained real growth probably undermine business confidence and slow the recovery. Favorable interest rate spreads together with an infusion of public funds should improve the banking situation gradually. In any case, a resolution of the banking situation may be necessary, but it is probably not sufficient for a resumption of strong economic growth.

Also at work to some extent are three "real" factors. The Japanese economy is undergoing sectoral reallocation. As industries are moving offshore to take advantage of cheaper labor, others must take their place. And deregulation requires some restructuring within certain sectors. Sectoral reallocation and restructuring could be particularly difficult in Japan where the expectation of lifetime employment with a single firm has been the rule. The third real factor at work is the maturation of the Japanese economy, which may be bringing trend productivity growth down from "growth miracle" status closer to OECD norms. There is little monetary or banking policy can or should do to block the adjustment to these real factors.

Real GDP growth has remained near or below 1 percent per year from 1992 through 1995 and the unemployment rate remains high for Japan at 3 percent, about where it was at the end of the 1985–6 recession. Based on my reading of developments, however, I do not think monetary policy made mistakes in the 1991–3 recession and the early years of the current recovery. Monetary policy eased substantially during that period as the multiple sources of drag on the economy became more evident.

Since 1994, however, policy has had to confront an increasingly deflationary economy. Wholesale prices in Japan have been falling slowly since 1992, and CPI prices have been increasingly deflationary. The GDP deflator, for its part, was running at –1 percent (year over year) as of the second quarter of 1995.[8] Dealing adequately with deflation requires some extraordinary measures as I will outline below. Here lies the potential for a third mistake.

Ordinarily a central bank implements monetary policy by targeting the overnight interbank rate on reserves. The interbank rate target provides the anchor for other short-term interest rates such as treasury securities, bank certificates of deposit, commercial paper, and bank loans.

A central bank eases policy by lowering its target for the interbank rate in order to lower short-term interest rates more generally. But the short-term interest rate channel by which monetary policy influences the economy is exhausted once rates have been bid down to zero. Short-term interest rates in Japan moved below 1 percent in 1995 as a result of deliberate monetary policy easing by the BOJ. Consequently, the conventional short-term interest rate channel for easing monetary policy has nearly been exhausted. The central bank cannot push interest rates below zero because no one will lend at negative nominal interest when they can hold cash instead.

There is nevertheless room for the BOJ to ease policy further. The BOJ could continue to inject cash into the economy with additional open market purchases. To ignore this possibility would be to risk making the same mistake as the Federal Reserve did in the early 1930s. At that time the Fed failed to pursue additional open market purchases vigorously once short rates had been driven near zero, and thus failed to stop the deflationary spiral.[9]

Determined open market purchases by the BOJ – now that short-term interest rates are near zero – would create a generalized excess yen demand for assets that would tend to drive up yen asset prices. In particular, such policy actions could push up bond and equity prices and depreciate the exchange rate. Higher yen asset prices would eliminate the deflationary pressure in goods markets by stimulating aggregate demand through a number of channels.

Most importantly the increased yen demand for dollar-denominated securities would decrease imports and increase exports by depreciating the foreign exchange value of the yen. Second, higher Japanese bond prices would bring yields down and stimulate investment demand. And higher equity prices would lower the cost of capital for firms and raise capital in those Japanese banks with significant equity holdings. Finally, the increased yen demand for durable goods would tend to raise aggregate demand directly.

To be effective, however, in preventing a deflationary spiral, determined open market operations might need to be accompanied by a public statement from the BOJ announcing its intention to use monetary policy in this way. If events seem to warrant it, a statement could be issued saying that the BOJ stands ready to use its full monetary policy powers to avert deflation, with the ultimate goal of stabilizing employment and output at a sustainable non-inflationary level. A bold announcement would help reverse immediately any gathering deflationary tendencies, and establish credibility for the BOJ's effort to break the deflation and maintain price stability.

Notes

1. See Ueda (1993), p. 195.
2. See McCallum (1995) for a related theoretical discussion.
3. Organization of Economic Cooperation and Development (1994), p. 12.
4. Ibid., p. 37.
5. Ibid., pp. 26, 35, and 40.
6. See Pauls (1990) and Ueda (1993).
7. See Goodfriend (1993).
8. Bank of Japan (1995), p. 11.
9. See Friedman and Schwartz (1963).

References

Bank of Japan (1995) *Quarterly Bulletin* (November).

Friedman, M. and Schwartz, A. (1963) *A Monetary History of the United States* (Princeton, NJ: Princeton University Press).

Goodfriend, M. (1993) "Interest Rate Policy and the Inflation Scare Problem," Federal Reserve Bank of Richmond *Economic Quarterly* (Winter), pp. 1–24.

McCallum, B. (1995) "Two Fallacies Concerning Central Bank Independence," *American Economic Review*, 85 (May), pp. 207–11.

Organization of Economic Cooperation and Development (1994) *OECD Economic Surveys: Japan*.

Pauls, B.D. (1990) "US Exchange Rate Policy: Bretton Woods to Present," *Federal Reserve Bulletin* (November), pp. 891–908.

Ueda, K. (1993) "Japanese Monetary Policy from 1970 to 1990: Rules or Discretion?," in K. Shigehara (ed.), *Price Stabilization in the 1990s* (London, Macmillan).

Part IV

Central Bank Independence and Accountability

10 Independence and Accountability*

Clive Briault, Andrew Haldane and Mervyn King

1 INTRODUCTION

Over the past few years many central banks have made significant strides toward greater accountability and transparency. There has been a dilution of what Karl Brunner (1981) once called the "peculiar and protective political mystique" that has traditionally surrounded central banking. Central banks in all of the countries which have recently adopted inflation targets have become more open about the formulation and presentation of their monetary policies (Haldane, 1995). Similar such moves have been evident among central banks recently granted greater independence through legislative changes – for example, in France. And in the United States there is active debate on the replacement of the Humphrey–Hawkins Act – and its multiple objectives – with a single inflation objective, and on the publication of the full transcripts of Federal Open Market Cammittee (FOMC) meetings.

How might we best explain this shift toward greater accountability and transparency? And what benefits might it confer? One answer to these questions is that greater accountability has run hand in hand with moves toward greater central bank independence: greater accountability is the government's *quid pro quo* for granting greater central bank autonomy. Why? Independence delegates responsibility for monetary policy to an ultimately unelected authority – the central bank. So making this authority accountable for its actions insures against a "democratic deficit"; it fulfills a fundamental political or even ethical demand for democracy.

But this politico-economic argument scarcely explains existing central bank practices. The Bundesbank is strongly independent yet has relatively

* We acknowledge the important contributions of Suzanne Hudson, Charles Nolan, Eric Schaling and Tony Yates in preparing this chapter and the thoughtful comments of our discussants; of other participants at the Bank of Japan conference; and of Bill Allen, Jag Chadha, Howard Davies, Charles Goodhart and Lars Svensson. Remaining errors are of course our own, as are the views expressed within.

few burdens imposed upon it in terms of accountability and transparency. And it is striking, too, that the statutes of the embryonic European Central Bank follow a similar blueprint. At the other end of the spectrum, the Bank of England has little formal central bank independence. But the United Kingdom's new monetary framework is characterized by considerable transparency. New Zealand offers a different model again. Independence was granted in the context of a formal contract between the government and the Reserve Bank (the Policy Targets Agreement), with accountability imposed through the threat of dismissal of the Governor. It is clear from these examples that, in practice, the mappings between accountability and independence are far from straightforward. And, correspondingly, no one analytical model is able to account for all of them. But to begin to understand these mappings it is useful to consider a set of distinct models of monetary policy institutions.

There has been considerable recent interest in the design of monetary policy institutions (see, for example, Cukierman, 1992; and Persson and Tabellini, 1993). The typical approach takes as its starting point the idea that there is an "inflation bias" problem endemic in discretionary policymaking – the time-consistency problem first formalized by Kydland and Prescott (1977) and subsequently popularized in the monetary policy game of Barro and Gordon (1983a). Several resolutions to this inflation bias have been put forward in the literature. These can be thought of as institutional frameworks which alter the policymakers' incentives in such a way as to secure a Pareto-improving policy outcome. The four solutions which have attracted most attention in the literature are: *non-contingent rules*, such as Friedman's (1959) celebrated *k*-percent rule; Rogoff's (1985) *"conservative" central banker*; solutions based on *reputation*, such as Barro and Gordon (1983b), Backus and Driffill (1985) and Barro (1986); and the Walsh (1995)/Persson and Tabellini (1993) *optimal performance contract* for a central bank. Each has – to a greater or lesser extent – some link with central bank independence. And each – implictly at least – suggests greater or lesser degrees of accountability and transparency. It is this, ultimately, which explains the complexity of the independence/accountability relationship observed in practice.

It is relatively straightforward to rank these competing models in welfare terms (see, for example, King, 1995). The conservative central banker dominates both the non-contingent rule and discretion, but is in turn dominated by the optimal contract which is typically able to secure a first-best. But where might some of the new monetary frameworks, such as those in New Zealand and the United Kingdom, be placed within this spectrum? For example, in the United Kingdom both monetary policy instruments and targets are set by government, so the Bank of England has little real goal or instrument independence – at least as formally defined. Arguably, then, this might position the United Kingdom at a worst-best – discretionary – solution. But much of the conventional literature underplays the role of accountability, and in particular transparency, within the policy problem – a key feature of the UK and other models. If there is uncertainty regarding inflation preferences, accountability and transparency can be shown to solve a time-consistency problem of their own, thereby generating welfare gains even without formal goal or instrument independence.

The next section seeks to define "accountability" and "independence," since these are elusive concepts. Sections 3–5 then consider how the various monetary policy institutional set-ups outlined above might relate to these concepts. In each case we begin by describing the basic model and then consider potential real-world manifestations of such monetary policy institutions. Section 6 extends the existing literature by presenting a model in which accountability or transparency has a well-defined role. In Section 7 we present a simple and preliminary index of central bank accountability for 14 industrialized countries (see Appendix for details). Cross-country comparisons suggest that there is an inverse relationship between accountability and independence and that central banks in countries with a track record of low inflation are less transparent than central banks in countries with less good inflation performances. Section 8 concludes.

2 SOME DEFINITIONS: INDEPENDENCE AND ACCOUNTABILITY

On *independence*, it is useful to follow Fischer's (1994) dichotomy between central bank *goal* independence – the central bank setting its own targets (or at least determining how precisely these targets are specified) – and *instrument* independence – the central bank's ability to choose its own instrument settings. The two are easily confused and in the literature have often been conflated. But the difference between them is crucial in explaining why various monetary models may imply differing degrees of accountability.

Turning to *accountability*, the Oxford English Dictionary defines accountable as "obliged to give a reckoning or explanation for one's actions; responsible." And, in turn, it defines responsible as "legally or morally obliged to take care of something or to carry out a duty; liable to be blamed for loss or failure." So the natural context in which to consider accountability is within a principal–agent relationship. And, in a monetary policy context, these roles are typically taken by the government – as principal – and the central bank – as agent.

Within this principal–agent relationship, however, accountability might take a variety of forms. The simplest case to envisage is when there is a formal contract between the government and the central bank – a "legal" obligation to carry out a duty, or *de jure* accountability. This contract might specify what the central bank exercises discretion over – what is its "duty"; what it is to be held accountable for – for what it is "responsible"; what needs routinely to be monitored to ensure effective accountability – a "reckoning" or "explanation"; and what penalty will be imposed for non-compliance – apportioning the blame for "loss or failure."

But, equally, it is possible to envisage more subtle forms of accountability or transparency. These may be desirable even when relatively little formal – or legal – responsibility is delegated to the agent by the principal. For example, even a non-independent central bank could perceive advantages in explaining its actions, intentions and objectives as a means of influencing public expectations – and thus lowering the costs of delivering the central bank's goals; of influencing the public's social welfare function – by educating the public about the benefits of price stability; and of enhancing its reputation and credibility – by providing a means for it to be judged against the coherence and persuasiveness of its analysis. This results in greater central bank accountability – *de facto* if not *de jure*. Making the central bank's actions, intentions or analysis transparent subjects the central bank's reputation to a "reckoning," for which it will suffer "loss or failure" if it is found wanting. Such a set-up is thus qualitatively similar to a fully specified legal contract between the government and the central bank.

3 THE TIME-CONSISTENCY PROBLEM: RULES AND DISCRETION

3.1 Inflation Bias and Discretionary Policymaking

We use the familiar Barro–Gordon framework. In a given period, output is described by a reduced-form Lucas surprise supply function:

$$y = y^* + b\,(\pi - \pi^e) + \varepsilon \qquad (10.1)$$

where (the natual log of) output is denoted by y and its natural rate by y^*; π denotes the observed inflation rate; π^e is the mathematical expectation of this on the part of private sector agents, conditional on their information set at $t-1$; and ε is a white noise supply shock, with zero mean and variance σ_ε^2. Assuming a constant velocity of circulation and normalizing the previous period's price level to unity, we have:

$$m = \pi + y \tag{10.2}$$

where m denotes the money stock, which is assumed to be controlled deterministically by the central bank. Finally, we have the loss function of the authorities, which is quadratic in inflation and output. The target level of inflation is zero, but the target level of output, ky^*, exceeds the natural rate of output:[1]

$$L = aE\pi^2 + E(y - ky^*)^2 \quad a > 0, k > 1 \tag{10.3}$$

We assume that each period the money supply is set by the central bank following the realization of the supply shock. But the inflation expectations of private sector agents are formed, and wage contracts are agreed, prior to their observation of this shock. It is this asymmetry in reacting to the supply shock that provides the policymaker with the ability to inflate the economy beyond its natural rate temporarily when given complete discretion over monetary policymaking.

We can solve for this *discretionary solution* by minimizing L, taking expected inflation as predetermined this period. Under rational expectations the private sector's expected inflation rate must equate, in equilibrium, with the policymaker's optimal inflation rate under discretion. Equilibrium inflation in this setting is hence given by:

$$\pi_D = (b/a)z - (b/(a + b^2))\varepsilon \tag{10.4}$$

where the D subscript denotes discretion, and $z \equiv (k-1)y^*$. The first term in (10.4) defines the familiar inflation bias. Note that this is positive and state-independent. And since the socially optimal inflation rate is assumed to be zero, this inflation bias is clearly suboptimal from society's point of view. The second term in (10.4) defines the authorities' stabilization effort in the face of supply shocks.[2] Discretion imparts the freedom to respond flexibly to shocks, thus stabilizing output. So the discretionary solution secures optimal policy stabilization – lower output variance – but at the expense of a higher inflation rate than is socially optimal – an inflation bias.

3.2 A Non-Contingent Rule

This discretionary outcome is usefully contrasted with a *non-contingent rule* – a rule that fixes m independently of realizations of the supply shock, ε. This can be thought of as exactly analogous to Friedman's k-percent rule. Inflation under the rule (denoted R) can be shown to be:

$$\pi_R = -(1/(1 + b))\varepsilon \tag{10.5}$$

Comparing (10.4) and (10.5), it is clear that the rule succeeds in eliminating completely the inflation bias – the first part of (10.4); it precommits policy to zero inflation. But it does so at the expense of a suboptimal degree of stabilization in response to supply shocks – compare (10.5) with the second part of (10.4).[3] The non-contingent rule takes no heed of supply shocks when setting policy and so minimizes stabilization effort. Herein lies the well-known credibility–flexibility tradeoff, familiar from Canzoneri (1985), Rogoff (1985) and Lohmann (1992), among many others. In the absence of some means of precommiting to the optimal state contingent rule, inflation bias can be reduced only by foregoing stabilization effort: lower inflation outcomes can be traded off against greater output variance or vice versa.

3.3 Accountability, Rules and Discretion in Practice

The non-contingent rule, taken by itself, involves no delegation of power to any agency, such as a central bank. Consequently, it is characterized by no central bank independence – whether goal or instrument independence – and no accountability. Formally, there is no distinction between principal and agent under the rule and so nothing for an agent to be held accountable for. So a non-contingent rule, if it were observed in the real world, would tell us very little about independence–accountability mappings.

In practice, however, it is difficult to pinpoint any real-world examples of a strict non-contingent rule having been adhered to by developed countries, at least over the post-Bretton Woods period.[4] While many countries experimented with, for example, monetary targeting procedures in the 1970s and 1980s, in practice none of these frameworks worked in the rigidly inflexible fashion suggested by a non-contingent rule. Prior to the 1970s, the Gold Standard and Bretton Woods regimes did, in principle, come much closer to such a non-contingent rule. But both regimes were characterized by contingencies – whether revaluations or, on occasions, suspensions. And the lesser accountability of these regimes was probably due more to the unobtrusiveness of democracy upon government behavior over much of the period.

A significant body of research has looked instead at simple feedback, or *contingent*, rules of various forms. The policy rules of McCallum (1988) and Taylor (1993) are prominent examples. These – unlike non-contingent rules – allow some degree of feedback from state variables, typically prices or money GDP, so as to secure a greater degree of policy stabilization. They can perhaps be thought to offer a compromise between a strict non-contingent rule and the fully optimal state contingent outcome. It is probably unrealistic to think that any central bank would ever set policy according to the automatic pilot suggested by these policy rules. But it is not unrealistic to think that such rules could actively form part of a central banker's information set. Indeed, in this respect, it is striking how well John Taylor's policy rule does in tracking the path of US interest rates over recent years.

4 CENTRAL BANK INDEPENDENCE AND THE ROGOFF MODEL

4.1 The Rogoff Model

In a highly influential paper, Rogoff (1985) showed that a Pareto-improving point on the credibility–flexibility frontier – better than either the non-contingent rule or discretionary outcomes – could be secured by delegating monetary policymaking to an authority with greater inflation aversion than society as a whole: a "conservative" central banker. Such a model probably comes closest to matching what many people would think of as central bank independence: delegation of monetary policy to an inflation-averse authority with instrument independence.

To formalize matters, denote the *absolute* inflation-aversion parameter of Rogoff's "conservative" central banker by α (where $\alpha > a$), and thus its *relative* degree of inflation aversion by $\rho = a/\alpha$ (where $\rho < 1$). Solving for inflation under this model:

$$\pi_I = (\rho b/a)z - ((\rho b/a)/(1 + \rho\theta))\varepsilon \qquad (10.6)$$

where I denotes the independence outcome.

Equation (10.6) neatly encapsulates the benefits – and costs – which central bank independence is deemed to confer. On the benefits side, the inflation bias implied by (10.6) is clearly lower than in the discretionary case, by an amount related to the relative inflation aversion of the conservative central bank. Against this, the conservative central banker now falls short of offering optimal stabilization policy – the second parts of (10.4) and (10.6) also differ. So the lower inflation bias is bought at the expense of potentially greater output variability. The credibility–flexibility tradeoff is thus preserved. The interesting point, however, is that when ρ is chosen optimally, Rogoff's conservative central banker secures a welfare outcome which is preferable to either the rules or the discretion solutions: it achieves a Pareto-preferred point on the credibility–flexibility frontier.[5] *Prima facie*, this lends strong support to independent central banking solutions to the time-consistency problem.

4.2 Empirical Evidence on Central Bank Independence

There have been a plethora of empirical studies which have attempted to shed light on the validity of the reduced-form implications of the Rogoff central bank independence model. From equation (10.6), the two most important of these implications are that an independent central bank should: (i) attenuate inflation biases (lower average inflation); and (ii) accentuate stabilization biases (raise output variability).

Existing empirical evidence (beginning with Bade and Parkin, 1987, and including Alesina and Summers, 1993; Grilli, Masciandaro and Tabellini, 1991; Cukierman, 1992; and Eijffinger and Schaling, 1993, 1995) appears to lend strong support to the first of the Rogoff model's predictions: in the cross-section greater (goal and instrument) independence does tend to be associated with lower inflation, both in mean and variance.[6] Whether we can tell a causal story from these correlations is, of course, another matter. Some have suggested that the observed correlations are instead the result of some third common driving factor: for example, the inflation preferences of agents in an economy; or the influence of pressure groups, such as those within the financial community (Posen, 1993); or the nature of the wage-bargaining process (Hall, 1994). But that said, the negative correlation between independence and inflation seems about as close to a "stylized fact" as central banking scholars are ever likely to get.

The second of the Rogoff model's predictions – that independence should result in greater output variability – raises deeper-seated questions. Most empirical studies have failed to find any significant link between independence and the mean or variability of output growth or employment (see De Long and Summers, 1992; and Alesina and Summers, 1993). Taken by itself, this evidence would imply that independence delivers a "free lunch": an inflation gain, without any of the countervailing output costs. Why might this be? Fischer (1994) offers differences in the susceptibility of different economies to shocks, and differences in their capacity to deal with these shocks, as perhaps the two most important explanations. On the second of these, it could be that independence serves to limit policy-induced, discretionary monetary policy disturbances, which more than counterbalances any loss from suboptimal supply shock stabilization (Alesina and Gatti, 1995). Or it could be that independent central banks are simply more efficient in the way they set their monetary policies; their policy "engineering" is more precise and effective.

4.3 Accountability and Central Bank Independence in Practice

Because the Rogoff solution involves delegation of monetary policy responsibility to a non-government agency, it clearly raises questions of accountability. Formally, there is now a clear principal–agent relationship at work, in a way not true of the non-contingent rule or discretionary outcomes. But the model also suggests there is no need for monitoring of the central bank or the imposition of *ex post* penalties upon it for failure. The conservative central banking solution – unlike the contract approach – is not designed to make a zero-inflation bias *incentive-compatible* for the central bank. Instead, the intention is that a central bank be chosen with the right set of incentives – in particular, inflation preferences – in the first place. Simply leaving an inflation-averse institution to its own devices is enough to ensure a preferred inflation outcome.[7] Put differently, if the central bank has goal as well as instrument independence, then accountability makes no sense: the institution is judged against targets it sets itself, so an accountability constraint on behavior never binds. So the Rogoff case can perhaps be characterized by (almost) complete goal and instrument independence and relatively little accountability.

Real-world examples of the Rogoff model could, in principle, be held to include any independent central bank. In practice, however, very few real-world institutions combine both high instrument and goal independence with little accountability in the strict way implied by the Rogoff model. The Bundesbank offers one possible exception. It has complete instrument independence; its objectives are not very precisely specified, so it has a high degree of goal independence; and at the same time, the Bundesbank has relatively little formal accountability to anyone.[8] By contrast, and despite having instrument independence, the US Federal Reserve system does not fit neatly within the Rogoff model. It is required to aim for the multiple objectives embodied in the Humphrey–Hawkins Act, which can be thought to dilute its "conservatism" and goal independence; it is formally accountable to the United States government through the Chairman's twice-yearly appearances at Humphrey–Hawkins hearings and through frequent other testimonies to congressional committees; and the Chairman is formally appointed by the President.

This raises a second question about the Rogoff model as a blueprint for an independent central bank. While the economics of this model are crystal-clear, the *politics* are much muddier. Delegation of power to an unelected authority might be interpreted as a dilution of democracy: an empowered, but unaccountable, central bank gives rise to a "democratic deficit."[9] Indeed, it was largely this democratic motive that lay beyond the Roll Committee's (1993) recommendation that independence for the Bank of England should be accompanied by greater parliamentary accountability for its actions. Lohmann (1992) presents a hybrid of the Rogoff model which goes some way toward addressing this "democratic deficit." Responsibility for monetary policy is still delegated to an independent central bank. But there is an override clause whereby government can intervene in the face of "large" supply shocks to secure more effective output stabilization. So the Lohmann model does involve accountability of a fashion: the central bank is held to account – overridden – in the event of significant shocks. And the outcome of this game is then a Pareto improvement over Rogoff. Moreover, the Lohmann model has some clear real-world analogs. For example, the New Zealand Policy Targets Agreement has explicit exemptions in the event of "significant" shocks to, for example, the terms of trade; and in the Netherlands and Canada, the Minister of Finance has the right to issue an "instruction" to the central bank on monetary policy.

5 OPTIMAL CONTRACTS FOR CENTRAL BANKERS

5.1 The Walsh Model

In recent papers, Walsh (1995) and Persson and Tabellini (1993) have demonstrated that, in principle at least, resolution of the credibility–flexibility tradeoff is remarkably straightforward. The Walsh solution is typically thought to take the form of a contract between the government (the principal) and the central bank (the agent). The contract levies a linear tax on the central bank for any inflation outturn in excess of the inflation target, and pays a linear subsidy if the outturn is below the target. In all other respects, the central bank is given complete discretion when setting policy. A suitably specified contract can be shown to offset fully the inflation bias, while at the same time leaving stabilization policy unaffected:

that is, a linear tax can make a first-best attainable.[10] Intuitively, this is straightforward to see. The inflation bias in (10.4) is constant; it is invariant to the shocks that lie at the heart of the stabilization problem. Raising the marginal cost of inflation by a *fixed* amount – equal to the inflation bias – thus offsets fully this bias, without in any way interfering with stabilization effort. The credibility–flexibility tradeoff is resolved.

To see this formally, augment the central bank's loss function with a linear tax levied at a rate on the observed inflation rate:

$$L = aE\pi^2 + E(y - ky^*)^2 + \omega\pi \quad a > 0, k > 1, \omega > 0 \tag{10.7}$$

If we then design the tax in such a way that the marginal cost of inflation is raised by an amount equal to the inflation bias:

$$\omega = (b/a)z \tag{10.8}$$

then the tax will fully offset the (constant) incentive to generate an inflation bias. This can be seen by solving (10.7) for the inflation rate subject to (10.8). This gives:

$$\pi_C = (-b/(a + b^2))\varepsilon \tag{10.9}$$

where the *C* subscript denotes the contract solution. Comparing (10.4) and (10.9) it is clear that the inflation bias is fully offset, while stabilization effort remains the same as that under the optimal state contingent rule – hence the first-best.[11]

5.2 Svensson's Inflation Target Interpretation

Recently, Svensson (1995) has shown that the same optimal outcome can result from a suitably specified inflation target. To see this, imagine that the central bank is charged with hitting an inflation target π^*, which is below the socially optimal inflation rate. The central bank's objective function thus takes the modified form:[12]

$$L = aE(\pi - \pi^*)^2 + E(y - ky^*)^2 \quad a > 0, k > 1 \tag{10.10}$$

But this can be rewritten trivially as:

$$L = aE\pi^2 + E(y - ky^*)^2 + (2a\pi^*)\pi + \varphi \tag{10.11}$$

where $\varphi \equiv a\pi^{*2}$. We can see that this is formally identical to the Walsh linear tax, up to a constant φ. Equating (10.11) and (10.7), it is easily seen that the Walsh first-best can be replicated by setting an inflation target satisfying:

$$\pi^* = -(b/a)z \tag{10.12}$$

That is, the inflation target is set equal to the negative of the inflation bias.[13] So the Svensson model implies that setting a suboptimally low inflation target can completely resolve the credibility–flexibility tradeoff – even if an inflation target congruent with the socially optimal inflation rate cannot.

5.3 Accountability and Optimal Central Bank Contracts in Practice

Under the Walsh contract, there is a clear principal–agent relationship at work. But unlike in the Rogoff model, the central bank is assigned instrument but *not* goal independence, since inflation objectives are written into the terms of the contract drawn up by government. This means that the central bank clearly has something to be accountable for; it does not decide itself what it is to be judged against. The contract, in turn, uses this accountability to impose a constraint upon the central bank, penalizing (or sometimes rewarding) it for target misses. The role of such penalties, again unlike in Rogoff, is explicitly to alter the central bank's inflationary incentives – in particular, to make a non-inflationary-biased equilibrium incentive-compatible for the central bank. The accountability constraint imposed under the Walsh contract – a linear tax – is clearly minimalist: it requires only that actual inflation outcomes are monitored, so that the tax can be levied on them. But with a clearly specified target and an appropriate set of penalties, the agent is provided with exactly the right incentives to "do the right thing." This is precisely the beauty of the optimal contract literature.

But to what extent is Walsh's optimal contract, or Svensson's inflation target, replicated in the real world? The optimal contract approach can be questioned on at least four counts. First, the original argument for an independent central bank was that the government could not credibly precommit to a rule. But, equally, it may be unable credibly to precommit to enforcing a contract. Because of this, some authors have observed that the Walsh solution is really a way of *relocating* the time-consistency problem rather than actually *resolving* it (Canzoneri *et al.*, 1995).

Second, the non-state contingency of the inflation bias in the Barro–Gordon game is crucial for the simple form of the contract to work. Canzoneri *et al.* (1995), for example, show how this result can break down. The contract would then achieve the first-best only if the tax on observed inflation became state-dependent – a contract that would probably be impossible to write, let alone enforce.

Third, how far are the features of a Walsh contract (or Svensson-style inflation target) mirrored in reality? Many countries have announced clearly specified targets which might reasonably be interpreted as a performance contract of sorts. This would encompass countries with monetary and exchange rate, as well as inflation, targets. But few of these frameworks impose *explicit* penalties for target misses. For example, the optimal contract literature usually envisages the penalty taking a pecuniary form: for example, linking the Governor's salary, or the central bank's budget, to inflation performance. Very few countries have such a pecuniary penalty mechanism in place. In principle, the penalty under the Walsh contract could be non-pecuniary: for example, embarrassment costs could serve as the disincentive mechanism. But, in practice, it is difficult to think how such costs could be accurately calibrated, so that the principal was sure that the right amount of the medicine was being administered to the agent.

This brings us to the fourth point: imposing a linear tax. Almost all targeting arrangements are quadratic in nature. For example, there is no presumption that any central bank at present reaps benefits – pecuniary or otherwise – from *under*shooting its targets. Yet this would be a logical implication of the Walsh contract. Another way of delivering the first-best, following Svensson, is if there are real-world examples of central banks with inflation targets set below the socially optimal inflation rate. But most countries appear in practice to be targeting rates of inflation above, rather than below, the socially optimal rate.[14] Moreover, it is questionable whether, under Svensson's inflation target, the central bank would want to be set an objective which it would rarely be seen to hit. That would surely be credibility-depleting over the longer run.

Taking these points together, the only country that perhaps comes close at present to the Walsh contract (or some variant of it) is New Zealand. There, the Policy Targets Agreement is an explicit, and precisely specified, contract between the government and the Reserve Bank. Explicit penalties are written into this contract, in that the Governor can be dismissed for failures to meet the target; he or she is held directly accountable for inflation target misses. Walsh (1995) has shown that this punishment mechanism can mimic perfectly an optimal contract, since the *expected* probability of dismissal is linear in inflation.[15] Other countries fare well on some features of Walsh's optimal contract, but fail to satisfy fully all the criteria that might deliver a first-best. For example, the United Kingdom has a clearly specified inflation target, which allows simple monitoring. This target, in turn, is intended to impose embarrassment costs on the authorities in the event of the target being breached – so it is a performance contract of sorts. Similarly, moves elsewhere toward clear and quantitative price stability objectives – for example, the inflation targets recently put in place in Australia, Canada, Finland, Israel, New Zealand, Sweden and Spain – are a step in the right direction, if not the final word. And the fact that these targets are not set as low as the negative of inflation bias does not of course preclude them from securing *some* welfare benefit, by pushing inflation in the direction of its socially optimal rate. Moreover, the introduction of an inflation target is not the full extent of the recent changes in the United Kingdom and elsewhere. As important has been the move toward a more transparent system of monetary policy implementation. These developments go well beyond the accountability and transparency implied even by the optimal contract. It is reasonable to ask, then, what role accountability and transparency about monetary policymaking – defined in the general sense of Section 2 – may play in a world of second-best or worse.

6 ACCOUNTABILITY WITH UNCERTAIN CENTRAL BANK PREFERENCES

6.1 Private Information and Monetary Policymaking

The Barro–Gordon model is often rationalized as a game in which the central bank has private information on realizations of one of the state variables – information assumed to be unavailable to private sector agents (see, for example, Canzoneri, 1985). This informational asymmetry in turn gives the authorities either a first-mover advantage (when setting policy) over private sector agents (when forming their inflation expectations) or an incentive not to divulge all their private information. So requiring the central bank to disclose this information may offer a way of resolving the inflation bias problem.

Yet it is questionable just how realistic the assumption of private information on the part of the central bank is – at least as far as supply shocks are concerned.[16] Certainly, having worked in a central bank, we find it difficult to think of many practical examples! To illustrate, if the supply shock is induced by the *government* – for example, a change in distortionary taxes

– then it is as transparent to private sector agents as to the authorities themselves. If the supply shock is *external* in origin – for example, a shock to the oil price – it is unclear where the authorities' informational advantage would lie. And if the supply shock is rooted in *private sector* behavior – greater competitiveness among retailers is a topical example in the United Kingdom – then it is possible the authorities could be at an informational *dis*advantage to the agents actually experiencing the supply shock. None of these examples offer compelling reasons for believing that the authorities have an absolute informational advantage over other agents in the economy.

So what informational advantage might the authorities have? The one thing the authorities do clearly possess more information on than outside agents is their own preferences. If the authorities know anything, it is their own minds. But in the standard Barro–Gordon game, the authorities' preferences are common knowledge and certain. In practice, at least in countries with less than perfect monetary policy credibility, this is rarely the case. For example, inflation preferences may be subject to short-run political pressures. And these pressures may vary in their severity according to the state of the political and economic business cycle. Even when monetary policy is delegated to an independent monetary authority, it is unlikely such an institution will have preferences that are known with certainty – at least when reputation and credibility are initially low. Private sector agents then face a tricky signal-extraction problem. They are subject to uncertainties both from additive supply shocks and from multiplicative preference shocks. Such a setting can be shown to afford a distinct role for accountability and transparency.

6.2 A Model of Inflation Preference Uncertainty

To formalize these thoughts, consider generalizing the loss function, (10.3):

$$L = a_t E\pi^2 + E(y - ky^*)^2 \quad k > 1 \tag{10.13}$$

where a_t – the authorities' inflation preferences – are now assumed to be a random variable satisfying $a_t = a^* - x_t$, where x_t is a mean–zero normal variate with *conditional* variance σ_x^2.[17] So from the viewpoint of the public, the authorities' preferences are subject to periodic white-noise shocks, distributed around a^*. x is unobservable for private sector agents, but is of course known to the authorities themselves. Agents face uncertainty about the authorities' true inflation preferences each period at the time they enter into the nominal wage bargain.

Moreover, agents care about both the mean and variance of inflation outturns.[18] So when forming their inflation expectations each period, they internalize the information on the distribution of x as well as its mean. Indeed, because they are inflation risk-averse, agents require compensation for the conditional variation in x – a risk premium of sorts – to guard against an adverse preference shock eroding real wages. This insurance premium becomes factored into agents' nominal wage expectations and thus, in turn, is reflected in actual inflation under rational expectations. This can be seen formally by solving the model (10.1), (10.2) and (10.13) for agents' inflation expectations under discretionary policy (now denoted DU):[19]

$$\pi^e_{DU} = \Phi(.)(b/a^*)z \tag{10.14}$$

where:

$$\Phi(.) = \frac{[a^*((a^* + b^2)^2 + \sigma^2_x)]}{[a^*(a^* + b^2)^2 - b^2\sigma^2_x]} \tag{10.15}$$

which compares with inflation expectations under discretion of:

$$\pi^e_D = (b/a^*)z \tag{10.16}$$

It is easily seen from (10.14) that $\Phi(.) > 1 \ \forall \ \sigma^2_x > 0$. In the special case where $\sigma^2_x = 0$, $\Phi(.) = 1$, and the model collapses to the certainty-equivalent preferences case given by (10.16). Consequently, any uncertainty regarding inflation preferences – a non-zero σ^2_x – will generate an upward bias to inflation expectations and hence to the inflation rate itself. It is also clear from (10.14), however, that preference uncertainty only worsens the existing inflation bias problem; it cannot generate an inflationary bias of its own. For example, setting $k = 1$ in (10.14) removes the inflation bias independently of σ^2_x.

For completeness, actual inflation in this set-up is given by:

$$\pi_{DU} = [b^2/(a_t + b^2)]\ [\Phi(b/a^*) + 1]z - [b^2/(a_t + b^2)]\varepsilon \tag{10.17}$$

where the upward bias to actual inflation – in excess of the conventional inflation bias – is evident from the first part of (10.17). But note also that stabilization effort is now dictated by *realized* outcomes for a_t, rather than its mean a^*. And so each period – if not on average – there is the potential for the authorities' stabilization effort to differ from that which is optimal for private sector agents. All of this clearly implies that a reduction in preference uncertainty is a "free lunch": it will both lower inflation biases and improve stabilization effort. The extent of the additional inflation bias is clearly conditional on σ_x^2.[20] It is also larger, the lower the inflation aversion of the authorities (the lower a*); or, put differently, the less the degree of central bank independence. So reductions in preference uncertainty are significantly welfare-enhancing for low-independence/low-credibility central banks; and conversely for highly independent central banks. These points are best illustrated with some numerical examples.

6.3 Some Simple Numerical Examples

Let $k = 1.1$ – that is, the authorities target a rate of output 10 percent above its natural rate.[21] A larger k would obviously generate bigger inflation biases, as it would signify a greater incentive to inflate. Further, we normalize the natural rate of output, y^*, to unity, and set b – the coefficient in the surprise supply function – equal to 4.[22] Take initially the case where $a^* = 0.4$ – a relatively low degree of inflation aversion or independence. If we consider first the certainty-equivalent case – $\sigma_x^2 = 0$ – then the expected inflation rate will be 1 percent. Now consider letting $\sigma_x^2 = 3.35$. Expected inflation doubles to more than 2 percent. And while the variance in this example is extreme, this at least illustrates the potential for preference uncertainties to increase signficantly inflation biases.

Consider now the case of a more inflation-averse or independent central bank – one with $a^* = 2$. As we would expect, expected inflation in the certainty-equivalent case falls, to 0.2 percent. And, perhaps most interestingly, if we now set $\sigma_x^2 = 3.35$, this raises expected inflation only marginally, to 0.22 percent. What this seems to suggest is that for countries with relatively little independence, or perhaps a poor inflationary track record, significant reductions in inflation bias can be achieved by lowering preference uncertainty. These reductions are much smaller for inflation-averse central banks, when preference uncertainty is reduced by the same absolute amount. This result has some relevance when we look at the empirical link between central bank accountability, independence and credibility in Section 7.

6.4 Reputation

Disclosure of private information on inflation preferences by the central bank can secure clear welfare benefits. But there is more than one way such disclosure could be achieved. Reputation – or monetary policy credibility more generally – is one way: a good track record shrinks the conditional distribution of inflation outcomes, by revealing information on the distribution of the authorities' "true" inflation preferences over time.

Intuitively, this way of capturing reputation sounds quite appealing.[23] After all, "price stability" is as much or more to do with the *variation* in inflation as with its mean value. For example, in Japan revealing information on inflation preferences through stability-oriented policy actions has arguably been central in helping to maintain low inflation, in the absence of formal central bank independence.

6.5 Accountability, Transparency and Central Bank Secrecy

Reputation amounts to revealing preference information by "deeds". Transparency, or *de facto* accountability, can be thought to do it by "words". There are a variety of forms these words might take: speeches, press statements, appearances before parliament, bulletins and inflation reports, and publication of the minutes of monetary policy council meetings are among the more common. All of these reveal information on the authorities' reaction function – its actions, objectives and intentions – and thus on the distribution of the authorities' inflation preferences. Correspondingly, agents will demand less compensation for inflation uncertainty – and a lower inflation bias will obtain.

The United Kingdom provides a good case study of how this might work in practice. The Bank of England has no formal goal or instrument independence; it too is perhaps at (10.14) above. But recently its advice has been made transparent, thereby forcing into the open whether – in the event of any disagreement – the government has different inflation preferences to the Bank, or whether instead it simply disagrees with the Bank's technical judgment. The three most important vehicles for this greater transparency have been the inflation target itself, which makes clear the authorities' medium-term price stability objectives; the published minutes of the Chancellor/Governor meetings, at which monetary policy decisions are made and discussed on the record each month; and the *Inflation Report*, which offers the Bank's own independent analysis of inflationary trends. None of this is to say that the United Kingdom model could not be improved upon: either by granting central bank independence – shifting the mean of a^* upwards; or by writing a Walsh-type contract – provided this is feasible.[24] But at the same time the model carries the implication that a little bit of transparency – a small reduction in preference uncertainty – may go a long way.

It is interesting, too, that the countries which have become noticeably more transparent in recent years are precisely those with low initial endowments of credibility. For example, it is striking how many inflation target countries – whose monetary regimes have no real track record because of their newness – have also recently sought greater transparency. Central banks in the United Kingdom, Sweden, Spain, Canada and New Zealand, for example, have all recently decided to publish inflation or monetary policy reports explaining their actions and intentions relative to their inflation target. Such a development would fit neatly within our model. These low-credibility countries with new monetary frameworks cannot rely on reputation – "actions" – to reveal information on the distribution of their inflation preferences. So instead they rely on "words" to improve their credibility. Recent shifts towards greater transparency may be serving as a surrogate for reputation or credibility in countries whose monetary regimes have yet to establish cast-iron inflationary credentials.[25]

This analysis stands in some contrast to the central bank "secrecy" literature, some of which has attempted to explain secrecy in monetary policymaking as a rational Pareto-improving outcome.[26] The rationale behind recent moves towards greater transparency stands in sharp contrast to this literature. Central banks have sought greater transparency precisely to help prevent private sector agents thinking the worst of them and factoring inflation biases into their price expectations. Openness can then serve as a demonstration effect of a central bank's unwillingness to countenance inflation surprises for short-term output gain, by voluntarily forgoing one means of camouflaging inflation surprises.

Karl Brunner (1981) wrote of central bank secrecy:

> The mystique thrives on a pervasive impression that Central Banking is an esoteric art. Access to this art and its proper execution is confined to the initiated elite. The esoteric nature of the art is moreover revealed by an inherent impossibility to articulate its insights in explicit and intelligible words and sentences.

Part of the motivation behind the Bank of England's *Inflation Report* was precisely to overcome this problem. As any self-respecting academic will tell you, "one learns a subject by teaching it." The self-same principle applies to the setting of monetary policy. And we hope the *Inflation Report*, and developments like it, might continue to serve as an educational tool – not just for private sector agents, but for the "initiated elite" too.

7 ACCOUNTABILITY, CREDIBILITY AND INDEPENDENCE IN THE CROSS-SECTION

So far we have attempted to link our models to existing central bank practices through "words." Now we see what evidence there is from some "numbers." To do this, we need to create an index of accountability, in a similar spirit to the central bank independence indices. To our knowledge, only one author has so far attempted this (Havrilesky, 1995). But because his estimates overlap in some respects with existing central bank independence indices, they are not best-placed to help assess accountability–independence mappings. So instead we have constructed our own accountability index (see Appendix). This is based on four criteria: (a) whether the central bank is subject to external monitoring by parliament (as, for example, in France, the USA and the UK); (b) whether the minutes of meetings to decide monetary policy are published (as in the USA and UK); (c) whether the central bank publishes an inflation or monetary policy report of some kind, in addition to standard central bank bulletins; and (d) whether there is a clause that allows the central bank to be overridden in the event of certain shocks (as in Lohmann, 1992). These are obviously simple proxies.[27] Some of them could, in certain circumstances, be used to diminish the independence of a central bank through political interference. And they might not capture the extent to which some central banks have influenced and cultivated public opinion through other means. But they cover most of the main features of accountability, as defined in Section 2.

We distinguish goal and instrument indices of independence. For goal independence we use four criteria, namely: (a) whether the statutes of the central bank make it independent of the government; (b) whether more than half the appointments to the central bank board are made independently of the government; (c) whether there are government officials on the board; and (d) whether the central bank does in practice set its own goals (for example monetary or inflation targets). An index of instrument independence would add little value, however, since of the fourteen industrialized countries we consider (Australia, Belgium, Canada, France, Germany, Italy, Japan, the Netherlands, New Zealand, Spain, Sweden, Switzerland, the United Kingdom and the United States), all but one (the United Kingdom) have significant instrument independence.

Figure 10.1 plots central bank goal independence against our accountability index. The correlation is clearly negative.[28] Interestingly, this is precisely the relationship the Rogoff and optimal contract models, when taken together, would predict. The greater is a central bank's goal independence, the less it is accountable for: setting your own objectives makes it difficult for you to be held accountable for them. But as goal independence lessens – government sets down the terms and conditions, for example via a Walsh contract – then accountability rises. However, the negative correlation in Figure 10.1 is inconsistent with a purely democratic or political

Figure 10.1 Central bank goal independence and accountability

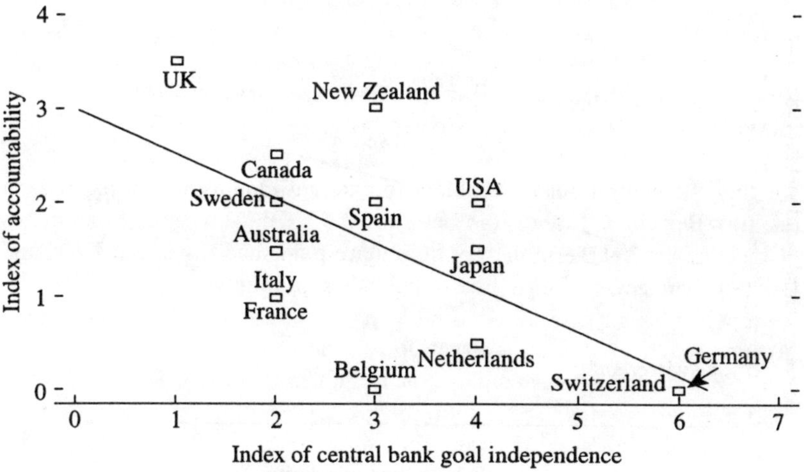

explanation of accountability, which would assert that independence and accountability should run in parallel.

Of course, there are many other factors at work when explaining such a correlation. And from Section 6 we know that monetary policy credibility – or reputation more generally – is one of the more important of them. High-credibility countries have earned their counter-inflationary spurs by deeds, and so do not need to reveal further information on their preferences by words. Figure 10.2 plots the accountability index against the average level of bond yields over the past decade – a crude proxy for (the inverse of) credibility – for our fourteen countries. The correlation is clearly positive.[29] It is particularly striking to note how many inflation target countries lie in the low credibility–high accountability segment. They have seemingly used transparency as a surrogate for credibility – indeed, in the United Kingdom case, perhaps as a partial substitute for independence.

8 CONCLUSIONS

Making a central bank independent imposes a constraint on government interference in monetary policy, while making the central bank accountable imposes a constraint on how it exercises this independence. Both these constraints are generally viewed as desirable aspects of monetary policymaking.

In this chapter we have tried to extend this conventional wisdom in

Figure 10.2 Accountability and average bond yields

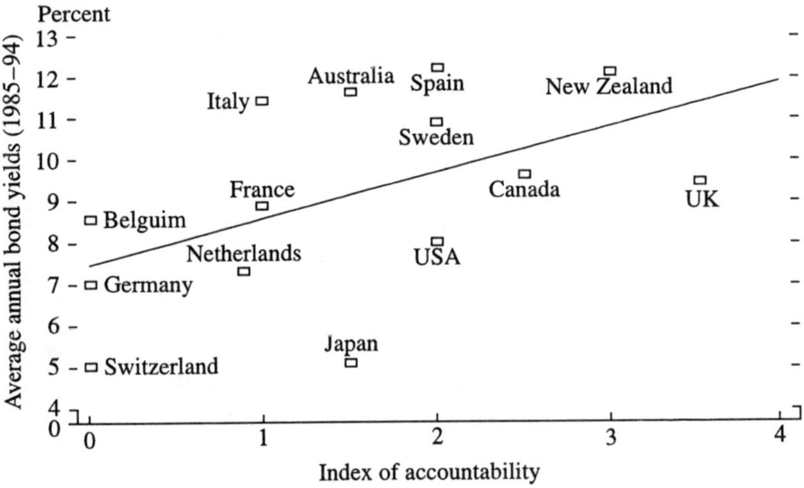

three ways. First, we have used a formal model to illustrate the potential role and value of accountability and transparency. This does not imply that accountability by itself is necessarily sufficient for a monetary institution; merely that it could help reduce inflation bias, either by itself or in conjunction with other institutional procedures (conservative central banks, optimal contracts and so on).

Second, we have considered the forms which accountability might take. And we have illustrated this by attempting to match each of the existing theoretical solutions for the inflation bias problem to existing real-world central banking institutions: for example, Rogoff's conservative central banker and the Bundesbank; Walsh's optimal contract and New Zealand's Policy Targets Agreement; and our preference-uncertainty model and the United Kingdom's new monetary framework.

Third, we have constructed a very preliminary and simple index of central bank accountability. Two features are striking here: first, that cross-section correlations point toward an inverse relationship between accountability and independence – consistent with accountability and transparency having served as a partial substitute for independence, rather than as a complement; and second, that countries with a good reputation for low inflation seem to be characterized by relatively low degrees of accountability, and vice versa. This is consistent with accountability having also served as a partial substitute for reputation among central banks whose monetary frameworks have yet fully to establish themselves.

Appendix: Index of Central Bank Accountability

Our constructed index of central bank accountability is based on four criteria:

- whether the central bank is subject to external monitoring by parliament;
- whether the minutes of meetings to decide monetary policy are published;
- whether the central bank publishes an inflation or monetary policy report of some kind, in addition to standard central bank bulletins; and
- whether there is a clause that allows the central bank to be overridden in the event of certain shocks. We allow for both *explicit* and *implicit* override procedures. If the central bank law mentions an explicit escape clause – for example New Zealand – a country receives a score of unity. If overriding the central bank is not *a priori* excluded it receives a score of one-half.

The accountability index is a simple sum of these criteria.

Table 10.1 Central bank accountability Index

	Parliamentary monitoring	*Minutes published*	*Inflation/ monetary policy report published*	*Override clause*	*Total*
Australia	*	–	–	1/2	1 1/2
Belgium	–	–	–	–	0
Canada	*	–	*	1/2	2 1/2
France	*	–	–	–	1
Germany	–	–	–	–	0
Italy	*	–	–	–	1
Japan	*	–	–	1/2	1 1/2
Netherlands	–	–	–	1/2	1/2
New Zealand	*	–	*	*	3
Spain	*	–	*	–	2
Sweden	*	–	*	–	2
Switzerland	–	–	–	–	0
United Kingdom	*	*	*	1/2	3 1/2
United States	*	*	–	–	2

Notes

1. There are a variety of factors that might generate $k > 1$. For example, Barro and Gordon (1983a) highlight distortionary income taxes and unemployment benefits as factors that might hold employment below its socially optimal level. See also Cukierman (1992), chapters 2–5.
2. Formally, the loss function under discretion is:

$$L_D = (1 + \theta)z^2 + (1/(1 + \theta))\sigma_\varepsilon^2$$

where $\theta = b^2/a$. This compares with a loss function under the optimal state contingent rule of:

$$L_O = z^2 + (1/(1 + \theta))\sigma_\varepsilon^2$$

The second parts of these expressions are clearly the same; only the first terms differ, which derives from the inflation bias under discretion (see King, 1995).

3. Again, comparing the loss function under the rule:

$$L_R = z^2 + ((1 + a)/(1 + b)^2)\sigma_\varepsilon^2$$

with the loss function under the optimal state contingent rule clarifies this.

4. Though it is easier to identify potential non-contingent rules among developing countries – for example, the currency boards which operate in Estonia and Argentina.
5. Rogoff shows that the optimal degree of conservativeness lies in the interval $0 < \rho < 1$. Welfare under the conservative central banker is given by:

$$L_I = (1 + \theta\rho^2)z^2 + ((1 + \theta\rho^2)/(1 + \theta\rho)^2)\sigma_\varepsilon^2$$

where $L_I < L_D$ if ρ is chosen optimally.

6. See also De Haan and Sturm (1992), and Debelle and Fischer (1994).
7. McCallum (1995) discusses a variant of this argument: a situation where a government just "does the right thing" in its monetary policy operations.
8. Though the Bundesbank President is appointed by the government.
9. Fischer (1994) uses precisely this argument to pinpoint a potential danger facing the Bundesbank – the desire to target inflation below its socially optimal level. And, of course, such a danger then applies equally to the embryonic European Central Bank.
10. Provided society and the monetary authority share the same preferences over output and inflation. In the event that they do not, an optimal contract is still feasible, but it is rather more complex than the simple linear tax.
11. Correspondingly, the value of the loss function under the Walsh contract is exactly equal to L_O.
12. We are again simplifying by assuming the socially optimal inflation rate is zero.
13. In the more general case where the socially optimal rate of inflation is non-zero, the inflation target should be set equal to the socially optimal inflation rate minus the inflation bias in order to secure a first-best.
14. It is difficult to make objective judgments about where the socially optimal rate of inflation might lie. But if we make the assumption that the public at large have read and fully digested Michael Woodford's chapter on the "Optimum Quantity of Money" in the *Handbook of Monetary Economics*, then it is quite difficult to mount a wholly convincing case for an optimal rate of inflation much different than zero.

15. Although because of the escape clauses in the Policy Targets Agreement, Walsh (1995) ultimately concludes that the New Zealand model falls short of an optimal contract.
16. In Canzoneri (1985), the private information of the authorities was assumed to be on money demand shocks; but the general point carries across to most types of shocks we can think of.
17. Technically, we require a_t to be strictly positive. But, clearly, when working with a normal distribution there exists a finite probability of a negative outcome for a_t. We are assuming that this probability is sufficiently small that it can be ignored here.
18. When forming inflation expectations, they minimize their squared inflation forecast errors. So, implicitly, agents are risk-averse and have a linear–quadratic utility function.
19. We have used a second-order Taylor series approximation to solve for the expectation of the ratio of two random variables when deriving (10.14). This is consistent with agents being mean-variance optimizers. Further details of this model are given in Nolan and Schaling (1996).
20. Moreover, the risk premium rises at an increasing rate with σ_x^2. Formally, $\partial\pi_{DU}^e/\partial\sigma_x^2 > 0$ and $\partial^2\pi_{DU}^e/(\partial\sigma\pi_x^2)^2 > 0$.
21. This is probably a conservative estimate. For example, economists' *unbiased* estimates of the NAIRU in the United Kingdom can often differ by as much as 50 percent.
22. Assuming technology to be Cobb–Douglas and the supply of other (than labor) factors of production to be fixed in the short run, it can be shown that $b = \beta/(1 - \beta)$, where β is labor's income share. In the UK, β is around 0.8, which gives $b = 4$. Obviously, different assumptions could generate different values for b.
23. Typically in the literature, reputation is modeled in a dynamic repeated game (see, for example, Barro and Gordon, 1983b; Backus and Driffill, 1985; Barro, 1986). But analytically this can prove cumbersome, as an infinity of solutions is often liable to obtain.
24. From (10.14), admitting preference uncertainty would complicate the optimal contract solution, by requiring that the linear tax depend upon the moments of the distribution of preference shocks. But provided these moments are stable, this would not be an insurmountable task. A trickier problem is to ask who this tax should be levied on and by whom, now that the government and private sector agents' utility functions differ. Alternatively, countries could attempt to establish over time a reputation for monetary rectitude. There is no implication here that a "words" approach is preferable to a "deeds" approach; most likely the reverse is true.
25. Transparency may also be useful in helping reveal information on the authorities' preferred "model" of how the world works. This might also generate inflation biases through a risk premium effect. Making b – the inflation surprise coefficient – stochastic within our analytical model would have similar consequences to making a stochastic, which illustrates this point.
26. See, for example, Stein (1989), Cukierman and Meltzer (1986), Dotsey (1987) and Garfinkel and Oh (1995). Goodfriend (1986) provides a good summary and critique of the arguments used by the Fed to rationalize secrecy.
27. Two additional proxies were suggested at the Bank of Japan conference.

First, Don Kohn commented that if the Governor of a central bank can be reappointed at the end of his or her term of office this might make the central bank more accountable. But this would not make much difference to our index, since central bank Governors can be reappointed in twelve of the fourteen countries we consider. Second, Professor Franco Bruni noted that it might be more difficult to make a central bank accountable if it has multiple objectives, for example being responsible for both monetary policy and banking supervision. Since there appears to be, for whatever reason, a weak but positive correlation across countries between the rate of inflation over the past decade and whether a central bank is responsible for banking supervision (see Goodhart and Schoenmaker, 1995), the inclusion of such a proxy would tend to have the effect of making central banks from low (high) inflation countries appear to be more (less) accountable.

28. This relationship is statistically significant at 95 percent; the *t*-ratio is 2.84.
29. This relationship is also statistically significant at 95 percent; the *t*-ratio is 2.16.

References

Aizenman, J. and Frenkel, J. (1985) "Optimal Wage Indexation, Foreign Exchange Intervention, and Monetary Policy," *American Economic Review*, 75, pp. 402–23.

Alesina, A. and Gatti, R. (1995) "Independent Central Banks: Low Inflation at No Cost?," *American Economic Review, Papers and Proceedings*, May, pp. 196–200.

Alesina, A. and Summers, L.H. (1993) "Central Bank Independence and Macroeconomic Performance: Some Comparative Evidence," *Journal of Money, Credit and Banking*, 25 (2) (May), pp. 151–62.

Backus, D. and Driffill, J. (1985) "Inflation and Reputation," *American Economic Review*, 75, pp. 530–8.

Bade, R. and Parkin, M. (1987) "Central Bank Laws and Monetary Policy," mimeo, University of Ontario.

Barro, R.J. (1986) "Reputation in a Model of Monetary Policy with Incomplete Information," *Journal of Monetary Economics*, 17, pp. 3–20.

Barro, R.J. and Gordon, D. (1983a) "A Positive Theory of Monetary Policy in a Natural Rate Model," *Journal of Political Economy*, 91, pp. 589–610.

Barro, R.J. and Gordon, D. (1983b) "Rules, Discretion and Reputation in a Model of Monetary Policy," *Journal of Monetary Economics*, 12, pp. 101–22.

Brunner, K. (1981) "The Art of Central Banking", *Centre for Research in Government Policy and Business*, Working Paper No. Gp B 81–6, June.

Canzoneri, M.B. (1985) "Monetary Policy Games and the Role of Private Information," *American Economic Review*, 75, pp. 1056–70.

Canzoneri, M.B., Nolan, C. and Yates, A. (1995) "Mechanisms for Achieving Monetary Stability: Inflation Targeting versus the ERM," *Journal of Money, Credit and Banking*, forthcoming.

Cukierman, A. (1992) *Central Bank Strategy, Credibility and Independence: Theory and Evidence* (Cambridge, Mass.: MIT Press).

Cukierman, A. and Meltzer, A. (1986) "A Theory of Ambiguity, Credibility and

Inflation under Discretion and Asymmetric Information," *Econometrica*, 54, pp. 1099–1128.

Debelle, G. and Fischer, S. (1994) "How Independent Should a Central Bank Be?," mimeo, MIT.

De Haan, J. and Sturm, J.E. (1992) "The Case for Central Bank Independence," *Banca Nazionale del Lavoro Quarterly Review*, 182, pp. 305–27.

De Long, J.B. and Summers, L.H. (1992) "Macroeconomic Policy and Long-Run Growth," *Economic Review*, Federal Reserve Bank of Kansas City, 77, pp. 5–29.

Dotsey, M. (1987) "Monetary Policy, Secrecy and Federal Funds Rate Behaviour," *Journal of Monetary Economics*, 20, pp. 463–74.

Eijffinger, S. and Schaling, E. (1993) "Central Bank Independence in Twelve Industrial Countries," *Banca Nazionale del Lavoro Quarterly Review*, 184, pp. 49–89.

Eijffinger, S. and Schaling, E. (1995) "The Ultimate Determinants of Central Bank Independence," Tilburg University, Centre for Economic Research Discussion Paper 9505, January.

Fischer, S. (1994) "Modern Central Banking," in F. Capie, C. Goodhart, S. Fischer and N. Schnadt (eds), *The Future of Central Banking* (Cambridge: Cambridge University Press).

Friedman, M. (1959) *A Program for Monetary Stability* (New York: Fordham University Press).

Garfinkel, M.R. and Oh, S. (1995) "When and How Much to Talk: Credibility and Flexibility in Monetary Policy with Private Information," *Journal of Monetary Economics*, 33, pp. 341–57.

Goodfriend, M. (1986) "Monetary Mystique: Secrecy and Central Banking," *Journal of Monetary Economics*, 17, pp. 63–97.

Goodhart, C.A.E. and Schoenmaker, D. (1995) "Should the Functions of Monetary Policy and Banking Supervision be Separated?," *Oxford Economic Papers*, 47, pp. 539–60.

Grilli, V., Masciandaro, D. and Tabellini, G. (1991) "Political and Monetary Institutions and Public Financial Policies in the Industrial Countries," *Economic Policy*, 6 (13) (October), pp. 342–92.

Haldane, A.G. (1995) "Introduction," in A.G. Haldane (ed.), *Targeting Inflation* (Bank of England).

Hall, P.A. (1994) "Central Bank Independence and Co-ordinated Wage Bargaining: Their Interactions in Germany and Europe," in *German Politics and Society*. Autumn, pp. 1–23.

Havrilesky, T. (1995) "Central Bank Autonomy, Central Bank Accountability and Inflation Performance," mimeo, Duke University, February.

King, M.A. (1995) "Changes in UK Monetary Policy: Rules and Discretion in Practice," paper delivered at the Swiss National Bank Conference, Gerzensee, March.

Kydland, F. and Prescott, E. (1977) "Rules Rather than Discretion: The Inconsistency of Optimal Plans," *Journal of Political Economy*, 85, pp. 473–92.

Lohmann, S. (1992) "Optimal Commitment in Monetary Policy: Credibility versus Flexibility," *American Economic Review*, 82, pp. 273–86.

McCallum, B.T. (1988) "Robustness Properties of a Rule for Monetary Policy," *Carnegie–Rochester Conference Series on Public Policy*, 29 (Autumn), pp. 173–204.

McCallum, B.T. (1995) "Two Fallacies Concerning Central Bank Independence," *American Economic Review, Papers and Proceedings*, May, pp. 207–11.

Nolan, C. and Schaling, E. (1996) "Monetary Policy Uncertainty and Central Bank Accountability," mimeo, Bank of England.

Persson, T. and Tabellini, G. (1993) "Designing Institutions for Monetary Stability," *Carnegie–Rochester Conference Series on Public Policy*, 39, pp. 53–84.

Posen, A. (1993) "Central Bank Independence Does Not Cause Low Inflation: The Politics Behind the Institutional Fix," mimeo, Harvard University, December.

Rogoff, K. (1985) "The Optimal Degree of Commitment to an Intermediate Monetary Target," *Quarterly Journal of Economics* (November), pp. 1169–90.

Roll Committee Report (1993) *Independent and Accountable: A New Mandate for the Bank of England* (London: CEPR).

Stein, J. (1989) "Cheap Talk and the Fed: A Theory of Imprecise Policy Announcements," *Journal of Political Economy*, 87, pp. 1190–1219.

Svensson, L.E.O. (1995) "Optimal Inflation Targets, "Conservative" Central Banks and Linear Inflation Contracts," mimeo, Institute for International Economics, University of Stockholm.

Taylor, J.B. (1993) *Macroeconomic Policy in the World Economy: From Econometric Design to Practical Operation* (New York: W.W. Norton).

Walsh, C. (1995) "Optimal Contracts for Central Bankers," *American Economic Review*, 85, pp. 150–67.

Comments

Robert Reynders

The chapter by Briault, Heldane and King attempts, successfully to shed an interesting light on the relationship between central bank independence and inflation and on the role played by accountability in this matter. Allow me first to give you some considerations about central bank independence and inflation.

Following traditional model-building and conventional formalization (accepting *k* being greater than unity), which is underpinned by the results of empirical studies, the authors suggest that a "conservative" central banker (the Rogoff model) secures a welfare outcome that is preferable to the other "discretion" or "rules" solution.

The Walsh model and Svensson's inflation target interpretation are called "optimal contracts for central bankers." For different reasons these models do not seem feasible in the real world.

The authors' last model, called "inflation preference uncertainty," which represents a great extent of original analysis, shows that reductions in preference uncertainty are significantly welfare-enhancing.

All this is excellent news for the "conservative" central banker I am or am supposed to be, aiming at low inflation and at low variability of this objective. Figure 10.1 gives me even more comfort: the more independent you are, the less inflation you experience.

This now generally accepted wisdom was the inspiration for Article 7 of the Statute of the European System of Central Banks (ESCB) that enshrines the principle of independence for the ESCB in the Maastricht Treaty: "neither the *ECB* nor a *national central bank*, nor any member of their decision-making bodies shall seek or take instruction from . . . any other body." Emphasis added.

The principle of independence is substantiated further in some areas: the security of tenure of the members of the decision-making bodies of the ESCB, the system's functional independence and financial autonomy (I remember a newspaper in a small city in Texas with the name *The Independent* (with in small print under the title "as long as money lasts").

It goes without saying that independence is not an objective in itself. It is an essential precondition for the pursuit and realisation of the ESCB's primary objective, which is also enshrined in the treaty: the maintaining of price stability. Only without prejudice to this primary objective is the ESCB to support the general economic policies in the Community.

Let me now turn to the role and value of accountability and transparency, the main topic of the chapter. Throughout the whole chapter you can feel that central bank independence – and so inflation results – should be enhanced by accountability. For the authors there is no independence without accountability. Accountability is a perfume that should for ever have enshrined and have penetrated each independent central bank. It could even serve as a surrogate for independence . . .

However, when visiting central banks in Germany, the Netherlands, Switzerland, Austria, France or Belgium, countries with some of the best inflation records in the world, the authors found it difficult to perceive even a slight whiff of accountability's scent. This causes upheaval among the authors and leads to a paradoxical situation.

The key word for solving this paradox is of course "confidence," that is, at the heart of banking. These central banks earned their credentials over the past years or even decades. They built up their credibility and their reputation. Most of the time in these countries central banking rests on social consensus. The proof of the pudding has been in the eating. In this situation neither the authorities nor the public ask for *de jure* accountability as it is defined in the Appendix of the chapter.

The second element explaining this paradox is the existence in these countries, one way or another, of a *de facto* accountability in various subtle forms which are hardly noticeable to an outsider.

Allow me to take my own central bank (National Bank of Belgium) as an example to illustrate this point. As you have read, it received a minimum accountability index in the table in the Appendix. Our monetary policy is accountable in the following forms:

- it is accountable to the Council of Regency (composed among other of the most representative economic and financial groups);
- through formal and informal gatherings of the Governor with ministers, e.g., the Minister of finance in weekly meetings;
- through various press statements or conferences by the Governor;
- via publications of the Bank (Annual Report, Quarterly Bulletins) which have become media events.

My bank, like all the other totally independent European central banks, has explained its policy to the public and it is now well-known. As I have already indicated, you can consider there is social consensus about our monetary policy. This *de facto* accountability can exert a much sharper constraint than the *de jure* accountability. A more or less comparable scheme could develop for the coming ECB.

The treaty has assigned to the ECB the goal of maintaining price stability, against which the performance of the system and of the members of the decision-making bodies can be measured. The political authorities are involved in the appointment of the members of the decision-making bodies and the ECB will have to report to the Community institutions and, not least, to the public. Such reporting – albeit of an *ex post* nature – generally leads to rationalization of previous actions. Finally, the powers of the ECB are precisely circumscribed by the treaty and the statute as well as by some pieces of secondary Community legislation to complement the provision of primary Community law. The regulatory and administrative acts of the ECB will be subject to review by the judiciary.

To my mind these data seem to guarantee that the ECB will prove as independent and credible as the "conservative" central banks I have already mentioned. The ECB has inherited many characteristics of these central banks and will soon earn its credentials. Unlike the British authors, I do not see "potential problems" in that field.

Let me conclude. Like most central bankers, I do agree with the authors that there is no central bank independence without central bank accountability. Accountability without independence is better than no accountability and no independence. But even perfect accountability cannot be a surrogate for independence.

Accountability can take many forms. New subtle indexes have to be constructed to take account of all its features. The integration of these indexes in economic model-building could mean further progress in the already rich literature about central bank independence and accountability.

Comments*

Donald L. Kohn

In looking at the evolving institutional structures for making monetary policy, one cannot help but be struck by the extent of change still occurring twenty years after the breakup of Bretton Woods. Major reforms have been undertaken in recent years in many countries, suggesting fairly widespread dissatisfaction with the outcomes of the conduct of policy. Even in the United States, where macroeconomic results have been reasonably satisfactory, proposals are on thc table to clarify policy objectives.

Briault, Haldane, and King (BHK) attempt to bring order to an examination of this process by looking at the reforms in the framework of a principal–agent relationship embedded in a time-consistency model. McCallum and others in this volume have pointed out the shortcomings of this model: Most importantly, it does not seem to account for the disinflation of the past two decades, perhaps because it does not allow central banks to learn from their mistakes, to ignore short-run temptations, and hence to move to price stability. But, even with its limitations, the model can be a useful framework to think about the problems facing monetary policy. Specifically, it highlights potential conflicts between the longer-run goal of price stability and attention to short-run variations in output. In the model, the conflict arises from the combined effects of period-by-period optimization and of socially optimal output lying beyond the non-inflationary level of production. In practice the conflict is heightened by the short time horizons of politicians and by uncertainty about the level of non-inflationary output interacting with pressures from businesses, labor, and elected representatives to explore just how far an economy can be pushed. A lot of the changes in central bank structure can be viewed as attempts to reshape institutions to increase the odds on producing both long-run price stability and short-run output stabilization.

BHK have made a useful and important contribution. Not only have they systematized a lot of material in a structured model framework, they have extended previous work in two ways. First, they show that transparency, by reducing the uncertainty of a risk-adverse public about central bank intentions, can directly lower inflation expectations. Second, they construct an accountability/ transparency index to test various hypotheses.

* The views expressed are those of the author and not necessarily those of the Board of Governors of the Federal Reserve System or its other staff.

They conclude that, in contrast to the common "democratic" model of central bank structure, high accountability has not been associated with high independence. Rather, countries dissatisfied with monetary policy performance are going in two ways. One is toward low independence/high accountability; the other is toward high independence/low accountability, drawing lessons from the success of the Bundesbank by changing their own structures or by linking their currencies to the deutschmark. My comments are mostly in the nature of cautions in interpreting this sort of work and its implications – many of which I suspect would get agreement from BHK.

My first set of comments is on the indexes and their implications. Cross-country empirical analysis of the sort they have undertaken, including the construction of indexes, is very difficult. Laws and published material on practices within a country often do not reflect the reality of underlying relationships in the particular cultural and political circumstances of each country. Naturally, I turned to the classification of the United States to gauge BHK's indexes. Monetary policy in the United States is made only by the Federal Reserve, without override by either the executive or legislative branches of government. But the independence index, not constructed by BHK, has the United States with the same degree of independence over the past ten years as the Banque de France, which until very recently did not exercise a monetary policy lever independent of the Ministry of Finance. In addition, it ranks the United States as less independent than the Netherlands, whose monetary policy is effectively made by the Bundesbank through the tight exchange rate tie.

The accountability index suffers from omitting a key element – whether and how central bank Governors can be reappointed. A Governor that cannot be reappointed or does not want reappointment can have significantly more independence than a Governor who desires reappointment from those in political power. In the United States, Chairmen of the Federal Reserve can be reappointed and need to find favor in both the executive and legislative branches to serve another four-year term.

Thus, I see the Federal Reserve as both more independent and more accountable than registered on the BHK scales. Consequently the central bank structure in the United States would seem to be shaped by the traditional democratic tradeoff of high independence bounded by fairly high accountability – in contrast to the findings of BHK of a paucity of observations in this quadrant. This exception does not negate the general findings of BHK, but it does counsel caution in interpreting their results.

Three of the trends in central bank design and practice analyzed by BHK are increased emphasis on inflation targets, accountability, and transparency.

In the remainder of my comments, and only partly in response to BHK, I would like to raise some questions as to whether movement in the direction of these three generally laudable attributes cannot go so far as to hinder the ability of the monetary authorities to achieve their ultimate objective of promoting the general economic welfare.

Inflation targets obviously can compensate for inflation bias, whatever its root cause. However, excessively rigid targets may unduly constrain a central bank from leaning against output fluctuations in the short run and from choosing a sensible path to price stability once inflation occurs. Every central bank pays some attention to output variations; people expect us to, and it often makes sense, especially in the face of variations in aggregate supply. Attention to output does not imply having explicit targets for the level of output or unemployment over time, but it does imply leaning against many business cycle fluctuations within the constraint of an ultimate objective of price stability. In the United States we have experienced reasonably satisfactory economic performance with an independent central bank that paid close attention to output in the context of an objective, albeit vague, of eventual price stability that provided long-run focus and discipline.

Concern about output variability implies that any mechanism for setting hard inflation targets needs to leave room for maneuver – at a minimum, some form of opt-out clause in the face of supply shocks. As we have seen, for example, in Chapter 8 of this volume, New Zealand has such clauses, but is still wrestling with responses to price increases from certain sources. In many countries, needed flexibility in the face of unusual developments can be provided by renegotiation of the inflation targets between the government and the central bank. This solution would not work in the United States, because there is no single "government" with whom to talk; we have two separate branches of government, and within the legislative branch two separate entities, all three jealously protecting their prerogatives. The United States would face difficult questions of how to build structures that balance flexibility and discipline, independence and accountability, if it were to move toward more explicit inflation targets, say in the context of legislation clarifying that price stability was the primary long-run goal of the Federal Reserve.

The possibility of too much accountability – insufficient independence – for a central bank is an old point, but may bear repeating as we talk about new institutional structures for monetary policy. Perhaps one of the most important attributes of inflation targets and price stability objectives is their constraint on governments as they interact with their central banks. In this regard they perform a similar role to central bank independence.

Inflation or price stability targets induce governments to take the longer view in their assessment of monetary policy, and to support and reappoint Governors who bring inflation down, even at the cost of some modest output foregone.

When goals are clearly defined, as with an inflation target, considerable accountability can be healthy. But when goals are not clearly defined – a situation that, as I noted above, may be inevitable to some extent in the United States – accountability becomes an avenue for potentially damaging political pressure. In the United States, those who have in the past proposed greater accountability for the Federal Reserve are most often those who believe the institution pays too much attention to inflation.

BHK give considerable support to the benefits of greater transparency. But in this category as well, it may be possible to have too much of a good thing. The first responsibility of a central bank is to make the right decision – in terms of current procedures, to set the short-term interest rate at the level that will best further society's macroeconomic goals. For the most part, central banks withhold information from the public because they see release of this information as interfering with reaching this objective. They do not do so for the reason cited in some academic literature – that is, to have the opportunity to spring "inflation surprises"; this is too calculating, too short-sighted, and contrary to my experience with central banks in the United States and elsewhere.

Central banks have, in fact, little "private" information to release. BHK make this point with respect to information on the economy. But it is generally true for central bank intentions and policy strategies as well. Monetary policy decisions are dependent on the actual and prospective state of the economy and financial markets at the time they are made. Rarely can a central bank honestly say more about its intentions for short-term interest rates than the vague generalities the public seems to find unsatisfying.

It is in the interest of the central bank to explain its decisions to the public and the market as best it can. Such explanations will build public support, reduce uncertainty and raise the odds that market reactions will reinforce policy intent. They have gained in importance as financial intermediation has broadened and the initial effects of policy changes have shifted away from a few select institutions to markets more generally. Central bankers are no longer dealing with a small number of knowledgeable observers, often former colleagues.

But there are limits on disclosure. Some types of disclosure and transparency can unduly constrain the decision process itself; in the extreme, televising policy deliberations would surely have this effect, but certain types of delayed reports of meetings potentially also could hamper give and take. Even explaining decisions can be difficult. In the United States decisions are made by a committee whose individuals have diverse views of the policy process and who may arrive at a given decision by a number of different routes. Detailed explanations that encompass all views may not be possible, and if attempted could provoke disagreement, even dissent, despite general agreement on the policy decision itself. And the effects of these statements on expectations and on reactions to future developments are difficult to predict and not always desirable. Small phrases can reverberate in ways that were never intended, when they are interpreted against the background of circumstances that could not be anticipated. Some types of disclosures and statements risk raising barriers to appropriate actions by locking policymakers into position; for example, it may be harder for policymakers to alter their views in response to new information or arguments once their own analysis and predilections are on the public record.

These caveats should not be interpreted as arguments for returning to the practices of decades gone by, when central banks rarely explained themselves in public. But they do suggest that more is not always better, that quality rather than quantity counts, and that disclosure be structured carefully to avoid hindering decision-making.

Comments

Reiner König

One cannot but agree with Briault, Haldane and King that independence and accountability are interrelated. Our very understanding of democracy prevents us from viewing the independence of an official institution in absolute terms. It must be accompanied by a clear mandate, conferred by parliament, and by a maximum of transparency in the deployment of its instruments. Moveover, one can take advantage of accountability in order to reach final goals; the incentive systems that are inherent in it should help to induce decision-makers to conform to targets.

Similarly, one cannot but endorse the authors' statement that the concrete interaction of accountability and independence is "far from straightforward." The models they present document the spread within which individual countries may move. It will hardly be possible to find an optimum approach applying equally to all central banks. Instead, the choice of the respective national model depends on

- individual countries' past experience of inflation,
- their starting point when combating inflation,
- the "stability-mindedness" of the population, and
- general considerations of political, legal and economic expedience.

For the sake of the clarity of argument in the theoretical discussion, a sharp distinction between the various models is essential. Quite rightly, the authors of the chapter also state that "real-world institutions are not so easily pigeon-holed, but reflect features of a variety of models." I should like to illustrate this point, using the example of the Bundesbank.

The Rogoff model is certainly a good starting point for studies of the interaction of independence and accountability in the case of the Bundesbank. On closer inspection, however, there are in the German real world some serious divergences from the underlying theoretical approach, in three respects: in the definition of the final goal, in the scope of the accountability, and in the transparency practiced in the monetary policy strategy.

It is true that the Bundesbank enjoys "complete instrument independence." But that it allegedly at the same time enjoys a "high degree of goal independence" is consistent neither with the Bundesbank's statutory mandate nor with its actual behavior. The legislature, as the "principal," has assigned to the Bundesbank, as the "agent," the mandate of ensuring price stability. In other words, the final goal is clearly defined; for statistical reasons, an inflation rate of up to 2 percent is deemed to be in line with the stability requirement. At the most, on the road to price stability a certain discretionary latitude exists to tolerate higher inflation rates for a temporary period in order to preclude shock-like adjustments. But no kind of "goal independence" can be derived from that. It was precisely in order to achieve the preordained target of price stability that the Bundesbank was granted independence, which therefore extends only as far as the deployment of its policy instruments, and not by any means to the choice of the target.

Parliament has given the Bundesbank a clearly defined assignment in the context of overall economic policy, as well as the instruments it needs to perform that assignment. The Bundesbank does not act by virtue of a law it has made itself, but rather on the strength of a parliamentary decision which could in fact be amended (for instance, in the event of serious misconduct). To this extent, there is no lack of democracy evident here or a potential danger to the Bundesbank, as Stanley Fischer suggested in a quotation cited by the authors. The sovereign entity, that is, parliament, is the wielder of power over the Bundesbank at all times. The delegation of a limited degree of power by an Act of parliament passed in accordance with the constitution is altogether in line with the ground rules of democracy, especially since, in the event of a conflict, it is always the legislature that has the last word.

Nor can a lack of democracy be derived from an inadequate degree of accountability. Admittedly, it is true that "the Bundesbank has relatively little *formal* accountability to anyone" (emphasis added). There is no "parliamentary monitoring," no publication of "minutes," no "override clause," and no "inflation reports" or "monetary policy reports" have to be officially submitted. But such a way of looking at things is based on a decidedly narrow concept of accountability, which hinges exclusively on formal legal requirements. From the German standpoint, a broader concept seems to be more appropriate – one geared above all to responsibility to the public at large, and not merely to the national government or to parliament.

To this extent, the accountability index constructed by Briault, Haldane and King appears to be too narrow. In a more recent paper, Havrilevsky has proposed a more comprehensive index (see Table 10C.1), which is based on "implicit or explicit sanctions on central bankers for inflation

Table 10C.1 Another central bank accountability index (period from 1986 to 1993 only)

	Implicit or explicit sanctions on central bankers for inflation performance	*Adherence to preannounced targets whenever errors occurred*	*Public discussions of policy plans or recent performance*
Australia	*	–	–
Belgium	*	–	*
Canada	*	–	–
France	*	*	*
Germany	*	–	*
Italy	*	*	–
Japan	*	*	*
Netherlands	*	–	*
New Zealand	*	*	*
Spain	–	–	-
Switzerland	*	–	*
United Kingdom	*	*	*
United States	*	*	*

Source: Thomas Havrilesky (1995) "Central Bank Autonomy, Central Bank Accountability and Inflation Performance," mimeo, Duke University, 1 May 1995, p. 5 and pp. 31–2.

performance," "adherence to preannounced targets whenever errors occurred," and "public discussion of plans and performance." Judging by that index, the Bundesbank stands, in terms of accountability, in the mid-range of the countries investigated (compared with the bottom group, according to the index presented here).

A broad concept of accountability is advocated not least by the experience that, in the event of actions incompatible with stability, the sanctions for the central bank turn out to be all the stronger, the wider the range of those to whom it is accountable. For one thing, it is assumed in most models that governments (and probably parliament, too) tend to have an inflationary bias, which in itself is likely to mitigate the pressure on the central bank to step up its counter-inflationary efforts. For another, losses of reputation *vis-à-vis* the public at large count for more than responsibility to, say, a parliamentary committee – not only in the case of the central bank as an institution but also in the case of individual decision-makers. "Monitoring" by the general public provides an exceptionally strong incentive to act in a manner consistent with stability, especially if there is a marked aversion to inflation in the population.

It is in the light of these facts that the Bundesbank endeavors to explain its policies in an ongoing dialog with all sections of society, in order to enhance the social acceptability of its actions. It has a profusion of instruments available for this purpose, ranging from official statements (such as press communiqués), press conferences, and publications in the Monthly and Annual Reports to more personally coloured speeches and interviews by members of the Central Bank Council and background information supplied by the Bundesbank staff. At the different levels, there is also a continuous exchange of views with the German government and leading parliamentarians, which extends as far as the attendance of members of the Bundesbank Board at cabinet meetings or visits of members of the cabinet to meetings of the Central Bank Council. There is no shortage of first-hand information on the Bundesbank's policies, so that there should not really be any misunderstandings or misinterpretations of monetary policy. The great respect which the Bundesbank enjoys in the eyes of the general public owes much to this open and comprehensive information policy.

For the rest, it must not be forgotten that accountability and independence may very well conflict with one another. It is undisputed, of course, that an independent central bank is subject to a special duty to account for itself. Conversely, however, overly pronounced accountability may adversely affect independence, particularly if it is displayed primarily *vis-à-vis* the government and if – as in the authors' accountability index – an override clause is envisaged by means of which, in the event of conflicts of strategy with the central bank, the government can get its way.

The chapter by Briault, Haldane and King impressively documents the fact that "Disclosure of private information on inflation preferences by the central bank can secure clear welfare benefits." In this connection, direct inflation targeting is undoubtedly an important way for some countries to achieve transparency about the central bank's intentions. Intermediate monetary targets are another option, especially in countries which – like Germany – can count on the long-term stability of money demand. For over twenty years now the Bundesbank has published monetary targets which, in the light of their derivation, indicate very clearly that only as much money is going to be supplied as is necessary to finance a growth rate which, as far as possible, is non-inflationary.

It is true that the strategy of monetary targeting has been impaired by a number of short-term disturbances of the demand for money since German reunification. We have at times witnessed a substantial overshooting or – as at the moment – undershooting of monetary growth. However, it appears that the long-term relationships between the central bank's instruments, the money stock and inflation have remained intact, with the result that it was, and remains, possible to abide by this strategy in principle. This means that the Bundesbank's policies are subject to a high degree of transparency, not only in terms of the inflation preferences of the Bundesbank, as suggested in the chapter by Briault, Haldane and King, but also beyond that in terms of its strategic approach. Any departures from the target must be explained in detail – a task which the Bundesbank's economists have evidently succeeded in performing so far without much loss of credibility. At bottom, intermediate targets constitute a constraint the central bank has imposed on itself, and their publication gives rise to considerable justification pressure. In the light of this consideration, too, the Bundesbank's accountability should be rated high rather than low.

Accountability and transparency are undoubtedly major elements of a successful monetary policy geared to fighting inflation. In day-to-day operations, however, the requirement of openness is somewhat at variance with the actual behavior of central banks, which cannot dispense with some degree of secrecy. There is no central bank that carries transparency so far that its next interest rate policy measures become apparent to the financial markets. Interest rate policy does not merely implement market expectations, but rather aims to give the markets guidance, which inevitably also involves some surprises. The theoretical reasoning behind this kind of secrecy is based not least on the fact that the response function of the central bank does not depend on a once-and-for-all fixed weighting system of indicators, but also encompasses subjective and changing assessments, as a result of which it becomes unpredictable. The day-to-day deployment of monetary policy instruments does not conform to any "mechanistic system," fixed for all time, but represents an "art," including all available information and its assessment by the decision-makers.

It follows from this that, in central banks' day-to-day operations, natural limits are set, so to speak, to transparency. For instance, even in those cases in which minutes are published, a not inconsiderable period elapses between the day of the meeting and the date of publication. During this period secrecy is obviously regarded as essential, even by those central banks that otherwise tend toward openness.

In other words, transparency is concentrated in three areas:

- in the strategy underlying the monetary policy (final-goal targeting or intermediate-goal targeting),

- in the basic strategic orientation of monetary policy (restrictive, expansionary, neutral), and
- in the *ex post* explanation of specific monetary policy measures.

The chapter by Briault, Haldane and King demonstrates impressively that openness in these areas pays off. It is heartening that more and more central banks seem to be adopting such an approach.

11 Central Bank Independence in the European Union*

Franco Bruni

1 INTRODUCTION

The Maastricht Treaty requires the central banks of the countries in the European Union (EU) to become fully "independent" before the start of the third phase of Economic and Monetary Union (EMU) and the creation of the European Central Bank (ECB). The treaty dictates several conditions for a central bank to be considered "independent." Central bank independence (CBI) is therefore *a condition* for participating in the EMU, to be considered together with the macroeconomic convergence criteria on inflation, interest and exchange rates and on the governments' financial deficits and debts. In this sense the relationship between CBI and a credible and permanent commitment to fixed exchange rates is one of *complementarity.* Fixing exchange rates and unifying currencies requires a common monetary policy. In order to be able to delegate their monetary policies to a supernational agency, the countries must first free their central banks of national political influences.

But, from the point of view of an individual country, CBI can also serve as a *substitute* for the commitment to peg its exchange rate to the currency of another country reputed for its monetary stability. The market will consider the country's "monetary constitution" as a signal of its serious search for price stability. In fact CBI can become *more* valuable precisely when a country *abandons* a system of fixed exchange rates.

This two-faced nature of the relationship between CBI and exchange

* The author, keeping full responsibility for the chapter and for all possible remaining errors, is grateful for useful criticisms and observations to the discussants Robert Raymond, Cathy Minehan and Clive Briault. He also thanks: Ian Macfarlane and the participants in the seminar held at the H.C. Coombs Centre for Financial Studies, Sydney, where a previous version of the chapter was presented on 30 October 1995; Eduard Hochreiter, Sylvester Eijffinger and the other participants in a workshop at the Austrian Nationalbank, where the chapter was discussed on 15 December 1995. He owes a special debt of gratitude for valuable suggestions to Donato Masciandaro. He is also grateful for their comments to Mario Gilli, Andrea Ichino, Claudio Michelacci, Riccardo Rovelli, Fabrizio Saccomanni and Guido Tabellini.

rate regimes is evident in the recent monetary developments of the EU. Section 2 of this chapter summarizes and comments upon the institutional and legislative changes adopted in the Union to increase CBI. The picture shows that monetary reforms are discussed and enacted as a consequence of the Maastricht Treaty, but measures to strengthen CBI have been taken – or are under consideration – also in countries that have left the European Monetary System (EMS) and/or will not be able or wanting to join the third phase of EMU in the future. Italy is in this latter group of countries and Section 2 will devote special attention to the Italian case.

From the evidence presented in Section 2 it is probably correct to conclude that even if the European plan of monetary unification fails, progress toward CBI will continue, with different speeds, in the large majority of EU countries.

An element that creates important institutional differences among the EU's central banks is the degree of their involvement in financial regulation, supervision and in other prudential policies. Some theoretical and empirical work has been done to discuss whether it is right to give prudential responsibilities to central banks and if this can have a negative impact on their independence. Section 3 contains several comments on these issues, taking into account the European cases.

Section 4 is devoted to some general theoretical topics that are relevant for understanding the development of CBI in the EU. In particular the section deals with the issue of the "endogeneity" of CBI and analyzes the interaction of the autonomy of monetary policy with wage-setting policies and with fiscal adjustment.

The European System of Central Banks (ESCB) will be composed of national central banks (NCBs) and the ECB: for the latter's independence a perfect independence of NCBs is a necessary but insufficient condition. There are issues specifically concerning the independence of the future ECB: some of them are considered in Section 5.

Section 6 briefly recalls the main conclusions of the chapter.

2 INSTITUTIONAL INDEPENDENCE OF EU CENTRAL BANKS: STATUTORY AND LEGISLATIVE CHANGES

When considering the convergence of EU member countries toward the Maastricht conditions for being admitted to the final phase of EMU, it is often the case that only the macroeconomic criteria are mentioned and discussed. But no less importance is attributed by the treaty to the structural criteria that define the legislative and institutional convergence of the

Table 11.1 Convergence in legal requirements for central bank independence: EU-12 averages

Criteria	*After the reforms of the period: 1991–5*	*Previously*	*Difference = indicator of convergence*
I Price stability as a statutory objective	0.54	0.29	+0.25
II Independence in the formulation of monetary policy	0.65	0.33	+0.32
III Prohibition to lend to the public sector	0.79	0.17	+0.62
IV Status of Governor	0.64	0.40	+0.24
Total (average)	0.66	0.30	+0.36

Note: For each criterion the level of compliance is measured between 0 and 1. The total average is unweighted. The table considers only the EU-12 countries. For the sources of information, other details and comments see Section 2 of the text and Table 11.2.

countries' monetary authorities toward the requirements of CBI. One of these requirements, forbidding central bank financing of the public sector, had even to be met for entering EMU's second phase, started on 1 January 1994.

A very clear and careful review of this type of convergence was prepared and published by the Bank of Japan (BOJ, 1995, pp. 39–62, and particularly Table 6) in its *Quarterly Bulletin*. While it is based on information as of July 1994 it covers all the important changes of the past few years and can be considered sufficiently up to date even after the more recent surveys by the European Monetary Institute (EMI, 1995a, pp. 100–10; EMI, 1995b, pp. 100–36) and by the Bank for International Settlements (BIS, 1995, pp. 87–93). It would be useless to reproduce in this chapter what is analyzed in these reports. This section is therefore devoted to a very simple numerical synthesis of the information reported in the cited sources and to some comments on specific points, including the Italian case.

Four rows of Table 11.1 are labeled with the four criteria of institutional convergence that can be detected in the text of the Maastricht Treaty and that are used by BOJ (1995) to organize the relevant information. The columns of the table show the current levels of the average degree of CBI in the EU-12 countries and the changes resulting after 1991 in

Table 11.2 Convergence in legal requirements for central bank independence: individual countries

	Ia	*Ib*	*IIa*	*IIb*	*IIIa*	*IIIb*	*IVa*	*IVb*	*Total (average) a*	*Total (average) b*	*Total (average) a–b*
Belgium	0.33	0	1	0	1	0	0.33	0	0.66	0	0.66
Denmark	0.5	0.5	0.66	0.66	0.66	0	0.33	0.33	0.54	0.37	0.17
Germany	0.83	0.83	0.83	0.83	1	0.5	0.66	0.66	0.83	0.71	0.12
Greece	0	0	0	0	1	0	0.5	0.5	0.37	0.12	0.25
Spain	1	0	1	0	1	0	1	0.17	1	0.04	0.96
France	1	0	1	0.5	1	0.5	1	0	1	0.25	0.75
Ireland	0.5	0.5	0.5	0.5	0	0	1	1	0.5	0.5	0
Italy	0	0	1	0.5	1	0	0.5	0.5	0.62	0.25	0.37
Luxembourg	1	0.66	1	0.5	1	0	1	0.33	1	0.37	0.63
Netherlands	0.66	0.66	0.5	0.5	1	0.66	0.33	0.33	0.62	0.54	0.08
Portugal	0.33	0.33	0	0	0.5	0	0.33	0.33	0.29	0.17	0.12
UK	0.33	0	0.33	0	0.33	0.33	0.66	0.66	0.42	0.25	0.17
Total (average)	0.54	0.29	0.65	0.33	0.79	0.17	0.64	0.40	0.66	0.30	0.36
Austria									1		
Finland									0.5		
Sweden									0.2		
Total (average)									0.64		

Note: Column titles refer to the criteria for independence of Table 11.1; the suffix "a" means "after the reforms 1991–5," the suffix "b" means "before the reforms": the last column can therefore be interpreted as an index of convergence to the required criteria. For each of the four criteria of independence a compliance index has been assigned (before and after the reforms) ranging from 0 to 1, where 1 indicates full *formal* compliance with the *legal* Maastricht requirements. averages are unweighted. The pending reform in Luxembourg has been considered as enacted, while current reform projects in Greece, Ireland, the Nehterlands, Portugal, Finland and Sweden have not been accounted for. The poorest and most uncertain set of information available to the author when compiling the table was the one concerning the three new member countries.

Sources: BOI (1995), Table 6; EMI (1995).

the four criteria. Measures of compliance with the criteria of convergence have been assigned, ranging from 0 to 1. The total average degree is now around two-thirds of the legal maximum, more than doubled with the recent reforms. The largest improvement has been obtained in the requirement that prohibits lending to government, for two reasons: it was by far the least respected and the countries had to comply with it already at the beginning of the second phase, 1 January 1994. The criterion of independence based on the role of price stability in the statutory objectives of central banks has the lowest current level of compliance and records a small recent improvement. The political cost of this requirement is probably the highest.

Table 11.2 shows the situation of individual countries, which still appears rather diversified. Reforms are still needed in several countries. The conclusion is that much has been done but there is still scope for working toward a more complete reform of central banks.

In Italy reforms of the powers to set the discount rate and reserve requirements and of the monetary financing of the government were enacted in 1992 and in 1993, precisely when pessimism over EMU was increasing and/or the lira was floating dramatically. Spain is also an example of how CBI can be increased in spite of the difficulties to stick to the EMS parities and of the worsening prospects of adhering to EMU. Also in the UK, Greece and Portugal there are serious proposals or discussions for increasing CBI, which clearly often appears as a substitute for the possibility or the desire of commitment to fixing the exchange rate and to participating in an accelerated plan of monetary unification. The institutional reform process will therefore probably continue even if the unification were to fail.

It has to be noted that tables like 11.1 and 11.2 try to assess the *de jure* independence, which can be different from the *de facto* CBI. The difference can be substantial and not only because the adherence to the law can be imperfect, as pointed out by Cuckierman, particularly for LDCs (Cuckierman *et al.*, 1992; Cuckierman, 1993a) and by Hochreiter (1994) and Steinherr (Galimberti, 1994, p. 35) for Eastern European economies "in transition," but also because legal independence itself is bound to be imperfectly defined and full of gaps. By applying sufficient political pressure to at least one of the gaps, *de facto* CBI can be made appreciably lower than legal independence. Table 11.3 points to the main conceptual weaknesses in the definition of each of the independence requirements. Obviously it is also possible for a legally dependent but "conservative" (Rogoff, 1985) central banker to behave in a strongly "independent" fashion.

The state and the past and future evolution of CBI in the EU could

Table 11.3 Conceptual weaknesses in the definition of the legal requirements for central bank independence (examples)

Requirement I: statutory inflation target	*Requirement II: indepencence in the formulation of monetary policy*	*Requirement III: prohibition of lending to government*	*Requirement IV: status of the governor*
Price level or inflation targeting?	Potential conflicts between monetary and exchange rate policies	Indirect lending	Political appointment nearly unavoidable
Total or "domestically produced" inflation?	Potential conflict between monetary and regulatory policies	Highly implicit regulatory incentives to buy government bonds	Implicit political incentives for the post-governorship career
Which is the sufficient speed of convergence from a high inflation level?	No authority on the interest rate offered on government bond issues	No authority on the differential tax treatment of government bonds	Diffficulty in establishing sanctions for non-independent behavior

therefore look different if actual independence were considered instead of legal independence. The picture would look even more complicated and abounding in nuances if a third profile of CBI were taken into account: the *reputation* of independence enjoyed by each NCB. This is a crucial dimension of CBI because it ultimately determines its impact on the credibility of monetary policy. The relation between the three dimensions of independence can turn out to be rather subtle and contradictory, at least in the short and medium run. Reputation can depend on actual CBI but it is sometimes influenced by legal CBI, even if larger than *de facto* autonomy. In principle all the six possible orderings of the three dimensions are admissible. A hypothetical example is shown in Figure 11.1 conjecturing an association of each ordering with certain countries, based only on the author's personal impressions. Both Germany and the USA have a reputation of CBI which is probably higher than both the actual and the legal independence. The latter is very low in Britain which enjoys a better reputation due to a growing actual independence. Recently reformed EU central banks, like those of France, Spain and Belgium, have a very high

Figure 11.1 Conjectual association of countries with the six possible orderings of legal (L), actual (A) and reputed (R) central bank independence

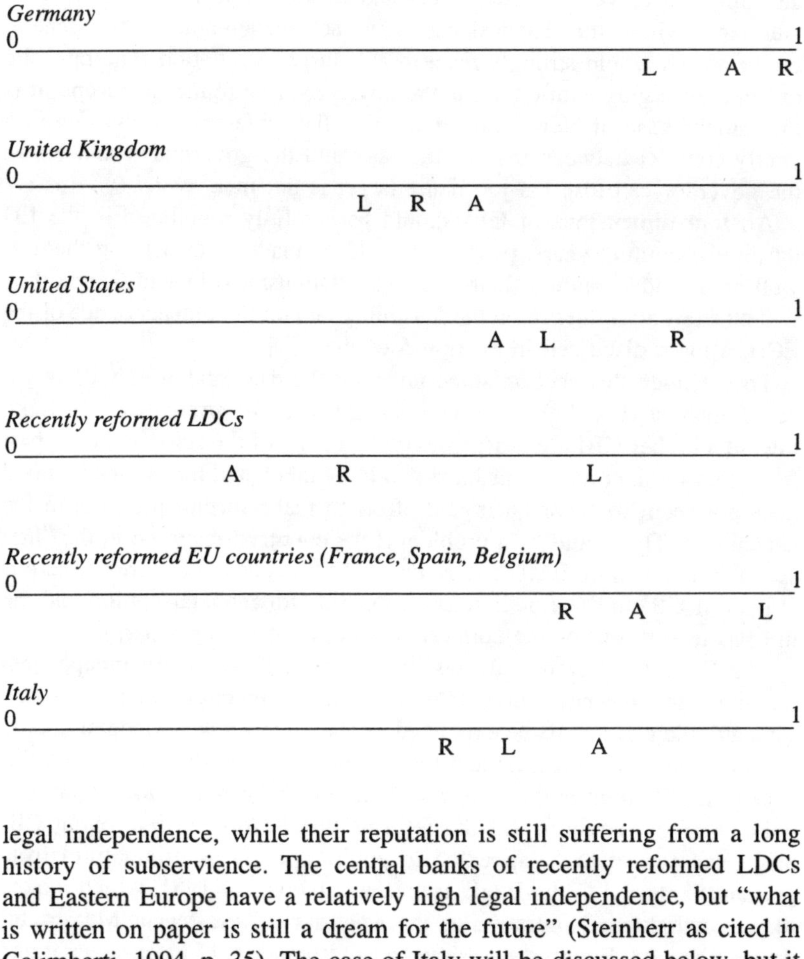

legal independence, while their reputation is still suffering from a long history of subservience. The central banks of recently reformed LDCs and Eastern Europe have a relatively high legal independence, but "what is written on paper is still a dream for the future" (Steinherr as cited in Galimberti, 1994, p. 35). The case of Italy will be discussed below, but it is probably an example of actual CBI higher than legal independence and where reputation must still get the full benefit of recent legal reforms.

From a certain point of view one could say that there is a fourth dimension of CBI: *accountability*. Without accountability independence is incomplete and insecure. But accountability is a somewhat vague concept, very difficult to assess in an objective way. It is very much connected with the existence of a statutory target of price stability, which becomes the basis for judging the behavior of the central bank and, at the same time, can serve as an objective criterion for the central bank to defend its policies. But even with a precise statutory target the accountability can be very indirect and informal or very precise, direct and explicit. The first is the case of Germany, where the Bundesbank is in fact accountable to the general public which would strongly react to any surge in inflation. The opposite example of highly explicit accountability cannot be found in Europe: it is the famous case of New Zealand where inflation targets are written in a yearly contract between the central bank and the government and where the governor can lose his job if the target is not met.

All four dimensions of CBI should be carefully monitored in the EU during the coming years; progress should be made in measuring them as well as in understanding their complex relationships. In due course they will all exert an influence on the feasibility and on the independence of the ECB, a topic discussed in Section 5 of this chapter.

To conclude this section some notes on the case of Italy's CBI might be of interest. For Italy international pressures to strengthen the trend toward a higher CBI are most welcome. In spite of the reforms of the past few years some crucial steps have still to be taken and the domestic mood does not seem to favor an urgent effort to make further progress in the near future. This could be a problem if the country tries to be in the "first speed" group toward EMU's third phase. But it is an even more dangerous attitude if CBI has to function as a substitute for monetary union and the lira has to stay out of the common currency for a longer period.

The Bank of Italy has always presented itself as a very independent institution and has never insisted on obtaining an increase of its autonomy. This attitude can in part be explained by the widely acknowledged quality and prestige of its directors and by the know-how and the *de facto* influence of the Bank in monitoring and designing the general macroeconomic policies of the country. All the reforms that have been improving CBI originated (or, at least, appeared to public opinion as originating) from pressures external to the Bank: from the "divorce" in 1981, which looked like an enlightened initiative of the Treasury, to the recent Maastricht-driven changes. Economists asking for a stronger CBI have never found clear consent and support from the Bank of Italy's officials, researchers and publications.

In fact, while the legal independence of the Bank of Italy is now very high with respect to the second and third criteria of Table 11.1, there is not even a plan to comply with the first (and probably the most important) Maastricht requirement for an explicit statutory price stability objective, notwithstanding an increasing weight of price stability in Italian monetary policy's announcements. As far as the fourth criterion of Table 11.1

is concerned, after Governor Ciampi became Prime Minister the existing procedures for appointing the Governor and the directorate, while ending, according to the Bank's tradition, with top quality designations, could not prove to be sufficiently quick, transparent and above political gossip. Moreover the appointment for life (which is equivalent to the possibility of being dismissed any time) should probably be transformed into a long but limited term of office with explicit provisions on dismissal similar to the ones contained in the statute of the ECB.

It is worthwhile reporting the Bank of Italy's argument against the reform of its statute introducing an explicit primary objective of price stability. In fact the argument has two parts, that lend themselves very well to introducing the topics of the next two sections of this paper: the separation between supervisory and monetary agencies (section 3) and the interaction between CBI, wage-setting policies and fiscal adjustment (section 4).

The first part of the argument is that "the safeguarding of savings and the connected quest for monetary stability called for in the Italian Constitution are basic principles that [sufficiently] motivate the Bank's determined anti-inflation commitment" (Visco, 1995, p. 10). The problem is that "the safeguarding of savings" implies both monetary and prudential targets, both monetary and financial stability: to the extent that some conflicts might develop between these targets, the primacy of price stability is not guaranteed. This issue will be touched upon in the next section. Here suffice it to say that the Bank of Italy's prudential and regulatory powers are among the greatest in European central banks (see Table 11.6 below) and that during the past few decades the use of these powers has often produced measures to facilitate the financing of the public sector and to engineer financial repression with the justification of preserving financial stability.

The second part of the argument is that "to maintain monetary stability in Italy, and specifically to achieve a low medium-term inflation target, the commitment of the central bank will have to be supported by a rational wage bargaining process and adjustment of the imbalance in the public finances" (Visco, 1995, p. 13). "No degree of autonomy can guarantee the objective of price stability if other areas of economic policy are set on divergent paths. Indeed, central bank autonomy offers no escape from the consequences of mismanagement of fiscal and incomes policies" (Padoa-Schioppa, 1994, p. 544). This reasoning seems to go beyond the usual caveat that *short-run* inflation is not under direct control of the central bank. It looks like a sort of unwarranted generalization of the extreme case of the "unpleasant arithmetic" by Sargent and Wallace (1981). Section 4 of this chapter tries to support the opposite idea: that both fiscal and incomes policies might find that CBI makes it easier to optimize their objective functions.

Table 11.4 Central banks in the EU with and without prudential responsibilities

With supervisory and prudential powers	*Without supervisory and prudential powers*
Greece	Belgium
Spain	Denmark
Ireland	Germany
Italy	France*
Luxembourg	Austria
The Netherlands	Finland
Portugal	Sweden
United Kingdom	
Total: 8	Total: 7

* France is placed on the right side of the table because: (i) it exerts its supervisory functions only through the "Commission Bancaire" and (ii) after the December 1993 reform monetary policy management is thoroughly separated from the other functions of the Banque de France.
Source: EMI (1995), Table 13 (point 5 of the third row, except for France).

3 CENTRAL BANK INDEPENDENCE AND PRUDENTIAL RESPONSIBILITIES

After Austria, Finland and Sweden entered the EU, only half (8/15) of the member countries' central banks have supervisory and prudential responsibilities (see Table 11.4). There is a line of thought according to which the separation between the agencies responsible for monetary and prudential policies is a necessary condition for the complete independence of monetary policy management. In fact, while no correlation seems evident between the most common measures of independence and the degree of involvement of central banks in prudential management, empirical evidence supports the thesis that central banks without supervisory responsibility have a better inflation track record (Table 11.5).

The most common argument for the separation of the two functions is that their combination might lead to a conflict of interest and to an inflationary bias of central banks' monetary management caused by concern with banks' health, with the stability of bank clients' income, of interest rates and security prices as well as by moral hazard in bailout policies. "There might be a temptation to delay or moderate a monetary tightening with a view to averting a sudden collapse in asset prices precisely at a

Table 11.5 Inflation performance and institutional separation between supervisory and monetary agencies

	Countries with monetary and supervisory functions combined	*Countries with monetary and supervisory functions separated*
Industrial countries: 1980–7	11.1	5.9
Industrial countries: 1980–91	9.5	5.3
All countries: 1980–7	21.5	6.8
All countries: 1980–91	48.4	7.1

Source: Goodhart and Shoenmaker (1993), Appendix 2, Table 1.

time when the inflation outlook is deteriorating; alternatively, a preventive tightening designed to contain the buid-up of speculative pressures and hence broader financial instability could risk weakening the real economy" (BIS, 1995, p. 117). Another important argument is that there is the danger that "those in charge of monetary policy are tarred with the supervisors' brush" (*Financial Times*, 1995b) and that losses of credibility in prudential controls can contaminate the reputation of the central bank in conducting monetary policy. A connected danger is that "a central bank that intervenes in a too wide range of activities is likely to find it harder to justify keeping political pressures at bay" (*The Economist*, 1993, p. 68). The most important argument against separation is that the effectiveness of prudential policies benefits by the information collected by the central bank when it manages the payment system and conducts its stardard monitoring as a regular lender to many banks. A thorough discussion of the issue is not among the purposes of this chapter. It is enough for this section to make a series of specific points on the matter.

The first point is that, at least in the EU and in preparation of EMU, the problem should be discussed openly and more comprehensively, disregarding the bureaucratic interests that tend to keep the status quo. Currently only in the UK does the debate seem to acquire some weight, due to the gaps in prudential controls emerging from the BCCI and Barings cases (see, for instance, *Financial Times*, 1995b) and to the rather recent official entrustment of supervisory powers to the Bank of England: but also "the Old Lady clings to the poisoned chalice" (*Financial Times*, 1995c). It is important to deepen the analysis of this issue also because the substantial differences between the EU countries regarding the organization of prudential responsibilities (see Table 11.6) could endanger

Table 11.6 Central bank involvement in the supervision and regulation of the banking system and of financial markets (in % of the maximum possible involvement)

	Considering only banks	*Global involvement index, considering also non-bank intermediaries*
United Kingdom	92	73
Greece	85	71
Italy	74	63
Spain	61	51
France	54	46
Sweden	42	42
Belgium	37	35
Germany	36	28
Japan	25	25

Notes: The indexes have been calculated on the basis of a detailed classfication of types of controls (5 types of "structural" controls, 2 types of "liquidity" controls, 7 types of "prudential" controls, 2 types of interventions in banking crises, 2 types of "inspection" responsibilities), distinguishing between regulatory and executive powers. Two points have been assigned for each control which is entrusted to the central bank, 1 point for each control shared by the central bank with other agencies, no points if the central bank is not in charge of the control. The involvement index is the ratio of the sum of points assigned to each central bank to the maximum possible number of points (i.e., 2 per type of control).

Source: Michelacci (1993), p. 5.

the compactness of the ESCB: this argument will be taken up again in Section 6.

A second point is that the nature and importance of the problem of separating monetary and prudential policies depend on the kind of supervisory and prudential schemes that are in force in a country. With "light" forms of supervision, largely based on disclosure rules, with minimal discretionary powers and a credible exclusion of bailouts, the allocation of prudential responsibilities matters less and in a different sense than when supervisory processes are intensive, highly discretionary, "intrusive" and ready to support banks in distress. A stimulating example of the first type are the new banking supervision arrangements adopted by the very independent price-stabilizing Reserve Bank of New Zealand (1994; and 1995, pp. 73–8).

The third point is that it does not make any sense to plan the total exclusion of the central bank from taking part in the technical implementation of bank supervision. The Bundesbank model of separateness, for instance, allows a very important role for the collaboration of regional central banks with governmental supervisory authority. What is really at issue is the political responsibility of the central bank for the final results of prudential controls and regulations.

The fourth point is that there is not only a problem of independence and credibility of monetary policy, but also of independence and credibility of prudential policies. The optimality of the allocation of supervisory functions is required also to maximize the effectiveness of these same functions (Bruni, 1995). The literature on the credibility of prudential policies is very scarce. These policies can suffer from a time-inconsistency problem similar to the Barro–Gordon problem of monetary policy. Their credibility depends on rationally expected values of the parameters of the prudential authority's utility function. It can be argued (Bruni and Paternò, 1995, section 2) that two crucial parameters, from this point of view, are the sensitivity to the danger of systemic damages that can be caused by the difficulties of an individual bank (call it s) and the sensitivity to the social costs of allocative distortions that can be caused by prudential controls and bailouts (call it d). It is an intuitive result that a disciplining no-bailout policy is optimal and credible only for sufficiently low values of s and high values of d. It is also reasonable to think that for a central bank, which is in charge of the interbank payment system, the ratio s/d naturally tends to be on the high side. Therefore it is better, for the effectiveness and credibility of prudential policies and for the working of market discipline of banks' riskiness, that the political responsibility for certain prudential decisions is clearly located outside the central bank. The latter could be authorized, for instance, to lend to the *banking system* for coping with *liquidity* crises and could be responsible for authorizing bank openings (based on objective criteria), but should not be in charge of supporting *individual institutions* confronted with *solvency* problems or responsible for arranging bank closures and managing bank crises.

The fifth and last point, on the issue of keeping monetary and prudential policies in separate agencies, is about the consequences of the blurring of traditional boundaries between banks and the rest of the financial system. To the extent that the central bank has prudential responsibilities, this development enlarges its supervisory functions over a rapidly growing set of financial operations, contracts and institutions that have decreasing connections with its expertise in monetary affairs. Its bureaucratic power increases disproportionately, while the economies of scope of a joint exercise of monetary and prudential functions tend to vanish. The accountability and transparency of monetary responsibilities suffer. "Covering an increasing range of activities and institutions is not without potential costs" (Borio and Filosa, 1994, p. 28). This is an argument in favor of a carefully balanced framework for prudential policies and controls, clearly limiting the role of the central bank. In Italy a solution has been adopted (see Padoa-Schioppa, 1994, p. 545) based on the distinction between supervision aimed to foster the *efficiency* of financial markets and supervision aimed to preserve their *stability*. Only the latter is entrusted to the Bank of Italy which, from the "stability point of view," is the prudential authority for the whole financial system. To this author the distinction seems insufficient to delimit the involvement of the central bank, to restrain moral hazard and to avoid regulatory forbearance, excessive discretionality and the uncontrolled interference of political pressures in the management of financial crises. The objective of "stability" is too wide and pervasive: it goes so far as serving as a justification for the fact that even the administration of the anti-trust regulation in the banking system is delegated to the Bank of Italy. The scheme also causes costly duplications of controls: an example is the mutual funds industry which falls under the supervision of the securities commission but which is also minutely supervised and regulated by the Bank of Italy on the ground that it is crucial for financial stability.

A possible conclusion of this section is that the problem must be carefully defined: what is at issue is not whether national central banks should be entrusted with prudential tasks, but how an optimal prudential framework must be designed, leaving aside present bureaucratic interests. One characteristic of the optimal framework is that it sets a precise boundary of the central banks' prudential responsibilities. But an optimal prudential institutional setting has many other connected aspects that increase the credibility and the effectiveness of both monetary and prudential policies. Probably, a multiplicity of prudential authorities are needed, with well-defined goals, limited discretionality and clearly specified rules of behavior. At the EU level this increases the need for harmonization and centralization, to be touched upon below (in Section 5).

4 ENDOGENOUS INDEPENDENCE?

The "question of endogeneity" was formulated as a critique to the prevailing literature on CBI by Adam Posen (1993 and 1994b) who suggested that the autonomy of the central bank is "endogenous to the political effectiveness of opposition to inflation in the society." Among the relevant indicators of the strength of the social interest in price stability it is possible to include the power of the financial sector and the weakness of labor. Posen offers some empirical support to the idea including a disproof of the impact of CBI on the credibility of disinflation (Posen, 1994a) which explains the acknowledged direct correlation between CBI and price stability by the fact that both depend on structural factors determining the social opposition to inflation.

In a different spirit, an elegant model was built by Cukierman (1993b) which endogenizes CBI without implying any criticism of the normative theory based on the time inconsistency of monetary policy. Among other factors that cause the choice of a higher CBI, Cukierman shows the influence of political instability and of the degree of polarization of political parties with respect to the structure of public expenditure. Within his model a surprising result is also obtained according to which the central bank is granted less independence the larger the relative concern of political authorities for price stability, because this concern decreases the benefits of any institutional commitment. A similar concept has been expressed by Charles Goodhart (as quoted by Galimberti, 1994, p. 31): "a Labour party gains more credibility by granting independence, because it starts from a lower credibility base . . . and if you are a left-wing party, it does not very much if the levers of monetary policy are in the hands of a conservative government or of a central bank."

"Endogenous" explanations of CBI are also discussed by Sylvia Maxfield (1994) with reference to developing countries. Ceding authority to the central bank, the government provides a signal about the likelihood that the nation's future policies will protect the business climate; CBI means that the central bank is allowed to function more nearly as "agent" of private financiers rather than as "agent" of the government: this is most useful when the country is looking for international financing. According to Maxfield this argument is also applicable to EU countries where the impetus for the wave of change in central bank status comes from the Maastricht Treaty not only directly, as a consequence of the specific requirements for CBI, but also indirectly, as a consequence of the impact of Maastricht on capital mobility in the EU and on the need to prevent capital flight in order to maintain currency parity.

It is apparent that discussing the issue of "endogeneity" is a way to go through the whole theory of CBI and to analyze the relationship between the autonomy of the central bank and other institutional, political and social features of a country. This line of reasoning tends to bring the analysis beyond the time inconsistency argument for CBI toward a more general type of reason for CBI that might be called "preferred agency" motive (Bruni and Masciandaro, 1991; Bruni, 1994, p. 42): society, "the market," or prevailing interest groups desire to maximize the influence of the central bank on the making of monetary policy because its expected behavior is in their favor. In a sense the case where the government decides to "tie its hands" with CBI is a very special case of this "preferred agency" motive.

It would be interesting to analyze the factors that endogenously explain the current and prospective degree of CBI in the different EU countries. But there is no room in this chapter for such an ambitious aim. The rest of this section will therefore be devoted to some notes on more specific issues. Consider two macroeconomic decision processes that can influence inflation in the short run: the wage-setting mechanism and the adjustment of fiscal imbalances. If they help disinflation, the value added of CBI is smaller (*à la* Posen); but the same is true if they act against price stability. In the latter case the argument can be made that for monetary stability CBI has to be "supported by a rational wage bargaining process and by the adjustment in the public finances" (see the Italian case as presented above in Section 2). It is therefore important to understand what is the *direct* interaction between these mechanisms and CBI. The argument is made below that, under certain conditions, the two decision processes favor CBI because it helps them to reach their own objectives, through its effect on monetary stability. This means that CBI is in part "endogenous," but it also means that there is no excuse for giving up CBI on the ground that fiscal and incomes policies are an obstacle to disinflation. The theoretical arguments that follow may be of help in understanding some institutional developments that are taking place in the EU.

4.1 CBI and Wage-Setting

In several countries one has the impression that in recent years the attitude of the labor unions (and of the left-wing political parties) toward inflation-prone policy styles has changed. A corresponding change has probably taken place in their opinion on CBI. The most striking example is the UK Labour Party which has been recently criticizing the government for its weak action toward CBI and calling for an expansion of the role and the operational responsibility of the Bank of England (*Financial Times*, 1995a). In the case of Italy and, in a sense, France, a similar increasing leftist support for monetary stability and CBI can be detected. There may be several explanations for this development, including the abolition (in the case of Italy) of contractual wage indexation, the increasing wealth/income ratio of workers and complex strategies in a two-party electoral game. But it is worthwhile exploring a particular rationale, based on the

Figure 11.2 The wage-setting mechanism

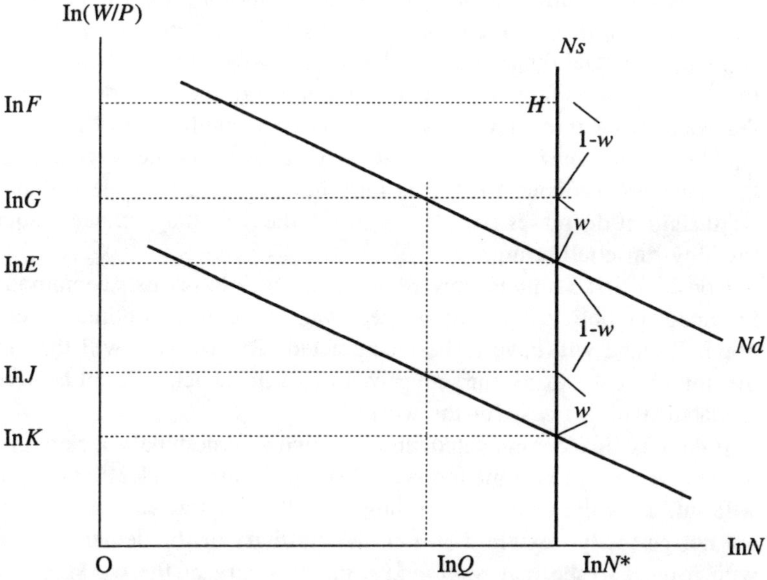

Notes: *Ns* is the supply of labor schedule; *Nd* the demand for labor. The horizontal axis measures the natural logarithm of employment *N*; the vertical axis the natural logarithm of the real wage *W/P*. *w* is a parameter expressing the degree of nominal downward wage rigidity. The model explaining the figure and its symbols is in Section 4 of the text.

increasing cost of recontracting nominal wages and guaranteeing *de facto* wage indexation.

Consider a situation where the nominal wage has been contracted in such a way as to optimize the expected real wage (*OE* in Figure 11.2), that is, to set it at the level where a negatively sloped demand for labor crosses the long-run supply schedule, which is rigid on the full employment level: in the long run the workers maximize employment.[1] But there is the possibility of short-run, temporary shocks causing deviations of actual from expected inflation. Only with CBI will the shocks be counteracted by monetary policy which will avoid their accommodation keeping the increase in prices on the expected track. In this "model" the relevant characteristic of CBI is that it prevents inflation from leaving its planned path. Four types of stochastic, transitory shocks can take place: nominal and real, upward and downward. Is CBI desirable from the workers' point of view?

Let us make the crucial hypothesis that there are short-run costs in recontracting nominal wages. When they are adjusted downward, these costs effectively limit the short-run adjustment to a proportion $(1 - w)$ of the change required in the long run: $0 \leq w \leq 1$ is a measure of downward wage rigidity, and the function $D(1 - w)$, $D' > 0$, is the total cost incurred by the workers.[2] When they are adjusted upward, the costs do not prevent the wage from immediately reaching its new equilibrium level and are equal to a constant r times the percentage increase in the wage. As far as the price level is concerned, it is fully flexible upward while it is downward rigid: it decreases only $(1 - p)$ times the percentage change required for long-run equilibrium.

Consider first a unitary upward nominal shock to prices, accommodated by monetary policy. To bring the real wage back to the optimal level, the nominal wage will have to be recontracted. The workers will then incur the unitary cost r of recontracting. With CBI the shock will not be accommodated, with no cost for the workers.

If there is an accommodated, unitary downward nominal shock to prices, the real wage will become too high (like OF in Figure 11.2): employment will suffer, in the short run, to the extent that contracted nominal wages are not perfectly flexible. Let e be the elasticity of the demand for labor with respect to the real wage and n the elasticity of the workers' utility function with respect to the level of employment (see note 1). Given the hypothesized downward nominal wage rigidity w, the cost of the shock for the workers will be $D(1 - w) + [wen - w(1 - n)]$, where the term in squared parenthesis is by hypothesis (a crucial one) a *positive* difference between the decrease in utility due to the sacrifice in employment ($N^* - Q$ in Figure 11.2) and the increase in utility due to the higher real wage (OG in Figure 11.2). Again, with CBI, the shock will not be accommodated and the workers will incur no cost.

Consider now a positive real shock, increasing (by one unit) the long-run equilibrium level of the real wage (in Figure 11.2 the demand curve for labor would shift upward crossing the supply in H). To adjust the latter, prices could be restrained. But to the extent that there is downward price rigidity (p, with: $0 \leq p \leq 1$) nominal wages will have to be increased, with a recontracting cost equal to pr. With CBI the cost is r, like with $p = 1$. Both with and without CBI the adjustment cost will be counterbalanced by the percentage increase in utility $(1 - n)$ derived by the higher real wage.

The opposite, negative real shock, without the pegging of the prices by the central bank, immediately produces the new equilibrium level of real wages (OK in Figure 11.2) both through a reduction of nominal wages (if there is not complete downward rigidity) and/or through an acceleration of

Table 11.7 The cost of shocks for the workers setting their wages

	Without CBI (1)	*With CBI* (2)	*Cost advantage of CBI* (1)–(2)
Nominal *upward* shock	r	0	r
Nominal *downward* shock	$D(1 - w) + wen - w(1 - n)$	0	$D(1 - w) + wen - w(1 - n)$
Real *upward* shock	$pr - (1 - n)$	$r - (1 - n)$	$-(1 - p)r$
Real *downward* shock	$D(1-w) + (1-n)$	$D(1 - w) + wen + (1 - w)(1 - n)$	$-wen + w(1 - n)$
		Total:	$pr + D(1 - w)$

price increases. The resulting cost for the workers is $D(1 - w) + (1 - n)$ where the loss of utility due to the lower equilibrium real wage has been accounted for. With CBI all the adjustment falls on wages with a total cost equal to $D(1 - w) + wen + (1 - w)(1 - n)$: the first term is the cost of partial downward recontracting, the second term is the decrease in utility caused by the disequilibium unemployment ($N^* - Q$ in Figure 11.2) and the third term is the decrease in utility due to the lower real wage (*OJ* in Figure 11.2).

Table 11.7 summarizes the costs of all the types of shocks, with and without CBI. Let us first suppose that all the four types of shocks are equally probable. Then the expected total cost for the workers is higher without CBI by the amount $pr + D(1 - w)$ times the probability of the shocks. The preference of workers for CBI increases with downward price rigidity and with the costs of recontracting nominal wages, and decreases when downward nominal wage rigidity increases. In recent years several factors have probably caused an increase in r: structural unemployment, international integration of the labor market and a lowering of the political power of the unions. There are also signs of a decrease of the downward rigidity of wages. These developments, according to the above model, would explain, particularly in certain European countries, an increasingly positive attitude of workers with respect to price stability and CBI. The behavior of wages, far from contrasting the impact of CBI on inflation, could be thought of as originating a "demand for CBI," as a cause of "endogeneity" of CBI. But this type of model can also be looked at from a different point of view. Suppose that the wage-setting mechanism is controlled by an oligarchic system of unions. Suppose also that the true social value of r and w are respectively higher and lower than the values of these parameters for the unions. Then a stronger CBI can be chosen by the general public on the basis of a "preferred agency" motive, that is, as an element of a political action to correct the undesired results of the unions' behavior.

When the different types of shocks have different probabilities, other results can be obtained that square with more general theories and intuition. The preference for price targeting policies increases, for instance, when the probability of nominal shocks is higher than the probability of real shocks. On the contrary, accommodative monetary policies are preferred when real shocks are more probable: in particular, if nominal wages are very rigid downward, when there is a high probability of a negative real shock.

4.2 CBI and the Adjustment of Fiscal Imbalances

Consider the relationship between CBI and the financing of the government deficit. In what follows the crucial aspect of CBI is that the independent central bank does not prevent the cost of public borrowing from fully reflecting the portfolio impact of excessive indebtedness. On the contrary, it is possible to define a subservient monetary policy as a policy that tries to keep the interest rate on public bonds relatively independent of the government's borrowing requirement.

To help the discussion a very simple model can be useful. Let S be the stock of preexisting public debt and F the current period's deficit net of interest costs, that is, the so called "primary" deficit. Both S and F consist in one-period public bonds floated each period. In each period a unique interest rate will be established on the market. Let R be one plus that interest rate. The total debt at the end of each period is:

$$D = RS + F \qquad (11.1)$$

The interest rate increases with the amount of bonds floated:

$$R = 1 + ab(S + F), \quad b > 0, \; 0 \leq a \leq 1 \qquad (11.2)$$

where b is the sensitivity of the interest rate to the borrowing requirement, while a is an index of central bank autonomy. With $a = 0$ a subservient central bank will finance the government with no interest cost; with $a = 1$ a completely independent central bank will let the whole risk premium enter the cost of debt.

Apart from the structural parameter a, F is the only policy variable in the model. Its level is chosen by the fiscal authorities minimizing the following loss function:

$$L = \tfrac{1}{2}(D - h)^2 + \tfrac{1}{2}(F - f)^2 \qquad (11.3)$$

where h and f are the preferred values of the debt and the primary deficit. While there is no well-established theory behind the two parameters of this type of function, one can refer to the reasoning that has inspired the long-run equilibrium fiscal parameters dictated by the Maastricht Treaty, and/or to the criteria that will characterize the coordination of national fiscal policies in the future EMU.

By substituting (11.2) into (11.1) and the latter into (11.3) and by setting to zero the total derivative of L with respect to F (checking the second derivative for a minimum), the optimal primary deficit F^* can be calculated:

$$F^* = \frac{f + (1 + abS)[h - S(1 + abS)]}{1 + (1 + abS)^2} \qquad (11.4)$$

The derivative of this expression with respect to a is negative. Increasing CBI raises the cost of debt and, not surprisingly, causes a reduction of the deficit: exogenously imposed CBI acts in favor of fiscal discipline. A less obvious result can be obtained by substituting (11.4) into (11.3) calculating the minimum value of the loss L^*. Setting the derivative of L^* with respect to a equal to zero and looking for a minimum, the "endogenous" optimal degree of CBI can be derived:

$$a^* = \frac{(h - S) - f}{[(S + f)bS]} \qquad (11.5)$$

It is easy to see that the corner solution $a^* = 0$ will be chosen if the inherited level of debt S is too large compared with the target level h. But a^* can also turn out to be positive and tend to unity. The derivative of a^* with respect to f is negative: if there is a large enough target primary surplus ($f < 0$) a high degree of CBI will be chosen even if S exceeds h.

Among the exercises that can be made using (11.5) consider what happens if S is at its short-run target level h, say the maximum Maastricht level equal to 60 percent of GDP. Suppose there is a target primary surplus equal to 3 percent of GDP (which implies a long-run target lower than 60 percent for S). From (11.2) the term bS appears to have the dimension of a nominal interest rate, say 6 percent. With these hypothetical values the optimal degree of CBI, according to (11.5), would be 3/(57.6 percent) ≅ 0.9: the authorities would choose to grant nearly full independence to the central bank in order to maximize their welfare function. But if the target level h is too ambitious compared to the inherited S a low level of CBI will be chosen. In a multi-period dynamic setting an adjustment path could be shown to exist where high CBI is compatible with the gradual approaching of h to its long-run desired (or Maastricht-imposed) value. This result seems instructive for an appropriate management of the coordinated convergence policies toward EMU.

Note that inflation and inflation surprises have been left out of this simple formulation of the model, to show how an "advantage of tying one's hands" can exist having no (direct and explicit) relation with the objective of price stability or with the problems of time inconsistency and credibility.

5 THE INDEPENDENCE OF THE ECB

It is generally agreed that "the European System of Central Banks is designed to have a high degree of independence" (Bank of Japan, 1995, p. 40), also because "the statutes of the ECB are closely modelled on those of the Bundesbank, historically the most independent of all Central Banks" (Goodhart, 1994, p. 3). It would therefore be superfluous to list here those aspects of the Maastricht Treaty that grant autonomy to the ECB. Consequently, the aim of this brief section is merely to mention some of the problems that could hinder its independence, in spite of the basic rules through which it is guaranteed.

First of all there is the issue of *accountability*: no agency can be truly autonomous without a precise definition of its accountability. "According to the statute this would be achieved by the ESCB reporting, *ex post*, to the European Parliament and the Council. Such ex post reporting, while taken seriously, generally leads to rationalizations of previous actions" (Goodhart, 1991, p. 43). But to make the ECB seriously accountable to a controlling body, a more robust and mature institutional design of the EU's political profile is necessary. Otherwise "the ECB appears as a disproportionately powerful entity placed in a still vaguely defined and weak institutional setting, where its same power looks fragile" (Bruni, 1993, p. 14). This means that to have a truly independent European monetary policy, progress must be made also on the fronts of European political unification and institutional reorganization. The 1996 Intergovernmental Conference is a crucial step to moving in this direction. Only when the political and institutional background is ready can several technical provisions serve to enhance the ESCB's accountability, including a more precise definition of the "primary objective to maintain price stability" (EU, 1992 Protocol, art. 2), a system of sanctions, a transparent mechanism to arbitrate the possible conflicts with political controlling bodies and, if necessary, a well-specified overriding clause. Before these delicate political and technical changes can happen, in the right way and in the right order, the importance of the accountability problem should not be exaggerated: the price stability rule, together with the other aspects of its autonomy and with the appointment of a credibly "conservative central banker" (*à la* Rogoff, 1985), will allow the ECB "to provide Europe with a beneficial, independent monetary policy, even before being sufficiently accountable" (Bruni, 1993, p. 8).

The independence of an "supranational" bank has several dimensions. The ECB must not only show its independence of national and EU governments: it must also be *independent of the Commission* and *of the NCBs* that hold its capital and, being "an integral part of the ESCB, shall act in accordance with the guidelines and instructions of the ECB" (EU, 1992 Protocol, art. 14.3).

As far as the Commission is concerned the problem could be one of bureaucratic conflict: the Commission has important roles in monetary and financial affairs. It is a technical body, potentially competent to deal with the tasks entrusted to the ECB, but it also has a political profile. Its contacts with the Parliament and the Council are continuous and validated by a precise institutional relationship. The duties of the Commission probably need clarification to exclude overlapping with the responsibilities delegated to the ECB. This is important for enabling the newly created agency to build its own reputation, not only in technical matters but also in matters of style and communication. Even if the EMI is not yet the ECB it is probably not too early to start favoring the birth of an atmosphere of conspicuous autonomy in monetary matters around the Institute. The recent publication of the Commission's Green Paper on the introduction of the single currency (COM, 1995) did not appear as a step in this direction. Certain articles of the treaty do not help to clarify the respective roles and responsibilities. For example: "The Commission *and* the EMI shall report on the progress made in the fulfilment by the Member States of their obligations regarding the achievement of economic and monetary union" (EU, 1992, art. 109j). The collaboration of the Commission with the EMI and, later, the ECB, will be valuable and crucial in many important instances, for example, when exchange rate regimes and policies will have to be decided and managed; but a good collaboration can only result from well-defined autonomies and specific responsibilities. The effectiveness of the actions of the European monetary agency depends on its credibility; national governments and financial markets must, as soon as possible, start looking at this agency as an autonomous centre of thought and decision-making, clearly distinct from the rest of the EU's bureaucracy which is often considered too abundant and intrusive.

The statute of the ECB has been organized in such a way as to favor the making of decisions in the "supernational interest." The votes in the Governing Council shall be weighted only for matters regarding the financial management of the Bank (EU, 1992 Protocol, art. 10.3). As regards monetary policy, the role of the Governors of the NCBs should not be to represent their national interests and form coalitions to this end, but to pursue the best for the EU. Still, the problem of avoiding centrifugal national pressures will certainly complicate the working of the ESCB. This problem will be more serious the larger are the differences between the statutes and the roles of the NCBs. From this point of view great progress will be made when each NCB fulfills the requirements of CBI. But, even after that, some dangers could come from the fact that several NCBs have other tasks besides monetary policy. These dangers are acknowledged by the statute of the ECB: "NCBs may perform functions other than those specified in this Statute unless the Governing Council finds, by a majority of two thirds of the votes cast, that these interfere with the objectives and tasks of the ESCB. Such functions shall be performed on the responsibility and liability of NCBs and shall not be regarded as being part of the functions of the ESCB" (EU, 1992 Protocol, art. 14.4). Among those functions the most delicate one is prudential policy.

The relation between CBI and *supervisory responsibilities* is an issue already dealt with in Section 3 of this chapter. As regards the independence of the ECB this issue has three connected aspects: (i) the consequences of the fact that NCBs are involved in very different degrees and ways in national prudential policies; (ii) the consequences of the lack of a European prudential policy; (iii) the type of involvement the ECB should have in case a European prudential authority were to be established. An entire chapter would be needed for a careful analysis of these three aspects. Suffice it to make some very short comments.

The introduction of a single currency seems to require, in compliance with the subsidiarity principle, some *centralization* of institutions, regulations and policies directed to maintain financial stability (Bruni, 1993).

The Basle Committee's work on *harmonization* is highly valuable but does not solve the problem without a central European agency taking explicit responsibility for prudential policies. As it stands, the text of the Maastricht Treaty makes it difficult for the ECB to be given a subtantial role in this field: prudential tasks may be performed by the ECB (EU, 1992 Protocol, art. 25.2) only after a decision of the Council following article 105.6 of the treaty which requires unanimity and assent of the European Parliament; for national political or bureaucratic interests it will be easy to prevent centralization. The fact that the treaty never uses the wording "lending of last resort" seems a bit of a hypocrisy, while article 3.3 of the statute can be interpreted in the sense that this function is left to NCBs, with very serious problems of coordination. In addition, if coordination takes place in the interests of the whole ESCB, it is not clear how the costs of the lending must be allocated (Aglietta and Moutot, 1993, p. 78): according to article 32.4 NCBs may be indemnified only in "exceptional circumstances." The whole picture looks dangerously inadequate to cope with the difficult prudential problems and pressures for bailouts that will probably attack the European financial markets in the next decade. This could hurt the independence of the ECB.

A final note on the independence of the ECB must be devoted to the very specific and important issue of exchange rate management. In this matter the position envisaged for the ECB is stronger than in the case of most NCBs, including the Bundesbank. To conclude formal agreements on an exchange rate system for the ECU in relation to non-Community currencies, and to adopt, adjust or abandon the central rates of the ECU within the exchange rate system, the Council will have to consult the ECB "in an endeavour to reach a consensus consistent with the objective of price stability" (EU, 1992, art. 109.1). "In the absence of an exchange rate system . . . general orientations for exchange rate policies [formulated by the Council] shall be without prejudice to the primary objective of the ECB to maintain price stability" (EU, 1992, art. 109.2). But, in spite of these provisions of the treaty, the potential conflict between exchange rate policies and monetary stability remains unavoidable and only experience will tell how much the ECB will be able to stand out against exchange rate policies that could endanger price stability. In this field its reputation will be affected not only by the ecu–dollar and ecu–yen policies that will prevail but also, and perhaps sooner and more importantly, by the decisions that will be taken with respect to the "second speed" currencies of EU countries. This will be a crucial theme for understanding how soon and how much the ECB will be able to take up positions that are independent (though cooperative) of the pressures of the member states, of the political behavior of the EU's Council, and of the opinions of the Commission.

6 CONCLUSIONS

This chapter has commented upon the institutional and legislative changes adopted in the EU to increase CBI. The conclusion is that much has been done but the reforms of the NCBs required by the Maastricht Treaty are still incomplete and there is much scope for further progress. Besides "legal" autonomy, three other dimensions of CBI independence should be carefully monitored in the EU in the future, in spite of the fact that they are much more difficult to measurc: *de facto* independence, the reputation of independence and accountability. In due time they will all exert an influence on the feasibility and on the independence of the ECB. But CBI can also serve as a substitute for fixing the exchange rates and it is probable that, even if the European plan of monetary unification fails, progress toward CBI will continue in the large majority of EU countries.

An element that creates important institutional differences among EU central banks is the degree of their involvement in prudential policies. In preparation of EMU this subject should be discussed comprehensively, disregarding the bureaucratic interests that tend to keep the status quo. CBI requires a correct allocation of regulatory and supervisory responsibilities, which is also a condition for the effectiveness and independence of prudential policies. Organizing an optimal institutional framework for supervision has become more difficult with the blurring of traditional boundaries between banks and the rest of the financial system. Probably, a multiplicity of prudential authorities are needed, with well-defined goals, limited discretionality and clearly specified rules of behavior.

The "question of endogeneity" of CBI has also been discussed, using theoretical arguments to illustrate some policy debates taking place in EU countries. Two macroeconomic decision processes have been considered that interact with CBI: the wage-setting mechanism and the adjustment of fiscal imbalances. The argument is made that, under certain conditions, both processes tend to favor CBI because it helps to reach their own objectives. In particular it is shown that, when the inherited stock of debt is not too large, fiscal authorities may like an autonomous central bank because it allows them to obtain a higher social and political utility, and also to be independent of any time inconsistency or credibility problems. It is also shown that, if the cost of recontracting nominal wages become sufficiently high, if there is downward price rigidity, and if the probability of short-run nominal macro shocks is sufficiently large with respect to the probability of shocks that change the equilibrium level of real wages, the workers prefer CBI to an accommodative monetary policy.

CBI is therefore, at least in part, "endogenous" and often there is no justification for giving up institutional monetary rigor on the ground that fiscal and incomes policies are an obstacle to disinflation.

A perfect independence of national central banks is a necessary but insufficient condition for the complete autonomy of the future ECB. Several issues regarding the independence of the ESCB have been discussed, including the problem of accountability, the potential centrifugal impact of excessively large differences between the non-monetary functions of the national central banks, the delicacy of the ECB's task of developing a profile independent of the EU Commission while collaborating with its policies, the dangers coming from the lack of substantial prudential tasks of the ECB, the complex interaction between the independence of Europe's monetary policy and the formulation of the Union's exchange rate strategies toward the non-Community currencies as well as the "second speed" EU currencies. The conclusion is that, while "on paper" the Maastricht Treaty grants a very strong autonomy to the ECB, it will not be easy to carry out a truly independent European monetary policy: this might even require some changes and integrations to the present design of the future monetary institutions of the EU.

Notes

1. Suppose the utility function of the workers and the demand curve for labour are as follows:

$$U = N^n\left(\frac{W}{p}\right)^{1-n} \tag{1}$$

$$N = \pi\left(\frac{W}{P}\right)^{-e}, \quad 0 \leq N \leq N^* \tag{2}$$

where π is a scale parameter for productivity. By substituting (2) into (1) the derivative of the utility with respect to the real wage can be shown to be negative (with positive second derivative) if the employment variable has sufficient importance in the utility function, that is, if $n > 1/(1 + e)$. The supply curve will therefore be rigid at the full employment level N^* and the utility will decrease along the whole demand curve, going toward lower levels of employment and higher real wages.
2. In a less descriptive and analytically better-developed model the degree of wage rigidity would be in part endogenously derived also on the basis of the function D.

References

Aglietta, M. and Moutot P. (1993) "L'évolution des structures financières des grands pays et la prévention du risque de système dans l'Union Economique et Monétaire," *Cahiers économiques et monétaires*, 41, pp. 55–81.

Bank for International Settlements (BIS) (1995) *65th Annual Report* (Basle), 12 June.

Bank of Japan (BOJ) (1995) "Developments in the European Union: Toward Economic Monetary Union," *Quarterly Bulletin* (February), pp. 39–62.

Borio, C.E.V. and Filosa, R. (1994) "The Changing Borders of Banking: Trends and Implications," Working Paper No. 23, Bank of International Settlements (Basle), October.

Bruni, F. (1993) "Monetary and Prudential Issues in the Planned European Monetary Union," in *Financial Markets in the Changing World* (Tokyo: Hitotsubashi University), pp. 1–34.

Bruni, F. (1994) "Introductory Remarks," in F. Bruni (ed.), *Centro di Economia Monetaria e Finanziaria "Paolo Baffi"*, Working Paper No. 82 (Milano: Università Bocconi).

Bruni, F. (1995) "Prudential Regulation and Supervisory Policies in an Integrated Financial Market: Issues of Optimality and Credibility," in G. Ferrarini (ed.), *Prudential Regulation of Banks and Securities Firms* (London: Kluwer Law International), pp. 89–100.

Bruni, F. and Masciandaro, D. (1991) "Evaluating Central Bank Independence: Theoretical Issues and European Perspectives," *Rivista Internazionale di Scienze Sociali*, 99 (January–March).

Bruni, F. and Paternò, F. (1995) "Market Discipline of Banks' Riskiness: A Study of Selected Issues," *Journal of Financial Services Research*, 9, pp. 303–25.

Commission of the European Communities (COM) (1995) *Green Paper on the Arrangements for the Introduction of the Single Currency* (com 95 333 final) (Brussels), 31 May.

Cukierman, A. (1993a) "Central Bank Independence, Political Influençe and Macroeconomic Performance: a Survey of Recent Developments," *Cuadernos de Economia*, 98 (December), pp. 271–91.

Cukierman, A. (1993b) "Commitment Through Delegation, Political Influence and Central Bank Independence," mimeo, preliminary version of a paper prepared for the Conference "A Framework for Monetary Stability," Amsterdam, De Nederlandsche Bank, October.

Cukierman, A., Webb, S.B. and Neyapti, B. (1992) "Measuring the Independence of Central Banks and Its Effect on Policy Outcomes," *The World Bank Economic Review*, 3, pp. 353–98.

The Economist (1993) "Too Many Pies for the Old Lady," 28 August, pp. 67–8.

European Monetary Institute (EMI) (1995a) *Annual Report 1994* (Frankfurt am Main), April.

European Monetary Institute (EMI) (1995b) *Progress Towards Convergence* (Frankfurt am Main), November.

European Union (EU) (1992) *Treaty on European Union* (Maastricht), February.

European Union (EU) (1992 Protocol) "Protocol on the Statutes of the ESCB and of the ECB," in *Treaty on the European Union* (Maastricht), February.

Financial Times (1995a) "Labour May Widen Central Bank's Role," by Kevin Brown, Thursday, 18 May, p. 9.
Financial Times (1995b) "Barings and the Bank," Wednesday, 19 July, p. 11.
Financial Times (1995c) "Old Lady Clings to Poisoned Chalice," by John Gapper, Thursday, 20 July, p. 11.
Galimberti, F. (1994) "Synthesis," in F. Bruni (ed.), *Centro di Economia Monetaria e Finanziaria "Paolo Baffi"*, Working Paper No. 82 (Milano: Università Bocconi).
Goodhart, C. (1991) "The Draft Statute of the European System of Central Banks: A Commentary," in CEPR, *The Road to EMU: Managing the Transition to a Single European Currency* (London: CEPR), pp. 41–4.
Goodhart, C. (1994) "Central Bank Independence," in F. Bruni (ed.), *Centro di Economia Monetaria e Finanziaria "Paolo Baffi"*, Working Paper No. 82 (Milano: Università Bocconi).
Goodhart, C. and Shoenmaker, D. (1993) "Institutional Separation between Supervisory and Monetary Agencies," in F. Bruni (ed.), *Prudential Regulation, Supervision and Monetary Policy: Theory, International Comparison and the ESCB Role* (Milano: Università Bocconi).
Hochreiter, E. (1994) "Central Banking in Economies in Transition," in F. Bruni (ed.), *Centro di Economia Monetaria e Finanziaria "Paolo Baffi"*, Working Paper No. 82 (Milano: Università Bocconi).
Maxfield, S. (1994) "The Politics of Central Banking in Developing Countries," mimeo, Yale University.
Michelacci, C. (1993) "Central Bank Involvement in the Supervision of the Banking System and of Financial Markets: A Comparative Analysis," Working Paper No. 72, Centro di Economia Monetaria e Finanziaria "Paolo Baffi" (Milano: Università Bocconi).
Padoa-Schioppa, T. (1994) "Adapting Central Banking to a Changing Environment," in T.J.T. Balino and C. Cottarelli (eds), *Frameworks for Monetary Stability: Policy Issues and Country Experiences* (Washington, DC: IMF), pp. 529–51.
Posen, A. (1993) "Why Central Bank Independence Does Not Cause Low Inflation: There is No Institutional Fix for Politics," in R. O'Brien (ed.), *Finance and the International Economy* (Oxford: Oxford University Press).
Posen, A. (1994a) "Central Bank Independence and Disinflationary Credibility: A Missing Link?," *Brookings Discussion Papers in International Economics*, 109 (Washington, DC: Brookings Institution).
Posen, A. (1994b) "Is Central Bank Independence the Result of Effective Opposition to Inflation?: Evidence of Endogenous Monetary Policy Institutions," mimeo, Harvard University.
Reserve Bank of New Zealand (1994) *Review of Banking Supervision: Reserve Bank's Policy Conclusions* (December).
Reserve Bank of New Zealand (1995) *Reserve Bank Bulletin*, 58 (June quarter).
Rogoff, K. (1985) "The Optimal Degree of Commitment to an Intermediate Monetary Target," *Quarterly Journal of Economics*, 100, pp. 1169–90.
Sargent, T.J. and Wallace, N. (1981) "Some Unpleasant Monetarist Arithmetic," *Federal Reserve Bank of Minneapolis Quarterly Review*, 5 (Fall), pp. 15–31.
Visco, I. (1995) "Inflation, Inflation Targeting and Monetary Policy. Notes for Discussion on the Italian Experience," in L. Leiderman and L. Svensson (eds), *Inflation Targets* (London: Centre for Economic Policy Research).

Comments
Robert Raymond

1 INTRODUCTION

Central bank independence has become a very important part of the credibility of the central bank's action to combat inflation. It has the effect of sheltering a central bank from political pressure aiming at a postponement of restrictive policies when warranted. In many countries where the central bank does not yet enjoy full independence there is a tendency to grant it.

I do not intend to criticize the chapter by Bruni, an expert in this field as in many others. I prefer to consider the main ingredients of central bank independence (CBI) as I see them – in some cases supplementing Bruni's chapter – and to show the limits of this delegation of powers.

2 THE MAIN INGREDIENTS

The main features of CBI are of an institutional, personal, functional and financial nature:

1. Institutional independence is the most obvious aspect of the concept. It means that the decision-making body and its members should not seek or receive any advice from political circles, should not be put under pressure by them. Symmetrically, the political sphere should refrain from exerting pressure of any kind.

   This clearly applies to relations of the central bank with the executive and legislative powers. It has a legal and a practical aspect, according to the distinction suggested by Bruni. The legal one is that institutional arrangements should not include any procedure which could be used to influence the central bank. Such precautions are necessary, but not sufficient. Much depends also on the type of relations between the top management of the central bank and political leaders or administrations.
2. Personal independence is also obvious. The Governor should be appointed for a definite period. He could therefore make a decision without being threatened with the possibility of losing his job before the end of his mandate.

In my view, this protection should also be extended to the other members of the Executive Board, if any, to the extent that they take part in the decision-making process and could possibly temporarily replace the Governor.

These two main features of CBI (institutional and personal) are explicit in the statute of the European System of Central Banks (ESCB) which is attached to the Maastricht Treaty, although the extension of personal independence to board members of national central banks is a controversial issue. They would not participate in the meetings of the ESCB Council, unless they had to replace their Governor.

3. Functional independence is less often recognized. Authorities should make sure that monetary policy operation are not hampered by legal restrictions or institutional arrangements. On the contrary, the central bank should be helped by public authorities when adopting a new system. Whilst previous features could be defined as abstaining, on the part of national authorities, this implies some positive contribution and should be the result of a cooperative approach.
4. The same is true with financial independence. Public authorities are quite often the main or single shareholder of the central bank. The latter needs some freedom to spend on projects which are necessary to support activities related to the elaboration and implementation of monetary policy. Financial independence also includes the possibility of having own funds in relation with the balance sheet and the risks involved.

Features 3 and 4 above fall within the field of practice rather than that of legislation. It should therefore be part of a "code of conduct."

3 LIMITS AND COUNTERPARTS

Democratic principles make it necessary for any delegation of power to be clearly assigned to a specific task and to be subject to public accountability. This is why the central bank has to be given an explicit mandate and to follow the appropriate procedure to be transparent *vis-à-vis* public opinion.

3.1 The Mandate

There is now full agreement that the central bank should be made responsible for low inflation. This was formerly a long-term objective. It has become either a medium-term target on which other intermediate targets should be based, or a substitute for targets based on monetary aggregates. Maintaining inflation at a low level now is usually enshrined in the statute of national central banks. So it is for the ESCB in the Maastricht Treaty. Any revision of the statute of a central bank to make this institution independent with the content above-mentioned would include a commitment to price stability, as the justification of CBI.

The role of the central bank with regard to the exchange rate policy is not clear-cut as it is for price developments. On the one hand, by steering short-term interest rates, the central bank is able to influence the exchange rate. In addition, the latter has a direct effect on prices, especially in open economies; to that extent, it falls within the competence of the central bank. On the other hand, the national currency is ruled by a monetary law. Everything related to the international or a regional monetary system has to be decided by the political powers. The same is true for a decision to change the parity in a fixed exchange rate system, to the extent that the parity is part of the official definition of the unit of account.

These principles apply to the European Union. Joining the EMS, announcing or changing the central rate in the ERM, require government action, with which the central bank has to be associated.

Therefore, the exchange rate policy is based on a cooperation between the government – which has the last word – and the central bank – which is responsible for executing interventions and for maintaining price stability. It is fortunate that devaluation has become unpopular, even for politicians.

Banking supervision is a field in which the competence of the central bank is very uneven, country by country. There are two extreme cases, that in which the central bank has no involvement at all, and that in which it is involved in the execution of the controls and is responsible for the decision to close a bank or to organize a rescue operation.

Bruni is in favor of the central bank not being responsible, in order not to pollute its independence for monetary policy implementation (i.e., interest rate management) and maybe its reputation (when a bank is about to collapse).

Personally, I think – but this is only my own opinion – that a central bank should be aware of the individual situations of banks. I see three reasons for this. First, the central bank is responsible for the smooth functioning of markets. Second, money is created by commercial banks to a great extent. Third, should a shock occur, the central bank will have to face the situation, even if it is not legally responsible for banking supervision.

Whichever institution is in charge of banking supervision, it should be independent.

Finally, I would like to mention an activity which is not often thought of as conflicting with CBI, although in my view it may be difficult to admit as a matter of principle. This is the role of the central bank as a fiscal agent. It is especially the case where the central bank is in charge of issuing public debt and enjoys some leeway to make the choice of the maturity. In such a case the central bank could influence the yield curve. We should therefore discuss first to what extent this is part of monetary policy and second if the way the PSBR is financed is an appropriate support.

3.2 Public Accountability

In a democracy, it is difficult to admit that one man would enjoy full delegation of power without any control. As a consequence, one could easily argue that an independent monetary policy should be run by a council with voting rights. The ESCB will be organized this way.

Transparency is a normal counterpart of CBI. Without it, the central bank would entail the risk of being accused of dictatorship, or of plotting against the general interest, or, at the very least, of arbitrary and ill-founded decisions. Therefore, there is a need to explain and justify. This can be done *ex post*, but the tendency is to do it with a shorter lag, if not immediately, either by publishing a communiqué or by disclosing minutes of preparatory meetings, as is the case in the United States or the UK. Transparency should also include some kinds of information given to members of parliament through hearings.

In general, we should not go so far as to recommend sanctions, at least to the extent that this would contradict the principle of independence. Sanctions, if any, could only be global, in the event of the final goal of low inflation being missed. However, I know of no example of a purely automatic rule. Applying a sanction, therefore, would involve another decision-making body which would judge in appeal, and this might also conflict with the principle of CBI.

Comments

Cathy E. Minehan

Many of the issues raised by Bruni with regard to the requirement that central banks of the countries of the European Union become fully "independent" before the start of the third phase of economic and monetary union and the creation of the European Central Bank are on the table for US central bankers as well. A bill currently under discussion in Congress would legislate price stability as the primary goal of the Fed, and would ask the Fed to announce numerical targets and a path over time for achieving price stability. So the questions of what constitutes central bank independence, how much of it should there be, and what are the proper goals for the monetary authority are just as relevant to the conduct of monetary policy in the United States as they are for the complex task of forming a European Central Bank.

Bruni has provided a comprehensive summary of a large number of issues of concern in the convergence to European Monetary Union. He begins by noting the four aspects of the Central Bank Independence condition of the EMU agreement. Bruni develops a numerical evaluation of convergence toward central bank independence among the original 12 countries of the Union and notes that convergence has been greatest in the area of prohibiting lending to the government, and least in the area of statutorily setting price stability as the objective of the central bank.

Bruni also discusses the relationship (and possible conflict) between the central bank's role as a monetary policymaker concerned with price stability, and its role as a supervisor for banks. A disproportionate concern by the central bank for the health of depository institutions might induce an inflationary bias into its monetary policy actions. On the other hand, the knowledge that the central bank gains from monitoring may be valuable in managing and stabilizing the payments system. Bruni makes five points here that emphasize his general discomfort with the appropriateness of joining monetary and prudential policy responsibility in the central bank, while recognizing it does not make sense to exclude the central bank totally from bank supervision.

Of interest is his notion that prudential policy setting needs independence and credibility as well. In that regard, he notes that a central bank in charge of the payment system may well have a fairly high sensitivity to the danger of systemic risk, and a fairly low sensitivity to the social costs of prudential controls and bailouts. He infers from this that it is better for the effectiveness and credibility of prudential policies and for the working of market discipline on banks that the *political* responsibility for at least *certain* prudential decisions is located outside the central bank. He concludes that what is at issue is not *whether* central banks should be invested with prudential tasks, but how an optimal prudential framework can be designed with the recognition that such a framework increases the credibility and effectiveness of both monetary and prudential policies.

Finally, Bruni draws distinctions among four aspects of central bank independence: legal, actual, reputational, and the dimension provided by accountability. He suggests that the more imprecisely independence is defined by legislation, the more leeway there is for political pressure to weaken the *de facto* independence of the central bank, and that reputational independence, such as that enjoyed by both Germany and the USA, may be more important for the credibility of monetary policy than measures of either *de jure* or *de facto* independence.

I found Bruni's paper useful in clarifying and distinguishing the sometimes murky and entangled issues surrounding central bank independence. His chapter suggests four questions that I would like to raise and answer immediately, but discuss more fully in the rest of my comments. First, should a government legislate a goal of price stability for the central bank? I think the answer here is unequivocally yes. Second, should price stability be the sole goal of monetary policy, to the exclusion of financial stability? The answer here is no. Third, should the legislated goal include numerical targets that define price stability? Again, the answer is no. Finally, should the central bank itself set numerical targets that it publicly communicates and is held accountable for? Maybe yes, maybe no. Now let me explain my positions more fully.

It is, of course, right and appropriate for a government to establish goals for a central bank. Certainly these exist for the Federal Reserve System, and have since its inception. It is also appropriate for such goals to change from time to time. A legislated mandate for price stability could serve as a wake-up call to the central bank, and give it a measure of authority it may not have had otherwise. Thus, I would view a legislated goal of price stability as clearly good, especially for countries with a history of high inflation.

Price stability as the sole goal of a central bank is more problematic. The ultimate objective of economic policy is to provide for continual improvement in standards of living. Price stability is a means to this end, but not an end in and of itself. To the extent that the single-minded pursuit of price stability precludes the central bank from, for example, any element of common sense in responding to cyclical or other shocks, I think it would be counter to achieving that ultimate objective.

Similarly, if setting price stability as the sole goal of monetary policy precludes the central bank from addressing issues of financial stability, it could also be harmful. In that regard, I am puzzled by the uncertainty in Bruni's chapter and in some of the literature about central bank involvement in bank regulation and supervision. A healthy banking system is key to financial stability and, far from being a distraction, financial stability is critical in practice to price stability. It may not be necessary for central banks to supervise all depository institutions to achieve some confidence that the state of bank health will not undermine monetary policy, but certainly an intimate knowledge of major banks, and the ability to intercede with them that comes only by being their regulator, seems to me to be key to maintaining financial stability.

On the third issue of numerical targets for price stability set by the legislature, I also have problems. Such targets are mentioned in some definitions of central bank independence. In some senses this is counter-intuitive since it seems to imply that a central bank can have little to say about what its goals and targets are, but still be considered "independent." More importantly, numerical targets set by legislatures can be revised by legislatures without assurance that this process will always result in the best outcome.

Finally, should central banks set their own numerical targets and time frames for achieving price stability and communicate them publicly? On the one hand, this could improve central bank accountability and if the choice is legislatively set targets or central bank set targets, I would always vote that the central bank set the targets. On the other hand, it is not clear whether targets achieve something for which the central bank wants to be accountable. In theory, numerical targets ought to buy the credibility necessary to achieve lower inflation at a lower cost in terms of unemployment, or to wring inflation premia out of long-term interest rates. To my knowledge, however, the available evidence does not indicate that countries with explicit inflation targets have lowered their sacrifice ratios or reduced inflation premia. Moreover, publicly set targets have the added downside of focusing attention on adherence to the target rather than the progress toward sound economic growth and price stability over the long run. In the USA, the good inflation performance since the early 1980s has been seen as a measure of central bank success. If explicit targets had been set, and perhaps exceeded, would the real progress be perceived in the same favorable light, with all that implies for credibility both with Congress and the general public? I think not, which makes me undecided on this issue.

Bruni also comments on the payment system responsibilities of central banks. He apparently believes that these activities make central banks more willing to bail out depository institutions, and less attracted to market discipline. This seems to me to ignore the very real central bank dilemma of moral hazard. To the extent that a central bank always was willing to bail out, and depository institutions knew this, there would be little incentive to improve risk controls. Central banks would in effect be underwriting private sector risk-taking in payment systems – something we do not want to do and worry about a lot. The answer seems to lie in being involved in prudential policy-setting which includes the establishment of standards related to risk control, and to be willing to intervene promptly to get the weak link out of the system (as is now required legislatively in the USA) – in short to be more involved in supervision and regulation rather than less because of payment system responsibilities.

My last point is an expansion on comments made by Bruni. He indicates he expects the existing central banks in the European Community to see their role diminish under the European Central Banking system. I think this has to happen if monetary union and a single currency come to be, but I can understand that such a prospect may not warm the hearts of many European central bankers. Perhaps I can provide a ray of partial hope based on my own experience as a regional Reserve Bank president.

The Federal Reserve System was designed specifically with both central and regional aspects that at least initially were to balance each other. Regional Reserve Banks set their own discount rates at first, but over time the forces of capital market development and the use of national open market operations as the main tool of monetary policy have pulled responsibility much more toward the center. However, regional Reserve Banks do continue to play a healthy role in the Federal Reserve System, as payments processors, as direct lenders to commercial banks using a single discount rate that is recommended by the individual Banks, but approved at the national level, and also as providers of vital input to the deliberations of the Federal Open Market Committee (FOMC). The Reserve Banks offer specific knowledge of economic developments in their region through their extensive ongoing contacts with local businesses and through information gained in the regulatory function.

A case in point is the New England experience in the 1980s. I am told that Frank Morris, then President of the Boston Fed, was a voice in the wilderness regarding the problems inherent in the excessive real estate lending in the mid-1980s. This fueled a sizeable economic boom in New England, but the recession that followed was much deeper as a result. The combination of a declining economy and a collapsing real estate market led to severe problems at the region's banks. As banks struggled to survive they cut back their lending which further exacerbated the regional recession. New England's problems were later echoed elsewhere; but because of New England's earlier experience, the FOMC was already sensitive to the contractionary effect of disruptions to the availability of credit.

The regional Reserve Banks also represent a variety of economic schools of thought, and bring many perspectives to the analysis of monetary policy. Because each Bank has relative autonomy, each Bank's research department has developed a distinctive analytical character. I may be naive here, but I believe such a rich variety has contributed to the System's relative success over the past fifteen years or so.

In sum, monetary union in the EC would not be easy, as Bruni points out. I think the points he makes about autonomy for the ECB are right on the mark if unity is to happen at all. The individual national central banks cannot represent their national interests but must pursue the best for the entire union. If this does not happen, if the system does not evolve to something like the Federal Reserve, it is hard to see that it will work at all.

Comments

Clive Briault

Bruni's chapter is interesting and wide-ranging and is highly pertinent to the current monetary debate in Europe. I welcome his call for a wider and deeper discussion of the issues he raises. I would like to comment on three particular aspects.

1 INDEPENDENCE AND ACCOUNTABILITY

Bruni's chapter adopts an overly narrow view of central bank independence, confined almost entirely not only to the model of a "conservative" central banker first set out by Rogoff (1985a), but also to an extreme version of this model in which the independent central banker places a weight of unity on inflation stabilization and of zero on output stabilization. This is particularly clear in the first half of Section 4 of his chapter, where the impacts of various types of shock on the price level are not accommodated at all under central bank independence. But, as the paper in chapter 10 of this volume demonstrates, there are many different models of central bank independence, many of which offer a welfare improvement over the Rogoff-type approach. And the extreme version of the Rogoff model used by Bruni will almost certainly generate a Pareto-inferior welfare outcome, as Rogoff himself observed.

I am also puzzled by Bruni's emphasis on the endogeneity of the optimal degree of central bank independence, given his later advocacy of the "perfect independence of national central banks" and a "truly independent European monetary policy." If central bank independence should indeed be determined endogenously, then the current and future structure of labor markets, fiscal intentions and other structural features in Europe might be consistent with less rather than greater central bank independence. Indeed, work on the optimal degree of central bank independence by Eijffinger and Schaling (1995a and 1995b) suggests that some central banks are too conservative while others are not conservative enough. This implies that the proposed statutory independence of a future European Central Bank may not coincide with the optimal level determined by economic conditions within European Monetary Union; and that the optimal degree of independence may change over time.

There is also an important question here as to how "conservative" a future European Central Bank might actually turn out to be if it takes the form of "monetary policy-making by committee." Perhaps we should turn for inspiration here to another paper by Rogoff (1985b), which showed that cooperation between the monetary authorities in two countries could lead to higher, rather than lower, inflation. Much of the analysis here may well be relevant to European Monetary Union. Sharing the time-consistency problem (or moving it from many individual countries to a single currency area) need not solve it; instead it could *increase* the inflation bias. Can we be sure that the members of the European Central Bank Council will collectively vote for *lower* inflation on average than the rate imposed on other members of the ERM through the leadership of the Bundesbank? This deserves to be studied further.

Turning to *accountability*, Bruni observes early in his chapter that independence may be "incomplete and insecure" without accountability, but he concludes later that "the importance of the accountability problem should not be exaggerated." This may be linked to his focus on Rogoff's "conservative central banker" model, which can be characterized as almost complete goal and instrument independence. But even here there could be an important role for accountability to play as a means of minimizing the "democratic deficit" and of reducing uncertainty about the preferences of the authorities. Moreover, accountability could perhaps be part of the answer to the problem of collective decision-taking which may face the European Central Bank. Why not publish the minutes of Council meetings and thereby expose the positions taken by Council members? Sensitivities over accountability should not be used as an excuse for having as little accountability as possible.

2 BANKING SUPERVISION

Bruni sets out clearly some of the potential advantages and disadvantages of combining supervisory and monetary policy functions within a central bank. However, it is very difficult to assess the importance of these and it may be worth searching for empirical evidence to assist us in this task.

How strong is the empirical evidence that central banks without supervisory responsibility have a better inflation track record? Figure 11C.1 shows a positive correlation between those countries where the central bank undertakes banking supervision[1] and those countries which have had relatively higher inflation over the past ten years. But there are notable outliers here, in particular Sweden and the Netherlands, and without a much clearer

Figure 11C.1 Central bank involvement in banking supervision and cumulative inflation

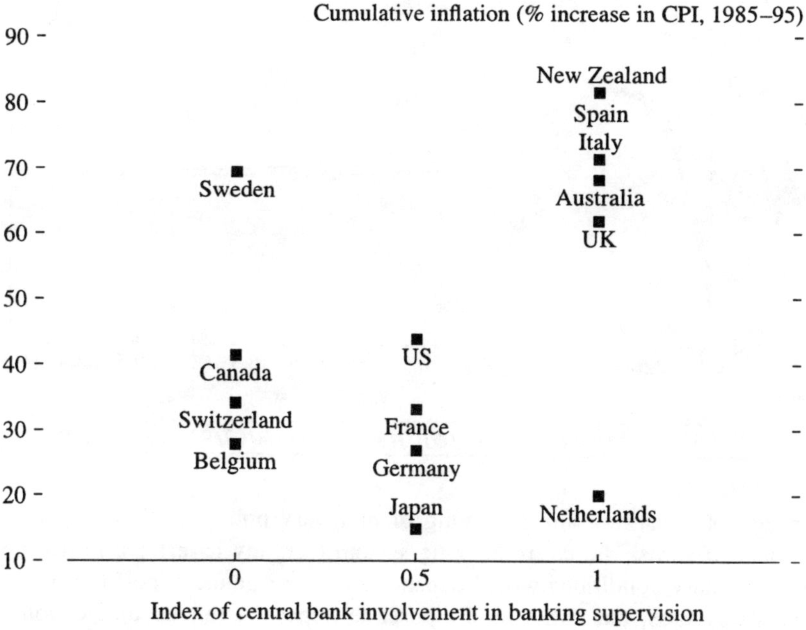

theoretical relationship it would be unwise to conclude that if only banking supervision was taken away from central banks then these countries would enjoy much lower rates of inflation.

It is difficult to find empirical evidence of the authorities deliberately loosening monetary conditions simply in order to support banks. Indeed, the conclusion drawn by Goodhart (1995) is that the monetary authorities usually make the opposite mistake of taking too little account of financial and asset prices in setting monetary policy. Do we really believe that the monetary authorities in Australia, Italy, New Zealand, Spain and the UK have deliberately *loosened* monetary policy over the past ten years in an attempt to support their banks?

Easing monetary policy would anyway be an extremely inefficient way of helping a single bank, or a relatively small number of banks. I think Bruni is too ready to assume here that any support of a bank must equate to a loosening of monetary policy. This depends on how the lender of last resort function is operated. Providing liquidity to an illiquid but solvent bank, on a fully collaterized basis and at a market or penal interest rate,

Figure 11C.2 UK inflation term structure: BCCI closure announced 5 July 1991

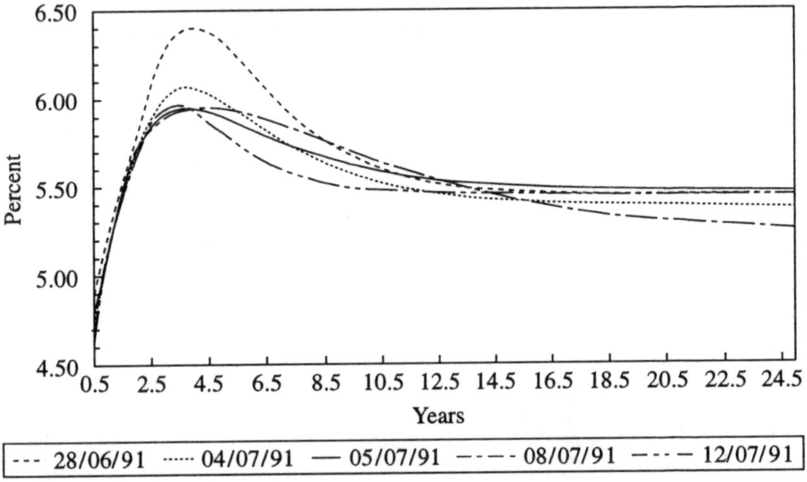

need not constitute any loosening of monetary policy. And if problems extended across the entire banking system then any case for a loosening in monetary conditions would depend not on the financial position of the banks as such, but rather on the possible impact of this on the economy more generally. For example, if banks were to cut back on their lending and if banks are "special" because of their inside information about the creditworthiness of their borrowers, then problems facing the banking sector could be communicated to the real economy. The reason for loosening monetary policy would then be to prevent this from putting excessive downward pressure on activity and prices.

Could criticisms of the way a central bank has discharged its prudential responsibilities damage the credibility of its monetary policy? This is even more difficult to test, but one approach available to us using UK data is to look at the inflation expectations curve immediately before and after some supervisory events which might have been interpreted as damaging the credibility of the Bank of England. Consider, for example, the closure of BCCI in July 1991 and the publication in October 1992 of the report on this by Lord Bingham; and the more recent problems at Barings (which emerged in February 1995) and the subsequent publication (in July 1995) of a report on this episode by the Board of Banking Supervision. Figures 11C.2–11C.5 show that these events had very little impact on – and certainly did not worsen significantly – inflation expectations in the UK, which might be taken to be a reasonable proxy for the credibility of monetary

Figure 11C.3 UK inflation term structure: Bingham Report published 22 October 1991

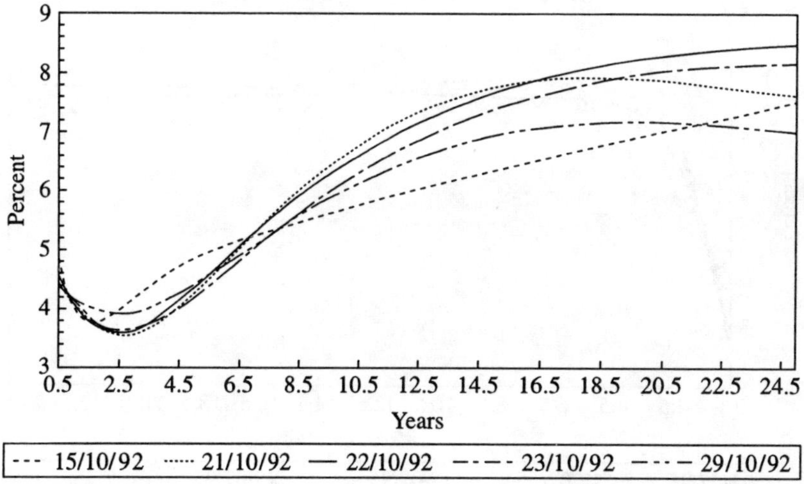

Figure 11C.4 UK inflation term structure: Barings problems emerged 27 February 1995

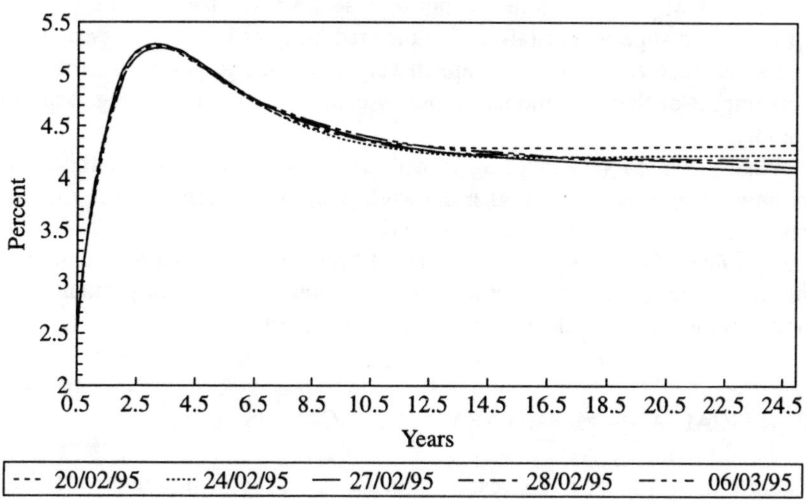

Figure 11C.5 UK inflation term structure: BOBS Report on Barings published 18 July 1995

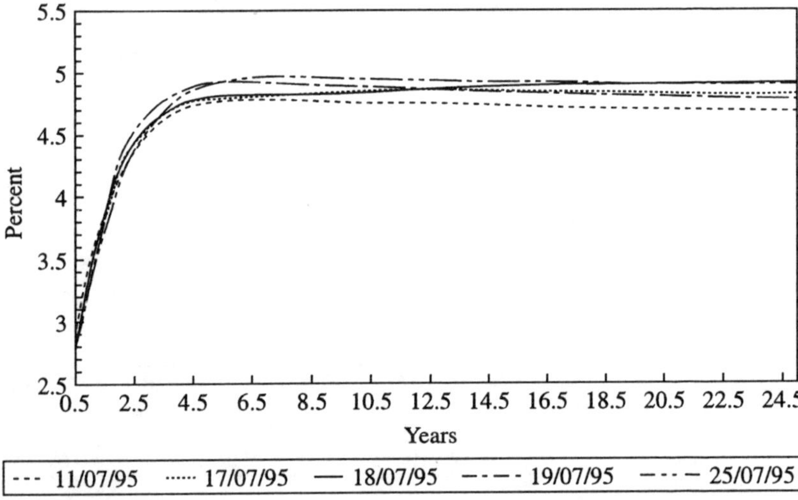

policy. The largest movements in the inflation expectations curve coincide with the publication of the Bingham Report in October 1992 (Figure 11C.3), but it is extremely difficult to isolate the impact of this from the shifts in market expectations which were occurring just one month after sterling's withdrawal from the European Exchange Rate Mechanism. There are plenty of reasons why these figures do not represent a perfect test of the impact of perceived supervisory failings on the credibility of UK monetary policy, but since such events do not happen very often one might have expected any impact of them on monetary policy credibility to have emerged quite rapidly.

Finally, while I very much agree with Bruni that the key issue in this area is how an optimal prudential framework could be designed, I see this in terms of the optimal setting of supervisory standards as a means of correcting market failures (along the lines of Miles, 1995), rather than in terms of how many supervisory institutions there should be; who they should be; and whether this should be harmonized across Europe.

3 FISCAL AND MONETARY INTERACTIONS

Bruni's fiscal model is interesting because it highlights a potential "knife edge" situation. But there are a number of problems which make it difficult to interpret his results. In particular, although there are a number of important intertemporal aspects of the model, the problem facing the authorities is solved as if they were playing a one-shot game. Richer dynamics would of course complicate the model, but without them it is difficult to understand how the model relates to the real world. For example, it might be useful to distinguish between short- and long-term debt, since the monetary policy pursued by the central bank (and the central bank's credibility) will have important implications for both the level and the shape of the yield curve. Indeed, many theoretical models suggest that debt structure can play a crucial role in counteracting dynamic inconsistency problems. Monetary policy laxity might reduce the cost of borrowing this period, but it might also generate an explosive *dynamic* solution to the model if economic agents respond to loose monetary policy this period by increasing their expectations of inflation in subsequent periods.

It is also interesting to think about the dynamic path following an upward shift in central bank independence, assuming that this shift in monetary policy regime leads to a lower average inflation rate. What if, as seems likely, this new regime does not immediately gain full credibility? An increase in the effective real interest rate on government debt will generate higher debt financing costs during the transitional period before full credibility is established. Expected inflation declines more slowly than actual inflation so the primary surplus consistent with a constant debt to GDP ratio will initially increase. Is it perhaps because of this "unpleasant fiscal arithmetic" (see King, 1995) that the Bank of Italy regards the Italian fiscal position as a constraint on sound monetary policy even if, as Bruni's model demonstrates, society would be better off over the long run if price stability can be achieved?

Note

1. The classification of countries is based on Goodhart and Schoenmaker (1995). A score of nil represents no central bank involvement in banking supervision; a score of 0.5 reflects partial involvement; and a score of unity indicates that banking supervision is undertaken entirely by the central bank.

References

Eijffinger, S. and Schaling, E. (1995a) "The Ultimate Determinants of Central Bank Independence," Centre for Economic Research Discussion Paper No. 9505, Tilburg University, January.

Eijffinger, S. and Schaling, E. (1995b) "Optimal Commitment in an Open Economy: Credibility versus Flexibility," Centre for Economic Research Discussion Paper No. 9579, Tilburg University, July.

Goodhart, C. (1995) "Price Stability and Financial Stability," in K. Sawamoto, Z. Nakajima and H. Taguchi (eds), *Financial Stability in a Changing Environment* (New York: St Martin's Press).

Goodhart, C. and Schoenmaker, D. (1995) "Should the Functions of Monetary Policy and Banking Supervision be Separated?," *Oxford Economic Papers*, 47, pp. 539–60.

King, M.A. (1995) "Monetary Policy Implications of Greater Fiscal Discipline," Comments on a paper by John Taylor given at the Federal Reserve Bank of Kansas City Conference on "Budget Deficits and Debt: Issues and Options," Jackson Hole, September.

Miles, D. (1995) "Optimal Regulation of Deposit Taking Financial Intermediaries," *European Economic Review*, 39, pp. 1365–84.

Rogoff, K. (1985a) "The Optimal Degree of Commitment to an Intermediate Monetary Target," *Quarterly Journal of Economics* (November), pp. 1169–90.

Rogoff, K. (1985b) "Can International Monetary Policy Co-operation be Counterproductive?," *Journal of International Economics*, 18, pp. 199–217.

Part V
Concluding Summary

12 Towards More Effective Monetary Policy: Concluding Remarks*

Guido Tabellini

1 INTRODUCTION

This conference addressed some fundamental and long-standing problems in monetary policy. A discussion of these issues between policymakers and academic researchers is always important, both to improve the conduct of monetary policy and for the advancement of knowledge. In this conference, the discussion has been particularly fruitful and exciting; I am grateful to the Bank of Japan for having made this possible, and for having given me the opportunity to take part in it. My task is daunting, however. It is impossible to completely and adequately summarize the many ideas and insights that emerged over the course of two full days, about many aspects of monetary policy. Therefore, I do not even attempt to provide an exhaustive summary. Instead, I organize my concluding remarks around a number of questions that repeatedly came up in the discussion and in the contributions. I then try to summarize the consensus answer, or to identify the nature of the disagreement or the extent to which the question remains open.

These questions can be divided in two groups: one concerning the design of the institutional framework for monetary policy; the other concerning the operational conduct of policy. It is important to keep these two kinds of questions distinct, since they reflect different underlying problems. The first set of problems typically arises from the distorted incentives that policymakers may have in specific environments. Institution design is an attempt to correct (or protect) the policymakers' incentives, so as to influence both the conduct of monetary policy as well as the private sector expectations about future monetary policy. The second set of problems, instead, arises from our imperfect information about the consequences of monetary policy.

* I am grateful to Torsten Persson for several discussions on the general topics of this conference.

2 THE INSTITUTIONAL FRAMEWORK

The first and most fundamental question about monetary policy is: *Which goals should monetary policy have?* There are really two parts to this question: (a) Which goals should *society* have with regard to monetary policy? and (b) Should the central bank have distorted preferences relative to society, and how?

Let us start with the first part. Probably everyone agrees that the ultimate macroeconomic goals ought to be price stability, high and stable sustainable growth, and financial stability. But making these goals more precise raises a number of difficulties. Do we want to stabilize prices or inflation? Why do we want it – that is, what is the nature of the cost of inflation? Is the cost duc to expected inflation, or to price level unpredictability? And how do we measure inflation? Similarly, do we want low volatility of output growth, or small deviations of output from trend?

Many of these questions are still open. Nevertheless, some answers are clearly ruled out and a consensus view has emerged from the conference. First of all, there is no long-run tradeoff between output and inflation. Hence, with a long enough horizon, monetary policy should aim at price stability only. Moreover, as David Laidler put it in chapter 4 of this volume, the key goal now is to consolidate a low inflation environment – that is, aim for a rate of inflation of about 2 percent per year. Given that measured CPI inflation has an upward measurement bias that could be as large as 1–1.5 percent, this would come pretty close to a goal of zero inflation. Aiming for a low inflation rate, naturally, would entail accepting some price level drift. But the output costs of removing the drift could be large, if there are nominal rigidities. Moreover, at a moderate rate of inflation, the resulting price level uncertainty would be small, even over a relatively long planning horizon.[1] In the short run, on the other hand, there is a tradeoff between price and output (or employment) volatility. In the face of supply shocks, therefore, the policymaker cannot escape some tough choices.

I now turn to the second part of the question, of whether the central bank ought to have distorted preferences relative to society. The answer here is more controversial. As McCallum noted in chapter 8 of this volume, there are two views in the literature, and both views were represented at this conference. According to the "*credibility view,*" monetary policy suffers from an endemic lack of credibility.[2] With sequential decision-making, monetary policy choices face a binding incentive constraint, lack of credibility, which in equilibrium results in excessively high average inflation. According to this view, the answer to question (b) is a clear and resounding yes. To offset the inflation bias, society ought to delegate monetary policy to an agency with distorted preferences relative to its own preferences. The optimal delegation reinforces the mandate to keep inflation low, and can be interpreted as an inflation target. This is the sense in which it is optimal to "give priority" to price stability over other goals. How exactly this priority should be stated – whether as a general mandate, or a numerical target, or as an exclusive mandate to only worry about price stability, is highly controversial. But, according to this view, it is clear that the central bank should give more weight to price stability than society itself does.

According to the "*pragmatic view*," instead, monetary policy does not lack credibility in general. The problem instead lies with the political process. Hence, the answer to question (b) is no. Central bank independence is still needed, and so is a clear mandate to price stability. But the reason is to prevent a distortion, namely to protect the central bank from distortions emanating from the political process, in particular, to protect it from excessive myopia, or even from its own mistakes. In the absence of these external distortions, monetary policy choices would maximize social welfare. Not surprisingly, this view appears to be shared by most policymakers, and perhaps is the dominant view at this conference.[3]

Thus, according, to both views, central bank independence, a mandate to price stability, transparency, accountability, are all desirable. And indeed the two views are not mutually exclusive. But the reasons offered for these institutional aspects are very different. These differences matter a lot when thinking about the more practical details of the institutional arrangement.

This takes me to the next question addressed at this conference: *Should monetary policy aim at meeting a prespecified quantitative nominal target, and if so which one?* Again, it is useful to break this question into several parts. The first and most obvious one is: (a) *What are the benefits of a nominal target*?

According to the "*credibility view*" they are clear: to offset the incentive constraint and restore credibility. Missing a target is costly for the public officials in charge of the monetary policy, particularly if the target is assigned from the outside (less so if they are self-imposed). A nominal target therefore increases the cost of inflation and offsets the inflation bias. As a result, the nominal target also anchors inflation expectations more firmly.

According to the "*pragmatic view*," the benefits of a nominal target are also clear. If the central bank has been given the mandate to meet a target, then it is more likely to resist political pressures to accommodate shocks or to deviate from the optimal path. Hence, a nominal target defends the central bank in the pursuit of low inflation.

Naturally, according to both views, having a nominal target also has other benefits. It insures consistency of the internal decision-making process, it forces the central bank to think through a large number of possible contingencies, it can be used as a communication device to make policy more transparent.

It is important however to stress the differences implicit in these two views, because they have different implications for how to optimally design a nominal target. I provide three examples of this. First, according to the "*credibility view*," an ideal nominal target is closely tied to the incentive problem to be corrected. Hence, an inflation target is best. Other nominal targets, such as nominal income growth or money growth, would also do, but they become less useful if they are not closely correlated with inflation. This aspect is instead less important for the "*pragmatic view*," since the role of the target is not to correct an inflation bias.

Second, according to the "*credibility view*," a target is more effective if it is imposed from the outside (if it is an assigned target) than if it is self-imposed. The reason is that, if the target is assigned, it is not up to the central bank to abandon it. Moreover, it is probably more costly to miss an assigned target than a self-imposed one: missing an assigned target means that the agency fails precisely where it was responsible to its principals. According to the "*practical view*," instead, the distinction between self-imposed and assigned targets is again not so important. Indeed, it is commonly thought that the Federal Reserve chose to give more emphasis to M1 targets in 1979–82 because it wanted to be isolated from pressures to abandon its disinflation policy; when these pressures faded because the disinflation had been achieved, the targets were deemphasized.

Third, according to the "*credibility view*," the target should be formulated as an interval, not as a single value, because the central bank ought to be held responsible for hitting the target: a single reference value is impossible to meet exactly, and hence missing it carries no penalty. According to the "*pragmatic view*," instead, a single reference value could be better, since it is more easily understood and provides a more visible reference point.[4]

I now turn to the second part of the question: (b) *What are the costs of imposing a nominal target on monetary policy*?

Again, here there is some disagreement over the size and nature of these costs. This disagreement cuts across the two views summarized above. According to the more conventional position, the costs of a target are that it constraints or distorts the response to new information (that is, to shocks that hit the economy). In this sense, there is a tradeoff between variability of output and of prices. A nominal target reduces price volatility, at the expense of larger output volatility (see Rogoff, 1985).

This view has been challenged by some recent work on optimal institution design (Persson and Tabellini, 1993; Walsh, 1994). If the targeting arrangement is optimally designed, then there is not such a tradeoff. The optimal marginal penalty for missing the target is a (possibly state contingent) constant. That is, the optimal arrangement is to "tax" the central bank according to a linear function in the target. Such a linear tax affects average (and expected) inflation, but not the response to shocks. Thus, the tradeoff between price and output volatility only arises if, due to incomplete contracting, risk aversion of the agent, or other complications, the targeting arrangement cannot impose such a linear penalty. The empirical evidence supports the claim that there is no tradeoff (see, for instance, Grilli, Masciandaro and Tabellini, 1990), but naturally other forces may be at work.

According to this more recent view, the relevant tradeoff in designing the target is between information and incentives. For instance, adding contingencies or escape clauses in the targeting arrangement enables one to exploit more information, but weakens the incentive effects of the target. Or, in choosing between money and inflation, the latter is closer to the source of the incentive problem, but the former is more easily controllable and with less delay, so that there is more information about what the central bank is really doing.

On the basis of this assessment of the benefits and costs of a nominal target, what is the verdict? *Should monetary policy follow a nominal target, or not?* Despite the disagreements mentioned above, some consensus did emerge from the conference. With regard to the real-world arrangements, we do observe a trend in favor of explicit nominal targets. The industrial countries that do not target either inflation or money or the exchange rate are becoming a minority. There exist countries where the central bank does not explicitly target any nominal variable, most notably the USA and Japan. But even in some of these countries (e.g., the USA and Italy), it can be said that the authorities are implicitly targeting inflation. It is a fact that policymakers seem to be abandoning what Tommaso Padoa-Schioppa in his opening remarks labeled the "classic style" of monetary policy.

With regard to the choice of variable, the ideal target should have the following properties. It should be closely related to inflation. It should be simple, precise and easily observable. It should be controllable, though possibly with error. It should allow the central bank to accommodate to some extent the impact effect on prices of purely exogenous shocks, such as changes in indirect taxes or in world commodity prices. Some of these properties are mutually exclusive. Hence, the optimal target inevitably entails some tradeoffs. The tradeoffs could vary across countries, and thus it is not surprising if the solution and the details of the arrangement also vary across countries. Nevertheless, here too the empirical evidence discussed at this conference points to some trends. Money demand has become more unstable everywhere. Thus, we observe a trend away from intermediate money targets in many countries. Moreover, the globalization of financial markets and the removal of capital controls has made exchange rate targeting unfeasible for many countries. On the other hand, we do observe a trend in favor of inflation targeting, with money and the exchange rate used as important *indicators* of future inflation, but no longer as exclusive targets. I think that this trend is indeed supported by economic theory.

A third question received much attention in the conference: *Should monetary policy be conducted according to a rule?* This question is related to the previous one. But it is not a very good question. If by a rule we mean a mapping from the state of the world to a setting for the policy instrument, then in practice monetary policy always follows a rule. Rather, the relevant issues concern the properties of alternative rules, in terms of social welfare but also in terms of their enforceability.

There is a weak answer to this question, which essentially says that policymakers should at least be aware that they are following a rule. Thus, they should always plan for all contingencies, pay attention to the consistency of their behavior, and communicate their intentions in the form of a policy rule. Behaving in this way clearly facilitates communications and helps to avoid mistakes.

There is also a stronger answer to the question, which however is much more controversial. It is that monetary policy ought to be conducted according to a mechanical rule, such as a *k*-percent money growth rule, or a more sophisticated feedback rule such as stabilizing the forecast of nominal income, where the forecast is taken from a vector autoregression model, or from outside forecasters (for example, Hall and Mankiw, 1993).

Several objections to this strong answer were voiced at the conference. The first and most simple objection is that it leads to suboptimal policy responses, because it forces the policymaker to neglect other information. A second objection is a version of the Lucas critique (or, more narrowly, of Goodhart Law): the underlying structure of the economy is probably not stable across alternative policy regimes. Hence, the welfare gains of following a specific rule, or the choice among alternative feedback rules, cannot be reliably assessed on the basis of past evidence. But perhaps the most fundamental objection is that simple or sophisticated feedback rules are not enforceable. In practice monetary policy will never abandon some elements of judgment and reoptimization. Hence, we should not search for the optimal rule when thinking about institution design. Rather, we should let the central bank solve that problem sequentially (i.e., with reoptimization), and instead focus the institution design problem on how to correct its possibly distorted incentives, by giving it sufficient independence, and by assigning an appropriate mandate, such as maintaining price stability or meeting a specific quantitative target.

Despite these objections, the analysis of alternative feedback rules can play a useful role as an operational guide to policy. But before turning to the operational issues, I want to briefly discuss one last institution design question that received attention at the conference: *Should the central bank fully disclose its information?*

In the real world there is clearly a trend in favor of more disclosure. Central banking is no longer a secretive art. Nevertheless, a distinction was suggested at the conference, between goals and operating procedures. Full disclosure of the policy goals is generally regarded as desirable, because it increases the accountability of monetary policy and it enhances policy credibility. Exactly how to make the central bank more accountable is problematic, because of the lags in the effects of monetary policy. But there is no doubt that more information about the policy goals increases accountability, and this is desirable.

On the other hand, policymakers seem to be generally less enthusiastic about full and timely disclosure of the operating targets and procedures of monetary policy. They fear that full disclosure here could be destabilizing, as financial markets sometimes over-react to information, and monetary policy could become less effective. This concern is supported by economic theory, under specific circumstances.[5]

3 THE OPERATING PROCEDURES

Several issues discussed at the conference concerned the actual implementation of monetary policy within a given institutional framework. A question that received much attention was: *What are the properties of an optimal "feedback mechanism" to control inflation?*

That is, how do central banks forecast inflation (over what horizon, with the help of which variables), how do they respond to this forecast, and how should they do it? In the work done by John Taylor for the USA and other industrial countries, it is found that a *k*-percent money growth rule can be improved upon by letting money respond to output growth but not to prices. McCallum and others have found that it is possible to do even better by allowing the feedback mechanism to also respond to velocity shocks. These automatic feedback rules, however, are only one of several other bits of information used by most central banks to forecast inflation and respond to it. In general, there is not a single optimal procedure, and different countries rely on different variables and methods. Two variables generally regarded as important indicators of future inflation are money growth and the exchange rate (the latter particularly, and not surprisingly, in smaller and hence more open economies).

The general rule, however, seems to be that we still know very little about the answer to this question. The link between policy instruments and inflation is very indirect, and changes across countries and time. Policymakers need to rely on lots of information and inevitably make use of judgment and discretion.

A puzzle was noted, that deserves attention. In theory and in the numerical simulations of optimal feedback rules, policy ought to respond immediately to any new information. Yet, in the real world, we generally observe a very gradual policy response to the shocks that hit the economy. Why this gradualism? There is probably more than one answer, but none of them is very well understood. Often the policymaker is ignorant about the nature and permanence of the shocks, or about the response of the economy to a monetary policy innovation. In this case, gradualism reflects the learning of the policymaker. But sometimes a gradual response reflects a genuine desire for smoothing interest rate changes, perhaps for fear of financial instability. Some conference participants also hinted that a sudden and very sharp policy response could generate some form of "instrument instability"; that is, the dynamic response of the economy could force the policymaker to sharp policy reversals to avoid destabilizing the macroeconomy.

Another question that was much discussed, but about which little is known, is the following: *Should monetary policy respond to asset prices?* Clearly, monetary policy should endeavor to avoid a collapse of the financial system. In exceptional circumstances, this may call for a policy response to sudden changes in asset prices, such as after the US stock market crash of October 1987 or as in Japan currently.

A more controversial question is to what extent monetary policy ought to respond to the exchange rate. As already remarked, the exchange rate is an important indicator of future inflation in a number of countries; it is also used in the construction of the so-called "monetary conditions index," a measure of the monetary policy stance in many small open economies.

It is therefore generally accepted that an interest rate response to exchange rate changes may be appropriate, with reference to the goal of controlling and stabilizing aggregate demand. However, a policy response directed at influencing the exchange rate itself would be more controversial, as witnessed by the experience of Japan in the 1990s. Moreover, the numerical simulations conducted by John Taylor and others concerning the properties of alternative feedback mechanisms have generally indicated that it is better not to respond to the exchange rate.

An even more controversial question is whether monetary policy should deliberately attempt to avoid "speculative changes" in asset prices. The argument in favor is that movements in asset prices could reflect speculative bubbles. If the authorities could identify the bubble and break it, then they would avoid destabilizing effects on the economy. The recent stock market and land price "bubbles" in Japan are an often quoted example. What is a bubble, however, is often clear *ex post*, but not *ex ante*. Moreover, sometimes asset prices give conflicting signals, and choosing which one to stabilize or respond to could be extremely difficult. In Japan, for instance, when the stock market was booming, indicating that monetary policy was perhaps too loose, the yen was rapidly appreciating, indicating the opposite.

The general conclusion seems to be that monetary policy ought to respond to asset prices, because they often carry information about market expectations, and because they influence prices and aggregate demand. But monetary policy should not directly aim at influencing or stabilizing asset prices, except in very exceptional circumstances.

4 CONCLUDING REMARKS

Many other questions were raised and discussed at the conference. For instance, should monetary and regulatory policies be run by different agencies? How do we measure the stance of monetary policy? Shall monetary policy instruments also include derivative instruments? Space constraints prevent me from addressing them all.

Going through the questions discussed in the previous pages, as well as the others that I did not talk about, left me with a very clear impression. We seem to know more about the answers to the first set of questions, concerning institution design, than to the second, more practical questions. This impression could reflect my bias as a researcher, and it is possible that policymakers have left the conference with just the opposite impression. But it is a fact that monetary policy institutions have changed remarkably over the past decade, and so has our way of thinking about the long-run goals of monetary policy and the general features of an optimal institutional framework. It is now commonly accepted that price stability ought to be the primary concern of monetary policy; that central bankers ought to be independent in the pursuit of such goals; that their decision-making process ought to be structured and consistent, but also transparent; that some form of precommitment is desirable because it makes monetary policy more credible and effective. These are all dramatic changes in the monetary policy regime relative to that prevailing in most countries in the late 1970s or early 1980s, and they are clearly changes for the better.

The same consensus and the same uniformity of real-world experiences does not exist with regard to the operational aspects of monetary policy. This points to a fruitful direction for economic research. But it would not be surprising if the practical aspects of monetary policy depended much more on specific circumstances than the general principles and strategies. If so, the search for optimal operational procedures in monetary policy is not likely to give general and definitive answers. The practice of monetary policy, within a given institutional framework, is likely to remain an art, guided by experience, trial and error.

Notes

1. Svensson (1995) provides a recent analysis of price level inflation targeting and discusses many of these issues. He presents several convincing arguments in favor of price level targeting.
2. Credibility is a better word than dynamic inconsistency, since it is easily understood in terms of modern game theory. Dynamic inconsistency is the term originally introduced in the seminal contribution of Kydland and Prescott, but has generated (and probably continues to generate) much confusion because sometimes it is used with reference to non-equilibrium outcomes.
3. Policymakers are generally reluctant to accept the idea that they have an incentive to create surprise inflation. If anything, they rather see themselves as trying to bring inflation down, sometimes unsuccessfully. But this subjective attitude of policymakers is entirely consistent with the "credibility view." According to this view, *in equilibrium* there is really no incentive to create surprise inflation. On the contrary, inflation and expected inflation are too high. Lack of credibility manifests itself in that policymakers tend to lose control of private sector expectations. Once that happens, bringing inflation down can only be done by reducing output growth below potential.
4. This argument was suggested at the conference by Rick Mishkin in the comments to chapter 9.
5. See in particular Cukierman and Meltzer (1986), Dotsey (1986), and Tabellini (1987).

References

Cukierman, A. and Meltzer, A. (1986) "A Theory of Ambiguity, Credibility and Inflation under Discretion and Asymmetric Information," *Econometrica*, 54 (September), pp. 1099–1128.

Dotsey, M. (1986) "Monetary Policy, Secrecy and Federal Funds Rate Behavior," *Journal of Monetary Economics*, 20, pp. 463–74.

Grilli, V., Masciandaro, D. and Tabellini, G. (1990) "Political and Monetary Institutions and Monetary and Financial Policies in the Industrial Countries," *Economic Policy*, 13 (October), pp. 341–92.

Hall, R. and Mankiw, G. (1993) "Nominal Income Targeting," NBER Working Paper No. 4439.

Persson, T. and Tabellini, G. (1993) "Designing Institutions for Monetary Stability," Carnegie–Rochester Conference Series in Public Policy (Fall), pp. 53–84.

Rogoff, K. (1985) "The Optimal Degree of Commitment to an Intermediate Monetary Target," *Quarterly Journal of Economics*, 100, pp. 1169–90.

Svensson, L. (1995) "Price Level Targeting versus Inflation Targeting: A Free Lunch?," mimeo, University of Stockholm.

Tabellini, G. (1987) "Secrecy of Monetary Policy and the Variability of Interest Rates," *Journal of Money Credit and Banking*, 19 (November), pp. 425–36.

Walsh, C. (1994) "Optimal Contract for Central Bankers," *American Economic Review*, 85, pp. 150–67.

Part VI
Background Paper

13 The Policy Objectives and the Optimal Institutional Framework of a Central Bank*

Kunio Okina

I INTRODUCTION

In recent years, an inflation targeting approach to monetary policy has been gaining popularity among European and Oceanian policymakers while the monetary targeting approach, which once dominated policy discussions in the 1970s, has been somewhat losing support, especially in the United States. In Europe, the scheduled emergence of Economic and Monetary Union and establishment of the European System of Central Banks have stimulated discussions on the desirable institutional framework for a central banking system to achieve price stability. At the same time, France, Italy, Belgium, and Spain have amended their statutory frameworks to strengthen the independence of their central banks.

Japan, in the meantime, seems to have succeeded in maintaining price stability since the late 1980s, although its economy has experienced a large swing in the business cycle due to the emergence and collapse of the so-called "bubble economy." The bursting of the bubble economy has also placed stress on the financial system and this, together with an observation of a large swing in the money supply, has caused some to argue that the Bank of Japan should have tightened its monetary policy during the bubble economy period even if this might have led to a decline in the consumer price level (Figure 13.1). An amendment to the Bank of Japan Act that would strengthen its independence is often discussed, but has rarely focused on the issue of what might be the most optimal

* Views presented here are those of the author, and not necessarily those of the Bank of Japan. I am grateful to David Laidler and John Taylor, as well as to Kazumasa Iwata, Keimei Kaizuka, Kazuo Ueda, Hiroshi Yoshikawa, and other participants in a workshop at the Institute for Monetary and Economic Studies in the Bank of Japan for many helpful comments.

Figure 13.1 Money supply and prices

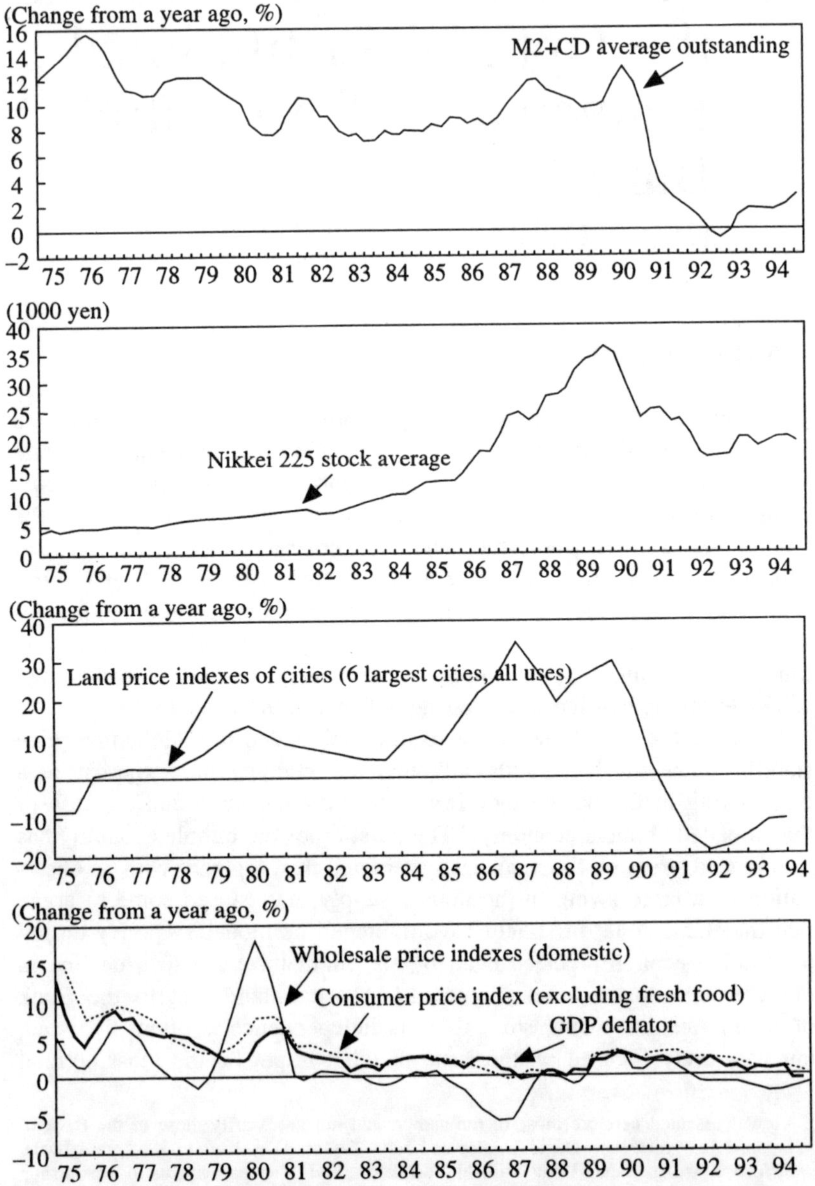

Sources: Economic Planning Agency, "Annual Report on National Acounts"; Management and Cordination Agency, "Consumer Price Index"; Bank of Japan, "Economic Statistics Monthly"; Japan Real Estate Institute, "Land Price Indexes of Cities."

institutional framework to help achieve the objectives of monetary policy more effectively.

With this situation in mind, the following two questions are discussed in this chapter. First, what policy objectives should a central bank pursue? Second, what is the optimal institutional framework in which a central bank can most effectively achieve those objectives?

Section 2 discusses sustainable economic growth and its relationship with price stability, which is regarded as the main objective of monetary policy by many central banks. Section 3 examines the operational definition of price stability. In Sections 4 and 5, the issue of the independence of a central bank and the optimal institutional framework to achieve the policy objectives are discussed. Section 4 examines the usefulness of independence in achieving the policy objectives. Section 5 asks what institutional framework helps a central bank gain credibility and hence achieve its policy objective most effectively. Finally, Section 6 summarizes the main conclusions.

2 THE OBJECTIVES OF MONETARY POLICY

2.1 Economic Policy and Sustainable Growth

The ultimate objective of economic policy is to improve the economic welfare of the people. This general policy principle seems to embrace many specific goals such as higher real income, fairer income distribution, a better natural environment, and the higher efficiency and utility of economic activities.

In fact, the reduced efficiency and utility of economic activities or increased unfairness of income distribution could undermine the economy's ability to achieve sustainable economic growth. Conversely, sustainable economic growth could make it possible for an economy to achieve continuous improvement in economic welfare without wasting limited resources and without intensifying social conflict arising from unfair income distribution. Therefore, if an economy has achieved sustainable economic growth, then its economic policy may be judged to have been successful.

From this viewpoint, price stability and financial system stability are important not only for their own sake but for achieving sustainable economic growth, which translates into a continuous improvement in economic welfare.[1] Even though price stability helps achieve sustainable economic growth, it cannot realize sustainable economic growth by itself because economic growth depends on many other factors. Therefore, the central bank alone cannot be held responsible for the policy of achieving sustainable growth.

2.2 Price Stability as the Main Objective of Monetary Policy

In recent years, a view that monetary policy should only aim at achieving price stability is gaining popularity. The central banks of the United Kingdom, Canada, Sweden, New Zealand, Finland, Australia, and Spain have started practicing inflation targeting policies which aim at containing the rate of inflation within a certain target range.

There are at least three reasons for this development. First, these countries previously experienced relatively high and persistent inflation under a monetary policy which used monetary aggregates or exchange rates as an intermediate target. Second, they might believe in the argument that money is neutral with respect to real economic activity and only affects the price level in the long run, and that therefore monetary policy should only aim at maintaining price stability. Even so, it cannot be denied that monetary policy affects real economic activity such as output and employment. I will discuss later how these inflation targeting countries deal with this problem. Third, it can be argued from the perspective of political economy that by setting price stability as the sole objective of monetary policy, the central bank can achieve sustainable economic growth more easily because it mitigates a disruptive inflationary bias in the policymaking process. In fact, political considerations often produce an inflationary bias in the economic policymaking process. If this bias undermines the economy's ability to achieve sustainable economic growth, then a central bank can improve macroeconomic performance by persistently pursuing the objective of price stability because this helps offset the politically induced inflationary bias. Later we will discuss this issue in connection with the related issue of the policy independence of a central bank.

Granting that price stability is important not only for its own sake but for achieving sustainable growth, a central banker then has to know the precise relationship between sustainable economic growth and price stability. Moreover the operational definition of price stability becomes important in the actual implementation of monetary policy. For example, the following questions arise. Should the price index relevant for monetary policy be the standard price indexes such as WPI and CPI, or some new indexes which include asset prices (i.e., land price, stock price)? Should the inflation rate so measured be kept to zero, or mildly positive or negative?

3 THE OPERATIONAL DEFINITION OF PRICE STABILITY

3.1 Importance of a Cost–Price Relationship

From the perspective of achieving sustainable growth, what is the operational definition of price stability? The traditional answer has been to maintain a representative price index such as the Consumer Price Index (CPI) at zero growth. This helps prevent inflationary expectations of households and firms from developing, and helps reduce uncertainty arising from price volatility that may adversely affect consumption and investment decisions. In theory, it may be sufficient to maintain a constant rate of moderate inflation, not necessarily zero inflation, to avoid the uncertainty of the future developments of inflation. However, in practice, many central bankers have learned that it is difficult to prevent moderate inflation not only from fluctuating but also from accelerating. Consequently the idea of a zero inflation target has many strong proponents among central bankers.[2]

The idea of zero inflation as the sole monetary policy target, however, finds fewer proponents in Japan because of its recent experience with the bursting of the bubble economy, which produced a large swing in the business cycle under relatively stable consumer prices. A policy designed to offset some shocks may contribute to realizing sustainable economic growth even if it means tolerating some price fluctuations in the short run.

There are two possibilities regarding the relationship between economic growth and volatility of economic fluctuations: one is that economic fluctuations lead to high growth if the cause of such fluctuations is technological innovation; the other possibility is that they reduce growth and investment by increasing uncertainty about future economic conditions. Some empirical evidence seems to support the latter view, although it does not necessarily follow that policymakers must smooth out economic fluctuations caused by technological innovation.[3] In short, identifying the cause of shocks becomes crucial for implementing proper economic policy.

A standard solution to this policy problem is to distinguish between demand shocks and supply shocks, and then to determine appropriate monetary policy according to the cause. In practice, however, it is sometimes difficult to distinguish between demand and supply shocks; to do so, some additional information such as the markup between production costs and product prices becomes necessary. For example, even if product prices are stable, production costs are not necessarily stable; and if the markup or profit fluctuates widely, so do output volume and investment. This magnifies the business cycle and increases uncertainty about future economic conditions, which undermines the economy's ability to achieve sustainable economic growth. Therefore, a central banker should pay close attention to price–cost movements in determining monetary policy. The importance of price–cost movements has been suggested from both an empirical and a theoretical[4] point of view. Economists who emphasize historical experience claim that, based on the experience of the United States in the 1920s, monetary policy should be tightened even under price stability if costs are declining; it is considered as a sort of inflation when prices do not decline despite a decline in costs. According to this view, the objective of monetary policy should be the maintenance of price level consistent with the cost rather than mere maintenance of a price level. Kosai (1992) referred to Rothbard (1963) as an example of this argument.

For example, because of the yen's appreciation, general price stability can coexist with an increase in corporate profits and stock prices because the lower production costs can offset inflationary pressure stemming from increased demand. In such a case, the proponents who emphasize the importance of the cost–price relationship would argue that monetary policy should be aimed at reducing product prices in line with their production costs. Such monetary policy would help realize a price level that would be consistent with sustainable economic growth.

In fact, Japan's recent experience seems to suggest the importance of this cost–price relationship. For example, in an application of the analysis of Hall (1988), Baba (1996) finds that the marginal markup for the non-manufacturing sector significantly exceeded its trendline at the time of the yen's appreciation following the 1985 Plaza Agreement (Figure 13.2). Moreover, the movement of marginal markup appears to have slightly preceded the movement of the current profit to sales ratio (Figure 13.3). Unfortunately, it is difficult to obtain timely and accurate information on the marginal markup and to determine the acceptable extent of a change in the cost–price structure.[5] Furthermore, there remains an important though somewhat technical problem in distinguishing between the primary and secondary effects of a supply shock.

A related traditional idea with respect to monetary policy is to prevent an inflationary (deflationary) spiral of wage and price increases (decreases). The spiral increase in wages and prices is a typical example of inflation and the traditional response is to nip such "wage inflation" in the bud. Therefore, the appropriate policy prescription is to tighten monetary policy when an exogenous shock increases factor costs which spill over to prices as well as wages, thereby triggering an inflationary wage–price spiral. The same argument applies to an exogenous shock which triggers a deflationary wage–price spiral.

Figure 13.2 Markup rate for the non-manufacturing industry

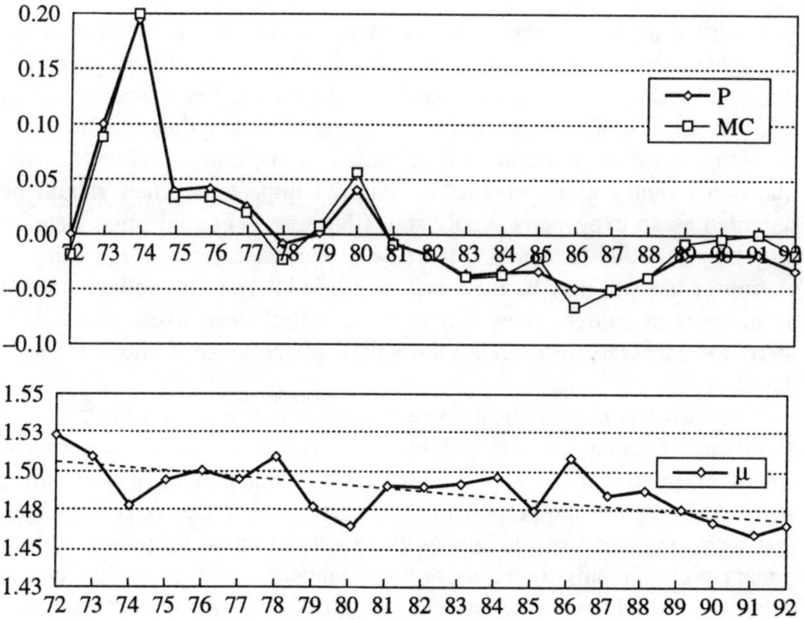

P: Price.
MC: Marginal cost.
μ: Markup rate.

Source: Baba (1996).

Figure 13.3 Markup rate for the non-manufacturing industry and current profits to sales ratio

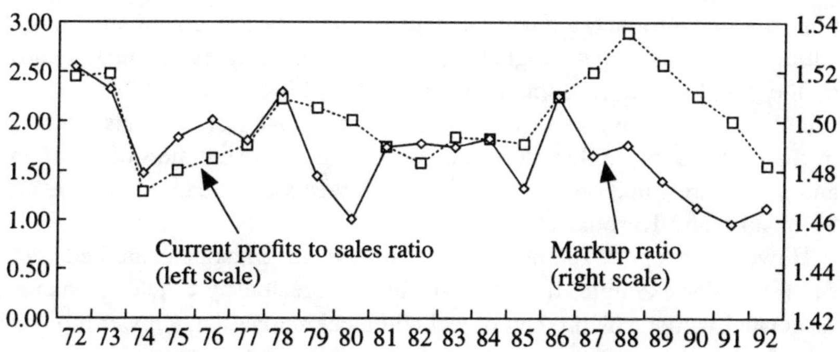

Source: Baba (1996).

3.2 Caveats in the Use of the Markup and a Price Index

In reality, a purely exogenous shock like an earthquake is rather unusual, and most shocks – even if they may appear exogenous at first – are generally related to domestic economic developments. For example, an oil price shock, a sudden depreciation of the yen, and an indirect tax increase are often cited as examples of exogenous price shocks. However, the question remains as to whether their initial impact on prices should be regarded as an exogenous supply shock because (1) an oil price increase may be partly due to a sudden increase in domestic demand; (2) a depreciation of the yen may be the result of a low interest rate policy; and (3) an increase in indirect taxes may be the result of loose fiscal policy. It is therefore necessary to examine the nature of the original shock in more detail.

A tentative policy implication seems to be that a central bank should avoid large fluctuations in output and employment as well as markups and wages originating from supply shocks while maintaining general price stability. However, the proponents of a rule-based monetary policy argue that with long and variable lags in the effects of monetary policy, discretionary policy is only too likely to make matters worse rather than better, either in a deflationary or an inflationary direction (Laidler, 1995), and that flexible policy actions are deemed discretionary, and will produce an inflationary bias. Since the first issue is discussed in chapter 4 of this volume, the latter issue will be discussed in this chapter.

In addition to the examination of the above cost–price relationship, the reliability of a price index is another important issue that needs to be addressed in considering the operational definition of price stability. There is a substantial accumulation of research in the United States concerning (1) the extent of a bias in CPI and (2) the cause of such a bias (introduction of a new product, a quality change due mainly to technological innovation, problems in the weighing method and price index formula, a shift in the retail location from high-priced downtown shops to low-priced suburban shops, and so on). This is an important issue because a bias in the price index could result in a substantial overestimation of inflation and an underestimation of real growth (Shiratsuka, 1995a, 1995c, 1995d; Shiratsuka and Kuroda, 1995).

However, the policy implications of such a bias must be examined very carefully. For example, if an upward bias is created by a quality change associated with a new product or technological innovation, a lower product price and higher profit can coexist. Such a bias in the price index is not necessarily deflationary from the macroeconomic viewpoint, even though it does not accurately represent the cost of living for consumers. In this case, a central bank does not have to offset such price decline, taking into account the bias. Thus, it would be a mistake to jump to the conclusion that an upward bias in measuring the cost of living for consumers immediately leads to a deflationary bias in monetary policy.

The policy implications of a bias in the price index may differ across countries and across time. For example, in the United States, the issue of a bias in CPI has been recently discussed in terms of its impact on tax revenue and government expenditure. Chairman Greenspan of the Federal Reserve Board stated in the Senate Budget Committee that because CPI had an upward bias, government expenditures indexed to it should be reexamined thoroughly by professional economists instead of being automatically indexed along with the increase in CPI. He listed the following factors that may produce an upward bias in CPI: (1) the use of fixed weights which ignores the substitution effects of relative price changes, (2) the appearance of many discount stores, (3) difficulties in measuring improvements in product and service qualities, and (4) sampling lag for including new products, such as PCs and video cameras, in the CPI basket (Greenspan, 1995). O'Neill, Director of the Congressional Budget Office (CBO), stated that the upward bias in CPI is estimated to be about 0.2–0.8 of a percentage point; and that, in view of the need to restrain government expenditures, recommended a review of the methodology of determining inflation-indexed expenditures.[6]

3.3 Nominal GDP Targeting and Money Supply Targeting

Another approach to monetary policy aimed at realizing sustainable economic growth is nominal GDP targeting. The proponents argue that nominal GDP, rather than money supply, should be an intermediate target for monetary policy. They point out that the average rate of nominal GDP growth necessary to yield a desired rate of inflation can be more accurately determined than that of money supply; that the maintenance of steady nominal GDP growth has better automatic stabilization properties in response to some kind of shocks; and that the operation of nominal GDP targeting has greater immunity to regulatory changes and technological innovation in the monetary and financial sector.[7]

However, some potential problems of nominal GDP targeting can be pointed out: (1) nominal GDP is difficult to control by monetary policy; (2) nominal GDP targeting tends to be inflationary if a government forecasts higher growth than warranted, but a central bank should nevertheless use this forecast as a target; and (3) nominal GDP data are available only after a significant time lag. In addition, even if nominal GDP targeting is to be adopted, it does not mean that money supply becomes irrelevant. In fact, the correlation between M2+CDs and nominal GDP in Japan appears to have strengthened since 1990 even though that between money supply and the general price level – which the monetarists emphasized – has broken down. If so, nominal GDP targeting may strengthen the importance of money supply as an information variable for nominal GDP that is available in a timely manner.

Furthermore, apart from a nominal GDP targeting approach, it could still be argued that stable money supply would contribute to achieving sustainable economic growth by preventing itself from becoming a source of monetary disturbances that could develop into real disturbances in the financial sector. For example, Japan's experience of the bubble economy in the late 1980s suggests that when asset prices are sharply rising under price stability, restrictive monetary policy to stabilize the growth of monetary aggregates might be appropriate even if it might mean a fall in prices owing to the price reduction effect of the yen's appreciation.

Since the latter half of 1990, the annual growth of M2+CDs has declined significantly from a double-digit figure to a negative one against the background of the slowdown in the Japanese economy. We have heard diverse arguments as to whether such a dramatic decline has provided useful information regarding the contraction of actual economic activity; some argue that the observed decline was an inevitable reaction because the level of monetary aggregates had reached a high level in mid-1990 due to the successive high annual growth since the late 1980s. However, the view which relates large decline in the growth of monetary aggregates to the contraction of economic activity became dominant as the economy turned out to be more stagnant than anticipated.

Nonetheless, even if money supply plays an important role in monetary policy, financial innovation makes money supply an illusive concept because the appropriate measure of money supply changes over time.[8] Therefore, a central bank that announces a money supply range as an intermediate target and commits itself to that target will risk losing credibility. For example, it may end up making policy errors by stubbornly committing itself to a target or it may have to frequently revise the target in view of changing economic conditions. Either way the central bank will lose credibility, making it more difficult to conduct effective monetary policy. The decision of many central bankers to adopt an inflation targeting approach with escape clauses seems to have been influenced by such a consideration.

4 MONETARY POLICY AND THE INDEPENDENCE OF A CENTRAL BANK

In the preceding sections, we have argued that the ultimate objective of monetary policy is to achieve sustainable economic growth; and that a central bank should pursue this objective by stabilizing prices and responding to exogenous shocks in such a way that it does not undermine the economy's ability to achieve sustainable growth. Conducting monetary policy toward this goal will require careful examination and use of information variables such as price markups and money supply.

The next question is how and under what conditions a central bank can achieve the monetary policy objective most effectively. "Rules versus discretion" in the conduct of monetary policy has been the well-known approach adopted when discussing these questions. In recent years, however, attention has been focused on an empirical study of the relationship between the independence of a central bank and success in attaining the monetary policy objective.[9] A typical argument is that the more independent a central bank is, the lower inflation will be.

If it is indeed the case that greater independence of a central bank raises its credibility, which in turn lowers the cost of reducing inflation, then strengthening independence would be a "free lunch" for a central bank pursuing the policy objective of price stability without any serious economic costs.

The independence of a central bank is also increasingly recognized as a very important issue by policymakers. For example, with a view to the scheduled establishment of the European System of Central Banks, some European countries have strengthened the independence of their central banks since the agreement of the Maastricht Treaty. In the United Kingdom, which left the Exchange Rate Mechanism, the Roll Committee of the Centre for Economic Policy Research (CEPR) and the Treasury and Civil Service Committee of the House of Commons published reports in October and December 1993, respectively, proposing the independence of the Bank of England from the government. In the United States, active discussions are under way regarding reform of the Federal Reserve System, including the publication of the minutes of the Federal Open Market Committee.

Two important questions emerged from these discussions: First, what is the relationship between the argument of the need for the independence of a central bank and the traditional debate of "rules versus discretion" in the conduct of monetary policy? Second, what is the optimal institutional framework in which independent central banks are consistent with democratic

Figure 13.4 Inflation rate and central bank independence (1955–88)

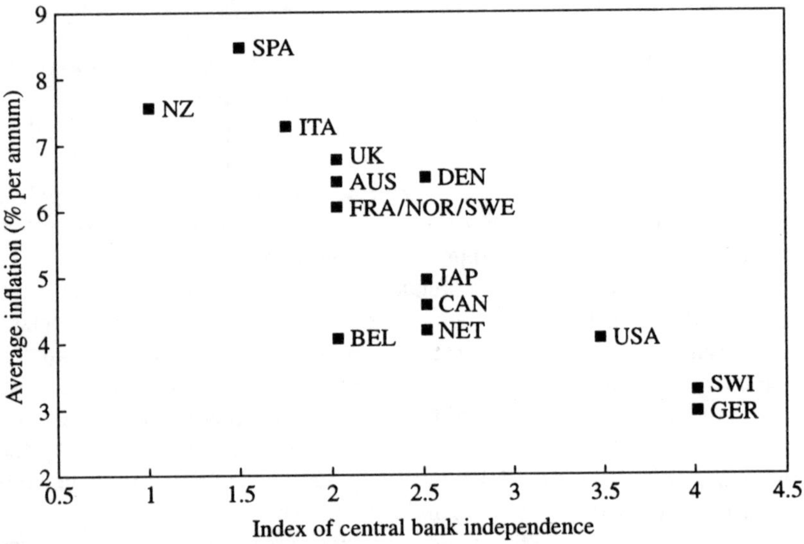

Source: Alesina and Summers (1993).

controls and institutions? In the following sections, we will discuss the conduct of efficient monetary policy and central bank independence for the purpose of realizing non-inflationary sustainable economic growth.

4.1 Reasons for Central Bank Independence

There are various reasons why central bank independence is necessary. The independence of a central bank should be examined from a broad perspective, though in this chapter we review only some of the recent discussions among academic economists.

Recent advocates of greater central bank independence often base their arguments on the empirical finding that inflation tends to be lower in countries which have an independent central bank (Figure 13.4). The report of the Roll Committee also points out this fact as well as that of the weak correlation between the degree of central bank independence and economic growth (Figure 13.5), and argues that strengthening the independence of a central bank provides a costless way to reduce inflation without adversely affecting long-term growth.

Figure 13.5 Economic growth and central bank independence (1955–88)

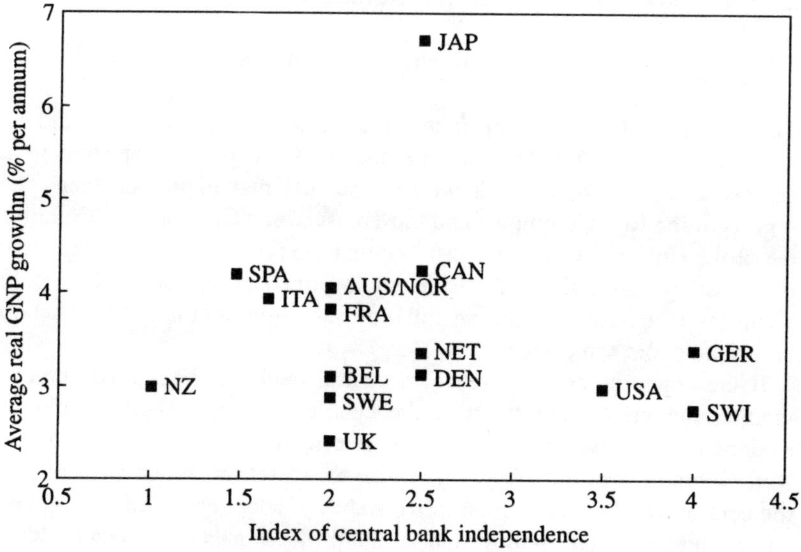

Source: Alesina and Summers (1993).

Nevertheless, it is very difficult to confirm this proposition empirically. Even the interpretation of Figures 13.4 and 13.5 needs reservation. First, there are too many ways to quantify the degree of central bank independence. Second, the negative correlation between the degree of central bank independence and the rate of inflation may not prove that there is a causal relationship. For example, it may be the case that while those people holding strong anti-inflation sentiments may give the central bank full backing for its independence, they may at the same time vote for the government which supports an anti-inflationary economic policy. In this case there would be a negative correlation between the degree of central bank independence and the observed inflation rate; but no causal relationship between the two would exist. Third, the report of the Roll Committee seems to imply that there is no relationship between inflation and growth or between monetary policy and growth. However, some of the recent empirical studies found a negative correlation between inflation and the growth rate of total factor productivity and income per capita. There are also studies which find a positive correlation between the degree of central bank independence and the growth rate of income per capita, conditioning on other factors such as the level of education and terms of trade which are both known to affect growth performance.[10]

4.2 The Task of an Independent Central Bank

The question of whether the independence of a central bank should be strengthened must be discussed in line with the policy objective of a central bank, which we dealt with in the first part of this chapter. The reports of the Roll Committee and the Treasury and Civil Service Committee of the House of Commons propose that the primary or single objective of monetary policy should be to maintain price stability. Many European countries that have adopted an inflation targeting approach to monetary policy hold the same view.

If the objective and the task of a central bank can be agreed upon as maintaining price stability, then the central banking system should be designed to achieve that objective most effectively. The proposal of the Roll Committee offers an example: that is, to set the single objective of the central bank as maintaining price stability, adopt an inflation targeting approach to monetary policy, and let the professionals in the central bank formulate and implement monetary policy to achieve that objective.

An important reason why such a monetary framework may present an effective way to control inflation is that the public can believe in the objective of price stability because it is explicitly presented as the single objective of a central bank.

This point has been discussed among economists in the context of "rules versus discretion" with respect to the conduct of monetary policy. Economists in favor of rules argue that a central bank can bring about a better economic outcome by committing itself to a fixed policy rule that is designed to control inflation, thereby leaving no room for adopting a time-inconsistent policy. The institutionalization of an inflation targeting approach to monetary policy and the Governor's contract with the government or parliament may be viewed as an example of such "commitment technology."

However, the report of the Roll Committee proposes that with approval of parliament, the government can temporarily stop the central bank from pursuing the policy objective of price stability. This implies that the Committee recognizes the importance of examining the nature of shocks to the economy from the viewpoint of effective monetary policy, even though inflation might not affect the growth rate in the long run. In fact, few would argue to keep the hands of a central bank tied all the time even in the face of large exogenous shocks to the economy.

5 HOW TO ESTABLISH POLICY CREDIBILITY: FOUR MAIN APPROACHES

We will now restate the guiding principle for monetary policy and relate it to the policy objective and the institutional framework of an effective central bank. The starting point is the recognition that offsetting price changes originating from supply shocks may impede the achievement of sustainable economic growth because they magnify output volatility and increase investment uncertainty. Therefore it seems appropriate for a central bank to accommodate supply-induced price shocks while offsetting demand-induced price shocks to maintain price stability. With this guiding principle in mind, the next question is what is the best way to secure credibility of a central bank's commitment to price stability while realizing the ultimate policy objective of sustainable economic growth. In this section we will examine the four main approaches: (1) the inflation targeting approach, (2) the state contingent rule approach, (3) the conservative central banker approach, and (4) the "option to override the policy rule" approach.

5.1 The Inflation Targeting Approach

One possible approach is to target an inflation rate without any escape clauses. This helps establish credibility that the central bank will stabilize the general price level. However, it increases the risk that supply shocks will disturb the real economy since no flexible price adjustment to supply shocks is possible. Therefore, the social cost adhering to a strict inflation targeting approach can be very large in some cases.

Instead of a final target such as inflation, policy commitment may be directed toward an intermediate target such as money supply. One advantage of monetary targeting is that it can enhance credibility of a central bank's commitment to price stability by maintaining stable money supply while allowing price flexibility so that the market mechanism can appropriately respond to various kinds of shocks.

In fact the Bundesbank, which has gained high credibility for its anti-inflation stance, continues its commitment to maintain stable money growth. The Swiss National Bank also adopts a similar policy approach. These examples seem to suggest an importance of money supply in maintaining the credibility of the policy commitment to price stability.

In this connection there is an argument in Japan that if the Bank of Japan had committed itself more strongly to maintaining stable money growth after the 1985 Plaza Agreement, it could have avoided the subsequent asset price bubble, the large swing in the business cycle, and the instability of financial system.

However, there are important differences between the German and Japanese arguments for money supply targeting. First, if there is a stable relationship between money supply and inflation, monetary targeting and inflation targeting become equivalent in the long run.[11] The Bundesbank's policy is based on this idea. In contrast, the above-mentioned Japanese case happened while there was a divergence between the developments of money supply and price. Furthermore, in many countries, including Japan, the presumed stable relationship (cointegration) between money supply and inflation is questioned. For example, Soejima (1995a, 1995b) has examined the long-term relationship between money supply and inflation in Japan, taking into account some structural changes. His studies presented a negative conclusion. It is widely observed in many countries that financial innovation has brought instability in the money demand function, and that money supply control is becoming more difficult to achieve through manipulating short-term interest rate instruments. Instability of the money demand function implies that exogenous shocks include financial innovation, which directly alters the relationship between money supply and inflation.

5.2 The State Contingent Rule Approach

The state contingent rule provides one possible way to avoid the disruptive effects of supply shocks while at the same time maintaining a rule-based and time-consistent monetary policy. The state contingent rule specifies a complete set of state contingent plans for all possible exogenous shocks. In fact, those countries which have adopted inflation targeting have also instituted a state contingent rule and/or decided to exclude such potentially volatile prices as food and energy prices from the price index used as an inflation target.

For example, in New Zealand, the state contingent rule explicitly allows a temporary divergence from the target price range when the price increase is initially caused by such shocks as a change in indirect tax rate or a change in the terms of trade, or caused by such emergencies as a natural disaster or spread of livestock disease. In such an event, a new target range of inflation has to be fixed immediately. In Canada, the rule also allows a departure from the target price range when faced with big supply and demand shocks such as a natural disaster or sharp increase in oil prices.

Although the idea of a state contingent rule is attractive, it becomes necessary to distinguish the sources of various shocks for policy purposes, and a natural classification seems to be between supply and demand shocks.

Since monetary policy is used to control aggregate demand, it seems appropriate that it be aimed at offsetting demand shocks while allowing some price increases if they are caused by supply shocks.[12]

Nevertheless, in practice, it is often difficult to distinguish between supply and demand shocks. For example, a price shock caused by an exchange rate change can be classified as either a demand shock or a supply shock, depending on the source of the exchange rate change. It will be a demand shock if the exchange rate change is caused by domestic demand-pull inflation, and a supply shock if the change is caused by innovation in an export industry. Furthermore it is often difficult to identify the source of an exchange rate change. In such a case, it becomes necessary to check the nature of a shock by examining the movement in the cost–price relationship. Naturally, the central bank prefers to maintain a certain degree of discretion regarding the choice of an appropriate monetary policy while examining the exogenous shock carefully. As a result, the question of how to maintain the credibility of monetary policy still remains.

An ideal situation will be where a central bank has made the right policy decisions in the past and the public has confidence in its ability to effect appropriate monetary policy. In this case, the central bank can enjoy a good reputation and maintain credibility in its discretional monetary policy to bring a desirable economic outcome, without explaining its commitment to maintain price stability. However, a central bank is not an omnipotent organization that makes no mistakes. And even if it had not made any mistakes in the past, it does not follow that it will not make mistakes in the future. Indeed, a single mistake could easily demolish any reputation that has been built up.

One possible solution to this credibility problem is to publicize the policy analysis and decision-making process of the central bank, and to demonstrate the time consistency of its monetary policy, which is free from short-sighted policy change to temporarily boost output and employment. In other words, if the fundamental argument for the central bank's independence is to improve monetary policy by enhancing the credibility of its commitment to maintain price stability, then the same argument also requires enhanced transparency of the decision-making process as it relates to discretionary monetary policy.

This requires disclosure of information that is necessary to explain the central bank's policy action. Such disclosure will benefit the central bank so long as its policy action is based on a clear objective and is backed by solid economic analysis. Instead of weakening the effectiveness of a policy action, disclosure should enhance the credibility and effectiveness of monetary policy just as it improves the reputation of a corporation in the capital market resulting in lower capital costs for that corporation.

Traditionally, the central bank's stance with regard to the conduct of monetary policy can often be described as "a policy action without apology." This practice is in complete opposition to the above argument for disclosure. One possible reason why this practice was prevalent in the past is that the central bank used to regard its primary role as being the "lender of last resort" rather than as a "maker of monetary policy"; and therefore it was very cautious about disclosing information which might have caused a "run on a bank." This consideration is still relevant to some extent, and therefore a central bank cannot disclose all the information it has.[13]

5.3 The Conservative Central Banker Approach

The main argument against a state contingent rule is that constructing a complete set of all state contingent plans is impossible in practice, and consequently monetary policy must be either based on a simple policy rule or the discretion of a central bank. Although some countries which adopt an inflation targeting approach such as New Zealand have a state contingent rule that distinguishes between supply and demand shocks, it is not possible to describe *all* possible contingencies *ex ante* or to verify them *ex post* because an actual economy is constantly subject to *unexperienced* shocks. Therefore, what kind of policy approach is desirable in a situation where a state contingent rule is always incomplete?

One idea is to incorporate a mechanism in which a central bank can flexibly respond to certain shocks that may adversely affect the achievement of sustainable growth while maintaining credibility of its policy commitment to price stability. The idea of a "conservative central banker" by Rogoff (1985) represents such an example. He has shown that it is possible to improve economic welfare by reducing inflation bias by delegating the formulation and implementation of monetary policy to a conservative central banker who puts relatively high priority on maintaining price stability. This strengthens the case for enhancing the independence of a central bank because the conservative central banker who puts high priority on price stability can produce better inflation performance than the government which must reflect the preferences of the general public.

5.4 The "Option to Override the Policy Rule" Approach

The report of the Roll Committee attempts to strike a balance between rules and discretion in the conduct of monetary policy through the following proposal: that the government decides the ultimate objective of monetary policy, but leaves the choice of monetary instrument and its target to the discretion of the central bank; and that the government can temporarily override the central bank in an emergency. Although this is a kind of state contingent rule, it may be better characterized as an escape clause which defines the condition for temporary reversion of monetary control to the government. The purpose of this proposal is to maintain the credibility of the central bank's commitment to price stability by making it explicit that the government is responsible for the temporary departure from price stability in an emergency.[14]

Granted that in a democratic world, the government should retain the option to override the central bank, the important question remains as to under what conditions and how this option should be exercised. In view of the argument of Rogoff (1985) that emphasizes the advantage of delegating the conduct of monetary policy to a conservative central banker, it seems undesirable to use an overriding option too frequently because the central bank should be by nature more anti-inflationary than the government. It is therefore necessary to limit the use of that option to only very serious emergencies because a monetary policy which the government regards as optimal is likely to introduce an inflationary bias in the long run. The Roll Committee seems to hold the same view. But if this is the case, it can be argued that it may not be necessary to explicitly introduce the overriding option in a central banking Act itself; instead, the government may choose to revise provisions to override monetary policy in the case of a real emergency. This would reduce the potential risk of inflation by limiting the undisciplined use of the overriding option.

6 CONCLUDING REMARKS

The main arguments of this chapter may be summarized as follows:

1. The ultimate objective of monetary policy is to improve the economic welfare of the people. This requires achieving non-inflationary sustainable economic growth. Price stability is a necessary but not sufficient condition for achieving sustainable economic growth.
2. Therefore, it becomes necessary not only to maintain price stability but also to check the underlying situation behind such price stability. For example, even if the general price level is stable on the surface, an excessive boom and asset price inflation might be developing together with a rise in profit margins. In this case, monetary policy needs to be

tightened even if it might lead to a decline in the general price level. Conversely, monetary policy needs to be relaxed in the opposite case.

3. In more general terms, within the general condition of price stability, the guiding principle of monetary policy should be to offset a price increase originating from the demand side while allowing some price increases originating from the supply side. When it is difficult to distinguish between supply and demand shocks, this guiding principle needs to be supplemented by an analysis of the cost–price relationship.[15]
4. Potential problems in conducting monetary policy according to this principle are that it ignores various lags and uncertainties, and may weaken the credibility of the central bank's commitment to maintain price stability by allowing price increases in some cases, thereby introducing an inflationary bias to the economy.
5. In order to avoid the latter problem, the following four main approaches were discussed: (1) the adoption of inflation targeting or monetary targeting; (2) the use of a state contingent rule; (3) the delegation of the responsibility of monetary control to an independent and conservative central bank; and (4) the adoption of a non-inflationary monetary rule with a governmental option to override that rule. Since they are not necessarily mutually exclusive, we can combine some of these approaches. In fact, a combination of inflation targeting and independence of the central bank are now practiced in European countries, with some countries additionally adopting a state contingent rule. The effectiveness of these approaches deserves attention in the coming years.
6. In any case, central banks can never gain automatic credibility unless they make no mistakes. One effective way to gain credibility of central banks and their policy is to publicize the information that is necessary to understand policy actions. As long as such actions are aimed at achieving a clear objective and are backed by solid economic analysis, a transparent decision-making process of monetary policy will enhance the central banks' credibility and its effectiveness in conducting monetary policy, just as disclosure of its financial condition improves the reputation of a corporation in the capital market and induces lower capital costs.

Walsh (1993) and Persson and Tabellini (1993) have shown that a contract between the government and the central banker in which the central banker's salary declines in proportion to inflation can attain the first-best equilibrium. But, in reality, it is not easy to apply this well-known scheme to the real world. Goodhart (1994) explains what will happen. "As an external adviser to the Reserve Bank of New Zealand before the 1989 Act, I advocated relating bonus payments to senior officials to the outcome, relative to the target. Although many thought that such a scheme had been introduced, it was actually rejected on the presentable argument that it would evoke headlines such as 'Governor makes $500000 by taking action to throw 500000 out of work'."

These examples indicate that an important future research topic is to narrow the gap between actual behavior and theoretical analysis.

Notes

1. Former Governor Mieno of the Bank of Japan stated in May 1994 as follows: "It goes without saying that the central bank's missions are (1) stabilizing the value of money; and (2) maintaining and fostering the financial system; in other words, to achieve price stability and financial system stability. 'Price stability,' in this case, does not mean stability of current price indices. There can be stability of prices in the medium to long run only when the economy is on a well-balanced and sustainable growth path. Therefore, one of the objectives of monetary policy should be to realize non-inflationary sustainable economic growth from medium- to long-term perspectives" (Mieno, 1994). This statement clearly indicates that the Bank of Japan views its policy objective of price stability from the long-term perspective of achieving sustainable economic growth.
2. Goodfriend (1995), however, suggests that moderate inflation may be desirable for monetary policy that focuses on markup rate as the main economic indicator.
3. Ramey and Ramey (1994), for example, present some empirical evidence on the relationship between a long-term growth rate and a short-term growth variation.
4. There are two theoretical arguments which employ a framework of imperfect competition. The first is represented by menu-cost theory and near-rationality theory. The essence of these theories is that the existence of menu cost prevents firms from changing producer prices consistent with its marginal cost structure, thus causing a huge social loss. In such a case, monetary policy can allow firms to change prices by raising the opportunity cost of not changing prices. That is, monetary policy can improve social welfare by directly controlling the markup ratio of firms through an appropriate shift in the demand curve which firms confront.

   The second is an argument regarding the social welfare cost of inflation under markup pricing. Goodfriend (1995) argues that when there is markup pricing in goods markets, the social welfare cost of inflation will be equivalent to that under prefect competition, as suggested by Lucas (1993), multiplied by the marginal markup ratio. In this argument, the monetary authorities have the optimal choice of tightening monetary policy and bringing down inflation even under low and stable inflation, if they observe or anticipate that the markup ratio has remained high.

   For further discussion, see Baba (1996).

5. The estimated markup in this chapter uses industrial data from Capital Stock and National Income Statistics, and therefore suffers from the problem of significant time lag.
6. In addition to the CBO estimate, there are other estimates (such as 0.5–1.5 and 1.0–1.8 percentage points) on the upward bias in CPI in the United States. See Shiratsuka (1995c).
7. See McCallum (1993), for example.
8. Taylor (1995 p. 4), for example, referred to this problem: "Much has been made of the unreliability of any one measure of the money supply because of recent changes in technology and regulation. In fact, the demand for money function – at least for the M1 and the M2 definitions – seems to have shifted substantially in recent years."
9. See Cukierman (1992), for example.
10. See Fischer (1993), Englander and Gurney (1994), and Cukierman *et al.* (1994), for example.
11. See King (1995). It should be pointed out, however, that even if money supply and inflation have a stable relationship, money supply may be a better informational variable for monetary policy than inflation since movement of the former tends to precede the latter. Even if there were a perfect relationship between the rate of money supply and inflation, monetary targeting and inflation targeting would be operationally different from the viewpoint of implementing monetary policy.
12. The Reserve Bank of New Zealand explicitly adopts this view. See Archer (1995).
13. There is also some academic literature that argues for the advantages of central bank secrecy. For example, in a situation where a central bank sometimes considers whether it should put priority on employment over price stability, Cukierman and Meltzer (1986) shows that such a central bank has an incentive to adopt stimulative policy action that is less likely to reveal its policy goal to the public.
14. For a theoretical justification of this approach, see Lohmann (1992).
15. New Zealand's inflation targeting may be viewed as an application of this monetary policy principle.

References

Alesina, A. and Summers, L.H. (1993) "Central Bank Independence and Macroeconomic Performance: Some Comparative Evidence," *Journal of Money, Credit and Banking*, 25 (2) (May), pp. 151–162.

Archer, D. (1995) "Rules for Monetary Policy: The Rationale Underlying the New Zealand Approach," paper presented at a conference held by the Swiss National Bank at Studienzentrum Gerzensee on 16–18 March 1995.

Baba, N. (1995a) "Naigai Kakakusa ni tsuite – Survey wo Tsuujita Kangaekatano Seiri (Price Differentials between Domestic and Overseas Market)" (in Japanese), *Kin'yu Kenkyu*, 14 (2), Institute for Monetary and Economic Studies, Bank of Japan, pp. 47–70.

Baba, N. (1995b) "On the Causes of Price Differentials between Domestic and Overseas Market: Approach through Empirical Analyses of Markup Pricing,"

Monetary and Economic Studies, 13 (2), Institute for Monetary and Economic Studies, Bank of Japan.
Baba, N. (1996) "Markup Pricing and Monetary Policy," Discussion Paper Series, Institute for Monetary and Economic Studies, Bank of Japan, forthcoming.
Barro, R.J. and Gordon, D.B. (1983) "Rules, Discretion and Reputation in a Model of Monetary Policy," *Journal of Monetary Economics*, 12, pp. 101–22.
Cukierman, A. (1992) *Central Bank Strategies, Credibility and Independence: Theory and Evidence* (MIT Press). Cambridge Mass.
Cukierman, A. and Meltzer, A.H. (1986) "A Theory of Ambiguity, Credibility, and Inflation under Discretion," *Econometrica*, 54 (5) (September), pp. 1099–1128.
Cukierman, A. *et al.* (1994) "Central Bank Independence, Growth, Investment and Real Rates," Carnegie–Rochester Conference Series on Public Policy, 39, pp. 95–140.
Englander, A.S. and Gurney, A. (1994) "Medium-Term Determinants of OECD Productivity," *OECD Economic Studies*, 22.
Fischer, Stanley (1993) "The Role of Macroeconomic Factors in Growth," *Journal of Monetary Economics*, 32, pp. 485–512.
Fuhrer, J.C. (1994) "Goals, Guidelines, and Constraints Facing Monetary Policy-makers: An Overview," *New England Economic Review* (September/October), pp. 3–16.
Goodfriend, M. (1995) "A Framework for the Analysis of Moderate Inflations," paper presented at the Swiss National Bank Conference on Rules versus Discretion in Monetary Policy, March 1995.
Goodhart, C.A.E. (1994) "What Should Central Banks Do? What Should Be Their Macroeconomic Objectives and Operations?," *Economic Journal* (November), pp. 1424–36.
Greenspan, A. (1995) "Testimony before the Committee on Finance of United States Senates," 13 March.
Hall, R. (1988) "The Relation between Price and Marginal Cost in US Industry," *Journal of Political Economy*, 96 (October), pp. 921–47.
King, M. (1995) "Changes in UK Monetary Policy: Rules and Discretion in Practice," paper presented at the Swiss National Bank Conference on Rules versus Discretion in Monetary Policy, March 1995.
Kosai, Y. (1992) "Bubble no Hassei to Kin'yu Seisaku (Speculative Bubbles and Monetary Policy)" (in Japanese), *Japan Center for Economic Research Bulletin*.
Kydland, F.E. and Prescott, E.C. (1977) "Rules Rather than Discretion: The Inconsistency of Optimal Plans," *Journal of Political Economy*, 85, pp. 473–90.
Laidler, D. (1995) "Inflation Control and Monetary Policy Rules," paper presented at the Seventh International Conference on Towards More Effective Monetary Policy, Bank of Japan, 26–7 October 1995.
Lohmann, S. (1992) "Optimal Commitment in Monetary Policy: Credibility versus Flexibility," *American Economic Review* (March), pp. 273–286.
Lucas, R.E., Jr (1993) "On the Walfare Cost of Inflation," University of Chicago mimeo, Jan. 1993.
McCallum, B. (1993) "Specification and Analysis of a Monetary Policy Rule for Japan," *Monetary and Economic Studies*, 11 (2), Bank of Japan, pp. 1–46.
Mieno, Y. (1994) "The Conduct of Monetary Policy by the Bank of Japan," *Quarterly Bulletin*, 2 (3), Bank of Japan.

Okina, K. (1993) *Kin'yu Seisaku* (*Monetary Policy*) (in Japanese) (Toyo Keizai Shinposha). Tokyo.

Persson, T. and Tabellini, G. (1993) "Designing Institutions for Monetary Stability," Carnegie–Rochester Conference Series on Public Policy, 39, pp. 53–84.

Ramey, G. and Ramey, V.A. (1994) "Cross-Country Evidence on the Link between Volatility and Growth," NBER Working Paper No. 4959.

Rogoff, K. (1985) "The Optimal Degree of Commitment to an Intermediate Monetary Target," *Quarterly Journal of Economics*, 100, pp. 1169–90.

Roll, E. *et al.* (1993) "Independent and Accountable – A New Mandate for the Bank of England," The Report of an Independent Panel chaired by Eric Roll, London CEPR.

Rothbard, M. (1963) *America's Great Depression* (Van Nostrand). Princeton, NJ.

Shiratsuka, S. (1995a), "Joyosha Kakaku no Hendo to Hinshitsu Henka (Car Prices and Quality Changes)" (in Japanese), *Kin'yu Kenkyu*, 14 (3), pp. 99–120. Institute for Monetary and Economic Studies, Bank of Japan.

Shiratsuka, S. (1995b) "Effects of Quality Changes on the Price Index: A Hedonic Approach to the Estimation of a Quality Adjusted Price Index for Personal Computers in Japan," *Monetary and Economic Studies*, 13 (1), Bank of Japan, pp. 17–52.

Shiratsuka, S. (1995c) "Shohisha Bukka Shisu to Keisoku Gosa (Consumer Price Index and Measurement Errors)" (in Japanese), *Kin'yu Kenkyu*, 14 (2), Bank of Japan, pp. 1–46.

Shiratsuka, S. and S. Kuroda (1995) "Video Camera Kakaku no Hedonic Bunseki (A Hedonic Analysis of Video Camera Prices)" (in Japanese), *Kin'yu Kenyu*, 14 (4), pp. 43–62. Institute for Monetary and Economic Studies, Bank of Japan.

Soejima, Y. (1995a) "Nihon no Macro Hensu no Tan'ikon Kentei (The Long-Run Relationship between Real GDP, Money Stock, and the Price Level: Critical Examination of Cointegration Test)" (in Japanese), *Kin'yu Kenkyu*, 14 (4), pp. 1–42. Institute for Monetary and Economic Studies, Bank of Japan, mimeo.

Soejima, Y. (1995b) "A Unit Root Test with Structural Change for Japanese Macroeconomic Variables," *Monetary and Economic Studies*, 13 (1), Bank of Japan, pp. 53–68.

Taylor, J.B. (1995), "The Monetary Transmission Mechanism: An Empirical Framework," paper presented at the CEPR/Federal Reserve Bank of San Francisco Conference on Monetary Policy in Changing Financial Environment, February 1995.

The Treasury and Civil Service Committee (1993) *The Role of the Bank of England.*

Walsh, C. (1993) "Optimal Contracts for Independent Central Bankers: Private Information, Performance Measures and Reappointment," Working Paper 93–02, Federal Reserve Bank of San Francisco (May).

Index